Solutions Manual/
Test Bank/
Achievement Tests

Payroll Accounting
2014 Edition

Bernard J. Bieg
Bucks County Community College

Judith A. Toland
Bucks County Community College

CENGAGE
Learning®

Australia • Brazil • Japan • Korea • Mexico • Singapore • Spain • United Kingdom • United States

CONTENTS

CHAPTER 1

Note: Working space and special forms are provided for the Practical Problems and the Continuing Payroll Problem only. If students are required to prepare written answers to the Questions for Review, Questions for Discussion, and Case Problems, blank paper should be provided.

Learning Objectives

After studying this chapter, students should be able to:

1. Identify the various laws that affect employers in their payroll operations.

2. Examine the recordkeeping requirements of these laws.

3. Describe the employment procedures generally followed in a Human Resources Department.

4. Recognize the various personnel records used by businesses and know the type of information shown on each form.

5. Identify the *payroll register* and the *employee's earnings record*.

Contents

Chapter 1 outline:

Uniformed Services Employment and Reemployment Rights Act of 1994
Employee Retirement Income Security Act of 1974
   Disclosure Requirements
Affordable Care Act of 2010 (ACA)
OTHER STATE LAWS AFFECTING THE NEED FOR PAYROLL AND PERSONNEL RECORDS
Workers' Compensation Laws
State Disability Benefit Laws
HUMAN RESOURCES AND PAYROLL ACCOUNTING SYSTEMS
HUMAN RESOURCES SYSTEM
Job Descriptions
Requisition for Personnel
Application for Employment
Reference Inquiry
Hiring Notice
Employee History Record
Change in Payroll Rate
RECORDKEEPING SYSTEM
Employee Access—Personnel Files
PAYROLL ACCOUNTING SYSTEM
Payroll Register
Employee's Earnings Record
Paycheck
Outsourcing Payroll
KEY TERMS
CHAPTER SUMMARY

Matching Quiz (p. 1–23)

1.	B		**6.**	I
2.	D		**7.**	J
3.	F		**8.**	C
4.	A		**9.**	E
5.	H		**10.**	G

Questions for Review (p. 1–23)

1. The Fair Labor Standards Act sets the minimum wage rate, and the current minimum wage rate is $7.25 an hour.

2. To meet the requirements of the FLSA, the employer must keep records providing the following information with respect to each employee's wages earned:

    a. Day and time of day when workweek begins
    b. Regular hourly rate of pay
    c. Basis of wage payments
    d. Hours worked each day
    e. Hours worked each week
    f. Daily or weekly straight-time pay
    g. Amount and nature of exempt pay
    h. Weekly overtime pay
    i. Total additions to or deductions from wages
    j. Total remuneration for payroll period
    k. Date of payment
    l. Payroll period

3. FICA levies taxes on employers and employees to finance the Federal Old-Age and Survivors' Trust Fund, the Federal Disability Insurance Trust Fund, and the Health Insurance Plan—Medicare. SECA also imposes taxes on the net earnings of the self-employed individual.

4. The taxes paid to the federal government (FUTA tax) are used to pay the state and federal administrative expenses incurred in operating the overall unemployment insurance program. The taxes paid to the various state governments (SUTA tax) are used to pay the unemployment compensation benefits to the qualified unemployed workers.

5. The unfair employment practices prohibited by the Civil Rights Act of 1964, as amended, include:

    a. Discriminating in hiring, firing, promoting, compensating, or in any other condition of employment on the basis of race, color, religion, gender, or national origin.
    b. Unions may not include or segregate union members on these bases.
    c. Employment agencies may not refer or refuse to refer applicants for employment on the basis of race, color, religion, gender, or national origin.

6. The purpose of the Age Discrimination in Employment Act (ADEA) is to prohibit discrimination on the basis of age in the employment practices of employers, employment agencies, and labor unions that are engaged in an industry affecting interstate commerce.

7. A key exception is executives who are 65 or older and who have held high policy-making positions during the two-year period prior to retirement. If such an employee is entitled to an annual retirement benefit from the employer of at least $44,000, he or she can be forcibly retired.

8. The Walsh-Healey Public Contracts Act covers laborers for contractors who furnish materials, supplies, articles, and equipment to any agency of the United States, provided the minimum contract amount is $10,000.

9. OSHA sets specific occupational and health standards for employers and requires that records be kept of work-related injuries, illnesses, and death.

10. The employer is required to offer the employee as many as 12 weeks of unpaid leave.

11. ERISA was designed primarily to ensure that workers covered by private pension plans receive benefits from those plans in accordance with their credited years of service with their employers.

12. *Vesting* conveys to employees the right to share in a retirement fund in the event they are terminated before the normal retirement age. The vesting process is linked to the number of years needed for workers to earn equity in their retirement plans and to become entitled to full or partial benefits at some future date if they leave the company before retirement. Once vested, a worker has the right to receive a pension at retirement age, based on years of covered service, even though the worker may not be working for the firm at that time.

13. The administrator must furnish a statement, not more than once in a 12-month period, of the total benefits accrued and accrued benefits that are vested, if any, or the earliest date on which these accrued benefits will become vested.

14. The procedure that may be followed by the Human Resources Department in hiring new employees is:

   a. Receive request for new employee.
   b. Examine applications.
   c. Interview applicants.
   d. Administer tests.
   e. Check references.
   f. Select and notify successful applicant.
   g. Send information to Payroll Department.
   h. Prepare personnel file.

15. The application for employment form may provide information such as the following:

   a. Personal information, including name, address, telephone number, and social security number
   b. Educational background, including a summary of the schools attended, whether the applicant graduated, and degrees conferred
   c. Employment and experience record
   d. Type of employment desired
   e. References

16. The employer who is subject to the Civil Rights Act of 1964 and the Age Discrimination in Employment Act must make certain that all aspects of the prehire inquiries are free of discrimination on the basis of race, color, religion, gender, national origin, and age.

17. The Fair Credit Reporting Act of 1968 subjects employers to certain disclosure obligations when they seek an investigative report from a consumer reporting agency on a job applicant or, in certain instances, on present employees. Generally, whenever such a report is requested, the employer must notify the applicant or employee in writing that such a report is being sought. If employment is denied because of the facts on the investigative report, the employer must inform the applicant of this fact. In addition, the name of the consumer reporting agency must be furnished to the applicant.

18. A typical payroll accounting system includes the following procedures:
    a. Record hours worked or units produced.
    b. Compute gross pay, deductions, and net pay.
    c. Complete payroll register.
    d. Maintain payroll deduction records.
    e. Update employees' earnings records.
    f. Prepare paychecks.
    g. Record payroll in accounting books.
    h. Prepare various payroll reports.

19. The two basic records generated in a payroll accounting system are the payroll register and the employee's earnings record.

20. The earnings record provides the information needed to prepare periodic reports required by the various laws and to complete Form W-2 for each employee.

Questions for Discussion (p. 1–24)

1. A small retailer with only three employees would not need very detailed personnel records. There should be, however, an application form or some other record providing the employee's name, address, telephone number, social security number, date of employment, regular working hours, and information about wages.

2. Many employers do not check job applicants' references because former employers, who are afraid of lawsuits, tend to be less than candid in their comments about ex-workers. Some companies will not make any comment about former workers unless they have the written consent of those workers. Other companies have found that even a good recommendation can create a "potential liability."

3. Use of this approach in staffing an office may pose too great an opportunity for the development of cliques in the office. The applicant recommended may not be desirable, and this will cause some embarrassment or disappointment to the person who recommended the applicant. The advantages in most instances, however, outweigh these disadvantages. The advantages realized from the use of in-house referrals include the added prestige among present employees and a positive psychological effect. Firms may offer incentives, such as cash payments, U.S. savings

bonds, and company merchandise, for referrals after the newly employed worker has been on the job for a stipulated period of time. Some firms estimate the recruiting and advertising cost of a new hire to be $5,000.

4. Sources of potential employees include employment agencies, both public and private; newspaper advertisements (Help Wanted and Jobs Wanted); employment bureaus in schools and in social and philanthropic institutions; friends and relatives secured through present employees; and "through the gate" and unsolicited applications. Past national surveys have found that for employees without a college degree, the leading recruiting sources were (1) walk-in, (2) newspaper advertisements, (3) in-house referrals, (4) employment agencies, (5) requests to high schools, (6) high school career conferences, and (7) unions.

5. **a.** and **b.** Illegally. Answers to these two questions could reveal the national origin, race, religion, or color of the applicant. One exception to this is when information of this nature is required as a bona fide occupational qualification for reasons of national or state security.

    c. Legally. Companies subject to Title VII of the Civil Rights Act of 1964 must ask ap-plicants if they are U.S. citizens. Companies are also permitted to ask the applicant if he or she intends to become a U.S. citizen and if the applicant has legal sanction to remain in the United States.

    d. Legally. A company is within legal sanction to ask the applicant *what* languages he or she is capable of reading, writing, or speaking. These abilities can be acquired through study and thus do not necessarily reveal race, religion, color, or national origin. However, the company may be proceeding illegally in its preemployment practices if it inquires *how* the applicant acquired the language abilities, for this could easily determine ethnic background. Thus, the interviewer must be aware of the *what* and *how* aspects of this question when making prehire inquiries that could directly or indirectly establish ethnic background characteristics of the applicant.

Case Problem (p. 1–24)

Case 1–1

Even though it was the company's mistake, legally it was entitled to reimbursement from Ken. However, the cost of legal fees to follow through on the proceedings needed to reclaim the paychecks would probably exceed the total of the four paychecks. The company would be better off to absorb this loss and to solve the problems it has in interdepartmental communication.

CHAPTER 2

Learning Objectives

After studying this chapter, students should be able to:

1. Explain the major provisions of the Fair Labor Standards Act.
2. Define *hours worked*.
3. Describe the main types of records used to collect payroll data.
4. Calculate regular and overtime pay.
5. Identify distinctive compensation plans.

Contents

Chapter 2 outline:

Matching Quiz (p. 2–30)

1.	D		**6.**	C
2.	G		**7.**	J
3.	F		**8.**	B
4.	E		**9.**	I
5.	H		**10.**	A

Questions for Review (p. 2–30)

1. The two bases of coverage provided by the FLSA are enterprise coverage and individual employee coverage. Under *enterprise coverage*, all the employees of an enterprise are covered if the enterprise has at least two employees who engage in interstate commerce or produce goods for interstate commerce and if the enterprise has annual gross sales of at least $500,000.

   Under *individual employee coverage*, the FLSA covers a worker if the employee either engages in interstate commerce or produces goods for such commerce. Employment in a fringe occupation closely related and directly essential to the production of goods for interstate commerce constitutes engagement in the production of goods for interstate commerce.

2. The IRS groups the items of evidence into behavioral control, financial control, and the relationship of the parties.

3. Retail or service establishments, farms, and institutions of higher education may employ full-time students at 85 percent of the minimum wage.

4. The living wage in Miami is $12.06 per hour (if the employer provides health insurance) or $13.82 per hour without insurance.

5. A tipped employee engages in an occupation in which tips of more than $30 a month are customarily and regularly received. An employer can credit up to $5.12 of a tipped employee's minimum wage as coming from tips actually received.

6. State employees working in the area of public safety may accumulate compensatory time off up to 480 hours. (The 480-hour limit represents 320 hours of overtime actually worked at the one and one-half overtime rate.) The employees may "bank" their hours and use them later as time off at time and one-half during the course of their employment.

7. An employee would be paid for compensatory time off in the following two cases:

(1) At termination of employment.
(2) Upon reaching the "bank" maximum of 480 or 240 hours.

8. The following employees are exempt from some of the requirements of the FLSA:

a. Amusement park employees are exempt from the minimum wage, equal pay, and overtime provisions.
b. Taxicab drivers are exempt from only the overtime provision.
c. Casual baby sitters are exempt from the minimum wage, equal pay, and overtime provisions.
d. Elementary school teachers are exempt from the minimum wage and overtime provisions.
e. Outside salespersons are exempt from the minimum wage and overtime provisions.

9. The types of exempt white-collar employees are executives, administrators, professionals, highly compensated employees, computer professionals, creative professionals, and outside salespersons.

10. To be classified as a highly compensated employee, he or she must:

(1) Earn $100,000 or more.
(2) Perform nonmanual work.
(3) Regularly perform one of the exempt duties of an executive, administrator, or professional employee.

11. The following conditions must be met:

(1) All work must be performed outside school hours.
(2) There is a maximum 3-hour day and 18-hour week when school is in session (8 and 40, respectively, when not in session).
(3) Work must be performed between 7 A.M. and 7 P.M. (9 P.M. in summer).

12. The principal activities of employees are those they must perform and include any work of consequence performed for the employer. Principal activities include those that are indispensable to the performance of productive work and those that are an integral part of a principal activity.

13. The time spent by employees in traveling to and from work counts as time worked only if contract, custom, or practice so requires. In some instances, however, travel time between home and work counts as time worked. For example, when an employee receives an emergency call outside the regular working hours and must travel a substantial distance to perform a job away from the usual work site for one of the employer's customers, the travel time counts as time worked.

14. "Engaged to wait" is considered working time. An example would be workers required to be at a car wash at a scheduled time waiting for car wash service volume. "Waiting to be engaged" is not working time. This involves waiting for the start of the working hours.

15. Nonexempt employees must be paid for all hours worked, even those outside the regular workplace. This also applies when employees take work home on their own.

16. The time spent by employees in attending lectures or training sessions does not count as working time when all of the following conditions are met:

   a. Attendance by the employee is voluntary.
   b. The employee does not produce any goods or perform any other productive work during the meeting or lecture.
   c. The meeting or lecture takes place outside regular working hours.
   d. The meeting or lecture is not directly related to the employee's work.

17. Preliminary and postliminary activities would be counted as time worked if required by custom or contract. In addition, if these activities are integral or indispensable to the employee's main activities, compensation is required for this time.

18. A biometric time clock identifies an employee's unique fingerprint, handprint, voice, iris, or whole face.

19. The Wage and Hour Division allows employers to round off employees' worktime to the nearest five, six, or fifteen minutes. This process must be applied consistently to all employees.

20. The overtime premium pay is calculated by multiplying the overtime hours by an overtime premium rate of one-half the regular hourly rate.

21. To calculate the overtime hourly rate for employees who are paid biweekly, divide by 2 to arrive at the weekly salary. Divide the weekly salary by the regular number of hours worked to obtain the hourly rate. Multiply this rate by one and one-half to obtain the overtime rate.

22. The regular rate of pay for a salaried nonexempt employee is found by dividing the number of hours expected to be worked each week into the weekly salary.

23. In the case of a salaried employee with fluctuating workweeks, overtime pay is found by dividing the normal salary by the total hours worked, and then dividing in half to get the extra half-rate which is paid for all the overtime hours.

   An alternative method would be to divide the fixed salary by 40 hours to determine a fixed hourly rate of pay, and then divide this in half to get the fixed extra half-rate.

24. Commissions are considered to be payments for hours worked and must be included in determining the regular hourly rate.

25. Bonuses that are known in advance or that are set up as inducement to achieve goals are nondiscretionary bonuses. This type of bonus is part of the employees' wage rates.

Questions for Discussion (p. 2–31)

1. The FLSA requires overtime pay for hours physically worked over 40 in a workweek. Hours that are paid for, but not actually worked, do not count toward the 40 hours. In addition, the hourly rate of pay is determined by dividing the total regular pay actually earned by the total number of hours actually worked.

2. No. Sanchez Printers, like other employers, may be inadvertently violating the FLSA by giving employees a four-day Thanksgiving weekend and then expecting them to make up the lost time later. Although there is no problem when an employer grants Thanksgiving Day and the following Friday as holidays, either with or without pay, a violation arises if the employees are asked to work extra hours without proper compensation in some other workweek to make up for the time lost. Such an arrangement could violate payment of time and one-half for hours over 40 in any workweek.

3. Under the Fair Labor Standards Act, if the correct amount of overtime compensation cannot be determined until after the regular pay period, the company may make the overtime payment as soon as is practicable but no later than the next payday.

4. In a case similar to the one described (69 LA 573), it was noted that the employer was more diligent in trying to correct paycheck errors that involved more than $30. It was decided that there is no sufficient business reason why an error in a small amount cannot be corrected as promptly as an error in a large amount. It was ruled that the employer should look into the matter and inspect its records at the earliest practicable moment. Further, it was concluded that errors should be attended to as soon as feasible, irrespective of the amount due.

5. First of all, the company pays Banta at two different wage rates based on the hours worked at each separate job. As far as the overtime pay, there are three options: (1) pay him one and one-half the higher rate for the overtime hours, (2) calculate an average overtime rate based on the total time worked, or (3) if agreed in advance, base the overtime rate on the job actually worked during the overtime hours.

Practical Problems (p. 2–33)

The principles and practices of payroll accounting discussed in Chapter 2 are applied in the Practical Problems as shown below.

Principle or Practice	Practical Problem No. (A and B)
1. *Paying less than the minimum wage* (exception to the FLSA)	2–1
2. Computing the *tip credit*	2–2, 2–5
3. Computing *gross earnings*	2–3
4. Computing *regular earnings, overtime earnings,* and *total gross earnings*	2–4 through 2–22
5. Computing salary—*exempt employee*	2–6
6. Reading *time cards* to determine hours worked	2–9, 2–10 2–11 (continental system)
7. *4/40 workweek*	2–11
8. *Converting monthly* and *annual salary rates* to hourly rates	2–14, 2–15
9. Using the *decimal system* for "docking"	2–10
10. *Piece-rate systems*	2–18, 2–19
11. *Commissions*	2–20, 2–21
12. *Bonuses*	2–22

Solutions—Series A Problems

2–1A. (a) 37 hours × $4.20 = $155.40

(b) Yes. Beck, a full-time student in a university, may be employed by a retail establishment for at least 85% of the minimum wage, or $6.17 (85% × $7.25 = $6.1625, which the government rounds to $6.17). Since Beck is being paid a rate less than $6.17, the wage rate violates the FLSA.

(c) 37 hours × $6.17 = $228.29

2–2A.   (a) $2.13 × 40 = $85.20* minimum weekly wages.

        (b)

$ 85.20	minimum weekly wages
– 80.00	weekly wage regularly paid
$ 5.20	additional weekly wage due

            *In order to be able to pay just the minimum ($85.20) for a 40-hour week, the employee must receive at least $204.80 in tips ($290.00 – $85.20).

2–3A.   (a)

Employee	Gross Earnings
Darley, R.	$ 368.60
Waxman, B.	334.00
Isaac, J.	333.00
Bruner, H.	310.00
Kellogg, P.	273.00
(b) Total gross earnings	$1,618.60

2–4A.   (a)

Employee	Regular Earnings	Overtime Rate	Overtime Earnings	Total Gross Earnings
Carman, T.	$378.00	$14.18	$ 99.26	$ 477.26
Galasso, A.	476.00	17.85	35.70	511.70
Jones, B.	354.00	13.28	106.24	460.24
Rodna, G.	330.00	12.38	49.52	379.52
Wilmon, W.	296.00	11.10	61.05	357.05
(b) Total gross earnings				$2,185.77

2–5A.   (a) 40-hour pay (40 hours × $2.13) $85.20

        (b) Overtime pay {2 hours × $5.76 [($7.25 × 1.5) – $5.12]} $11.52

2–6A. $80,000 ÷ 52 weeks = $1,538.46 × 2/5 = $615.38

2–7A.   (a) Overtime earnings: $22.20 ($14.80 × 1.5) × 7 hours = $155.40

        (b) Total earnings: $592.00 + $155.40 = $747.40

2–8A.   (a) Regular pay (46 × $12.96) $596.16

        (b) Overtime premium pay (6 × $6.48) 38.88

        (c) Gross pay $635.04

2–9A.   (a)   Hours worked each day:

Monday	8	hours
Tuesday	10	hours
Wednesday	8	hours
Thursday	10 1/2	hours
Friday	9 1/2	hours
Saturday	4	hours
Sunday	4	hours

      (b)   Total hours worked 54   hours

      (c)   Regular earnings = 40 hours × $13.50 .... $540.00

      (d)   Overtime earnings:

           Overtime earnings for hours beyond 8 daily and
           for Saturday:
               10 hours × $20.25 ($13.50 × 1.5) $202.50
           Overtime earnings for Sunday:
               4 hours × $27.00 ($13.50 × 2) 108.00   310.50

      (e)   Total earnings $850.50

2–10A.   (a)   Hours worked each day:

Monday	8		hours
Tuesday	7	9/10	hours
Wednesday	7	6/10	hours
Thursday	7	6/10	hours
Friday	7	8/10	hours

      (b)   Total hours worked .... 38 9/10   hours

      (c)   Gross earnings for the week:
          38 9/10 hours × $12.15 .... $472.64

2–11A.   (a)   Daily total hours:

Tuesday	10	hours
Wednesday	10	hours
Thursday	9 3/4	hours
Friday	10	hours
Saturday	4	hours

      (b)   Total hours for the week .... 43 3/4   hours

      (c)   Regular weekly earnings = 40 hours × $8.45 .... $338.00

      (d)   Overtime earnings = 3 3/4 hours × $12.675 .... 47.53

      (e)   Total weekly earnings $385.53

2–12A. (a) Earnings, Job I: 40 × $14.00   = $ 560.00
Earnings, Job II: 7 × $11.80   =   82.60

One-half overtime rate:
($560.00 + $82.60) ÷ 47 hours × 1/2 = $6.84

Extra overtime pay: 7 × $6.84   =   47.88

Gross pay $690.48

(b) 40 × $14.00   = $560.00
7 × ($11.80 × 1.5)   =   123.90

Gross pay   = $683.90

OR

40 × $14.00   = $560.00
7 × $11.80   =   82.60
7 × $5.90   =   41.30

Gross pay   = $683.90

2–13A. $695 ÷ 40 = $17.38 hourly rate

$17.38 × 1.5 = $26.07 overtime rate

(a) Regular earnings $695.00

(b) Overtime earnings (5 hours × $26.07) 130.35

(c) Total earnings $825.35

2–14A. Yearly earnings: $2,875 × 12   = $34,500

Weekly earnings: $34,500 ÷ 52 = $663.46

(a) Hourly rate: $663.46 ÷ 40 = $16.59

(b) Overtime rate: $16.59 × 1.5 = $24.89

2–15A. Yearly earnings: $2,575 × 12   = $30,900

Weekly earnings: $30,900 ÷ 52 = $594.23

Hourly rate: $594.23 ÷ 35 = $16.98

Overtime rate: $16.98 × 1.5 = $25.47

(a) Regular semimonthly earnings $1,287.50

(b) Overtime earnings:
Up to 40 hrs. (8 × $16.98)........................ $135.84
Over 40 hrs. (2 × $25.47) 50.94   186.78

(c) Total earnings $1,474.28

2–16A. Gross pay = $675 + [2 hours × ($18.00* × 1.5)] = $729.00

*$675 ÷ 37 1/2 hours

2–17A. (a) Overtime earnings: $1,050 ÷ 48 = $21.88 ÷ 2 = $10.94 × 8 . $87.52

(b) Total earnings: $1,050.00 + $87.52....................................... $1,137.52

(c) BELO pay: [($22.00 × 53 hours) + (13 hours × $22.00 × 0.5)] $1,309.00

2–18A. (a) Piecework earnings = 1,275 units × $0.35.................... $446.25

(b) Regular hourly rate:
   $446.25 ÷ 45.5 hours = $9.81
   Overtime hourly rate:
   1/2 of $9.81 = $4.91

(c) Overtime earnings = 5.5 hours × $4.91 ....   27.01

(d) Total earnings... $473.26

2–19A. (a) Piecework earnings = 1,075 units × $0.35.................... $376.25

(b) Overtime earnings = 200 units × $0.53 ($0.35 × 1.5) 106.00

(c) Total earnings... $482.25

2–20A. (a) Regular annual salary.. $29,500

(b) Commission:
   Commission on sales of $50,000 in
      excess of $150,000 ($50,000 @ 8.5%) $4,250
   Commission on sales in excess of
      $200,000 ($95,000 @ 10%)................   9,500
   Commission   13,750

(c) Total annual earnings $43,250

2–21A. (a) Weekly base salary $340.00

   Weekly gross sales $2,215.00
      Less customer returns.............................   187.00
   Weekly net sales $2,028.00

(b) Commission: $2,028.00 × 2%..   40.56
   Weekly gross sales of cashmere sweaters .... $ 995.00
      Less customer returns.............................   75.00
   Weekly net sales of cashmere sweaters .... $ 920.00

(c) PM: $920.00 × 2%...   18.40

(d) Total weekly earnings.. $398.96

2–22A. $975 ÷ 13 weeks = $75/week
            $75 ÷ 43 hours = $1.74 bonus per hour
            $1.74 × 0.5 = $0.87 extra overtime rate
            $0.87 × 3 overtime hours/week × 13 weeks = $33.93

Solutions—Series B Problems

2–1B.   (a)   33 1/4 hours × $5.25 = $174.56

         (b)   Yes. Cross, a full-time student in a university, may be employed by a retail establishment for at least 85% of the minimum wage, or $6.17 (85% × $7.25 = $6.1625, which the government rounds to $6.17). Since Cross is being paid a rate less than $6.17, the wage rate violates the FLSA.

         (c)   33 1/4 hours × $6.17 = $205.15

2–2B.   (a) $2.13 × 40 = $85.20* minimum weekly wages.

         (b) $ 85.20   minimum weekly wages
               – 75.00   weekly wage regularly paid
               $ 10.20   additional weekly wage due

         *In order to be able to pay just the minimum ($85.20) for a 40-hour week, the employee must receive at least $204.80 in tips ($290.00 – $85.20).

2–3B.   (a)

Employee	Gross Earnings
Duffy, M.	$ 416.50
Hazelton, G.	396.20
Inman, T.	430.55
Palmer, C.	401.80
Diaz, O.	399.90
(b) Total gross earnings	$2,044.95

2–4B.   (a)

Employee	Regular Earnings	Overtime Rate	Overtime Earnings	Total Gross Earnings
Wilson, H.	$476.00	$17.85	$ 53.55	$ 529.55
Aha, C.	568.00	21.30	42.60	610.60
Shoup, K.	396.00	14.85	103.95	499.95
Carlyn, D.	428.00	16.05	24.08	452.08
McMurray, J.	684.00	25.65	128.25	812.25
(b) Total gross earnings				$2,904.43

2–5B.   (a)   40-hour pay (40 hours × $2.13) $85.20

          (b)   Overtime pay {3 1/2 hours × $5.76 [($7.25 × 1.5) − $5.12]} $20.16

2–6B. $77,000 ÷ 52 weeks = $1,480.77 × 2/5 = <u>$592.31</u>

2–7B.   (a)   Overtime earnings: $25.35 ($16.90 × 1.5) × 7 hours = $177.45

          (b)   Total earnings: $676.00 + $177.45 = $853.45

2–8B.   (a)   Regular pay (44 × $13.76)....................................... $605.44

          (b)   Overtime premium pay (4 × $6.88)............................   <u>27.52</u>

          (c)   Gross pay ....   <u>$632.96</u>

2–9B.   (a)   Hours worked each day:

Monday	8	hours
Tuesday	11	hours
Wednesday	7 3/4	hours
Thursday	10	hours
Friday	10	hours
Saturday...	4	hours
Sunday	<u>4</u>	hours

          (b)   Total hours worked .... 54 3/4 hours

          (c)   Regular earnings = 39.75 hours × $14.10 .... $560.48

          (d)   Overtime earnings:

               Overtime earnings for hours beyond 8 daily and
               for Saturday:

                   11 hours × $21.15 ($14.10 × 1.5) $232.65
               Overtime earnings for Sunday:
                   4 hours × $28.20 ($14.10 × 2) ....   <u>112.80</u>   <u>345.45</u>

          (e)   Total earnings..   <u>$905.93</u>

2–10B.   (a)   Hours worked each day:

Monday	7 6/10	hours
Tuesday	7 9/10	hours
Wednesday	7 7/10	hours
Thursday	7 9/10	hours
Friday	<u>7 7/10</u>	hours

          (b)   Total hours worked .... 38 8/10 hours

          (c)   Gross earnings for the week:
               38 8/10 hours × $12.95 ....   <u>$502.46</u>

2–11B. (a) Daily total hours:

Tuesday	10	hours
Wednesday	10	hours
Thursday	9 1/2	hours
Friday	10	hours
Saturday	4	hours

(b) Total hours for the week .... 43 1/2 hours

(c) Regular weekly earnings = 40 hours × $9.35................... $374.00

(d) Overtime earnings = 3 1/2 hours × $14.025..................... 49.09

(e) Total weekly earnings $423.09

2–12B. (a) Earnings, Job I: 40 × $15.00 = $600.00

Earnings, Job II: 9 × $13.10 = 117.90

One-half overtime rate:
($600.00 + $117.90) ÷ 49 hours × 1/2 = $7.33

Extra overtime pay: 9 × $7.33 = 65.97

Gross pay $783.87

(b) 40 × $15.00 = $600.00
9 × ($13.10 × 1.5) = 176.85

Gross pay = $776.85

OR

40 × $15.00 = $600.00
9 × $13.10 = 117.90
9 × $6.55 = 58.95

Gross pay = $776.85

2–13B. $725 ÷ 40 = $18.13 hourly rate

$18.13 × 1.5 = $27.20 overtime rate

(a) Regular earnings $725.00

(b) Overtime earnings (4 hours × $27.20) 108.80

(c) Total earnings $833.80

2–14B. Yearly earnings: $3,875 × 12 = $46,500

Weekly earnings: $46,500 ÷ 52 = $894.23

(a) Hourly rate: $894.23 ÷ 40 = $22.36

(b) Overtime rate: $22.36 × 1.5 = $33.54

2–15B.

Yearly earnings:	$2,650 × 12	= $31,800	
Weekly earnings:	$31,800 ÷ 52	= $611.54	
Hourly rate:	$611.54 ÷ 37.5	= $16.31	
Overtime rate:	$16.31 × 1.5	= $24.47	

(a) Regular semimonthly earnings $1,325.00

(b) Overtime earnings:

Up to 40 hrs. (4 × $16.31)	$65.24	
Over 40 hrs. (2 × $24.47)	48.94	114.18

(c) Total earnings... $1,439.18

2–16B. Gross pay = $735 + [2 hours × ($21.00* × 1.5)] = $798.00

*$735 ÷ 35 hours

2–17B.

(a) Overtime earnings: $920 ÷ 42 = $21.90 ÷ 2 = $10.95 × 2 .... $ 21.90

(b) Total earnings: $920.00 + $21.90... $941.90

(c) BELO pay: [($21.00 × 45 hours) + (5 hours × $21.00 × 0.5)] $997.50

2–18B.

(a) Piecework earnings = 1,450 units × $0.38....................... $551.00

(b) Regular hourly rate:
    $551.00 ÷ 46 hours = $11.98
  Overtime hourly rate:
    1/2 of $11.98 = $5.99

(c) Overtime earnings = 6 hours × $5.99 ....   35.94

(d) Total earnings... $586.94

2–19B.

(a) Piecework earnings = 1,120 units × $0.38......................... $425.60

(b) Overtime earnings = 330 units × $0.57 ($0.38 × 1.5) 188.10

(c) Total earnings... $613.70

2–20B.

(a) Regular annual salary.. $34,500

(b) Commission:

Commission on sales of $50,000 in		
excess of $150,000 ($50,000 @ 9.5%)	$ 4,750	
Commission on sales in excess of		
$200,000 ($115,000 @ 12%)...............	13,800	
Commission		18,550

(c) Total annual earnings... $53,050

2–21B.   (a)   Weekly base salary.. $400.00

                 Weekly gross sales.. $2,715.00

                    Less customer returns............................. 217.00

                 Weekly net sales... $2,498.00

      (b)   Commission: $2,498.00 × 1%... 24.98

                 Weekly gross sales of cashmere sweaters..... $ 895.00

                    Less customer returns............................. 75.00

                 Weekly net sales of cashmere sweaters......... $ 820.00

      (c)   PM: $820.00 × 3% 24.60

      (d)   Total weekly earnings $449.58

2–22B. $2,000 ÷ 52 weeks = $38.46/week

           $38.46 ÷ 44 hours = $0.87 bonus per hour

           $0.87 × 0.5 = $0.44 extra overtime rate

           $0.44 × 4 overtime hours/week × 52 weeks = $91.52

Continuing Payroll Problems (p. 2–45)

See the completed payroll registers on pages CPP–1 through CPP–6.

Case Problems (p. 2–47)

Case 2–1

Some potential solutions that Delgado should consider are:

1.   Limit vacation accruals to a maximum, such as two or three weeks. This move would reduce the current cost of payouts for earlier vacations granted at lower wage rates.

2.   Combine sick leave and vacation leave into one category called "annual leave." This practice enables a worker to use the leave time for any purpose—sick leave, vacation time, child care, parental care, etc.

3.   Adopt flexible time scheduling to enable workers to handle personal business, such as medical and dental appointments, while they are flexing during the workday.

Case 2–2

John should be made aware of the fact that the FLSA requires overtime pay for hours physically worked over 40 in a workweek. Time paid for but not worked because of holidays, vacations, sickness, jury duty, etc., is not included in the employee's regular rate of pay and does not count toward 40 hours *worked.*

CHAPTER 3

Learning Objectives

After studying this chapter, students should be able to:

1. Identify, for social security purposes, those persons covered under the law and those services that make up employment.
2. Identify the types of compensation that are defined as wages.
3. Apply the current tax rates and wage base for FICA and SECA purposes.
4. Describe the different requirements and procedures for depositing FICA taxes and income taxes withheld from employees' wages.
5. Complete Form 941, Employer's Quarterly Federal Tax Return.

Contents

Chapter 3 outline:

A SELF-EMPLOYED PERSON
> Self-Employment Income
>> *Self-Employment OASDI/HI Taxes*
>> *Taxable Year*
>> *Reporting Self-Employment Income*

EMPLOYER IDENTIFICATION NUMBER

EMPLOYEE'S APPLICATION FOR SOCIAL SECURITY CARD (FORM SS-5)
> Verifying Social Security Numbers

RETURNS REQUIRED FOR SOCIAL SECURITY PURPOSES
> Deposit Requirements (Nonagricultural Workers)
>> *Monthly*
>> *Semiweekly*
>> *One-Day*
>> *Credit Against the Required Deposits*
>> *The Safe Harbor Rule (98 Percent Rule)*
>> *Deposit Requirements for Employers of Agricultural Workers*
>> *Deposit Requirements for Employers of Household Employees*
>> *Deposit Requirements for State and Local Government Employers*
>> *Procedures for Making Deposits*
>>> *Electronic Deposits*

PREPARING FORM 941 (EMPLOYER'S QUARTERLY FEDERAL TAX RETURN)
> Completing the Return
>> *Part 1*
>> *Part 2*
>> *Part 3*
>> *Part 4*
>> *Part 5*
> Filing Form 941
> Electronic Filing of Form 941
> Non-Filers
> Form 941-X
> Form 944

FAILURE-TO-COMPLY PENALTIES
> Failure to File Employment Tax Returns
> Failure to Fully Pay Employment Taxes
> Failure to Make Timely Deposits
> Failure to Furnish Payee Statements
> Failure to Furnish Information Returns
> Bad Checks

KEY TERMS

CHAPTER SUMMARY

Matching Quiz (p. 3–33)

1.	E	6.	I
2.	D	7.	C
3.	H	8.	B
4.	A	9.	G
5.	J	10.	F

Questions for Review (p. 3–33)

1. To be classified as a "covered" employer, the person must employ one or more individuals for the performance of services in the United States, unless such services or employment are specifically exempted by the law. As long as the common-law relationship of employer and employee exists, the employer is covered.

2. To be classified as a "covered" employee, an individual must perform services in a covered employment. As long as the common-law relationship of employer and employee exists and the employment is not exempt from the provisions of the law, the employee is covered.

3. A common-law relationship exists between an employee and an employer when the employer tells, or has a right to tell a worker how, when, and where to work.

4. Refer to Figure 3–2, which lists the *Test for Independent Contractor Status*. By definition, an *independent* contractor follows an *independent* trade, business, or profession, and offers services to the *public*.

5. a. Employers must collect the employee's FICA taxes on tips reported by each employee. The employee's FICA taxes are deducted from the wages due the employee or from other funds the employee makes available. Employers are also liable for their share of the FICA taxes on the tips that are subject to the employee's FICA taxes.

   b. Employers deduct the employee's FICA taxes from the wages due the employee, and they also are liable for their share of the FICA taxes on the wages paid tipped employees.

6. Payments of sick pay made after the expiration of six calendar months following the last month in which the employee worked for the employer are not taxed. The first six months of sick pay that employees receive are considered wages and thus are subject to withholding for FICA tax purposes. The period off the job must be continuous for six months. (A relapse after a return to work starts a new six-month period.)

7. Employees' pretax contributions into a qualified deferred compensation plan are subject to FICA tax. However, the employers' matching contributions are tax free.

8. Yes. If individuals such as Luis paid OASDI taxes on wages in excess of $113,700 because of having worked for more than one employer, they are entitled to a refund of their overpayment. The amount of the overpayment should be credited against

Luis's federal income taxes for that year, as directed in the instructions accompanying his U.S. Individual Income Tax Return (Form 1040).

9. For 2013, the SECA tax rates for self-employed persons are OASDI—12.4 percent and HI—2.9 percent. The actual tax calculation is done on Schedule SE of Form 1040—Self-Employment Tax.

10. The employer must file Form SS-4 with the IRS. This application form should be sent to the IRS service center where the employer will file future federal tax returns.

11. The deposit rules for nonagricultural employers are:

    a. *Total taxes $50,000 or less in the lookback period:* Deposit taxes monthly.

    b. *Total taxes more than $50,000 in the lookback period:* Deposit taxes semi-weekly.

    c. *Accumulated taxes of $100,000 or more:* Deposit by the next banking day.

    d. *If you fell under the one-day rule at any time during this year or last year:* Deposit taxes semiweekly.

    e. *Less than $2,500 for the quarter:* Deposit by the end of the month following the quarter, or mail taxes with Form 941.

12. All employers must deposit electronically with the exception of those with $2,500 or less in quarterly tax liabilities.

13. There are two electronic methods of deposit:

    a. ACH debit method—employer instructs the Treasury Financial Agent to withdraw funds from the employer's account and route them to the Treasury's account at the Federal Reserve Bank.

    b. ACH credit method—employer instructs the bank to send the payment directly to the Treasury's account at the Federal Reserve Bank.

14. Generally, an employer must file Form 941 each calendar quarter. Form 941 is due on or before the last day of the month following the close of the calendar quarter for which the return applies. If, however, the employer has made timely deposits of the taxes for a quarter, Form 941 may be filed on or before the 10th day of the second month following the close of the calendar quarter for which the return is made.

15. The following penalties may be imposed:

    a. If the employer does not file Form 941 by the due date, a percentage of the tax will be added to the amount due. If the failure to file is for not more than one month, the penalty is 5 percent of the *net* amount of tax required to have been reported. An additional 5 percent is levied for each additional month or fraction of a month during which the failure continues, not to exceed 25 percent in the aggregate.

If, however, the employer shows to the satisfaction of the IRS that the failure to file was due to reasonable cause and not to willful neglect, the addition to the tax will not apply.

If the employer *willfully* tries to evade the payment of taxes by not filing a return (or files a false return), upon conviction he or she may be fined up to $25,000 or imprisoned for not more than one year, or both.

b. If the employer is seven days late in making a monthly deposit, the penalty is 5 percent of the undeposited taxes.

c. If the employer gives the IRS a bad check for $2,000, the penalty is 2 percent of the amount of the taxes, or $40. However, the penalty will not apply if the employer can prove that the check was tendered in good faith and there was reasonable cause to believe it would be paid upon presentment.

Questions for Discussion (p. 3–33)

1. By diverting his payroll tax money to business uses, Emerald faces a penalty. It may take the IRS as much as a year to do anything more than send overdue tax notices. However, when the agency does move, the consequences can be severe. In addition to assessing penalties and interest, the IRS can file a lien against Emerald's assets to collect the past-due taxes.

2. The 65 percent credit for the continuation premiums would be claimed as a credit against the company's payroll tax liability (Employer's FICA, Employee's FICA, and FIT). The credit is claimed on line 12a on Form 941. This credit is treated like a deposit against the company's quarterly deposit requirement and is applied on the first day of the quarter.

3. Yes. If a union member is acting as an employee of the union, the payments made for services rendered will be wages. In this very common example of Volmer being employed by the union as a union representative, the amounts he receives from the union for these services are wages and thus are subject to FICA (and FUTA and federal income tax withholding).

4. Under FICA (as well as under FUTA and for purposes of federal income tax withholding), amounts paid to employees that represent the difference between the employee's regular wages and the amount received for jury duty are wages, even though the amounts were paid for a period when the employee was absent from work. Thus, for her first week of jury duty, the employee would be subject to FICA withholding on $300 ($365 weekly salary less $65 received for jury duty).

Practical Problems (p. 3–35)

The principles and practices of payroll accounting discussed in Chapter 3 are applied in the Practical Problems as shown below.

Principle or Practice	Practical Problem No. (A and B)
1. Calculating *employee's* FICA taxes to be withheld	3–1 through 3–7, 3–9 through 3–10, 3–17
2. Calculating *employer's* FICA taxes	3–1, 3–3, 3–6, 3–7, 3–9 through 3–10, 3–17
3. FICA taxes on *regular earnings* and *self-employment income*	3–8
4. Computing monthly gross earnings, deductions for FICA, and net earnings	3–10
5. Completing Form 941	3–11 through 3–15
6. Calculating penalty for failure to make timely deposit	3–16

Solutions—Series A Problems

3–1A.

Employee No.	Employee Name	Biweekly Taxable Wages	FICA Taxes OASDI	FICA Taxes HI
711	Castro, Manny	$ 493.28	$ 30.58	$ 7.15
512	Corrales, Pat	870.00	53.94	12.62
624	Guitar, Joseph	419.80	26.03	6.09
325	Moore, Connie	523.20	32.44	7.59
422	Morrison, Harry	1,100.00	68.20	15.95
210	Robertson, Catherine	950.00	58.90	13.78
111	Swarez, Joseph	489.75	30.36	7.10
	Totals	$4,846.03	$300.45	$70.28

Employer's OASDI $\dfrac{\$4,846.03}{\text{Total Taxable Wages}}$ $\dfrac{\$300.45}{\text{Employer's OASDI Tax}}$

Employer's HI Tax $\dfrac{\$4,846.03}{\text{Total Taxable Wages}}$ $\dfrac{\$70.27}{\text{Employer's HI Tax}}$

3–2A.

		OASDI	HI
(a)	9th paycheck	$421.60	$98.60
(b)	17th paycheck [$113,700 − ($6,800 × 16 pays) = $4,900 OASDI taxable]..................................	303.80	98.60
(c)	24th paycheck	0	98.60

3–3A.

		OASDI	HI
(a)	The amount of FICA taxes that the employer should withhold from Gilmore's wages during July ($525 + $390)	$56.73	$13.27
(b)	The amount of the employer's FICA taxes on Gilmore's wages and tips during July	56.73	13.27

3–4A.

(a) $800 + $900 = $1,700 × 0.062 = $105.40

(b) $800 + $900 = $1,700 × 0.0145 = $24.65

3–5A.

		November 14			
		OASDI		**HI**	
	Annual	**Taxable**	**OASDI**	**Taxable**	**HI**
Name and Title	**Salary**	**Earnings**	**Tax**	**Earnings**	**Tax**
Hanks, Timothy, President	$134,400	$1,700.00*	$105.40	$5,600.00	$81.20
Grath, John, VP Finance	114,000	4,750.00	294.50	4,750.00	68.88
James, Sally, VP Sales	69,600	2,900.00	179.80	2,900.00	42.05
Kimmel, Joan, VP Manufacturing	54,000	2,250.00	139.50	2,250.00	32.63
Wie, Pam, VP Personnel	51,600	2,150.00	133.30	2,150.00	31.18
Grant, Mary, VP Secretary	49,200	2,050.00	127.10	2,050.00	29.73

*[$113,700 – ($5,600 × 20)]

		December 31			
		OASDI		**HI**	
	Annual	**Taxable**	**OASDI**	**Taxable**	**HI**
Name and Title	**Salary**	**Earnings**	**Tax**	**Earnings**	**Tax**
Hanks, Timothy, President	$134,400	$ 0.00	$ 0.00	$5,600.00	$81.20
Grath, John, VP Finance	114,000	4,450.00**	275.90	4,750.00	68.88
James, Sally, VP Sales	69,600	2,900.00	179.80	2,900.00	42.05
Kimmel, Joan, VP Manufacturing	54,000	2,250.00	139.50	2,250.00	32.63
Wie, Pam, VP Personnel	51,600	2,150.00	133.30	2,150.00	31.18
Grant, Mary, VP Secretary	49,200	2,050.00	127.10	2,050.00	29.73

**[$113,700 – ($4,750 × 23)]

3–6A.

		OASDI		**HI**	
		Taxable	**OASDI**	**Taxable**	**HI**
Name and Position	**Salary**	**Earnings**	**Tax**	**Earnings**	**Tax**
Zena Vertin, Office	$ 535 per week	$ 535.00	$ 33.17	$ 535.00	$ 7.76
Nicole Norge, Sales	2,980 per month	687.69	42.64	687.69	9.97
Bob Mert, Delivery	485 per week	485.00	30.07	485.00	7.03
Audrey Martin, Partner	950 per week*	0.00	0.00	0.00	0.00
Beth James, Partner	950 per week*	0.00	0.00	0.00	0.00
	Totals	$1,707.69	$105.88	$1,707.69	$24.76

Employer's OASDI Tax $105.88
Employer's HI Tax $24.76

*The $950 that each partner receives each week is considered a drawing or withdrawal, not a salary payment.

3–7A.

Employees' total OASDI	$263.50 ($850 × 6.2% × 5)
Employees' total HI.....................	$61.65 ($850 × 1.45% = $12.33 × 5 = $61.65)
Employer's total OASDI..............	$263.50 (6.2% × $4,250)
Employer's total HI	$61.63 (1.45% × $4,250)

3–8A.

(a) The amount of FICA taxes that was withheld from his earnings during 2014 by Odesto Company.

    OASDI $4,005.20
    HI $ 936.70

(b) Henwood's self-employment taxes (will receive a credit on his federal income tax return for these paid taxes) on the income derived from the public accounting business for 2014.
[$49,100 taxable ($113,700 – $64,600) × 0.124]
($60,000 taxable × 0.029)

    OASDI $6,088.40
    HI $1,740.00

3–9A.

Employee	Annual Salary	OASDI Taxable Wages	OASDI Tax	HI Tax
Utley, Genna	$ 22,150	$ 1,845.83	$ 114.44	$ 26.76
Werth, Norm	48,900	4,075.00	252.65	59.09
Bass, John	24,000	2,000.00	124.00	29.00
Ruiz, Sam	120,000	3,700.00*	229.40	145.00
Compton, Sue	20,900	1,741.67	107.98	25.25
Williams, Mary	19,500	1,625.00	100.75	23.56
Patel, Raymond	106,080	8,840.00	548.08	128.18
Carson, Abe	56,900	4,741.67	293.98	68.75
Livinsky, Sarah	37,850	3,154.17	195.56	45.74
Harper, Mark	51,200	4,266.67	264.53	61.87
Totals		$35,990.01	$2,231.37	$613.20

Employer's OASDI Tax ($35,990.01 × 0.062) $2,231.38
Employer's HI Tax ($42,290.01 × 0.0145) $613.21

*[$113,700 – ($120,000 × 11/12)]

3–10A.

Full-Time Office:

Employees	Total Monthly Payroll	OASDI Taxable Wages	HI Taxable Wages	OASDI Tax	HI Tax
Adaiar, Gene	$ 1,400.00	$ 1,400.00	$ 1,400.00	$ 86.80	$ 20.30
Crup, Jason	1,300.00	1,300.00	1,300.00	80.60	18.85
Essex, Joan	1,975.00	1,975.00	1,975.00	122.45	28.64
Garza, Irma	1,985.00	1,985.00	1,985.00	123.07	28.78
Leason, Mel	1,900.00	1,900.00	1,900.00	117.80	27.55
Pruit, Marne	7,000.00	7,000.00	7,000.00	434.00	101.50
Rubble, Deanne	2,400.00	2,400.00	2,400.00	148.80	34.80
Simpson, Dick	3,985.00	3,985.00	3,985.00	247.07	57.78
Truap, Ann	5,000.00	5,000.00	5,000.00	310.00	72.50
Wilson, Trudy	1,500.00	1,500.00	1,500.00	93.00	21.75

Part-Time Office:

	Hours Worked	Hourly Rate	Total Monthly	OASDI Taxable Wages	HI Taxable Wages	OASDI Tax	HI Tax
Kyle, Judy	170	$ 8.25	1,402.50	1,402.50	1,402.50	86.96	20.34
Laird, Sharon	170	8.35	1,419.50	1,419.50	1,419.50	88.01	20.58
Maxwell, Sara	140	10.10	1,414.00	1,414.00	1,414.00	87.67	20.50
Nelson, Donna	145	8.20	1,189.00	1,189.00	1,189.00	73.72	17.24
Scott, Kim	162	9.65	1,563.30	1,563.30	1,563.30	96.92	22.67
Totals			$ 35,433.30	$35,433.30	$35,433.30	$2,196.87	$513.78

Employer's FICA taxes   OASDI _____ $2,196.86   HI _____ $513.78

3–11A.

Form **941** for 20--: Employer's QUARTERLY Federal Tax Return
(Rev. January 2013)   Department of the Treasury — Internal Revenue Service

OMB No. 1545-0029

Employer identification number (EIN) 0 0 — 0 0 0 6 5 0 9

Name (not your trade name) Carlos Cruz

Trade name (if any) Cruz Company

Address 901 Keystone
Number   Street   Suite or room number

Sacramento   CA   95916
City   State   ZIP code

Report for this Quarter of 20--
(Check one.)

☐ 1: January, February, March

☐ 2: April, May, June

☒ 3: July, August, September

☐ 4: October, November, December

Instructions and prior year forms are available at www.irs.gov/form941.

Read the separate instructions before you complete Form 941. Type or print within the boxes.

Part 1: Answer these questions for this quarter.

1	Number of employees who received wages, tips, or other compensation for the pay period including: *Mar. 12* (Quarter 1), *June 12* (Quarter 2), *Sept. 12* (Quarter 3), or *Dec. 12* (Quarter 4) ... **1**	14
2	Wages, tips, and other compensation ... **2**	79750 . 17
3	Income tax withheld from wages, tips, and other compensation ... **3**	9570 . 00
4	If no wages, tips, and other compensation are subject to social security or Medicare tax ☐ Check and go to line 6.	

		Column 1		Column 2	
5a	Taxable social security wages ..	79750 . 17	× .124 =	9889 . 02	
5b	Taxable social security tips ...	.	× .124 =	.	
5c	Taxable Medicare wages & tips. .	79750 . 17	× .029 =	2312 . 75	
5d	Taxable wages & tips subject to Additional Medicare Tax withholding	.	× .009 =	.	

5e	Add Column 2 from lines 5a, 5b, 5c, and 5d ... **5e**	12201 . 77
5f	Section 3121(q) Notice and Demand—Tax due on unreported tips (see instructions) .. **5f**	.
6	Total taxes before adjustments (add lines 3, 5e, and 5f) ... **6**	21771 . 77
7	Current quarter's adjustment for fractions of cents ... **7**	. 06
8	Current quarter's adjustment for sick pay ... **8**	.
9	Current quarter's adjustments for tips and group-term life insurance ... **9**	.
10	Total taxes after adjustments. Combine lines 6 through 9 ... **10**	21771 . 83
11	Total deposits for this quarter, including overpayment applied from a prior quarter and overpayment applied from Form 941-X or Form 944-X filed in the current quarter ... **11**	21771 . 83
12a	COBRA premium assistance payments (see instructions) ... **12a**	.
12b	Number of individuals provided COBRA premium assistance .	
13	Add lines 11 and 12a ... **13**	21771 . 83
14	Balance due. If line 10 is more than line 13, enter the difference and see instructions ... **14**	.
15	Overpayment. If line 13 is more than line 10, enter the difference ____ . ___ Check one: ☐ Apply to next return. ☐ Send a refund.	

► You MUST complete both pages of Form 941 and SIGN it.

Next ►

For Privacy Act and Paperwork Reduction Act Notice, see the back of the Payment Voucher.   Cat. No. 17001Z   Form **941** (Rev. 1-2013)

3–12A.

Name *(not your trade name)*	Employer identification number (EIN)
Carlos Cruz	00-0006509

Part 2:   Tell us about your deposit schedule and tax liability for this quarter.

If you are unsure about whether you are a monthly schedule depositor or a semiweekly schedule depositor, see Pub. 15 (Circular E), section 11.

16   Check one: ☐   Line 10 on this return is less than $2,500 or line 10 on the return for the prior quarter was less than $2,500, and you did not incur a $100,000 next-day deposit obligation during the current quarter. If line 10 for the prior quarter was less than $2,500 but line 10 on this return is $100,000 or more, you must provide a record of your federal tax liability. If you are a monthly schedule depositor, complete the deposit schedule below; if you are a semiweekly schedule depositor, attach Schedule B (Form 941). Go to Part 3.

☒   **You were a monthly schedule depositor for the entire quarter.** Enter your tax liability for each month and total liability for the quarter, then go to Part 3.

Tax liability:	Month 1	7193.10
	Month 2	7000.95
	Month 3	7577.78
Total liability for quarter		21771.83 **Total must equal line 10.**

☐   **You were a semiweekly schedule depositor for any part of this quarter.** Complete Schedule B (Form 941), Report of Tax Liability for Semiweekly Schedule Depositors, and attach it to Form 941.

Part 3:   Tell us about your business. If a question does **NOT** apply to your business, leave it blank.

17   If your business has closed or you stopped paying wages . . . .   ☐ Check here, and

enter the final date you paid wages   ☐ / /   .

18   If you are a seasonal employer and you do not have to file a return for every quarter of the year . .   ☐ Check here.

Part 4:   May we speak with your third-party designee?

Do you want to allow an employee, a paid tax preparer, or another person to discuss this return with the IRS? See the instructions for details.

☐ Yes.   Designee's name and phone number

Select a 5-digit Personal Identification Number (PIN) to use when talking to the IRS.   ☐ ☐ ☐ ☐ ☐

☒ No.

Part 5:   Sign here. You **MUST** complete both pages of Form 941 and SIGN it.

Under penalties of perjury, I declare that I have examined this return, including accompanying schedules and statements, and to the best of my knowledge and belief, it is true, correct, and complete. Declaration of preparer (other than taxpayer) is based on all information of which preparer has any knowledge.

✗ Sign your name here	*Carlos Cruz*	Print your name here	Carlos Cruz
		Print your title here	President
Date	10/31/14	Best daytime phone	916-555-9739

Paid Preparer Use Only   Check if you are self-employed . . . ☐

Preparer's name		PTIN	
Preparer's signature		Date	/ /
Firm's name (or yours if self-employed)		EIN	
Address		Phone	
City		State	ZIP code

Form **941** (Rev. 1-2013)

Source: Internal Revenue Service.

3–13A.

Form 941 for 20--: Employer's QUARTERLY Federal Tax Return
(Rev. January 2013)   Department of the Treasury — Internal Revenue Service

OMB No. 1545-0029

Employer identification number (EIN) 0 0 – 0 0 0 5 8 7 4

Name (not your trade name) Karen Kluster

Trade name (if any) Lube and Wash

Address 234 Oak
Number   Street

Suite or room number

Austin   TX   78711-0234
City   State   ZIP code

Report for this Quarter of 20--
(Check one.)

[X] **1:** January, February, March

[ ] **2:** April, May, June

[ ] **3:** July, August, September

[ ] **4:** October, November, December

Instructions and prior year forms are available at *www.irs.gov/form941*.

Read the separate instructions before you complete Form 941. Type or print within the boxes.

Part 1: Answer these questions for this quarter.

1	Number of employees who received wages, tips, or other compensation for the pay period including: *Mar. 12* (Quarter 1), *June 12* (Quarter 2), *Sept. 12* (Quarter 3), or *Dec. 12* (Quarter 4)	1	4
2	Wages, tips, and other compensation	2	31290 . 00
3	Income tax withheld from wages, tips, and other compensation	3	3546 . 00
4	If no wages, tips, and other compensation are subject to social security or Medicare tax		[ ] Check and go to line 6.

		Column 1		Column 2
5a	Taxable social security wages	31290 . 00	× .124 =	3879 . 96
5b	Taxable social security tips	.	× .124 =	.
5c	Taxable Medicare wages & tips	31290 . 00	× .029 =	907 . 41
5d	Taxable wages & tips subject to Additional Medicare Tax withholding	.	× .009 =	.

5e	Add Column 2 from lines 5a, 5b, 5c, and 5d	5e	4787 . 37
5f	Section 3121(q) Notice and Demand—Tax due on unreported tips (see instructions)	5f	.
6	Total taxes before adjustments (add lines 3, 5e, and 5f)	6	8333 . 37
7	Current quarter's adjustment for fractions of cents	7	. 03
8	Current quarter's adjustment for sick pay	8	
9	Current quarter's adjustments for tips and group-term life insurance	9	
10	Total taxes after adjustments. Combine lines 6 through 9	10	8333 . 40
11	Total deposits for this quarter, including overpayment applied from a prior quarter and overpayment applied from Form 941-X or Form 944-X filed in the current quarter	11	8333 . 40
12a	COBRA premium assistance payments (see instructions)	12a	.
12b	Number of individuals provided COBRA premium assistance		
13	Add lines 11 and 12a	13	8333 . 40
14	Balance due. If line 10 is more than line 13, enter the difference and see instructions	14	.
15	Overpayment. If line 13 is more than line 10, enter the difference ____ . ___ Check one: [ ] Apply to next return. [ ] Send a refund.		

▶ **You MUST complete both pages of Form 941 and SIGN it.**

Next ▶

For Privacy Act and Paperwork Reduction Act Notice, see the back of the Payment Voucher.   Cat. No. 17001Z   Form **941** (Rev. 1-2013)

3–13A. Concluded

Name *(not your trade name)*	Employer identification number (EIN)
Karen Kluster	00-0005874

Part 2: Tell us about your deposit schedule and tax liability for this quarter.

If you are unsure about whether you are a monthly schedule depositor or a semiweekly schedule depositor, see Pub. 15 (Circular E), section 11.

16 Check one: ☐ Line 10 on this return is less than $2,500 or line 10 on the return for the prior quarter was less than $2,500, and you did not incur a $100,000 next-day deposit obligation during the current quarter. If line 10 for the prior quarter was less than $2,500 but line 10 on this return is $100,000 or more, you must provide a record of your federal tax liability. If you are a monthly schedule depositor, complete the deposit schedule below; if you are a semiweekly schedule depositor, attach Schedule B (Form 941). Go to Part 3.

☒ **You were a monthly schedule depositor for the entire quarter.** Enter your tax liability for each month and total liability for the quarter, then go to Part 3.

Tax liability:	Month 1	2777. 80
	Month 2	2777. 80
	Month 3	2777. 80
Total liability for quarter		8333. 40	Total must equal line 10.

☐ **You were a semiweekly schedule depositor for any part of this quarter.** Complete Schedule B (Form 941), Report of Tax Liability for Semiweekly Schedule Depositors, and attach it to Form 941.

Part 3: Tell us about your business. If a question does NOT apply to your business, leave it blank.

17 If your business has closed or you stopped paying wages . . . .   ☐ Check here, and

enter the final date you paid wages   [/ /] .

18 If you are a seasonal employer and you do not have to file a return for every quarter of the year . . ☐ Check here.

Part 4: May we speak with your third-party designee?

Do you want to allow an employee, a paid tax preparer, or another person to discuss this return with the IRS? See the instructions for details.

☐ Yes. Designee's name and phone number

Select a 5-digit Personal Identification Number (PIN) to use when talking to the IRS. ☐ ☐ ☐ ☐ ☐

☒ No.

Part 5: Sign here. You MUST complete both pages of Form 941 and SIGN it.

Under penalties of perjury, I declare that I have examined this return, including accompanying schedules and statements, and to the best of my knowledge and belief, it is true, correct, and complete. Declaration of preparer (other than taxpayer) is based on all information of which preparer has any knowledge.

✗	**Sign your name here**	*Karen Kluster*	Print your name here	Karen Kluster
			Print your title here	President
	Date	4/30/14	Best daytime phone	512-555-1111

Paid Preparer Use Only   Check if you are self-employed . . . ☐

Preparer's name		PTIN	
Preparer's signature		Date	/ /
Firm's name (or yours if self-employed)		EIN	
Address		Phone	
City		State	ZIP code	

Page **2**   Form **941** (Rev. 1-2013)

Source: Internal Revenue Service.

3–14A.

Form **941 for 20--:** **Employer's QUARTERLY Federal Tax Return**
(Rev. January 2013)　　Department of the Treasury — Internal Revenue Service

OMB No. 1545-0029

Employer identification number (EIN)　9　0　–　0　0　0　3　6　0　7

Name *(not your trade name)*　Diane R. Peters

Trade name *(if any)*　Bayview Inn

Address　404 Union Avenue
　　　　Number　　　　Street　　　　　　　　　Suite or room number

Memphis　　　　　　　　　TN　　38112
City　　　　　　　　　　　　State　　ZIP code

Report for this Quarter of 20--
(Check one.)

☐ 1: January, February, March

☐ 2: April, May, June

☒ 3: July, August, September

☐ 4: October, November, December

Instructions and prior year forms are available at *www.irs.gov/form941*.

Read the separate instructions before you complete Form 941. Type or print within the boxes.

Part 1:　Answer these questions for this quarter.

1　Number of employees who received wages, tips, or other compensation for the pay period including: *Mar. 12* (Quarter 1), *June 12* (Quarter 2), *Sept. 12* (Quarter 3), or *Dec. 12* (Quarter 4)　**1**　　10

2　Wages, tips, and other compensation . . . .　**2**　49363 . 26

3　Income tax withheld from wages, tips, and other compensation . . . .　**3**　5720 . 00

4　If no wages, tips, and other compensation are subject to social security or Medicare tax　☐ Check and go to line 6.

		Column 1		Column 2
5a	Taxable social security wages . .	39284 . 96	× .124 =	4871 . 34
5b	Taxable social security tips . . .	10078 . 30	× .124 =	1249 . 71
5c	Taxable Medicare wages & tips. .	49363 . 26	× .029 =	1431 . 53
5d	Taxable wages & tips subject to Additional Medicare Tax withholding	.	× .009 =	.

5e　Add Column 2 from lines 5a, 5b, 5c, and 5d . . . .　**5e**　7552 . 58

5f　Section 3121(q) Notice and Demand—Tax due on unreported tips (see instructions) . .　**5f**　　.

6　Total taxes before adjustments (add lines 3, 5e, and 5f) . . . .　**6**　13272 . 58

7　Current quarter's adjustment for fractions of cents . . . .　**7**　　. 29

8　Current quarter's adjustment for sick pay . . . .　**8**　　.

9　Current quarter's adjustments for tips and group-term life insurance . . . . .　**9**　　.

10　Total taxes after adjustments. Combine lines 6 through 9 . . . .　**10**　13272 . 87

11　Total deposits for this quarter, including overpayment applied from a prior quarter and overpayment applied from Form 941-X or Form 944-X filed in the current quarter . . .　**11**　13272 . 87

12a　COBRA premium assistance payments (see instructions) . . . .　**12a**　　.

12b　Number of individuals provided COBRA premium assistance .　　　　　　　

13　Add lines 11 and 12a . . . .　**13**　13272 . 87

14　Balance due. If line 10 is more than line 13, enter the difference and see instructions . . .　**14**　　.

15　Overpayment. If line 13 is more than line 10, enter the difference　　　　　. 　Check one: ☐ Apply to next return. ☐ Send a refund.

▶ You MUST complete both pages of Form 941 and SIGN it.　　　　　Next ▶

For Privacy Act and Paperwork Reduction Act Notice, see the back of the Payment Voucher.　　Cat. No. 17001Z　　Form **941** (Rev. 1-2013)

3–14A. Concluded

Name *(not your trade name)*	Employer identification number (EIN)
Diane R. Peters	00-0003607

Part 2:   Tell us about your deposit schedule and tax liability for this quarter.

If you are unsure about whether you are a monthly schedule depositor or a semiweekly schedule depositor, see Pub. 15 (Circular E), section 11.

16 Check one: ☐ Line 10 on this return is less than $2,500 or line 10 on the return for the prior quarter was less than $2,500, and you did not incur a $100,000 next-day deposit obligation during the current quarter. If line 10 for the prior quarter was less than $2,500 but line 10 on this return is $100,000 or more, you must provide a record of your federal tax liability. If you are a monthly schedule depositor, complete the deposit schedule below; if you are a semiweekly schedule depositor, attach Schedule B (Form 941). Go to Part 3.

☒ **You were a monthly schedule depositor for the entire quarter.** Enter your tax liability for each month and total liability for the quarter, then go to Part 3.

Tax liability:	Month 1	5104 . 95
	Month 2	4083 . 96
	Month 3	4083 . 96
Total liability for quarter		13272 . 87 Total must equal line 10.

☐ **You were a semiweekly schedule depositor for any part of this quarter.** Complete Schedule B (Form 941), Report of Tax Liability for Semiweekly Schedule Depositors, and attach it to Form 941.

Part 3:   Tell us about your business. If a question does NOT apply to your business, leave it blank.

17 **If your business has closed or you stopped paying wages** . . . .   ☐ Check here, and

enter the final date you paid wages   [/ /] .

18 **If you are a seasonal employer and you do not have to file a return for every quarter of the year** . .   ☐ Check here.

Part 4:   May we speak with your third-party designee?

Do you want to allow an employee, a paid tax preparer, or another person to discuss this return with the IRS? See the instructions for details.

☐ Yes.   Designee's name and phone number   [   ]   [   ]

Select a 5-digit Personal Identification Number (PIN) to use when talking to the IRS.   ☐ ☐ ☐ ☐ ☐

☒ No.

Part 5:   Sign here. You MUST complete both pages of Form 941 and SIGN it.

Under penalties of perjury, I declare that I have examined this return, including accompanying schedules and statements, and to the best of my knowledge and belief, it is true, correct, and complete. Declaration of preparer (other than taxpayer) is based on all information of which preparer has any knowledge.

X **Sign your name here** *Diane R. Peters*	Print your name here	Diane R. Peters
	Print your title here	Owner
Date 10/31/--	Best daytime phone	901-555-7959

Paid Preparer Use Only   Check if you are self-employed . . . ☐

Preparer's name	[ ]	PTIN	[ ]
Preparer's signature	[ ]	Date	[/ /]
Firm's name (or yours if self-employed)	[ ]	EIN	[ ]
Address	[ ]	Phone	[ ]
City	[ ] State [ ]	ZIP code	[ ]

Page **2**   Form **941** (Rev. 1-2013)

Source: Internal Revenue Service.

3–15A. (a)

Schedule B (Form 941):

Report of Tax Liability for Semiweekly Schedule Depositors

(Rev. June 2011)   Department of the Treasury — Internal Revenue Service

OMB No. 1545-0029

(EIN)
Employer identification number   0 0 – 0 0 0 1 4 6 2

Name *(not your trade name)*   STEVE HAZELTON

Calendar year   2 0 1 4   *(Also check quarter)*

Report for this Quarter...
(Check one.)

[X] **1:** January, February, March

[ ] **2:** April, May, June

[ ] **3:** July, August, September

[ ] **4:** October, November, December

Use this schedule to show your TAX LIABILITY for the quarter; DO NOT use it to show your deposits. When you file this form with Form 941 or Form 941-SS, DO NOT change your tax liability by adjustments reported on any Forms 941-X. You must fill out this form and attach it to Form 941 or Form 941-SS if you are a semiweekly schedule depositor or became one because your accumulated tax liability on any day was $100,000 or more. Write your daily tax liability on the numbered space that corresponds to the date wages were paid. **See Section 11 in Pub. 15 (Circular E), Employer's Tax Guide, for details.**

Month 1

1		9		17		25		**Tax liability for Month 1**			
2		10		18		26					
3		11		19		27					13693.20
4		12		20		28					
5		13		21		29					
6		14		22		30					
7		15	6933.50	23		31	6759.70				
8		16		24							

Month 2

1		9		17		25		**Tax liability for Month 2**			
2		10		18		26					
3		11		19		27					14667.18
4		12		20		28	7403.10				
5		13		21		29					
6		14	7264.08	22		30					
7		15		23		31					
8		16		24							

Month 3

1		9		17		25		**Tax liability for Month 3**			
2		10		18		26					
3		11		19		27					14442.66
4		12		20		28					
5		13		21		29					
6		14	7202.36	22		30					
7		15		23		31	7240.30				
8		16		24							

Fill in your total liability for the quarter (Month 1 + Month 2 + Month 3) ▶
Total must equal line 10 on Form 941 or Form 941-SS.

Total liability for the quarter

42803.04

For Paperwork Reduction Act Notice, see separate instructions.   Cat. No. 11967Q   Schedule B (Form 941) (Rev. 6-2011)

Source: Internal Revenue Service.

3–15A. Concluded

(b) Due Dates:

    1.   January 22
    2.   February 5
    3.   February 19
    4.   March 5
    5.   March 19
    6.   April 4

3–16A.

1. Date to be filed: by April 15.

2. (a) Penalty for failure to make timely deposit (17 days late):
       $2,505 × 10%.. $250.50

    (b) Penalty for failure to fully pay tax: $2,505 × 1/2%......................   12.53

    (c) Interest on taxes due and unpaid:

$$\frac{\$2,505}{1} \times \frac{3}{100} \times \frac{17}{365}$$ 3.50

    (d) Total penalty imposed $266.53

3–17A.

VISION CLUB COMPANY

(a)

Weekly Payroll for Period Ending December 12, 2014

Employee	Annual Bonus	(1) Regular Earnings	(2) Overtime Earnings	(3) Total Earnings	(4) FICA Taxable Wages This Pay Period OASDI	(4) HI	(5) FICA Taxes to Be Withheld OASDI	(5) HI
Marx, A.	$30,000	$1,870.00		$ 31,870.00	$22,070.00*	$ 31,870.00	$1,368.34	$ 462.12
Boxer, C.	25,000	1,750.00		26,750.00	26,750.00	26,750.00	1,658.50	387.88
Lundy, R.	20,000	1,440.00		21,440.00	21,440.00	21,440.00	1,329.28	310.88
Ruth, B.	15,000	1,080.00		16,080.00	16,080.00	16,080.00	996.96	233.16
Gehrig, L.	8,000	1,130.77	$339.28	9,470.05	9,470.05	9,470.05	587.14	137.32
Totals	$98,000	$7,270.77	$339.28	$105,610.05	$95,810.05	$105,610.05	$5,940.22	$1,531.36

(b) Employer's FICA taxes for week ended December 12, 2014:

OASDI = $95,810.05 × 0.062 = $5,940.22

HI = $105,610.05 × 0.0145 = $1,531.35

*[$113,700 − ($1,870 × 49 pays)]

Solutions—Series B Problems

3–1B.

Employee No.	Employee Name	Biweekly Taxable Wages	FICA Taxes	
			OASDI	HI
711	Adams, Jane	$ 631.24	$ 39.14	$ 9.15
512	Candy, James	892.00	55.30	12.93
624	Guiterrez, Roberta	499.75	30.98	7.25
325	Harrison, Ken	1,250.00	77.50	18.13
422	Lowland, Harriet	1,600.00	99.20	23.20
210	Ranger, Ralph	975.50	60.48	14.14
111	Sweat, Rudy	819.45	50.81	11.88
	Totals	$6,667.94	$413.41	$96.68

Employer's OASDI $\dfrac{\$6,667.94}{\text{Total Taxable Wages}}$ $\dfrac{\$413.41}{\text{Employer's OASDI Tax}}$

Employer's HI Tax $\dfrac{\$6,667.94}{\text{Total Taxable Wages}}$ $\dfrac{\$96.69}{\text{Employer's HI Tax}}$

3–2B.

		OASDI	HI
(a)	9th paycheck	$322.40	$75.40
(b)	22nd paycheck [$113,700 – ($5,200 × 21 pays) = $4,500 OASDI taxable]	279.00	75.40
(c)	24th paycheck	0	75.40

3–3B.

		OASDI	HI
(a)	The amount of FICA taxes that the employer should withhold from Sherm's wages during May ($630 + $475 = $1,105 taxable)	$68.51	$16.02
(b)	The amount of the employer's FICA taxes on Sherm's wages and tips during May	68.51	16.02

3–4B.

(a) $900 + $860 = $1,760 × 0.062 = $109.12

(b) $900 + $860 = $1,760 × 0.0145 = $25.52

3–5B.

| | | October 31 | | | | |
Name and Title	Annual Salary	OASDI Taxable Earnings	OASDI Tax	HI Taxable Earnings	HI Tax
Perez, Paul, President	$136,800	$5,400.00*	$334.80	$5,700.00	$82.65
Donald, Donna, VP Finance	117,600	4,900.00	303.80	4,900.00	71.05
Funke, Jack, VP Sales	76,800	3,200.00	198.40	3,200.00	46.40
Weis, Al, VP Manufacturing	92,400	3,850.00	238.70	3,850.00	55.83
Lang, Hope, VP Personnel	78,000	3,250.00	201.50	3,250.00	47.13
Lee, Amy, VP Secretary	52,800	2,200.00	136.40	2,200.00	31.90

*[$113,700 – ($5,700 × 19)]

| | | December 31 | | | | |
Name and Title	Annual Salary	OASDI Taxable Earnings	OASDI Tax	HI Taxable Earnings	HI Tax
Perez, Paul, President	$136,800	$ 0.00	$ 0.00	$5,700.00	$82.65
Donald, Donna, VP Finance	117,600	1,000.00**	62.00	4,900.00	71.05
Funke, Jack, VP Sales	76,800	3,200.00	198.40	3,200.00	46.40
Weis, Al, VP Manufacturing	92,400	3,850.00	238.70	3,850.00	55.83
Lang, Hope, VP Personnel	78,000	3,250.00	201.50	3,250.00	47.13
Lee, Amy, VP Secretary	52,800	2,200.00	136.40	2,200.00	31.90

**[$113,700 – ($4,900 × 23)]

3–6B.

Name and Position	Salary	OASDI Taxable Earnings	OASDI Tax	HI Taxable Earnings	HI Tax
Kelly Simon, Office	$ 650 per week	$ 650.00	$ 40.30	$ 650.00	$ 9.43
Jim Tress, Sales	3,450 per month	796.15	49.36	796.15	11.54
May Aha, Delivery	520 per week	520.00	32.24	520.00	7.54
Amanda Autry, Partner	1,900 per week*	0.00	0.00	0.00	0.00
Carley Wilson, Partner	1,900 per week*	0.00	0.00	0.00	0.00
	Totals	$1,966.15	$121.90	$1,966.15	$28.51

Employer's OASDI Tax $121.90
Employer's HI Tax $28.51

*The $1,900 that each partner receives each week is considered a drawing or withdrawal, not a salary payment.

3–7B.

Employees' total OASDI	$325.50 ($1,050 × 6.2% × 5)
Employees' total HI	$76.15 ($1,050 × 1.45% = $15.23 × 5 = $76.15)
Employer's total OASDI	$325.50 (6.2% × $5,250)
Employer's total HI	$76.13 (1.45% × $5,250)

3–8B.

(a) The amount of FICA taxes that was withheld from his earnings during 2014 by Umberger Company.

     OASDI $4,631.40
     HI $1,083.15

(b) Parker's self-employment taxes (will receive a credit on his federal income tax return for these paid taxes) on the income derived from the public accounting business for 2014.
[$39,000 taxable ($113,700 – $74,700) × 0.124]
($50,000 taxable × 0.029)

     OASDI $4,836.00
     HI $1,450.00

3–9B.

Employee	Annual Salary	OASDI Taxable Wages	OASDI Tax	HI Tax
Stern, Myra	$ 42,150	$ 3,512.50	$ 217.78	$ 50.93
Lundy, Hal	30,500	2,541.67	157.58	36.85
Franks, Rob	36,000	3,000.00	186.00	43.50
Haggerty, Alan	161,280	0.00	0.00	194.88
Ward, Randy	40,800	3,400.00	210.80	49.30
Hoskin, Al	29,600	2,466.67	152.93	35.77
Wee, Pam	106,800	8,900.00	551.80	129.05
Prince, Harry	76,800	6,400.00	396.80	92.80
Maven, Mary	24,000	2,000.00	124.00	29.00
Harley, David	68,960	5,746.67	356.29	83.33
Totals		$37,967.51	$2,353.98	$745.41

Employer's OASDI Tax ($37,967.51 × 0.062) $2,353.99
Employer's HI Tax ($51,407.51 × 0.0145) $745.41

3–10B.

Full-Time Office:

Employees	Total Monthly Payroll	OASDI Taxable Wages	HI Taxable Wages	OASDI Tax	HI Tax
Hutchings, Jean	$ 2,300.00	$ 2,300.00	$ 2,300.00	$ 142.60	$ 33.35
Florio, Anne	1,900.00	1,900.00	1,900.00	117.80	27.55
Trabert, Judy	3,500.00	3,500.00	3,500.00	217.00	50.75
Williams, Justin	2,875.00	2,875.00	2,875.00	178.25	41.69
Galzano, Jared	4,250.00	4,250.00	4,250.00	263.50	61.63
Sussex, Jude	8,000.00	8,000.00	8,000.00	496.00	116.00
Robinson, Dave	6,300.00	6,300.00	6,300.00	390.60	91.35
Prender, Hank	4,985.00	4,985.00	4,985.00	309.07	72.28
Sorenson, Deb	5,600.00	5,600.00	5,600.00	347.20	81.20
Hutchinson, Wendy	5,200.00	5,200.00	5,200.00	322.40	75.40

Part-Time Office:

Employees	Hours Worked	Hourly Rate	Total Monthly	OASDI Taxable Wages	HI Taxable Wages	OASDI Tax	HI Tax
Fox, Mandy	180	$ 8.25	1,485.00	1,485.00	1,485.00	92.07	21.53
Billings, Clara	160	10.90	1,744.00	1,744.00	1,744.00	108.13	25.29
Nau, Kevin	170	9.75	1,657.50	1,657.50	1,657.50	102.77	24.03
Millis, Toby	142	12.10	1,718.20	1,718.20	1,718.20	106.53	24.91
Cummings, Cheryl	162	13.40	2,170.80	2,170.80	2,170.80	134.59	31.48
Totals			$53,685.50	$53,685.50	$53,685.50	$3,328.51	$778.44

Employer's FICA taxes   OASDI $3,328.50   HI $778.44

3–11B.

Form **941 for 20--:**   **Employer's QUARTERLY Federal Tax Return**
(Rev. January 2013)   Department of the Treasury — Internal Revenue Service

OMB No. 1545-0029

Employer identification number (EIN)   0   0 — 0   0   0   6   5   0   9

Name *(not your trade name)*   James Gallagher

Trade name *(if any)*   Gallagher Company

Address   901 Keystone
      Number   Street   Suite or room number

      Sacramento   CA   95916
      City   State   ZIP code

Report for this Quarter of 20--
(Check one.)

- ☐ **1:** January, February, March
- ☐ **2:** April, May, June
- ☒ **3:** July, August, September
- ☐ **4:** October, November, December

Instructions and prior year forms are available at *www.irs.gov/form941*.

Read the separate instructions before you complete Form 941. Type or print within the boxes.

Part 1:   Answer these questions for this quarter.

1	Number of employees who received wages, tips, or other compensation for the pay period including: *Mar. 12* (Quarter 1), *June 12* (Quarter 2), *Sept. 12* (Quarter 3), or *Dec. 12* (Quarter 4) **1**	15
2	Wages, tips, and other compensation **2**	89352 . 18
3	Income tax withheld from wages, tips, and other compensation **3**	10195 . 00
4	If no wages, tips, and other compensation are subject to social security or Medicare tax	☐ Check and go to line 6.

		Column 1		Column 2
5a	Taxable social security wages	89352 . 18	× .124 =	11079 . 67
5b	Taxable social security tips	.	× .124 =	.
5c	Taxable Medicare wages & tips	89352 . 18	× .029 =	2591 . 21
5d	Taxable wages & tips subject to Additional Medicare Tax withholding	.	× .009 =	.

5e	Add Column 2 from lines 5a, 5b, 5c, and 5d **5e**	13670 . 88
5f	Section 3121(q) Notice and Demand—Tax due on unreported tips (see instructions) **5f**	.
6	Total taxes before adjustments (add lines 3, 5e, and 5f) **6**	23865 . 88
7	Current quarter's adjustment for fractions of cents **7**	. 04
8	Current quarter's adjustment for sick pay **8**	.
9	Current quarter's adjustments for tips and group-term life insurance **9**	.
10	Total taxes after adjustments. Combine lines 6 through 9 **10**	23865 . 92
11	Total deposits for this quarter, including overpayment applied from a prior quarter and overpayment applied from Form 941-X or Form 944-X filed in the current quarter **11**	23865 . 92
12a	COBRA premium assistance payments (see instructions) **12a**	.
12b	Number of individuals provided COBRA premium assistance	
13	Add lines 11 and 12a **13**	23865 . 92
14	Balance due. If line 10 is more than line 13, enter the difference and see instructions **14**	.
15	Overpayment. If line 13 is more than line 10, enter the difference [.] Check one: ☐ Apply to next return. ☐ Send a refund.	

▶ **You MUST complete both pages of Form 941 and SIGN it.**   **Next ➡**

For Privacy Act and Paperwork Reduction Act Notice, see the back of the Payment Voucher.   Cat. No. 17001Z   Form **941** (Rev. 1-2013)

3–12B.

Name (not your trade name)	**Employer identification number (EIN)**
James Gallagher	00-0006509

Part 2:   Tell us about your deposit schedule and tax liability for this quarter.

If you are unsure about whether you are a monthly schedule depositor or a semiweekly schedule depositor, see Pub. 15 (Circular E), section 11.

16   Check one: [ ]   Line 10 on this return is less than $2,500 or line 10 on the return for the prior quarter was less than $2,500, and you did not incur a $100,000 next-day deposit obligation during the current quarter. If line 10 for the prior quarter was less than $2,500 but line 10 on this return is $100,000 or more, you must provide a record of your federal tax liability. If you are a monthly schedule depositor, complete the deposit schedule below; if you are a semiweekly schedule depositor, attach Schedule B (Form 941). Go to Part 3.

           [X]   **You were a monthly schedule depositor for the entire quarter.** Enter your tax liability for each month and total liability for the quarter, then go to Part 3.

	Tax liability:	Month 1	7891 . 75	
		Month 2	7984 . 90	
		Month 3	7989 . 27	
	Total liability for quarter		23865 . 92	Total must equal line 10.

           [ ]   **You were a semiweekly schedule depositor for any part of this quarter.** Complete Schedule B (Form 941), Report of Tax Liability for Semiweekly Schedule Depositors, and attach it to Form 941.

Part 3:   Tell us about your business. If a question does NOT apply to your business, leave it blank.

17   If your business has closed or you stopped paying wages . . . .   [ ] Check here, and

     enter the final date you paid wages | /   / | .

18   If you are a seasonal employer and you do not have to file a return for every quarter of the year . .   [ ] Check here.

Part 4:   May we speak with your third-party designee?

Do you want to allow an employee, a paid tax preparer, or another person to discuss this return with the IRS? See the instructions for details.

[ ]   Yes. Designee's name and phone number | | | |

         Select a 5-digit Personal Identification Number (PIN) to use when talking to the IRS.   [ ] [ ] [ ] [ ] [ ]

[X]   No.

Part 5:   Sign here. You MUST complete both pages of Form 941 and SIGN it.

Under penalties of perjury, I declare that I have examined this return, including accompanying schedules and statements, and to the best of my knowledge and belief, it is true, correct, and complete. Declaration of preparer (other than taxpayer) is based on all information of which preparer has any knowledge.

X	**Sign your name here**	*James Gallagher*	Print your name here	James Gallagher
			Print your title here	President
	Date	10/31/14	Best daytime phone	916-555-9739

Paid Preparer Use Only   Check if you are self-employed . . . . [ ]

Preparer's name		PTIN	
Preparer's signature		Date	/ /
Firm's name (or yours if self-employed)		EIN	
Address		Phone	
City		State	ZIP code

Page **2**   Form **941** (Rev. 1-2013)

Source: Internal Revenue Service.

3–13B.

Form **941 for 20--:** **Employer's QUARTERLY Federal Tax Return**
(Rev. January 2013)   Department of the Treasury — Internal Revenue Service

OMB No. 1545-0029

Employer identification number (EIN) `0` `0` – `0` `0` `0` `5` `8` `7` `4`

Name *(not your trade name)* Stan Barker

Trade name *(if any)* Quik-Stop Market

Address 234 Oak
         Number   Street   Suite or room number

         Austin   TX   78711-0234
         City   State   ZIP code

Report for this Quarter of 20--
(Check one.)

[X] **1:** January, February, March

[ ] **2:** April, May, June

[ ] **3:** July, August, September

[ ] **4:** October, November, December

Instructions and prior year forms are available at *www.irs.gov/form941.*

Read the separate instructions before you complete Form 941. Type or print within the boxes.

Part 1:	**Answer these questions for this quarter.**

1 Number of employees who received wages, tips, or other compensation for the pay period including: *Mar. 12* (Quarter 1), *June 12* (Quarter 2), *Sept. 12* (Quarter 3), or *Dec. 12* (Quarter 4)   **1** | 4 |

2 Wages, tips, and other compensation . . . .   **2** | 18630 . 00 |

3 Income tax withheld from wages, tips, and other compensation . . . .   **3** | 2556 . 00 |

4 If no wages, tips, and other compensation are subject to social security or Medicare tax   [ ] Check and go to line 6.

	Column 1		**Column 2**
5a Taxable social security wages . .	18630 . 00	× .124 =	2310 . 12
5b Taxable social security tips . . .	.	× .124 =	.
5c Taxable Medicare wages & tips .	18630 . 00	× .029 =	540 . 27
5d Taxable wages & tips subject to Additional Medicare Tax withholding	.	× .009 =	.

5e Add Column 2 from lines 5a, 5b, 5c, and 5d . . . . .   **5e** | 2850 . 39 |

5f Section 3121(q) Notice and Demand—Tax due on unreported tips (see instructions) . .   **5f** | . |

6 Total taxes before adjustments (add lines 3, 5e, and 5f) . . . .   **6** | 5406 . 39 |

7 Current quarter's adjustment for fractions of cents . . . .   **7** | . 03 |

8 Current quarter's adjustment for sick pay . . . .   **8** | . |

9 Current quarter's adjustments for tips and group-term life insurance . . . .   **9** | . |

10 Total taxes after adjustments. Combine lines 6 through 9 . . . .   **10** | 5406 . 42 |

11 Total deposits for this quarter, including overpayment applied from a prior quarter and overpayment applied from Form 941-X or Form 944-X filed in the current quarter . . .   **11** | 5406 . 42 |

12a COBRA premium assistance payments (see instructions) . . . .   **12a** | . |

12b Number of individuals provided COBRA premium assistance . . | |

13 Add lines 11 and 12a . . . .   **13** | 5406 . 42 |

14 Balance due. If line 10 is more than line 13, enter the difference and see instructions . . .   **14** | . |

15 Overpayment. If line 13 is more than line 10, enter the difference | . | Check one: [ ] Apply to next return. [ ] Send a refund.

▶ **You MUST complete both pages of Form 941 and SIGN it.**   Next ▶

For Privacy Act and Paperwork Reduction Act Notice, see the back of the Payment Voucher.   Cat. No. 17001Z   Form **941** (Rev. 1-2013)

3–13B.   Concluded

Name *(not your trade name)*	Employer identification number (EIN)
Stan Barker	00-0005874

Part 2:   Tell us about your deposit schedule and tax liability for this quarter.

If you are unsure about whether you are a monthly schedule depositor or a semiweekly schedule depositor, see Pub. 15 (Circular E), section 11.

16 Check one: ☐ Line 10 on this return is less than $2,500 or line 10 on the return for the prior quarter was less than $2,500, and you did not incur a $100,000 next-day deposit obligation during the current quarter. If line 10 for the prior quarter was less than $2,500 but line 10 on this return is $100,000 or more, you must provide a record of your federal tax liability. If you are a monthly schedule depositor, complete the deposit schedule below; if you are a semiweekly schedule depositor, attach Schedule B (Form 941). Go to Part 3.

☒ **You were a monthly schedule depositor for the entire quarter.** Enter your tax liability for each month and total liability for the quarter, then go to Part 3.

	Tax liability:	Month 1	1802 . 14
		Month 2	1802 . 14
		Month 3	1802 . 14
	Total liability for quarter		5406 . 42	Total must equal line 10.

☐ **You were a semiweekly schedule depositor for any part of this quarter.** Complete Schedule B (Form 941), Report of Tax Liability for Semiweekly Schedule Depositors, and attach it to Form 941.

Part 3:   Tell us about your business. If a question does NOT apply to your business, leave it blank.

17 If your business has closed or you stopped paying wages . . . . ☐ Check here, and

enter the final date you paid wages   [/   /   ] .

18 If you are a seasonal employer and you do not have to file a return for every quarter of the year . . ☐ Check here.

Part 4:   May we speak with your third-party designee?

Do you want to allow an employee, a paid tax preparer, or another person to discuss this return with the IRS? See the instructions for details.

☐ Yes. Designee's name and phone number   [   ]   [   ]

Select a 5-digit Personal Identification Number (PIN) to use when talking to the IRS. [   ][   ][   ][   ][   ]

☒ No.

Part 5:   Sign here. You MUST complete both pages of Form 941 and SIGN it.

Under penalties of perjury, I declare that I have examined this return, including accompanying schedules and statements, and to the best of my knowledge and belief, it is true, correct, and complete. Declaration of preparer (other than taxpayer) is based on all information of which preparer has any knowledge.

✗	Sign your name here	*Stan Barker*	Print your name here	Stan Barker
			Print your title here	President
	Date	4/30/14	Best daytime phone	512-555-1111

Paid Preparer Use Only   Check if you are self-employed . . . ☐

Preparer's name		PTIN	
Preparer's signature		Date	/ /
Firm's name (or yours if self-employed)		EIN	
Address		Phone	
City		State		ZIP code	

Page **2**   Form **941** (Rev. 1-2013)

3-14B.

Form **941 for 20--:**	**Employer's QUARTERLY Federal Tax Return**
(Rev. January 2013)	Department of the Treasury — Internal Revenue Service

OMB No. 1545-0029

Employer identification number (EIN) | 0 | 0 | — | 0 | 0 | 0 | 3 | 6 | 0 | 7

Name *(not your trade name)* Dawn Smedley

Trade name *(if any)* Beechtree Inn

Address 404 Union Avenue
Number   Street   Suite or room number

Memphis   TN   38112
City   State   ZIP code

Report for this Quarter of 20--
(Check one.)

- [ ] **1:** January, February, March
- [ ] **2:** April, May, June
- [X] **3:** July, August, September
- [ ] **4:** October, November, December

Instructions and prior year forms are available at *www.irs.gov/form941.*

Read the separate instructions before you complete Form 941. Type or print within the boxes.

Part 1:   Answer these questions for this quarter.

1   Number of employees who received wages, tips, or other compensation for the pay period including: *Mar. 12* (Quarter 1), *June 12* (Quarter 2), *Sept. 12* (Quarter 3), or *Dec. 12* (Quarter 4) **1** | 10

2   Wages, tips, and other compensation . . . . **2** | 78953 . 30

3   Income tax withheld from wages, tips, and other compensation . . . . . **3** | 8216 . 00

4   If no wages, tips, and other compensation are subject to social security or Medicare tax   [ ] Check and go to line 6.

		Column 1		Column 2
5a	Taxable social security wages . .	64875 . 00	× .124 =	8044 . 50
5b	Taxable social security tips . . .	14078 . 30	× .124 =	1745 . 71
5c	Taxable Medicare wages & tips. .	78953 . 30	× .029 =	2289 . 65
5d	Taxable wages & tips subject to Additional Medicare Tax withholding	.	× .009 =	.

5e   Add Column 2 from lines 5a, 5b, 5c, and 5d . . . . **5e** | 12079 . 86

5f   Section 3121(q) Notice and Demand—Tax due on unreported tips (see instructions) . . **5f** | .

6   Total taxes before adjustments (add lines 3, 5e, and 5f) . . . . . . **6** | 20295 . 86

7   Current quarter's adjustment for fractions of cents . . . . . . **7** | . 26

8   Current quarter's adjustment for sick pay . . . . **8** | .

9   Current quarter's adjustments for tips and group-term life insurance . . . . **9** | .

10   Total taxes after adjustments. Combine lines 6 through 9 . . . . . **10** | 20296 . 12

11   Total deposits for this quarter, including overpayment applied from a prior quarter and overpayment applied from Form 941-X or Form 944-X filed in the current quarter . . . **11** | 20296 . 12

12a   COBRA premium assistance payments (see instructions) . . . . **12a** | .

12b   Number of individuals provided COBRA premium assistance . . |

13   Add lines 11 and 12a . . . . **13** | 20296 . 12

14   Balance due. If line 10 is more than line 13, enter the difference and see instructions . . . **14** | .

15   Overpayment. If line 13 is more than line 10, enter the difference | .   Check one: [ ] Apply to next return. [ ] Send a refund.

▶ **You MUST complete both pages of Form 941 and SIGN it.**

Next ▶

For Privacy Act and Paperwork Reduction Act Notice, see the back of the Payment Voucher.   Cat. No. 17001Z   Form **941** (Rev. 1-2013)

3–14B. Concluded

Name *(not your trade name)*	Employer identification number (EIN)
Dawn Smedley	00-0003607

Part 2:   Tell us about your deposit schedule and tax liability for this quarter.

If you are unsure about whether you are a monthly schedule depositor or a semiweekly schedule depositor, see Pub. 15 (Circular E), section 11.

16   Check one: ☐   Line 10 on this return is less than $2,500 or line 10 on the return for the prior quarter was less than $2,500, and you did not incur a $100,000 next-day deposit obligation during the current quarter. If line 10 for the prior quarter was less than $2,500 but line 10 on this return is $100,000 or more, you must provide a record of your federal tax liability. If you are a monthly schedule depositor, complete the deposit schedule below; if you are a semiweekly schedule depositor, attach Schedule B (Form 941). Go to Part 3.

☒   **You were a monthly schedule depositor for the entire quarter.** Enter your tax liability for each month and total liability for the quarter, then go to Part 3.

Tax liability:	Month 1	7806 . 20	
	Month 2	6244 . 96	
	Month 3	6244 . 96	
	Total liability for quarter	20296 . 12	**Total must equal line 10.**

☐   **You were a semiweekly schedule depositor for any part of this quarter.** Complete Schedule B (Form 941), Report of Tax Liability for Semiweekly Schedule Depositors, and attach it to Form 941.

Part 3:   Tell us about your business. If a question does NOT apply to your business, leave it blank.

17   **If your business has closed or you stopped paying wages** . . . . ☐ Check here, and

enter the final date you paid wages   [/ /] .

18   **If you are a seasonal employer and you do not have to file a return for every quarter of the year** . . ☐ Check here.

Part 4:   May we speak with your third-party designee?

Do you want to allow an employee, a paid tax preparer, or another person to discuss this return with the IRS? See the instructions for details.

☐ **Yes.** Designee's name and phone number   [   ]   [   ]

Select a 5-digit Personal Identification Number (PIN) to use when talking to the IRS.   [ ] [ ] [ ] [ ] [ ]

☒ **No.**

Part 5:   Sign here. You MUST complete both pages of Form 941 and SIGN it.

Under penalties of perjury, I declare that I have examined this return, including accompanying schedules and statements, and to the best of my knowledge and belief, it is true, correct, and complete. Declaration of preparer (other than taxpayer) is based on all information of which preparer has any knowledge.

✗   **Sign your name here**   *Dawn Smedley*

Print your name here	Dawn Smedley
Print your title here	President

Date   10/31/--

Best daytime phone   901-555-7959

Paid Preparer Use Only
Check if you are self-employed . . . ☐

Preparer's name		PTIN	
Preparer's signature		Date	/ /
Firm's name (or yours if self-employed)		EIN	
Address		Phone	
City		State		ZIP code	

Page **2**

Form **941** (Rev. 1-2013)

Source: Internal Revenue Service.

3–15B. (a)

Schedule B (Form 941):

Report of Tax Liability for Semiweekly Schedule Depositors

OMB No. 1545-0029

(Rev. June 2011)   Department of the Treasury — Internal Revenue Service

(EIN)
Employer identification number `0` `0` – `0` `0` `0` `1` `4` `6` `2`

Name (not your trade name) Harry Conway

Calendar year `2` `0` `1` `4`   (Also check quarter)

Report for this Quarter...
(Check one.)

- [X] **1:** January, February, March
- [ ] **2:** April, May, June
- [ ] **3:** July, August, September
- [ ] **4:** October, November, December

Use this schedule to show your TAX LIABILITY for the quarter; DO NOT use it to show your deposits. When you file this form with Form 941 or Form 941-SS, DO NOT change your tax liability by adjustments reported on any Forms 941-X. You must fill out this form and attach it to Form 941 or Form 941-SS if you are a semiweekly schedule depositor or became one because your accumulated tax liability on any day was $100,000 or more. Write your daily tax liability on the numbered space that corresponds to the date wages were paid. See Section 11 in Pub. 15 (Circular E), Employer's Tax Guide, for details.

Month 1

#		#		#		#		Tax liability for Month 1
1	.	9	.	17	.	25	.	
2	.	10	.	18	.	26	.	**18536 . 30**
3	.	11	.	19	.	27	.	
4	.	12	.	20	.	28	.	
5	.	13	.	21	.	29	.	
6	.	14	.	22	.	30	.	
7	.	15	9412 . 60	23	.	31	9123 . 70	
8	.	16	.	24	.			

Month 2

#		#		#		#		Tax liability for Month 2
1	.	9	.	17	.	25	.	
2	.	10	.	18	.	26	.	**17083 . 18**
3	.	11	.	19	.	27	.	
4	.	12	.	20	.	28	8229 . 42	
5	.	13	.	21	.	29	.	
6	.	14	8853 . 76	22	.	30	.	
7	.	15	.	23	.	31	.	
8	.	16	.	24	.			

Month 3

#		#		#		#		Tax liability for Month 3
1	.	9	.	17	.	25	.	
2	.	10	.	18	.	26	.	**16693 . 60**
3	.	11	.	19	.	27	.	
4	.	12	.	20	.	28	.	
5	.	13	.	21	.	29	.	
6	.	14	8196 . 40	22	.	30	.	
7	.	15	.	23	.	31	8497 . 20	
8	.	16	.	24	.			

Fill in your total liability for the quarter (Month 1 + Month 2 + Month 3) ►
Total must equal line 10 on Form 941 or Form 941-SS.

Total liability for the quarter

52313 . 08

For Paperwork Reduction Act Notice, see separate instructions.   Cat. No. 11967Q   Schedule B (Form 941) (Rev. 6-2011)

Source: Internal Revenue Service.

3–15B. Concluded

(b) Due Dates:

      1.   January 22
      2.   February 5
      3.   February 19
      4.   March 5
      5.   March 19
      6.   April 4

3–16B.

1. Date to be filed: by July 15.

2. (a) Penalty for failure to make timely deposit (21 days late):
         $3,930 × 10%... $393.00

    (b) Penalty for failure to fully pay tax: $3,930 × 1/2% 19.65

    (c) Interest on taxes due and unpaid:

$$\frac{\$3,930}{1} \times \frac{3}{100} \times \frac{21}{365}$$ 6.78

    (d) Total penalty imposed $419.43

3–17B.

Gleeson Brewing Company

(a)

Weekly Payroll for Period Ending December 12, 2014

Employee	Annual Bonus	(1) Regular Earnings	(2) Overtime Earnings	(3) Total Earnings	(4) FICA Taxable Wages This Pay Period		(5) FICA Taxes to Be Withheld	
					OASDI	HI	OASDI	HI
Won, H.	$30,000	$1,920.00		$ 31,920.00	$19,620.00*	$ 31,920.00	$1,216.44	$ 462.84
Park, B.	25,000	1,850.00		26,850.00	23,050.00**	26,850.00	1,429.10	389.33
James, R.	20,000	1,680.00		21,680.00	21,680.00	21,680.00	1,344.16	314.36
Oho, J.	15,000	1,215.00		16,215.00	16,215.00	16,215.00	1,005.33	235.12
Mack, K.	8,000	784.62	$176.58	8,961.20	8,961.20	8,961.20	555.59	129.94
Totals.........	$98,000	$7,449.62	$176.58	$105,626.20	$89,526.20	$105,626.20	$5,550.62	$1,531.59

(b) Employer's FICA taxes for week ended December 12, 2014:

OASDI = $89,526.20 × 0.062 = $5,550.62

HI = $105,626.20 × 0.0145 = $1,531.58

*[$113,700 – ($1,920 × 49 pays)]

**[$113,700 – ($1,850 × 49 pays)]

Continuing Payroll Problems A and B (p. 3–65)

See the completed payroll register on pages CPP–1 through CPP–6.

Case Problems (p. 3–66)

Case 3–1

The following changes should be made on Form 941 before the final copy is prepared, signed, dated, and mailed:

1. *Line 2:* The amount of the total wages and salaries was incorrectly read from the ledger account. The correct amount is $77,900.83.

2. *Line 5a:* The transposition error noted above has been carried down to this line. The amount should be corrected to read $77,900.83, and the extension should be changed to read $9,659.70.

3. *Line 5c:* The transposition error noted above has been carried down to this line, too. The amount should be corrected to read $77,900.83, and the extension should be changed to read $2,259.12.

4. *Line 5e:* The total FICA taxes should read $11,918.82.

5. *Line 6:* Total taxes before adjustments should be corrected to read $23,995.82.

6. *Line 7:* After the corrections indicated above are made, there is an adjustment of FICA taxes. These lines should read –.02.

7. *Line 14:* Since the total deposits for the quarter equal the net taxes, this line should be left blank.

8. *Line 16:* Since the three liability accounts indicate that Coastal is a semiweekly depositor, the box for "Semiweekly depositors" should be checked. The tax liability section should be left blank. In addition, Schedule B, Report of Tax Liability for Semiweekly Schedule Depositors, should be completed.

Case 3–2

Jackson is not an employee of Nelson. A person in the trade or business of referring sitters to individuals is not considered the employer of the sitters if:

1. He or she does not pay the salary of the sitters.
2. He or she is paid a fee by the sitter or the person employing the sitter.

Jackson receives her salary directly from Mrs. Mock and is a household employee of Mrs. Mock.

CHAPTER 4

Learning Objectives

After studying this chapter, students should be able to:

1. Explain coverage under the Federal Income Tax Withholding Law by determining: (a) the employer-employee relationship, (b) the kinds of payments defined as wages, and (c) the kinds of pretax salary reductions.

2. Explain: (a) the types of withholding allowances that may be claimed by employees for income tax withholding and (b) the purpose and use of Form W-4.

3. Compute the amount of federal income tax to be withheld using: (a) the percentage method; (b) the wage-bracket method; (c) alternative methods such as quarterly averaging, annualizing of wages, and part-year employment; and (d) withholding of federal income taxes on supplementary wage payments.

4. Explain: (a) Form W-2, (b) the completion of *Form 941, Employer's Quarterly Federal Tax Return*, (c) major types of information returns, and (d) the impact of state and local income taxes on the payroll accounting process.

Contents

Chapter 4 outline:

Pretax Salary Reductions
    Cafeteria Plans
    Flexible-Spending Accounts
    Health Savings Accounts
    Archer Medical Savings Accounts
    Deferred Arrangements

TAX-DEFERRED RETIREMENT ACCOUNTS
    Individual Retirement Accounts
    Roth IRA

WITHHOLDING ALLOWANCES
    Personal Allowances
    Allowances for Dependents
    Additional Withholding Allowance
    Other Withholding Allowances
    Form W-4 (Employee's Withholding Allowance Certificate)
        Completing Form W-4
        Withholding Allowances
        Changing Form W-4
        Exemption from Income Tax Withholding
        Additional and Voluntary Withholding Agreements
        Electronic Filing of Form W-4
        Invalid Forms W-4
        Requested Forms W-4
        Employee Penalties
        Withholding on Nonresident Aliens
    Other Withholdings
        Withholding for Pension or Annuity Payments
        Withholding from Sick Pay
        Withholding on Government Payments

FEDERAL INCOME TAX WITHHOLDING
    Percentage Method
    Wage-Bracket Method

OTHER METHODS OF WITHHOLDING

SUPPLEMENTAL WAGE PAYMENTS
    Vacation Pay
    Supplemental Wages Paid with Regular Wages
    Supplemental Wages Paid Separately from Regular Wages
        Method A
        Method B
    Gross-Up Supplementals

WAGE AND TAX STATEMENTS
- Form W-2
- Form W-2c
- Form W-3
- Penalties
- Form W-3c
- Privately Printed Forms

RETURNS EMPLOYERS MUST COMPLETE

INFORMATION RETURNS

INDEPENDENT CONTRACTOR PAYMENTS

BACKUP WITHHOLDING
- Nonpayroll Reporting

ELECTRONIC FILING FORM W-2 AND INFORMATION RETURNS

WITHHOLDING STATE INCOME TAX
- State Income Tax Returns and Reports
- Withholding Local Income Taxes

KEY TERMS

CHAPTER SUMMARY

Matching Quiz (p. 4–35)

1.	J		**6.**	H
2.	E		**7.**	F
3.	I		**8.**	C
4.	A		**9.**	G
5.	B		**10.**	D

Questions for Review (p. 4–36)

Note: All answers and solutions are based on Tax Tables A and B in the textbook and the tax regulations presented in Chapter 4. Tax Tables A and B are used by employers, effective January 1, 2013.

1. The amount by which the fair market value of the fringe benefit exceeds what the employee paid, plus any amount the law excludes.

2. Cash tips of $20 or more received in a calendar month, in the course of employment with a single employer, are treated as remuneration subject to income tax withholding.

3. a. Nonexempt
   b. Exempt
   c. Exempt
   d. Exempt
   e. Exempt

4. The employer must match the employee's contribution up to a maximum of 3 percent of the employee's pay.

5. The maximum of deferred contributions that employees can make into their 401(k) plans is the lesser of $17,500 or 100 percent of their pay.

6. A personal allowance is a deduction allowed in computing taxable income. In 2013, the amount of a personal allowance was $3,900.

7. None. D'Amato would have been entitled to a *partial* tax-free deduction if his modified adjusted gross income had been less than $69,000.

8. Employer contributions into employees' health savings accounts are excluded from the employees' taxable income.

9. Employees who had no income tax liability in 2013 and do not expect to have any for 2014 qualify for exemption from withholding of federal income tax from their wages. Single persons who made less than $10,000 in 2013 owed no federal income tax. During 2013, a married couple entitled to file a joint return could earn combined wages up to $20,000 without incurring any federal income tax liability. However, if someone else claimed the employee as a dependent on his or her tax return, the employee probably would have to pay some income tax. For example, in 2013, employees were *not* exempt from withholding if they had any nonwage income, such as interest on savings or dividends (exceeding $350), and if their total income (wages and nonwage income) was more than $1,000; or if unearned income was less than $350 but total income exceeds $6,100.

   Employees who are exempt from the withholding of federal income taxes should complete and submit to their employer Form W-4 showing the exempt status.

10. The special period rule allows employers to use October 31 as the cutoff date for valuing noncash fringe benefits. This means that fringe benefits received in November and December can be treated as being received in the following year.

11. Oldt may elect to have no income tax withheld from his pension fund payments by so indicating on *Form W-4P, Withholding Certificate for Pension or Annuity Payments.*

12. $75.00

    $325.00 ($162.50 × 2)

13. The formula is:

$$\frac{\text{Intended payment}}{1 - \text{Applicable tax rates}}$$

14. When the federal income tax has already been withheld from the employee's regular wages, the employer may select one of two alternative methods for withholding the tax on the annual bonus payment. The employer may combine the bonus with the wages for the last preceding or the current payroll period. The amount to be withheld is then determined as if the bonus and the regular wages were a single payment. However, since the federal income tax has already been withheld from the regular wages, that amount is subtracted from the tax due on the total. Only the excess federal income tax is deducted from the payment of the bonus.

    Or, the employer may elect to withhold a flat 25 percent of the bonus payment. If the employer elects to withhold at the 25 percent rate, this must be done without considering any withholding allowances claimed by the employee.

15. Form 944 replaces Form 941 for employers who owe $1,000 or less in employment taxes for the year, and Form 944 has to be filed only once a year.

16. Employers who are required to prepare information returns (Form 1099 series) must file a Form 1096 to transmit each type of information return. For example, one Form 1096 is filed to transmit all Forms 1099-MISC.

17. The penalty is $50 per form.

18. Employees who willfully file false Forms W-4 are subject to fines of up to $1,000 or imprisonment for up to one year or both. A $500 civil penalty for each offense is imposed on employees claiming excess deductions.

19. Employers need to submit only those W-4s that are requested in writing by the IRS.

20. The payer's telephone number is required.

Questions for Discussion (p. 4–36)

1. No, Lagomarsino should not include the cash value of Oberstar's meals as part of his taxable wages. The general rule is that the value of meals and lodging furnished an employee is included in taxable wages. However, the tax does not apply if the employer furnishes the meals on the business premises and for the employer's convenience. Note that this exclusion does not apply if the employee is given a cash allowance for meals or lodging. Only meals and lodging furnished in kind are free from withholding.

2. Generally, a payroll period is the period of service for which a payment of wages is ordinarily made to an employee by the employer. When the payroll periods are of a uniform duration, there is no problem. However, in cases such as that of Nagle, the payroll periods may sometimes vary. The period for which payment is ordinarily made is controlling, even though that period may not coincide with the actual period for which a given payment is made. Thus, Nagle's payroll period for withholding purposes is still weekly, and Barbri Company must treat the wage payment as if it were three separate weekly wage payments.

3. This question gives students an opportunity to become acquainted with their state's income tax withholding law. If your state has no withholding law, you may assign one or more other states to be investigated. Or, you may divide the class and have students research several different state laws so that comparisons and contrasts may be drawn. You may ask students to prepare oral or written reports and develop an All-States Chart of Income Tax Withholding Laws.

4. There is no law against withholding more federal income taxes from a worker's pay than would be required under the wage-bracket or percentage method. Reynolds would be proceeding legally by amending her Form W-4 and would be joining many wage earners who give interest-free loans to Uncle Sam by overwithholding. For some workers, the only way to save money is via the payroll deduction route of overwithholding. Of course, the economic disadvantage in this approach to forced savings is that the monies deducted and turned over to the government earn no interest. But like many, Reynolds may lack the initiative or motivation to deposit $10 weekly in an interest-bearing savings account.

5. a. The IRS claims that several hundred casino waitresses and waiters fail to report about $10,000 in tips each year and owe an average of $2,400 in back taxes. Waiters and waitresses in casino hotels state they have received letters from the IRS indicating that federal agents have conducted surveillance operations at their places of employment and that a detailed analysis of the hotel-casino records was undertaken. From this information, the IRS reconstructs the amount of tips received by each tipped employee. In the IRS letters, the casino workers were informed that many factors affecting the hourly tip rate in each particular casino were taken into consideration in determining the amount of tips received. It was noted that the lifestyles of some waiters and waitresses did not correspond with their reported income.

b. No. Leland's employer is not subject to a penalty for not having withheld payroll taxes on her *unreported* tips. As indicated in Chapters 3 and 4, the liability for unreported tip income rests squarely on the shoulders of the person receiving the tips. The employer is not required to audit or verify the amount of tip income reported.

6. Since the fringe benefit is subject to federal income and social security taxes, it must be reported on a W-2 form. Because these taxes cannot be deducted from any wage payments, the value of the fringe benefit will have to be grossed-up (add taxes to the fringe value) in order to cover the appropriate taxes.

Practical Problems (p. 4–39)

The principles and practices of payroll accounting discussed in Chapter 4 are applied in the Practical Problems as shown below.

Principle or Practice	Practical Problem No. (A and B)
1. Using the *percentage method* to compute federal income taxes to withhold.	4–2, 4–3
2. Using the *wage-bracket method* to compute federal income taxes to withhold.	4–1, 4–3, 4–4, 4–5, 4–8 through 4–9
3. Computing the *withholdings for FICA, federal income taxes, state income taxes, and city income taxes* to determine net pay.	4–5, 4–8, 4–9
4. Computing *annual bonus to be paid with regular salaries.*	4–6, 4–8
5. Computing the *quarterly totals* (weekly and monthly paydays) for gross earnings, deductions, and net pay.	4–9
6. Gross-up supplementals.	4–10
7. Compute net pay with tax-free retirement withholdings.	4–7, 4–11
8. Completing *Form 941* and *Employer's Report of State Income Tax Withheld.*	4–12
9. Completing *Forms W-2* and *Form W-3* for calendar year.	4–13

Solutions—Series A Problems

4–1A.

Gross pay	$150.00
Federal income tax (on $650.00)	(35.00)
Social security taxes (6.2% × $650.00).....	(40.30)
(1.45% × $650.00)...	(9.43)
State income tax (2% × $650.00)..............	(13.00)
Net pay	$ 52.27

4–2A.

Employee No.	Employee Name	Marital Status	No. of Withholding Allowances	Gross Wage or Salary	Amount to Be Withheld
1	Amoroso, A.	M	4	$1,610 weekly	$155.35[a]
2	Finley, R.	S	0	825 biweekly	93.85[b]
3	Gluck, E.	S	5	9,630 quarterly	519.20[c]
4	Quinn, S.	M	8	925 semimonthly	0.00[d]
5	Treave, Y.	M	3	2,875 monthly	120.80[e]

[a] $1,610.00 − 4($75.00) = $1,310.00 − $503.00 = $807.00 × 0.15 = $121.05 + $34.30 = $155.35

[b] $825.00 − $0 = $825.00 − $428.00 = $397.00 × 0.15= $59.55 + $34.30 = $93.85

[c] $9,630.00 − 5($975.00) = $4,755.00 − $2,781.00 = $1,974.00 × 0.15 = $296.10 + $223.10 = $519.20

[d] $925.00 − 8($162.50) = $0

[e] $2,875.00 − 3($325.00) = $1,900.00 − $692.00 = $1,208.00 × 0.10 = $120.80

4–3A.

Employee	Marital Status	No. of Withholding Allowances	Gross Wage or Salary	Amount to Be Withheld	
				Percentage Method	Wage-Bracket Method
Corn, A.	S	2	$ 675 weekly	$ 63.85[a]	$ 64.00
Fogge, P.	S	1	1,960 weekly	387.04[b]	N/A*
Felps, S.	M	6	1,775 biweekly	55.60[c]	55.00
Carson, W.	M	4	2,480 semimonthly	185.40[d]	187.00
Helm, M.	M	9	5,380 monthly	190.10[e]	190.00

[a]$675.00 − 2($75.00) = $525.00 − $214.00 = $311.00 × 0.15 = $46.65 + $17.20 = $63.85

[b]$1,960.00 − $75.00 = $1,885.00 − $1,732.00 = $153.00 × 0.28 = $42.84 + $344.20
= $387.04

[c]$1,775.00 − 6($150.00) = $875.00 − $319.00 = $556.00 × 0.10 = $55.60

[d]$2,480.00 − 4($162.50) = $1,830.00 − $1,090.00 = $740.00 × 0.15 = $111.00 + $74.40
= $185.40

[e]$5,380.00 − 9($325.00) = $2,455.00 − $2,179.00 = $276.00 × 0.15 = $41.40 + $148.70
= $190.10

*Must use percentage method.

4–4A.

Employee	Marital Status	No. of Withholding Allowances	Payroll Period W = Weekly S = Semimonthly M = Monthly D = Daily	Wage	Amount to Be Withheld
Hal Bower	M	1	W	$1,350	$151.00
Ruth Cramden	S	1	W	590	63.00
Gil Jones	S	3	W	675	53.00
Teresa Kern	M	6	M	4,090	146.00
Ruby Long	M	2	M	2,730	140.00
Katie Luis	M	8	S	955	0.00
Susan Martin	S	1	D	96	9.00
Jim Singer	S	4	S	2,610	297.40**
Martin Torres	M	4	M	3,215	123.00

**$2,610 − 4($162.50) = $1,960.00 − $1,602.00 = $358.00 × 0.25 = $89.50 + $207.90
= $297.40

4–5A.

For Period Ending December 19

Employee Name	Marital Status	No. of W/H Allowances	Total Earnings	Deductions (a) FICA OASDI	HI	(b) FIT	(c) SIT	(d) CIT	(e) Net Pay
John, Matthew	M	3	$2,272.00	$ 6.20*	$32.94	$315.20**	$ 45.44	$34.08	$1,838.14
Smith, Jennifer	S	1	275.00	17.05	3.99	16.00	5.50	4.13	228.33
Bullen, Catherine	M	0	250.00	15.50	3.63	10.00	5.00	3.75	212.12
Matthews, Mary	S	3	320.25	19.86	4.64	6.00	6.41	4.80	278.54
Hadt, Bonnie	S	1	450.00	27.90	6.53	42.00	9.00	6.75	357.82
Camp, Sean	S	2	560.50	34.75	8.13	47.00	11.21	8.41	451.00
Wilson, Helen	S	1	475.50	29.48	6.89	45.00	9.51	7.13	377.49
Gleason, Josie	M	3	890.00	55.18	12.91	59.00	17.80	13.35	731.76
Totals			$5,493.25	$205.92	$79.66	$540.20	$109.87	$82.40	$4,475.20

Compute the employer's FICA taxes for the pay period ending December 19.

OASDI Taxes

OASDI taxable earnings	$3,321.25
OASDI taxes	$ 205.92

HI Taxes

HI taxable earnings	$5,493.25
HI taxes	$ 79.65

*113,700 – ($2,272.00 × 50) = $100 × 0.062 = $6.20

**Must use percentage method: $2,272.00 – 3($75.00) = $2,047.00 – $1,554.00 = $493.00 × 0.25 = $123.25 + $191.95 = $315.20

4–6A.

(a)

$$\frac{\$250}{1 - 0.25 \text{ (supplemental federal rate)} - 0.062 \text{ (OASDI)} - 0.0145 \text{ (HI)} - 0.07 \text{ (California tax)}}$$

(b) $250/(1 − 0.3965) = $250/0.6035 = $414.25

(c)

Gross bonus amount	$ 414.25
Federal income tax withheld	(103.56)
OASDI tax withheld	(25.68)
HI tax withheld	(6.01)
California income tax withheld	(29.00)
Take-home bonus check	$ 250.00

4–7A.

Gross pay	$ 930.00
HSA contributions	(25.00)
401(k) deductions	(100.00)
OASDI tax	(57.66)
HI tax	(13.49)
FIT (taxable $830.00)	(88.00)
Net pay	$ 645.85

4–8A.

For Period Ending December 26

Employee Name	Marital Status	No. of W/H Allowances	Earnings			Deductions					(g) Net Pay
			Regular	(a) Supp'l.	(b) Total	(c) FICA OASDI	HI	(d) FIT	(e) SIT	(f) CIT	
Hall, Michael	M	5	$ 5,000.00*	$ 4,800.00	$ 9,800.00	$ 607.60	$142.10	$1,531.00	$196.00	$ 98.00	$ 7,225.30
Short, Joy T.	M	2	2,750.00*	2,640.00	5,390.00	334.18	78.16	800.00	107.80	53.90	4,015.96
Abbott, Linda	S	1	520.00	2,163.20	2,683.20	166.36	38.91	593.80	53.66	26.83	1,803.64
Smith, Joseph	M	4	465.00	1,934.40	2,399.40	148.76	34.79	484.60	47.99	23.99	1,659.27
Tols, Sean M.	M	2	380.00	1,580.80	1,960.80	121.57	28.43	403.20	39.22	19.61	1,348.77
Gillespie, Michelle	S	1	350.00	1,456.00	1,806.00	111.97	26.19	391.00	36.12	18.06	1,222.66
Smart, Jennifer	M	2	575.00	2,392.00	2,967.00	183.95	43.02	625.00	59.34	29.67	2,026.02
White, Matthew J.	S	0	425.00	1,768.00	2,193.00	135.97	31.80	491.00	43.86	21.93	1,468.44
Totals			$10,465.00	$18,734.40	$29,199.40	$1,810.36	$423.40	$5,319.60	$583.99	$291.99	$20,770.06

*Monthly

Compute the employer's FICA taxes for the pay period ending December 26.

OASDI Taxes
OASDI taxable earnings $29,199.40
OASDI taxes $ 1,810.36

HI Taxes
HI taxable earnings $29,199.40
HI taxes $ 423.39

4–9A.

Employee Name	(a) Total Earnings	(b) FICA		(c) FIT	(d) SIT	(e) CIT	(f) Net Pay
		OASDI*	HI*				
Hall, Michael	$19,800.00	$1227.60	$ 287.10	$2,193.00	$ 396.00	$198.00	$15,498.30
Short, Joy T.	10,890.00	675.18	157.92	1,080.00	217.80	108.90	8,650.20
Abbott, Linda	8,923.20	553.24	129.39	1,229.80	178.46	89.23	6,743.08
Smith, Joseph	7,979.40	494.72	115.67	496.60	159.59	79.79	6,633.03
Tols, Sean M.	6,520.80	404.29	94.55	499.20	130.42	65.21	5,327.13
Gillespie, Michelle	6,006.00	372.37	87.15	715.00	120.12	60.06	4,651.30
Smart, Jennifer	9,867.00	611.75	143.10	949.00	197.34	98.67	7,867.14
White, Matthew J.	7,293.00	452.17	105.72	1,079.00	145.86	72.93	5,437.32
Totals	$77,279.40	$4,791.32	$1,120.60	$8,241.60	$1,545.59	$772.79	$60,807.50

Deductions

*To compute withholding, you must figure the rounded tax for each pay and multiply the tax by the number of pays in the quarter plus the withheld tax from Problem 4–8A.

4–10A.

(a)

$$\frac{\$100}{1 - 0.25 \text{ (supplemental rate)} - 0.062 \text{ (OASDI)} - 0.0145 \text{ (HI)} - 0.028 \text{ (state)}} = \$154.93^*$$

*Add $0.01 to $154.92 = $154.93 in order to receive $100.00 after taxes withheld.

(b) $100 − $25[a] − $6.20[b] − $1.45[c] − $2.80[d] = $64.55

    [a]0.25 × $100
    [b]0.062 × $100
    [c]0.0145 × $100
    [d]0.028 × $100

4–11A.

(a)	Clausen's maximum contribution	$12,000.00
(b)	Kline Company's contribution (3%)	$1,279.20

(c) Clausen's take-home pay with the
retirement contribution deducted:

Weekly pay	$ 820.00
FICA—OASDI	(50.84)
FICA—HI	(11.89)
FIT ($820.00 − $230.77 = $589.23 taxable)	(28.00)*
State income tax ($820.00 × 0.023)	(18.86)
Retirement contribution ($12,000 ÷ 52)	(230.77)
Take-home pay	$ 479.64

*Married, 2 allowances.

(d) Clausen's take-home pay without the
retirement contribution deducted:

Weekly pay	$820.00
FICA—OASDI	(50.84)
FICA—HI	(11.89)
FIT (on $820.00)	(60.00)
State income tax ($820.00 × 0.023)	(18.86)
Take-home pay	$678.41

4–12A.

(a)

FEDERAL DEPOSIT INFORMATION WORKSHEET

Employer Identification Number	00-0004701	**Name**	Quality Repairs
Month Tax Year Ends	12	**Amount of Deposit**	2033.04
Type of Tax (Form)	941	**Tax Period**	4th Quarter
Address	10 Summit Square	**Phone Number**	(501) 555-7331
City, State, ZIP	City, State 00000-0000		

To be deposited on or before November 17, 2014.

FEDERAL DEPOSIT INFORMATION WORKSHEET

Employer Identification Number	00-0004701	**Name**	Quality Repairs
Month Tax Year Ends	12	**Amount of Deposit**	1355.36
Type of Tax (Form)	941	**Tax Period**	4th Quarter
Address	10 Summit Square	**Phone Number**	(501) 555-7331
City, State, ZIP	City, State 00000-0000		

To be deposited on or before December 15, 2014.

4–12A. (Continued)

FEDERAL DEPOSIT INFORMATION WORKSHEET

Employer Identification Number	00-0004701	**Name**	Quality Repairs
Month Tax Year Ends	12	**Amount of Deposit**	1355.36
Type of Tax (Form)	941	**Tax Period**	4th Quarter
Address	10 Summit Square	**Phone Number**	(501) 555-7331
City, State, ZIP	City, State 00000-0000		

To be deposited on or before January 15, 2015.

4–12A. (Continued) Form 941

(b)

Form **941 for 20--:** **Employer's QUARTERLY Federal Tax Return**
(Rev. January 2013)   Department of the Treasury — Internal Revenue Service

OMB No. 1545-0029

Employer identification number (EIN) 0 0 – 0 0 0 0 4 7 0 1

Name *(not your trade name)* Quality Repairs

Trade name *(if any)*

Address 10 Summit Square
         Number   Street   Suite or room number

City   ST   00000-0000
City   State   ZIP code

Report for this Quarter of 20--
(Check one.)

☐ **1:** January, February, March

☐ **2:** April, May, June

☐ **3:** July, August, September

☒ **4:** October, November, December

Instructions and prior year forms are available at *www.irs.gov/form941.*

Read the separate instructions before you complete Form 941. Type or print within the boxes.

Part 1: Answer these questions for this quarter.

1 Number of employees who received wages, tips, or other compensation for the pay period including: *Mar. 12* (Quarter 1), *June 12* (Quarter 2), *Sept. 12* (Quarter 3), or *Dec. 12* (Quarter 4)   1 | 5

2 Wages, tips, and other compensation . . . .   2 | 18750 ▪ 00

3 Income tax withheld from wages, tips, and other compensation . . . .   3 | 1875 ▪ 00

4 If no wages, tips, and other compensation are subject to social security or Medicare tax   ☐ Check and go to line 6.

		Column 1	Column 2
5a	Taxable social security wages . .	18750 ▪ 00	× .124 =	2325 ▪ 00
5b	Taxable social security tips . . .	▪	× .124 =	▪
5c	Taxable Medicare wages & tips. .	18750 ▪ 00	× .029 =	543 ▪ 75
5d	Taxable wages & tips subject to Additional Medicare Tax withholding	▪	× .009 =	▪

5e Add Column 2 from lines 5a, 5b, 5c, and 5d . . . .   5e | 2868 ▪ 75

5f Section 3121(q) Notice and Demand—Tax due on unreported tips (see instructions) . .   5f | ▪

6 Total taxes before adjustments (add lines 3, 5e, and 5f) . . . .   6 | 4743 ▪ 75

7 Current quarter's adjustment for fractions of cents . . . .   7 | ▪ 01

8 Current quarter's adjustment for sick pay . . . .   8 | ▪

9 Current quarter's adjustments for tips and group-term life insurance . . . . . .   9 | ▪

10 Total taxes after adjustments. Combine lines 6 through 9 . . . .   10 | 4743 ▪ 76

11 Total deposits for this quarter, including overpayment applied from a prior quarter and overpayment applied from Form 941-X or Form 944-X filed in the current quarter . . .   11 | 4743 ▪ 76

12a COBRA premium assistance payments (see instructions) . . . .   12a | ▪

12b Number of individuals provided COBRA premium assistance . .

13 Add lines 11 and 12a . . . .   13 | 4743 ▪ 76

14 Balance due. If line 10 is more than line 13, enter the difference and see instructions . . .   14 | ▪

15 Overpayment. If line 13 is more than line 10, enter the difference | ▪ | Check one: ☐ Apply to next return. ☐ Send a refund.

▶ **You MUST complete both pages of Form 941 and SIGN it.**

Next ▶

For Privacy Act and Paperwork Reduction Act Notice, see the back of the Payment Voucher.   Cat. No. 17001Z   Form **941** (Rev. 1-2013)

4–12A. (Continued)

Name *(not your trade name)*	Employer identification number (EIN)
Quality Repairs	00-0004701

Part 2: Tell us about your deposit schedule and tax liability for this quarter.

If you are unsure about whether you are a monthly schedule depositor or a semiweekly schedule depositor, see Pub. 15 (Circular E), section 11.

16 Check one: ☐ Line 10 on this return is less than $2,500 or line 10 on the return for the prior quarter was less than $2,500, and you did not incur a $100,000 next-day deposit obligation during the current quarter. If line 10 for the prior quarter was less than $2,500 but line 10 on this return is $100,000 or more, you must provide a record of your federal tax liability. If you are a monthly schedule depositor, complete the deposit schedule below; if you are a semiweekly schedule depositor, attach Schedule B (Form 941). Go to Part 3.

☒ **You were a monthly schedule depositor for the entire quarter.** Enter your tax liability for each month and total liability for the quarter, then go to Part 3.

Tax liability:	Month 1	2033 . 04
	Month 2	1355 . 36
	Month 3	1355 . 36
Total liability for quarter		4743 . 76	**Total must equal line 10.**

☐ **You were a semiweekly schedule depositor for any part of this quarter.** Complete Schedule B (Form 941), Report of Tax Liability for Semiweekly Schedule Depositors, and attach it to Form 941.

Part 3: Tell us about your business. If a question does NOT apply to your business, leave it blank.

17 If your business has closed or you stopped paying wages . . . . ☐ Check here, and

enter the final date you paid wages [/ /] .

18 If you are a seasonal employer and you do not have to file a return for every quarter of the year . . ☐ Check here.

Part 4: May we speak with your third-party designee?

Do you want to allow an employee, a paid tax preparer, or another person to discuss this return with the IRS? See the instructions for details.

☐ Yes. Designee's name and phone number [   ] [   ]

Select a 5-digit Personal Identification Number (PIN) to use when talking to the IRS. ☐ ☐ ☐ ☐ ☐

☒ No.

Part 5: Sign here. You MUST complete both pages of Form 941 and SIGN it.

Under penalties of perjury, I declare that I have examined this return, including accompanying schedules and statements, and to the best of my knowledge and belief, it is true, correct, and complete. Declaration of preparer (other than taxpayer) is based on all information of which preparer has any knowledge.

X **Sign your name here**	*Student*	Print your name here	Student
		Print your title here	President
Date	2 / 2 / 15	Best daytime phone	501-555-7331

Paid Preparer Use Only   Check if you are self-employed . . . ☐

Preparer's name		PTIN	
Preparer's signature		Date	/ /
Firm's name (or yours if self-employed)		EIN	
Address		Phone	
City		State		ZIP code	

Form **941** (Rev. 1-2013)

Source: Internal Revenue Service.

4–12A. (Concluded) Employer's Report of State Income Tax Withheld

(c)

EMPLOYER'S REPORT OF STATE INCOME TAX WITHHELD

IMPORTANT, PLEASE REFER TO THIS NUMBER IN ANY CORRESPONDENCE →	WITHHOLDING IDENTIFICATION NUMBER	MONTH OF OR QUARTER ENDING
	00-0-3301	**DEC. 20--**

(DO NOT WRITE IN THIS SPACE)

IF YOU ARE A SEASONAL EMPLOYER AND THIS IS YOUR FINAL REPORT FOR THIS SEASON, CHECK HERE ☐

AND SHOW THE NEXT MONTH IN WHICH YOU WILL PAY WAGES

**QUALITY REPAIRS
10 SUMMIT SQUARE
CITY, STATE 00000-0000**

1.	GROSS PAYROLL THIS PERIOD......	$ 18,750	00
2.	STATE INCOME TAX WITHHELD	$ 1,312	50
3.	ADJUSTMENT FOR PREVIOUS PERIOD(S). (ATTACH STATEMENT)		
4.	TOTAL ADJUSTED TAX (LINE 2 PLUS OR MINUS LINE 3)........	$ 1,312	50
5.	PENALTY (35% OF LINE 4)		
6.	INTEREST		
7.	TOTAL AMOUNT DUE AND PAYABLE	$ 1,312	50

IF NAME OR ADDRESS IS INCORRECT, PLEASE MAKE CORRECTIONS. THIS REPORT MUST BE RETURNED EVEN IF NO AMOUNT HAS BEEN WITHHELD

Under penalties proscribed by law, I hereby affirm that to the best of my knowledge and belief this return, including any accompanying schedules and statements, is true and complete. If prepared by a person other than taxpayer, his affirmation is based on all information of which he has any knowledge.

SIGNATURE: **STUDENT** TITLE: President DATE: 2/2/15

MAIL THIS REPORT WITH CHECK OR MONEY ORDER PAYABLE TO THE DEPT. OF REVENUE ON OR BEFORE DUE DATE TO AVOID PENALTY.

4–13A. Wage and Tax Statement

(a)

22222 Void ☐	a Employee's social security number 000-00-4310	For Official Use Only OMB No. 1 545-0008			
b Employer identification number (EIN) 00-0000972		1 Wages, tips, other compensation 18980.00		2 Federal income tax withheld 1508.00	
c Employer's name, address, and ZIP code		3 Social security wages 21580.00		4 Social security tax withheld 1337.96	
Quigley Corporation *4800 River Road* *Philadelphia, PA 19113-5548*		5 Medicare wages and tips 21580.00		6 Medicare tax withheld 313.04	
		7 Social security tips		8 Allocated tips	
d Control number		9		10 Dependent care benefits	
e Employee's first name and initial Kelly B.	Last name Roach	Suff.	11 Nonqualified plans	12a See instructions for box 12 Code D 2600.00	
			13 Statutory employee ☐ Retirement plan ☒ Third-party sick pay ☐	12b Code	
54 Gradison Place Philadelphia, PA 19113-4054			14 Other	12c Code	
				12d Code	
f Employee's address and ZIP code					

15 State	Employer's state ID number	16 State wages, tips, etc.	17 State income tax	18 Local wages, tips, etc.	19 Local income tax	20 Locality name
PA	00-0-1066	21580.00	662.48	21580.00	847.60	Phila.

Form **W-2** Wage and Tax Statement **20--**

Department of the Treasury—Internal Revenue Service
For Privacy Act and Paperwork Reduction Act Notice, see back of Copy D.

Source: Internal Revenue Service.

4–13A. (Continued)

(b)

22222 Void ☐	a Employee's social security number 000-00-8804	For Official Use Only OMB No. 1 545-0008		
b Employer identification number (EIN) 00-0000972		**1** Wages, tips, other compensation 21580.00	**2** Federal income tax withheld 936.00	
c Employer's name, address, and ZIP code		**3** Social security wages 25220.00	**4** Social security tax withheld 1563.64	
Quigley Corporation 4800 River Road Philadelphia, PA 19113-5548		**5** Medicare wages and tips 25220.00	**6** Medicare tax withheld 365.56	
		7 Social security tips	**8** Allocated tips	
d Control number		**9**	**10** Dependent care benefits 950.00	
e Employee's first name and initial Ralph I.	Last name Volpe · Suff.	**11** Nonqualified plans	**12a** See instructions for box 12 Code **D** 3640.00	
		13 Statutory employee ☐ Retirement plan ☒ Third-party sick pay ☐	**12b** Code	
56 Andrews Court, Apt. 7 Philadelphia, PA 19103-3356		**14** Other	**12c** Code	
			12d Code	
f Employee's address and ZIP code				

15 State PA	Employer's state ID number 00-0-1066	**16** State wages, tips, etc. 25220.00	**17** State income tax 774.28	**18** Local wages, tips, etc. 25220.00	**19** Local income tax 990.60	**20** Locality name Phila.

Form **W-2** **Wage and Tax Statement**   **20--**   Department of the Treasury—Internal Revenue Service
For Privacy Act and Paperwork Reduction Act Notice, see back of Copy D.

(c)

22222 Void ☐	a Employee's social security number 000-00-3316	For Official Use Only OMB No. 1 545-0008		
b Employer identification number (EIN) 00-0000972		**1** Wages, tips, other compensation 18980.00	**2** Federal income tax withheld 2080.00	
c Employer's name, address, and ZIP code		**3** Social security wages 18980.00	**4** Social security tax withheld 1176.76	
Quigley Corporation 4800 River Road Philadelphia, PA 19113-5548		**5** Medicare wages and tips 18980.00	**6** Medicare tax withheld 275.08	
		7 Social security tips	**8** Allocated tips	
d Control number		**9**	**10** Dependent care benefits	
e Employee's first name and initial Randi A.	Last name Myer · Suff.	**11** Nonqualified plans	**12a** See instructions for box 12 Code	
		13 Statutory employee ☐ Retirement plan ☐ Third-party sick pay ☐	**12b** Code	
770 Camac Street Philadelphia, PA 19101-3770		**14** Other UNION DUES 102.00	**12c** Code	
			12d Code	
f Employee's address and ZIP code				

15 State PA	Employer's state ID number 00-0-1066	**16** State wages, tips, etc. 18980.00	**17** State income tax 582.92	**18** Local wages, tips, etc. 18980.00	**19** Local income tax 745.68	**20** Locality name Phila.

Form **W-2** **Wage and Tax Statement**   **20--**   Department of the Treasury—Internal Revenue Service
For Privacy Act and Paperwork Reduction Act Notice, see back of Copy D.

Source: Internal Revenue Service.

4–13A. (Continued)

(d)

22222	Void ☐	a Employee's social security number 000-00-6839	For Official Use Only OMB No. 1 545-0008		

b Employer identification number (EIN) 00-0000972	1 Wages, tips, other compensation 65262.75*	2 Federal income tax withheld 3536.00

c Employer's name, address, and ZIP code	3 Social security wages 70462.75*	4 Social security tax withheld 4368.69

Quigley Corporation
4800 River Road
Philadelphia, PA   19113-5548

	5 Medicare wages and tips 70462.75*	6 Medicare tax withheld 1021.96
	7 Social security tips	8 Allocated tips

d Control number	9	10 Dependent care benefits

e Employee's first name and initial Kenneth T.	Last name Ford	Suff.	11 Nonqualified plans	12a See instructions for box 12 Code **C** 262.75

13 Statutory employee ☐ Retirement plan ☒ Third-party sick pay ☐	12b Code **D** 5200.00

338 North Side Avenue
Philadelphia, PA 19130-6638

14 Other	12c Code
	12d Code

f Employee's address and ZIP code

15 State PA	Employer's state ID number 00-0-1066	16 State wages, tips, etc. 70200.00	17 State income tax 2155.40	18 Local wages, tips, etc. 70200.00	19 Local income tax 2757.56	20 Locality name Phila.

Form W-2 Wage and Tax Statement   **20--**

Department of the Treasury—Internal Revenue Service
For Privacy Act and Paperwork
Reduction Act Notice, see back of Copy D.

*Including cost of C, Group-Term Life Insurance, reported in Box 12a.

(e)

22222	Void ☐	a Employee's social security number 000-00-5771	For Official Use Only OMB No. 1 545-0008		

b Employer identification number (EIN) 00-0000972	1 Wages, tips, other compensation 16640.00	2 Federal income tax withheld 104.00

c Employer's name, address, and ZIP code	3 Social security wages 16640.00	4 Social security tax withheld 1031.68

Quigley Corporation
4800 River Road
Philadelphia, PA   19113-5548

	5 Medicare wages and tips 16640.00	6 Medicare tax withheld 241.28
	7 Social security tips	8 Allocated tips

d Control number	9	10 Dependent care benefits

e Employee's first name and initial Chrissy C.	Last name Carman	Suff.	11 Nonqualified plans	12a See instructions for box 12 Code

13 Statutory employee ☐ Retirement plan ☐ Third-party sick pay ☐	12b Code

4900 Gladwynne Terrace
Philadelphia, PA 19127-0049

14 Other UNION DUES 102.00	12c Code
	12d Code

f Employee's address and ZIP code

15 State PA	Employer's state ID number 00-0-1066	16 State wages, tips, etc. 16640.00	17 State income tax 510.64	18 Local wages, tips, etc. 16640.00	19 Local income tax 653.64	20 Locality name Phila.

Form W-2 Wage and Tax Statement   **20--**

Department of the Treasury—Internal Revenue Service
For Privacy Act and Paperwork
Reduction Act Notice, see back of Copy D.

Source: Internal Revenue Service.

4–13A. (Continued)

(f)

22222	Void ☐	a Employee's social security number 000-00-8703	For Official Use Only OMB No. 1 545-0008		

b Employer identification number (EIN) 00-0000972	1 Wages, tips, other compensation 17680.00	2 Federal income tax withheld 1352.00

c Employer's name, address, and ZIP code	3 Social security wages 20280.00	4 Social security tax withheld 1257.36
Quigley Corporation *4800 River Road* *Philadelphia, PA 19113-5548*	5 Medicare wages and tips 20280.00	6 Medicare tax withheld 294.32
	7 Social security tips	8 Allocated tips

d Control number	9	10 Dependent care benefits

e Employee's first name and initial	Last name	Suff.	11 Nonqualified plans	12a See instructions for box 12 Code **D** 2600.00
Hal B.	Zuber			

13 Statutory employee ☐ Retirement plan ☒ Third-party sick pay ☐	12b Code
14 Other EDUC. ASSIST 675.00	12c Code
	12d Code

480-A Hopkinson Tower
Philadelphia, PA 19101-3301

f Employee's address and ZIP code

15 State PA	Employer's state ID number 00-0-1066	16 State wages, tips, etc. 20280.00	17 State income tax 622.44	18 Local wages, tips, etc. 20280.00	19 Local income tax 796.64	20 Locality name Phila.

Form **W-2** **Wage and Tax Statement** **20--**

Department of the Treasury—Internal Revenue Service
**For Privacy Act and Paperwork
Reduction Act Notice, see back of Copy D.**

Source: Internal Revenue Service.

4–13A. (Concluded)

DO NOT STAPLE

a Control number 33333	For Official Use Only ▶ OMB No. 1545-0008	

b Kind of Payer (Check one): ☒ 941   ☐ Military   ☐ 943   ☐ 944   ☐ CT-1   ☐ Hshld. emp.   ☐ Medicare govt. emp.

Kind of Employer (Check one): ☒ None apply   ☐ 501c non-govt.   ☐ State/local non-501c   ☐ State/local 501c   ☐ Federal govt.

Third-party sick pay (Check if applicable): ☐

c Total number of Forms W-2 6	**d** Establishment number
1 Wages, tips, other compensation 159122.75	**2** Federal income tax withheld 9516.00
e Employer identification number (EIN) 00-0000972	
3 Social security wages 173162.75	**4** Social security tax withheld 10736.09
f Employer's name Quigley Corporation	
5 Medicare wages and tips 173162.75	**6** Medicare tax withheld 2511.24
7 Social security tips	**8** Allocated tips
4800 River Road Philadelphia, PA 19113-5548	
9	**10** Dependent care benefits 950.00
11 Nonqualified plans	**12a** Deferred compensation 14040.00
g Employer's address and ZIP code	
h Other EIN used this year	**13** For third-party sick pay use only	**12b**
15 State PA Employer's state ID number 00-0-1066	**14** Income tax withheld by payer of third-party sick pay
16 State wages, tips, etc. 172900.00 **17** State income tax 5308.16	**18** Local wages, tips, etc. 172900.00 **19** Local income tax 6791.72
Contact person Ralph I. Volpe	Telephone number (215) 555-0017	For Official Use Only
Email address NA	Fax number (215) 555-0010	

Under penalties of perjury, I declare that I have examined this return and accompanying documents and, to the best of my knowledge and belief, they are true, correct, and complete.

Signature ▶ *Kenneth F. Ford*   Title ▶ President   Date ▶ 3/2/15

Form **W-3** Transmittal of Wage and Tax Statements   20__   Department of the Treasury Internal Revenue Service

Source: Internal Revenue Service.

Solutions—Series B Problems

4–1B.

Gross pay	$160.00
Federal income tax (on $860.00)	(66.00)
Social security taxes (6.2% × $860.00).....	(53.32)
(1.45% × $860.00)...	(12.47)
State income tax (2% × $860.00)..............	(17.20)
Net pay	$ 11.01

4–2B.

Employee No.	Employee Name	Marital Status	No. of Withholding Allowances	Gross Wage or Salary	Amount to Be Withheld
1	Skymer, A.	M	4	$ 1,575 weekly	$ 150.10[a]
2	Wolfe, T.	S	0	990 biweekly	118.60[b]
3	Klein, G.	S	5	12,600 quarterly	964.70[c]
4	Carey, P.	M	8	1,090 semimonthly	0.00[d]
5	Wu, M.	M	3	8,120 monthly	934.80[e]

[a] $1,575.00 − 4($75.00) = $1,275.00 − $503.00 = $772.00 × 0.15 = $115.80 + $34.30 = $150.10

[b] $990.00 − $0 = $990.00 − $428.00 = $562.00 × 0.15 = $84.30 + $34.30 = $118.60

[c] $12,600.00 − 5($975.00) = $7,725.00 − $2,781.00 = $4,944.00 × 0.15 = $741.60 + $223.10 = $964.70

[d] $1,090.00 − 8($162.50) = $0

[e] $8,120.00 − 3($325.00) = $7,145.00 − $6,733.00 = $412.00 × 0.25 = $103.00 + $831.80 = $934.80

4–3B.

Employee	Marital Status	No. of Withholding Allowances	Gross Wage or Salary	Amount to Be Withheld	
				Percentage Method	Wage-Bracket Method
Ruiz, S.	S	2	$1,040 weekly	$133.70[a]	$135.00
Flume, X.	S	1	2,190 weekly	451.44[b]	N/A*
Farley, H.	M	6	1,890 biweekly	67.10[c]	67.00
Comey, P.	M	4	2,315 semimonthly	160.65[d]	160.00
Hanks, R.	M	9	4,200 monthly	58.30[e]	60.00

[a]$1,040.00 − 2($75.00) = $890.00 − $739.00 = $151.00 × 0.25 = $37.75 + $95.95
= $133.70
[b]$2,190.00 − 1($75.00) = $2,115.00 − $1,732.00 = $383.00 × 0.28 = $107.24 + $344.20
= $451.44
[c]$1,890.00 − 6($150.00) = $990.00 − $319.00 = $671.00 × 0.10 = $67.10
[d]$2,315.00 − 4($162.50) = $1,665.00 − $1,090.00 = $575.00 × 0.15 = $86.25 + $74.40
= $160.65
[e]$4,200.00 − 9($325.00) = $1,275.00 − $692.00 = $583.00 × 0.10 = $58.30

*Must use percentage method.

4–4B.

Employee	Marital Status	No. of Withholding Allowances	Payroll Period W = Weekly S = Semimonthly M = Monthly D = Daily	Wage	Amount to Be Withheld
Ed Boone	M	1	W	$1,250	$136.00
Ray Ortega	S	1	W	695	78.00
Carl Lopez	S	3	W	915	89.00
Terri Kim	M	6	M	5,070	288.00
Kathy Horace	M	2	M	3,730	285.00
John Gleam	M	8	S	995	0.00
Rob Abreu	S	1	D	115	12.00
Carmen Sanchez	S	4	S	3,040	404.90**
Howard Nee	M	4	M	4,500	302.00

**$3,040.00 − 4($162.50) = $2,390.00 − $1,602.00 = $788.00 × 0.25 = $197.00 + $207.90
= $404.90

4–5B.

For Period Ending December 19

Employee Name	Marital Status	No. of W/H Allowances	Total Earnings	(a) FICA		Deductions				(e) Net Pay
				OASDI	HI	(b) FIT	(c) SIT	(d) CIT		
Gold, Ken	M	3	$2,080.00	$128.96	$30.16	$267.20*	$ 64.48	$20.80		$1,568.40
Morton, Cam	S	1	490.00	30.38	7.11	48.00	15.19	4.90		384.42
Wendal, Hal	M	0	675.00	41.85	9.79	60.00	20.93	6.75		535.68
Cox, Debbie	S	3	510.00	31.62	7.40	29.00	15.81	5.10		421.07
Hurley, Don	S	1	1,010.00	62.62	14.65	146.00	31.31	10.10		745.32
Hand, Cheryl	S	2	850.00	52.70	12.33	91.00	26.35	8.50		659.12
Welsh, Ronda	S	1	490.90	30.44	7.12	48.00	15.22	4.91		385.21
Ruiz, Stacy	M	3	611.15	37.89	8.86	23.00	18.95	6.11		516.34
Totals			$6,717.05	$416.46	$97.42	$712.20	$208.24	$67.17		$5,215.56

Compute the employer's FICA taxes for the pay period ending December 19.

OASDI Taxes

OASDI taxable earnings	$6,717.05
OASDI taxes	$ 416.46

HI Taxes

HI taxable earnings	$6,717.05
HI taxes	$ 97.40

*Must use percentage method: $2,080.00 − 3($75.00) = $1,855.00 − $1,554.00 = $301.00 × 0.25 = $75.25 + $191.95 = $267.20

4–6B.

(a)

$$\frac{\$750}{1 - 0.25 \text{ (supplemental federal rate)} - 0.062 \text{ (OASDI)} - 0.0145 \text{ (HI)} - 0.05 \text{ (Utah tax)}}$$

(b) $750/(1 − 0.3765) = $750/0.6235 = $1,202.89

(c)

Gross bonus amount	$1,202.88*
Federal income tax withheld	(300.72)
OASDI tax withheld	(74.58)
HI tax withheld	(17.44)
Utah income tax withheld	(60.14)
Take-home bonus check	$ 750.00

*Need to subtract $0.01 in order to arrive at net of $750.00 (due to rounding).

4–7B.

Gross pay	$1,090.00
HSA contributions	(40.00)
401(k) deductions	(125.00)
OASDI tax	(67.58)
HI tax	(15.81)
FIT (taxable $965.00)	(81.00)
Net pay	$ 760.61

4–8B.

For Period Ending December 26

Employee Name	Marital Status	No. of W/H Allowances	Earnings (a) Regular	Earnings (a) Supp'l.	Earnings (b) Total	(c) FICA OASDI	(c) FICA HI	Deductions (d) FIT	Deductions (e) SIT	Deductions (f) CIT	(g) Net Pay
Wayne, Bret	M	5	$ 4,200.00*	$ 4,032.00	$8,232.00	$ 510.38	$119.36	$1,219.00	$164.64	$82.32	$ 6,136.30
Young, Gina	M	2	4,150.00*	3,984.00	8,134.00	504.31	117.94	1,341.00	162.68	81.34	5,926.73
Course, Rudy	S	1	810.00	3,369.60	4,179.60	259.14	60.60	938.40	83.59	41.80	2,796.07
Dickson, Emile	M	4	715.00	2,974.40	3,689.40	228.74	53.50	769.60	73.79	36.89	2,526.88
Woodrow, Walt	M	2	695.00	2,891.20	3,586.20	222.34	52.00	763.80	71.72	35.86	2,440.48
Noblet, Jim	S	1	525.00	2,184.00	2,709.00	167.96	39.28	599.00	54.18	27.09	1,821.49
Ono, Joan	M	2	800.00	3,328.00	4,128.00	255.94	59.86	889.00	82.56	41.28	2,799.36
Jones, Carrie	S	0	645.00	2,683.20	3,328.20	206.35	48.26	752.80	66.56	33.28	2,220.95
Totals			$12,540.00	$25,446.40	$37,986.40	$2,355.16	$550.80	$7,272.60	$759.72	$379.86	$26,668.26

*Monthly

Compute the employer's FICA taxes for the pay period ending December 26.

OASDI Taxes

OASDI taxable earnings	$37,986.40
OASDI taxes	$ 2,355.16

HI Taxes

HI taxable earnings	$37,986.40
HI taxes	$ 550.80

4-9B.

	(a) Total Earnings	(b) FICA		Deductions			(f) Net Pay
Employee Name		OASDI*	HI*	(c) FIT	(d) SIT	(e) CIT	
Wayne, Bret	$ 16,632.00	$1,031.18	$ 241.16	$ 1,641.00	$ 332.64	$ 166.32	$13,219.70
Young, Gina	16,434.00	1,018.91	238.30	2,031.00	328.68	164.34	12,652.77
Course, Rudy	13,899.60	861.78	201.60	2,090.40	277.99	139.00	10,328.83
Dickson, Emile	12,269.40	760.70	177.94	1,081.60	245.39	122.69	9,881.08
Woodrow, Walt	11,926.20	739.42	172.96	1,255.80	238.52	119.26	9,400.24
Noblet, Jim	9,009.00	558.56	130.60	1,235.00	180.18	90.09	6,814.57
Ono, Joan	13,728.00	851.14	199.06	1,573.00	274.56	137.28	10,692.96
Jones, Carrie	11,068.20	686.23	160.46	1,736.80	221.36	110.68	8,152.67
Totals	$104,966.40	$6,507.92	$1,522.08	$12,644.60	$2,099.32	$1,049.66	$81,142.82

*To compute withholding, you must figure the rounded tax for each pay and multiply the tax by the number of pays in the quarter plus the withheld tax from Problem 4–8B.

4–10B.

(a)

$$\frac{\$250}{1 - 0.25 \text{ (supplemental rate)} - 0.062 \text{ (OASDI)} - 0.0145 \text{ (HI)} - 0.0301 \text{ (state)}} = \$388.56$$

(b) $\$250 - \$62.50^a - \$15.50^b - \$3.63^c - \$7.53^d = \$160.84$

$^a 0.25 \times \$250$
$^b 0.062 \times \$250$
$^c 0.0145 \times \$250$
$^d 0.0301 \times \$250$

4–11B.

(a) Montgomery's maximum contribution $12,000.00

(b) Canon Company's contribution (3%) $1,872.90

(c) Montgomery's take-home pay with the
retirement contribution deducted:

Weekly pay	$ 1,200.58
FICA—OASDI	(74.44)
FICA—HI	(17.41)
FIT ($1,200.58 − $230.77 = $969.81 taxable)	(81.00)*
State income tax ($1,200.58 × 2.3%)	(27.61)
Retirement contribution ($12,000 ÷ 52)	(230.77)
Take-home pay	$ 769.35

*Married, 2 allowances.

(d) Montgomery's take-home pay without the
retirement contribution deducted:

Weekly pay	$ 1,200.58
FICA—OASDI	(74.44)
FICA—HI	(17.41)
FIT (on $1,200.58)	(117.00)
State income tax ($1,200.58 × 2.3%)	(27.61)
Take-home pay	$ 964.12

4–12B.

(a)

FEDERAL DEPOSIT INFORMATION WORKSHEET

Employer Identification Number	00-0004701	**Name**	Clarke's Roofing
Month Tax Year Ends	12	**Amount of Deposit**	3913.68
Type of Tax (Form)	941	**Tax Period**	4th Quarter
Address	20 Summit Square	**Phone Number**	(501) 555-1212
City, State, ZIP	City, State 00000-0000		

To be deposited on or before November 17, 2014.

FEDERAL DEPOSIT INFORMATION WORKSHEET

Employer Identification Number	00-0004701	**Name**	Clarke's Roofing
Month Tax Year Ends	12	**Amount of Deposit**	2609.12
Type of Tax (Form)	941	**Tax Period**	4th Quarter
Address	20 Summit Square	**Phone Number**	(501) 555-1212
City, State, ZIP	City, State 00000-0000		

To be deposited on or before December 15, 2014.

4–12B. (Continued)

FEDERAL DEPOSIT INFORMATION WORKSHEET

**Employer
Identification Number**   00-0004701   **Name**   Clarke's Roofing

Month Tax Year Ends   12   **Amount of Deposit**   2609.12

Type of Tax (Form)   941   **Tax Period**   4th Quarter

Address   20 Summit Square   **Phone Number**   (501) 555-1212

City, State, ZIP   City, State 00000-0000

To be deposited on or before January 15, 2015.

4–12B. (Continued) Form 941

(b)

Form **941 for 20--:** Employer's QUARTERLY Federal Tax Return
(Rev. January 2013)   Department of the Treasury — Internal Revenue Service   OMB No. 1545-0029

Employer identification number (EIN) 0 0 – 0 0 0 4 7 0 1

Name (not your trade name) Clarke's Roofing

Trade name (if any)

Address 20 Summit Square
         Number   Street   Suite or room number
         City   ST   00000-0000
         City   State   ZIP code

Report for this Quarter of 20--
(Check one.)

☐ 1: January, February, March

☐ 2: April, May, June

☐ 3: July, August, September

☒ 4: October, November, December

Instructions and prior year forms are available at *www.irs.gov/form941*.

Read the separate instructions before you complete Form 941. Type or print within the boxes.

Part 1: Answer these questions for this quarter.

1	Number of employees who received wages, tips, or other compensation for the pay period including: *Mar. 12* (Quarter 1), *June 12* (Quarter 2), *Sept. 12* (Quarter 3), or *Dec. 12* (Quarter 4)	1	5
2	Wages, tips, and other compensation	2	37450 . 00
3	Income tax withheld from wages, tips, and other compensation	3	3402 . 00
4	If no wages, tips, and other compensation are subject to social security or Medicare tax	☐ Check and go to line 6.	

		Column 1		Column 2	
5a	Taxable social security wages . .	37450 . 00	× .124 =	4643 . 80	
5b	Taxable social security tips . . .	.	× .124 =	.	
5c	Taxable Medicare wages & tips. .	37450 . 00	× .029 =	1086 . 05	
5d	Taxable wages & tips subject to Additional Medicare Tax withholding	.	× .009 =	.	

5e	Add Column 2 from lines 5a, 5b, 5c, and 5d	5e	5729 . 85
5f	Section 3121(q) Notice and Demand—Tax due on unreported tips (see instructions) . .	5f	.
6	Total taxes before adjustments (add lines 3, 5e, and 5f)	6	9131 . 85
7	Current quarter's adjustment for fractions of cents	7	. 07
8	Current quarter's adjustment for sick pay	8	.
9	Current quarter's adjustments for tips and group-term life insurance	9	.
10	Total taxes after adjustments. Combine lines 6 through 9	10	9131 . 92
11	Total deposits for this quarter, including overpayment applied from a prior quarter and overpayment applied from Form 941-X or Form 944-X filed in the current quarter . . .	11	9131 . 92
12a	COBRA premium assistance payments (see instructions)	12a	.
12b	Number of individuals provided COBRA premium assistance . .		
13	Add lines 11 and 12a	13	9131 . 92
14	Balance due. If line 10 is more than line 13, enter the difference and see instructions . . .	14	.
15	Overpayment. If line 13 is more than line 10, enter the difference [.] Check one: ☐ Apply to next return. ☐ Send a refund.		

▶ You MUST complete both pages of Form 941 and SIGN it.   Next ▶

For Privacy Act and Paperwork Reduction Act Notice, see the back of the Payment Voucher.   Cat. No. 17001Z   Form **941** (Rev. 1-2013)

4–12B. (Continued)

Name *(not your trade name)*	Employer identification number (EIN)
Clarke's Roofing	00-0004701

Part 2:   **Tell us about your deposit schedule and tax liability for this quarter.**

If you are unsure about whether you are a monthly schedule depositor or a semiweekly schedule depositor, see Pub. 15 (Circular E), section 11.

16   Check one: ☐   Line 10 on this return is less than $2,500 or line 10 on the return for the prior quarter was less than $2,500, and you did not incur a $100,000 next-day deposit obligation during the current quarter. If line 10 for the prior quarter was less than $2,500 but line 10 on this return is $100,000 or more, you must provide a record of your federal tax liability. If you are a monthly schedule depositor, complete the deposit schedule below; if you are a semiweekly schedule depositor, attach Schedule B (Form 941). Go to Part 3.

               ☒   **You were a monthly schedule depositor for the entire quarter.** Enter your tax liability for each month and total liability for the quarter, then go to Part 3.

Tax liability:	Month 1	3913 . 68	
	Month 2	2609 . 12	
	Month 3	2609 . 12	
	Total liability for quarter	9131 . 92	Total must equal line 10.

               ☐   **You were a semiweekly schedule depositor for any part of this quarter.** Complete Schedule B (Form 941), Report of Tax Liability for Semiweekly Schedule Depositors, and attach it to Form 941.

Part 3:   **Tell us about your business. If a question does NOT apply to your business, leave it blank.**

17   If your business has closed or you stopped paying wages . . . . ☐ Check here, and

     enter the final date you paid wages   / /   .

18   If you are a seasonal employer and you do not have to file a return for every quarter of the year . . ☐ Check here.

Part 4:   **May we speak with your third-party designee?**

Do you want to allow an employee, a paid tax preparer, or another person to discuss this return with the IRS? See the instructions for details.

  ☐ Yes. Designee's name and phone number

         Select a 5-digit Personal Identification Number (PIN) to use when talking to the IRS.   ☐ ☐ ☐ ☐ ☐

  ☒ No.

Part 5:   **Sign here. You MUST complete both pages of Form 941 and SIGN it.**

Under penalties of perjury, I declare that I have examined this return, including accompanying schedules and statements, and to the best of my knowledge and belief, it is true, correct, and complete. Declaration of preparer (other than taxpayer) is based on all information of which preparer has any knowledge.

X **Sign your name here**	*Student*	Print your name here	Student
		Print your title here	President
Date	2 / 2 / 15	Best daytime phone	501-555-1212

Paid Preparer Use Only   Check if you are self-employed . . . ☐

Preparer's name		PTIN	
Preparer's signature		Date	/ /
Firm's name (or yours if self-employed)		EIN	
Address		Phone	
City		State	ZIP code

Source: Internal Revenue Service.

4–12B. (Concluded) Employer's Report of State Income Tax Withheld

(c)

**EMPLOYER'S REPORT
OF STATE INCOME TAX WITHHELD**

(DO NOT WRITE IN THIS SPACE)

IMPORTANT, PLEASE REFER TO THIS NUMBER IN ANY CORRESPONDENCE ⟶

WITHHOLDING IDENTIFICATION NUMBER	MONTH OF OR QUARTER ENDING
00-0-8787	**DEC. 20--**

IF YOU ARE A SEASONAL EMPLOYER AND THIS IS YOUR FINAL REPORT FOR THIS SEASON, CHECK HERE ☐

AND SHOW THE NEXT MONTH IN WHICH YOU WILL PAY WAGES

**CLARKE'S ROOFING
20 SUMMIT SQUARE
CITY, STATE 00000-0000**

IF NAME OR ADDRESS IS INCORRECT, PLEASE MAKE CORRECTIONS. THIS REPORT MUST BE RETURNED EVEN IF NO AMOUNT HAS BEEN WITHHELD

1. GROSS PAYROLL THIS PERIOD	$ 37,450 00
2. STATE INCOME TAX WITHHELD	$ 2,621 50
3. ADJUSTMENT FOR PREVIOUS PERIOD(S). (ATTACH STATEMENT)	
4. TOTAL ADJUSTED TAX (LINE 2 PLUS OR MINUS LINE 3)	$ 2,621 50
5. PENALTY (35% OF LINE 4)	
6. INTEREST	
7. TOTAL AMOUNT DUE AND PAYABLE	$ 2,621 50

Under penalties proscribed by law, I hereby affirm that to the best of my knowledge and belief this return, including any accompanying schedules and statements, is true and complete. If prepared by a person other than taxpayer, his affirmation is based on all information of which he has any knowledge.

SIGNATURE: **STUDENT**   TITLE: President   DATE: 2/2/15

MAIL THIS REPORT WITH CHECK OR MONEY ORDER PAYABLE TO THE DEPT. OF REVENUE ON OR BEFORE DUE DATE TO AVOID PENALTY.

4–13B. Wage and Tax Statement

(a)

22222 Void ☐	a Employee's social security number 000-00-4310	For Official Use Only OMB No. 1 545-0008		
b Employer identification number (EIN) 00-0000972		1 Wages, tips, other compensation 29380.00		2 Federal income tax withheld 2444.00
c Employer's name, address, and ZIP code		3 Social security wages 31980.00		4 Social security tax withheld 1982.76
Omni Corporation		5 Medicare wages and tips 31980.00		6 Medicare tax withheld 463.84
4800 River Road *Philadelphia, PA 19113-5548*		7 Social security tips		8 Allocated tips
d Control number		9		10 Dependent care benefits
e Employee's first name and initial: Randy A. Last name: Kellison Suff.		11 Nonqualified plans		12a See instructions for box 12 Code D 2600.00
		13 Statutory employee ☐ Retirement plan ☒ Third-party sick pay ☐		12b Code
54 Gradison Place Philadelphia, PA 19113-4054				12c Code
		14 Other		12d Code
f Employee's address and ZIP code				

15 State	Employer's state ID number	16 State wages, tips, etc.	17 State income tax	18 Local wages, tips, etc.	19 Local income tax	20 Locality name
PA	00-0-1066	31980.00	981.76	31980.00	1256.32	Phila.

Form **W-2** Wage and Tax Statement   **20--**

Department of the Treasury—Internal Revenue Service
For Privacy Act and Paperwork Reduction Act Notice, see back of Copy D.

Source: Internal Revenue Service.

4–13B. (Continued)

(b)

22222	Void ☐	a Employee's social security number 000-00-8804	For Official Use Only OMB No. 1 545-0008		
b Employer identification number (EIN) 00-0000972			**1** Wages, tips, other compensation 47580.00		**2** Federal income tax withheld 3224.00
c Employer's name, address, and ZIP code			**3** Social security wages 51220.00		**4** Social security tax withheld 3175.64
Omni Corporation 4800 River Road Philadelphia, PA 19113-5548			**5** Medicare wages and tips 51220.00		**6** Medicare tax withheld 742.56
			7 Social security tips		**8** Allocated tips
d Control number			**9**		**10** Dependent care benefits 950.00
e Employee's first name and initial Vince T.	Last name Roper	Suff.	**11** Nonqualified plans		**12a** See instructions for box 12 Code **D** 3640.00
			13 Statutory employee ☐ Retirement plan ☒ Third-party sick pay ☐		**12b** Code
56 Andrews Court, Apt. 7 Philadelphia, PA 19103-3356			**14** Other		**12c** Code
					12d Code
f Employee's address and ZIP code					

15 State PA	Employer's state ID number 00-0-1066	16 State wages, tips, etc. 51220.00	17 State income tax 1572.48	18 Local wages, tips, etc. 51220.00	19 Local income tax 2011.88	20 Locality name Phila.

Form **W-2** Wage and Tax Statement   **20--**   Department of the Treasury—Internal Revenue Service
For Privacy Act and Paperwork Reduction Act Notice, see back of Copy D.

(c)

22222	Void ☐	a Employee's social security number 000-00-3316	For Official Use Only OMB No. 1 545-0008		
b Employer identification number (EIN) 00-0000972			**1** Wages, tips, other compensation 29380.00		**2** Federal income tax withheld 3640.00
c Employer's name, address, and ZIP code			**3** Social security wages 29380.00		**4** Social security tax withheld 1821.56
Omni Corporation 4800 River Road Philadelphia, PA 19113-5548			**5** Medicare wages and tips 29380.00		**6** Medicare tax withheld 425.88
			7 Social security tips		**8** Allocated tips
d Control number			**9**		**10** Dependent care benefits
e Employee's first name and initial Murray T.	Last name Rodson	Suff.	**11** Nonqualified plans		**12a** See instructions for box 12 Code
			13 Statutory employee ☐ Retirement plan ☐ Third-party sick pay ☐		**12b** Code
770 Camac Street Philadelphia, PA 19101-3770			**14** Other UNION DUES 102.00		**12c** Code
					12d Code
f Employee's address and ZIP code					

15 State PA	Employer's state ID number 00-0-1066	16 State wages, tips, etc. 29380.00	17 State income tax 902.20	18 Local wages, tips, etc. 29380.00	19 Local income tax 1153.88	20 Locality name Phila.

Form **W-2** Wage and Tax Statement   **20--**   Department of the Treasury—Internal Revenue Service
For Privacy Act and Paperwork Reduction Act Notice, see back of Copy D.

Source: Internal Revenue Service.

4–13B. (Continued)

(d)

22222	Void ☐	a Employee's social security number 000-00-6839	For Official Use Only OMB No. 1 545-0008		
b Employer identification number (EIN) 00-0000972			**1** Wages, tips, other compensation 92562.75*	**2** Federal income tax withheld 8195.20**	
c Employer's name, address, and ZIP code *Omni Corporation* *4800 River Road* *Philadelphia, PA 19113-5548*			**3** Social security wages 97762.75*	**4** Social security tax withheld 6061.29	
			5 Medicare wages and tips 97762.75*	**6** Medicare tax withheld 1417.69	
			7 Social security tips	**8** Allocated tips	
d Control number			**9**	**10** Dependent care benefits	
e Employee's first name and initial Frank A.	Last name Kent	Suff.	**11** Nonqualified plans	**12a** See instructions for box 12 Code **C** 262.75	
			13 Statutory employee ☐ Retirement plan ☒ Third-party sick pay ☐	**12b** Code **D** 5200.00	
338 North Side Avenue Philadelphia, PA 19130-6638			**14** Other	**12c** Code	
				12d Code	
f Employee's address and ZIP code					
15 State PA	Employer's state ID number 00-0-1066	**16** State wages, tips, etc. 97500.00	**17** State income tax 2993.12	**18** Local wages, tips, etc. 97500.00	**19** Local income tax 3829.80 **20** Locality name Phila.

Form **W-2**   Wage and Tax Statement   **20--**

Department of the Treasury—Internal Revenue Service
For Privacy Act and Paperwork
Reduction Act Notice, see back of Copy D.

Source: Internal Revenue Service.

*Including cost of C, Group-Term Life Insurance, reported in Box 12a.
**[($1,875 − $100) − 6($75.00) = $1,325.00 − $503.00 = $822.00 × 0.15 = $123.30 + $34.30 = $157.60 × 52]

4–13B.   (Continued)

(e)

22222	Void ☐	**a** Employee's social security number 000-00-5771	For Official Use Only OMB No. 1 545-0008		
b Employer identification number (EIN) 00-0000972			**1** Wages, tips, other compensation 24960.00		**2** Federal income tax withheld 0.00
c Employer's name, address, and ZIP code			**3** Social security wages 24960.00		**4** Social security tax withheld 1547.52
Omni Corporation 4800 River Road Philadelphia, PA 19113-5548			**5** Medicare wages and tips 24960.00		**6** Medicare tax withheld 361.92
			7 Social security tips		**8** Allocated tips
d Control number			**9**		**10** Dependent care benefits
e Employee's first name and initial Carlie C.	Last name Christian	Suff.	**11** Nonqualified plans	**12a** See instructions for box 12 Code	
			13 Statutory employee ☐ Retirement plan ☐ Third-party sick pay ☐	**12b** Code	
4900 Gladwynne Terrace Philadelphia, PA 19127-0049			**14** Other UNION DUES 102.00	**12c** Code	
f Employee's address and ZIP code				**12d** Code	

15 State	Employer's state ID number	**16** State wages, tips, etc.	**17** State income tax	**18** Local wages, tips, etc.	**19** Local income tax	**20** Locality name
PA	00-0-1066	24960.00	766.48	24960.00	980.20	Phila.

Form W-2   **Wage and Tax Statement**   **20--**   Department of the Treasury—Internal Revenue Service
For Privacy Act and Paperwork Reduction Act Notice, see back of Copy D.

(f)

22222	Void ☐	**a** Employee's social security number 000-00-8703	For Official Use Only OMB No. 1 545-0008		
b Employer identification number (EIN) 00-0000972			**1** Wages, tips, other compensation 22880.00		**2** Federal income tax withheld 2132.00
c Employer's name, address, and ZIP code			**3** Social security wages 25480.00		**4** Social security tax withheld 1579.76
Omni Corporation 4800 River Road Philadelphia, PA 19113-5548			**5** Medicare wages and tips 25480.00		**6** Medicare tax withheld 369.72
			7 Social security tips		**8** Allocated tips
d Control number			**9**		**10** Dependent care benefits
e Employee's first name and initial Zana W.	Last name Amelia	Suff.	**11** Nonqualified plans	**12a** See instructions for box 12 Code **D** 2600.00	
			13 Statutory employee ☐ Retirement plan ☒ Third-party sick pay ☐	**12b** Code	
480-A Hopkinson Tower Philadelphia, PA 19101-3301			**14** Other EDUC. ASSIST 675.00	**12c** Code	
f Employee's address and ZIP code				**12d** Code	

15 State	Employer's state ID number	**16** State wages, tips, etc.	**17** State income tax	**18** Local wages, tips, etc.	**19** Local income tax	**20** Locality name
PA	00-0-1066	25480.00	782.08	25480.00	1001.00	Phila.

Form W-2   **Wage and Tax Statement**   **20--**   Department of the Treasury—Internal Revenue Service
For Privacy Act and Paperwork Reduction Act Notice, see back of Copy D.

Source: Internal Revenue Service.

4–13B. (Concluded)

DO NOT STAPLE

33333	a Control number	For Official Use Only ▶ OMB No. 1545-0008

b Kind of Payer (Check one)	▶ 941 ☒ Military ☐ 943 ☐ 944 ☐ Hshld. emp. ☐ Medicare govt. emp. ☐ CT-1 ☐	Kind of Employer (Check one)	▶ None apply ☐ 501c non-govt. ☐ State/local non-501c ☒ State/local 501c ☐ Federal govt. ☐	Third-party sick pay (Check if applicable) ☐

c Total number of Forms W-2 6	d Establishment number	1 Wages, tips, other compensation 246742.75	2 Federal income tax withheld 19635.20
e Employer identification number (EIN) 00-0000972		3 Social security wages 260782.75	4 Social security tax withheld 16168.53
f Employer's name Omni Corporation		5 Medicare wages and tips 260782.75	6 Medicare tax withheld 3781.61
		7 Social security tips	8 Allocated tips
4800 River Road Philadelphia, PA 19113-5548		9	10 Dependent care benefits 950.00
g Employer's address and ZIP code		11 Nonqualified plans	12a Deferred compensation 14040.00
h Other EIN used this year		13 For third-party sick pay use only	12b
15 State Employer's state ID number PA 00-0-1066		14 Income tax withheld by payer of third-party sick pay	
16 State wages, tips, etc. 260520.00	17 State income tax 7998.12	18 Local wages, tips, etc. 260520.00	19 Local income tax 10233.08
Contact person Vince T. Roper		Telephone number (215) 555-0017	For Official Use Only
Email address NA		Fax number (215) 555-0010	

Under penalties of perjury, I declare that I have examined this return and accompanying documents and, to the best of my knowledge and belief, they are true, correct, and complete.

Signature ▶ *Frank A. Kent*   Title ▶ **President**   Date ▶ 3/2/15

Form **W-3** Transmittal of Wage and Tax Statements   **20 - -**   Department of the Treasury Internal Revenue Service

Source: Internal Revenue Service.

Continuing Payroll Problem A (p. 4–67)

See the completed payroll register on pages CPP–1 through CPP–3.

Continuing Payroll Problem B (p. 4–67)

See the completed payroll register on pages CPP–4 through CPP–6.

Case Problems (p. 4–68)

Case 4–1

1. To correct the errors, the employer must complete *Form W-2c, Statement of Corrected Income and Tax Amounts.* On Form W-2c, there is a place to show the incorrect information and the corrections. (Since the employer is correcting only the workers' social security numbers, there is no need to file Form W-3c.)

   To encourage employers to make corrections, the SSA guarantees that penalties will not be assessed. Employers should remember that their employees will not receive credit for these wages on their social security records until the errors are corrected.

2. The only form needed is *Form 941X, Adjusted Employment Tax Return.*

3. The employer is required by law to retain the employee's copies of Form W-2 for four years. However, Copy A should be forwarded to the SSA.

4. No. Titles used after a name can be read as initials or even as last names by the computer software used by the SSA. For example, "John Jones, M.D." looks like "John D." to the computer. As a result, the person's name and SSA number will not match the SSA earnings record.

Case 4–2

The IRS states that "dual status" arrangements can be valid. However, the work done as a contractor must be entirely distinct from the work done as an employee. The contractor work must not be subject to the direction or control of the employer.

CHAPTER 5

Learning Objectives

After studying this chapter, students should be able to:

1. Describe the basic requirements for an individual to be classified as an employer or an employee under the Federal Unemployment Tax Act.

2. Identify generally what is defined as taxable wages by the Federal Unemployment Tax Act.

3. Compute the federal unemployment tax, the credit against the tax, and any credit reductions that might apply.

4. Describe how an experience-rating system is used in determining employers' contributions to state unemployment compensation funds.

5. Complete the reports required by the Federal Unemployment Tax Act.

6. Describe the types of information reports under the various state unemployment compensation laws.

Contents

Chapter 5 outline:

UNEMPLOYMENT COMPENSATION TAXES AND CREDITS

    Tax Rate—FUTA

        Credits Against FUTA Tax

        Experience Rating

        Title XII Advances

    Tax Rates—SUTA

        Employer Contributions

        Employee Contributions

        Experience Rating

        Computing the Contribution Rate

        Voluntary Contributions

        Nonprofits

        Dumping

UNEMPLOYMENT COMPENSATION REPORTS REQUIRED OF THE EMPLOYER

    Annual FUTA Return—Form 940

        Completing the Return

            Part 1

            Part 2

            Part 3

            Part 4

            Part 5

            Part 6

            Part 7

        Schedule A

        Filing the Return

        Electronic Filing

        Amending the Return

        Final Return

    Quarterly Deposit Form—FUTA

        Taxes—Household Employers

    Penalties—FUTA

    Information Reports—SUTA

        Status Reports

        Contribution Reports

        Wage Information Reports

        Separation Reports

        Partial Unemployment Notices

    Penalties—SUTA

KEY TERMS

CHAPTER SUMMARY

Matching Quiz (p. 5–29)

1.	F		**6.**	B
2.	G		**7.**	C
3.	H		**8.**	E
4.	D		**9.**	J
5.	I		**10.**	A

Questions for Review (p. 5–29)

1. Under FUTA, a person or a business is considered an employer if either of the following two tests applies:

   a. Pays wages of $1,500 or more during any calendar quarter in the current or preceding calendar year, or

   b. Employs one or more persons, on at least some portion of one day, in each of 20 or more calendar weeks during the current or preceding taxable year.

2. If during the present or previous year, the household employer paid $1,000 or more during any quarter for household services in a private home, college club, or local fraternity or sorority club, the employer is covered.

3. Services performed by a student for the school where he or she is attending classes are exempt from FUTA coverage.

4. The three conditions are (1) the employee performs work in that state, (2) the employee lives in that state, or (3) the employer has a place of business in that state.

5. FUTA coverage includes service of any nature performed outside the United States by a citizen of the United States for an American employer. The major exception is service performed in Canada or any other adjoining country with which the United States has an agreement relating to unemployment.

6. Only (a), commissions as compensation for covered employment, and (e), dismissal payments, are taxable under FUTA.

7. To obtain the maximum credit of 5.4 percent, the employer must make the state contributions on or before the due date for filing the annual FUTA tax return (February 2, 2015). (January 31, 2015 is a Saturday.)

8. State contribution 1.5%

   Net FUTA tax 0.6%

   Total tax 2.1%

9. Two situations that could result in a net FUTA tax greater than 0.6 percent are:

   a. An employer is tardy in paying the state contributions. In this case, the credit is limited to 90 percent of the amount of the state contributions paid after February 2, 2015.

   b. An employer is located in a state that has not met the repayment provisions of Title XII advances. Employers in those states will have their credit against the gross FUTA tax reduced by 0.3 percent the second year after the advance. This penalty is increased by an additional 0.3 percent for each succeeding year up to a maximum of 0.6 percent.

10. The purpose of Title XII advances is to provide funds to states that cannot pay their unemployment compensation benefits. The funds are borrowed from the federal government by the states who are in need of financial assistance.

11. a. Massachusetts—1.26% to 12.27%

    b. Massachusetts—$674

    c. Washington—$39,800

12. Each state sets an initial contribution rate (not less than 1%) for new employers that will apply for a specific period of time. During this time, the new employer's employment record can be developed and an experience rating later established.

13. a. The basic form that must be filed is Form 940, Employer's Annual Federal Unemployment (FUTA) Tax Return.

    b. Form 940 must be filed by February 2, 2015 (January 31, 2015 is a Saturday). However, if all deposits of FUTA tax liability are made on a timely basis, Form 940 may be filed by February 10, 2015.

    c. The total taxable wages are computed by:

       (1) Determining the total payments (including exempt payments) made during the calendar year for services of employees.

       (2) Subtracting from this amount the total exempt payments and the aggregate amount of the wages paid each employee above $7,000.

14. Contributions made on a pretax basis to a cafeteria plan are included in Part 2, line 4, on Form 940 and then on line 6 as part of the subtotal.

15. The employer must complete a new Form 940 for the year being amended. The "Amended" box on the form should also be checked, and an explanation of the reasons for filing an amended return should be attached.

16. A final Form 940 is completed (a box on Form 940 is checked to indicate a final return), and the balance of the tax is paid. In addition, a statement giving the name and address of the person(s) in charge of the required payroll records must be included with Form 940.

17. If the employer's FUTA tax liability exceeds $500 at the end of a calendar quarter, the employer must pay the FUTA tax on or before the last day of the month following the end of the quarter.

18. The employer is required to deposit all federal depository tax liabilities electronically using EFTPS.

19. Contribution reports and wage information reports are usually filed together for each state on a quarterly basis.

20. A separation report provides a wage and employment record of an employee and the reason for leaving. Whenever workers become separated from their employers, the state unemployment compensation laws may require the employer to furnish such a report.

Questions for Discussion (p. 5–30)

1. Benefits cannot be paid to self-employed persons because persons in business for themselves on a full-time basis are not considered unemployed for compensation payment purposes. However, a person may operate a sideline business or a farm, in addition to regular full-time employment, and be eligible for benefits based on the full-time employment.

2. Stable employers should not be penalized with high minimum rates in order to keep a cap on the upper tax limits. Employers responsible for layoffs should pay for the cost of their employees' benefits. In addition, with higher upper limits of SUTA rates, employers with heavy layoffs would have a greater incentive to cut costs by challenging any questionable employee claims for benefits.

3. Students' answers to this question will vary, depending upon the state under consideration. The instructor may e-mail or visit the Web site of the state agency that administers the unemployment compensation program to obtain a copy of the law or special publications made available in many states, such as "Questions and Answers Regarding Unemployment Compensation."

4. a. Benefits for the employer include:

(1) The shared-work compensation program may be applied to selected departments rather than to the whole company.

(2) Substantial time and money are saved by avoiding retraining, rehiring, and recalling former employees after a companywide layoff.

Benefits for the employees include:

(1) The hardship is spread out over the entire workforce. And with partial unemployment benefits helping to make up for the day's pay lost, workers may obtain about 90 percent of their former full-time, take-home pay.

(2) Workers in the lower-paying, more junior jobs stand to gain the most. Junior workers—often women or minority group members—are most vulnerable to job cutbacks, and their pay is close to the benefit level. Thus, these workers are protected from LIFO—"last in, first out."

(3) Often, while on a reduced workweek, workers do not lose their health and welfare benefits. In the event of a companywide layoff, however, such benefits would be lost.

b. Because of the continuation of health and welfare benefits to the partially unemployed, the cost of the program may be a little more than under a companywide layoff in the short run. However, one must take into consideration the offsetting cost factor of recruiting new employees, especially those with hard-to-find skills, after a layoff. Work sharing also causes a drain on the employer's unemployment tax account. This eventually causes the employer to be assessed a higher state unemployment tax rate.

Organized labor feels that the program requires too great a sacrifice by the senior workers. It is seen as a program of sharing the misery of underemployment. Also, it is felt that the shared-work compensation subsidizes the seasonal or volatile industries that have large cyclical layoffs. Union leaders state that seniority clauses and layoff clauses have been negotiated in anticipation of economic hardship. Then, at the time of economic hardship, the people are asked to surrender their seniority under this kind of program. Also, organized labor is concerned that employers may try to make workers do five days' work in the shortened four-day workweek.

Practical Problems (p. 5–31)

The principles and practices of payroll accounting discussed in Chapter 5 are applied in the Practical Problems as shown below.

Principle or Practice	Practical Problem No. (A & B)
1. Calculating the *net FUTA* and *SUTA taxes*.	5–1 through 5–9, 5–11, 5-14
2. Determining *taxable wages* for FUTA and SUTA.	5–6 through 5–9, 5–14
3. *Transfer of employment*.	5–7
4. The amount of credit *against the FUTA tax* based on *late payments of SUTA tax*.	5–10
5. Calculating the *net SUTA and FUTA taxes* and the *amount of the employees' unemployment compensation tax*.	5–11
6. Determining the *SUTA contribution rate* based on a *reserve ratio*.	5–12, 5–13, 5–15
7. *Voluntary contributions*.	5–12, 5–13
8. *Employees' FICA taxes* and *the employer's payroll taxes* for one payroll period.	5–14
9. *Form 940* [Employer's Annual Federal Unemployment (FUTA) Tax Return].	5–16, 5–17
10. *State Quarterly Unemployment Compensation Tax Form*.	5–17

Solutions—Series A Problems

5–1A. (a) Net FUTA tax .... $123,400 × 0.006 = $ 740.40

(b) Net SUTA tax .... $123,400 × 0.048 = 5,923.20

(c) Total unemployment taxes $6,663.60

5–2A. Earnings subject to FUTA and SUTA:
$737,910 − $472,120 = $265,790

(a) Net FUTA tax...$265,790 × 0.006   = $1,594.74
(b) Net SUTA tax...$265,790 × 0.029   =   7,707.91
(c) Total unemployment taxes $9,302.65

5–3A. (a) Net FUTA tax...$67,900 × 0.006   = $ 407.40

(b) Net SUTA tax...$83,900 × 0.037   = $3,104.30

5–4A. (a) SUTA taxes paid to Massachusetts.......$18,000 × 0.04   = $ 720.00

(b) SUTA taxes paid to New Hampshire .....$24,000 × 0.0265   = $ 636.00

(c) SUTA taxes paid to Maine.....................$79,000 × 0.029   = $2,291.00

(d) FUTA taxes paid................................$103,500 × 0.006   = $ 621.00

5–5A. (a) Yes. Donner Company meets the test of having paid wages totaling more than $1,500 during any calendar quarter of the current year.

(b) Taxable wages ....$23,400 + $64,700   = $88,100.00
Net FUTA tax...$88,100 × 0.006   = $ 528.60

5–6A. (a) FUTA taxable wages:
Total wages .... $ 177,610
Less: Director's salary ....   (900)
Less: Nontaxable portion of president's and vice
    president's salaries [($20,000 − $7,000) + ($15,000
    − $7,000)]..   (21,000)
Less: Pretax cafeteria plan contributions..........................   (2,000)
Taxable wages .... $ 153,710

Net FUTA tax: $153,710 × 0.006.................................... $ 922.26

(b) SUTA taxable wages:
Total wages .... $ 177,610
Less: Director's salary ....   (900)
Less: Nontaxable portion of president's and vice
    president's salaries [($20,000 − $7,000) + ($15,000
    − $7,000)]..   (21,000)
Less: Pretax cafeteria plan contributions..........................   (2,000)
Taxable wages .... $ 153,710

SUTA tax: $153,710 × 0.035 .... $5,379.85

5–7A. (a) $2,800 \times 0.032 = 89.60$

(b) $(9,000 - 2,800) \times 0.038 = 235.60$

(c) $(7,000 \times 0.006) + [(7,000 - 2,800) \times 0.006] = 67.20$

5–8A. (a)

FUTA tax	$7,000 × 0.006 =	$ 42.00
SUTA tax	$22,000 × 0.046 =	1,012.00
	Total =	$1,054.00

(b)

FUTA tax	$7,000 × 0.006 =	$ 42.00
SUTA tax	$8,000 × 0.051 =	408.00
	Total =	$450.00

5–9A. (a)

Gross payroll	$ 314,800
Less: Payroll to partners (nontaxable)	(160,000)
Less: Salaries beyond $7,000 limit	(114,800)
Taxable payroll	$ 40,000
FUTA tax rate	× 0.006
FUTA tax	$ 240.00

(b)

Gross payroll	$ 314,800
Less: Payroll to partners (nontaxable)	(160,000)
Less: Salaries beyond $9,000 limit	(106,800)
Taxable payroll	$ 48,000
SUTA tax rate	× 0.0295
SUTA tax	$1,416.00

5–10A. (a)

$114,000 × 0.031 × 90%	$3,180.60
$114,000 × 0.023 (additional credit to 5.4%)	2,622.00
Total FUTA tax credit	$5,802.60

(b)

$114,000 × 0.060	$ 6,840.00
Less: Credit against tax [see (a) above]	(5,802.60)
Net FUTA tax	$ 1,037.40

(c)

Net FUTA tax	$1,037.40
FUTA tax without penalty: $114,000 × 0.006	684.00
Penalty	$ 353.40

5–11A. (a) $171,000 × 0.042 = $7,182.00

(b) $ 86,700 × 0.006 = $520.20

(c) $171,000 × 0.0066 = $1,128.60

5–12A. (a) $17,440 ÷ $850,000 = 2.05%

        (b) 4.9%

        (c) Balance needed to qualify for 4.6% rate: $850,000 × 0.022 = $18,700

Less: Actual balance	17,440
Contribution needed	$ 1,260

        (d)

Tax without voluntary contribution ....$980,000 × 0.049	=	$48,020
Tax with voluntary contribution ....$980,000 × 0.046	=	45,080
Tax decrease resulting from voluntary contribution		$ 2,940
Less: Amount of voluntary contribution.............................		1,260
Tax savings realized..		$ 1,680

5–13A. (a) $1,190

        (b)

Tax without voluntary contribution ....$660,000 × 0.072	=	$47,520
Tax with voluntary contribution ....$660,000 × 0.067	=	44,220
Tax decrease resulting from voluntary contribution		$ 3,300
Less: Amount of voluntary contribution.............................		1,190
Tax savings realized..		$ 2,110

5–14A. (a)

	Taxable Earnings	OASDI (6.2%)	HI (1.45%)
V. Hoffman....................................	$392.31	$24.32	$5.69
A. Drugan	288.46	17.88	4.18
G. Beiter	180.00	11.16	2.61
S. Egan..	220.00	13.64	3.19
B. Lin	160.00	9.92	2.32

Grady and Monroe (partners are not taxed under FICA)

        (b) Taxable payroll: $1,240.77

OASDI ....$1,240.77 × 0.062	=	$76.93
HI...$1,240.77 × 0.0145	=	$17.99

        (c) Taxable earnings:

G. Beiter	$180		
B. Lin	160		
	$340		
SUTA tax ....$340 × 0.031	=	$10.54

        (d) Taxable earnings:

B. Lin	$160		
Net FUTA tax..$160 × 0.006	=	$ 0.96

The remaining employees are beyond the $7,000 limit; therefore, there is no FUTA tax on their salaries.

        (e)

FICA	$ 94.92
SUTA...	10.54
Net FUTA	0.96
Total payroll taxes	$106.42

5–15A. (a)   State contributions:

2000 to 2009 inclusive			$14,695.00
2010	$48,500 × 0.027	=	1,309.50
2011	$47,000 × 0.027	=	1,269.00
2012	$51,450 × 0.027	=	1,389.15
2013	$28,650 × 0.027	=	773.55
Total reserve 9/30/13			$19,436.20
Less: Benefits paid			15,100.90
Balance in reserve account 9/30/13			$ 4,335.30

Total annual payroll for last three years:

2011

$ 13,000	
11,000	
11,500	
12,750	
	$ 48,250

2012

$ 12,500	
13,000	
12,750	
12,200	
	50,450

2013

$ 14,000	
10,000	
9,300	
9,350	
	42,650
Total	$141,350

Average annual payroll:
   Total payroll for last three years, $141,350, divided by 3 equals $47,116.67, the average annual payroll.
Computation of the rate for 2014:
   Balance in reserve account, 9/30/13, $4,335.30, divided by the average annual payroll, $47,116.67, equals 9.20%.

   Since the reserve is 9.20% of the average annual payroll, the rate for 2014 is 4.5%.

(b)   If $2,000 additional benefits had been charged against the account of Karlson Software Company by mistake, the total reserve on 9/30/13 would be $2,335.30. This converts to a reserve ratio of 4.96%, which yields a tax rate of 5.5% (between 0.0% to 7.9% on the chart).

5–16A.   Form 940

Form **940 for 20--:** **Employer's Annual Federal Unemployment (FUTA) Tax Return**

Department of the Treasury — Internal Revenue Service

OMB No. 1545-0028

Employer identification number (EIN)   0 0 – 0 0 0 3 7 9 3

Name *(not your trade name)*   Runson Moving Company

Trade name *(if any)*

Address   423 Bristol Pike
Number   Street   Suite or room number

Sacramento   CA   94203-4523
City   State   ZIP code

Type of Return
(Check all that apply.)

☐ **a.** Amended
☐ **b.** Successor employer
☐ **c.** No payments to employees in 20--
☐ **d.** Final: Business closed or stopped paying wages

Instructions and prior-year forms are available at *www.irs.gov/form940*.

Read the separate instructions before you complete this form. Please type or print within the boxes.

Part 1:   **Tell us about your return. If any line does NOT apply, leave it blank.**

1a If you had to pay state unemployment tax in one state only, enter the state abbreviation .   **1a**

1b If you had to pay state unemployment tax in more than one state, you are a multi-state employer . . . .   **1b** ☒   Check here. Complete Schedule A (Form 940).

2 If you paid wages in a state that is subject to **CREDIT REDUCTION** . . . .   **2** ☒   Check here. Complete Schedule A (Form 940).

Part 2:   **Determine your FUTA tax before adjustments for 20--. If any line does NOT apply, leave it blank.**

3 Total payments to all employees . . . .   **3**   120800 ▪ 00

4 Payments exempt from FUTA tax . . . .   **4**   3500 ▪ 00

Check all that apply: **4a** ☐ Fringe benefits   **4c** ☒ Retirement/Pension   **4e** ☐ Other
                      4b ☐ Group-term life insurance   **4d** ☐ Dependent care

5 Total of payments made to each employee in excess of $7,000 . . . .   **5**   36500 ▪ 00

6 Subtotal (line 4 + line 5 = line 6) . . . .   **6**   40000 ▪ 00

7 Total taxable FUTA wages (line 3 – line 6 = line 7) (see instructions) . . . .   **7**   80800 ▪ 00

8 FUTA tax before adjustments (line 7 x .006 = line 8) . . . .   **8**   484 ▪ 80

Part 3:   **Determine your adjustments. If any line does NOT apply, leave it blank.**

9 If ALL of the taxable FUTA wages you paid were excluded from state unemployment tax, multiply line 7 by .054 (line 7 × .054 = line 9). Go to line 12 . . . .   **9**   ▪

10 If SOME of the taxable FUTA wages you paid were excluded from state unemployment tax, OR you paid ANY state unemployment tax late (after the due date for filing Form 940), complete the worksheet in the instructions. Enter the amount from line 7 of the worksheet . .   **10**   ▪

11 If credit reduction applies, enter the total from Schedule A (Form 940) . . . .   **11**   463 ▪ 80

Part 4:   **Determine your FUTA tax and balance due or overpayment for 20--. If any line does NOT apply, leave it blank.**

12 Total FUTA tax after adjustments (lines 8 + 9 + 10 + 11 = line 12) . . . .   **12**   948 ▪ 60

13 FUTA tax deposited for the year, including any overpayment applied from a prior year   .   **13**   948 ▪ 60

14 Balance due (If line 12 is more than line 13, enter the excess on line 14.)
• If line 14 is more than $500, you must deposit your tax.
• If line 14 is $500 or less, you may pay with this return. (see instructions) . . . .   **14**   ▪

15 Overpayment (If line 13 is more than line 12, enter the excess on line 15 and check a box below.) . . . .   **15**   ▪

▶ You **MUST** complete both pages of this form and **SIGN** it.

Check one: ☐ Apply to next return.   ☐ Send a refund.

Next ▶

For Privacy Act and Paperwork Reduction Act Notice, see the back of Form 940-V, Payment Voucher.   Cat. No. 11234O   Form **940** (2012)

5–16A.   Form 940 (Continued)

Name (not your trade name)	Employer identification number (EIN)
Runson Moving Company	00-0003793

Part 5:   Report your FUTA tax liability by quarter only if line 12 is more than $500. If not, go to Part 6.

16   Report the amount of your FUTA tax liability for each quarter; do NOT enter the amount you deposited. If you had no liability for a quarter, leave the line blank.

16a   **1st quarter** (January 1 – March 31) . . . . **16a** | 220 ▪ 10 |

16b   **2nd quarter** (April 1 – June 30) . . . . **16b** | 107 ▪ 60 |

16c   **3rd quarter** (July 1 – September 30) . . . . **16c** | 101 ▪ 00 |

16d   **4th quarter** (October 1 – December 31) . . . . . . **16d** | 519 ▪ 90 |

17   **Total tax liability for the year** (lines 16a + 16b + 16c + 16d = line 17) **17** | 948 ▪ 60 | **Total must equal line 12.**

Part 6:   May we speak with your third-party designee?

Do you want to allow an employee, a paid tax preparer, or another person to discuss this return with the IRS? See the instructions for details.

☐ **Yes.**   Designee's name and phone number

Select a 5-digit Personal Identification Number (PIN) to use when talking to IRS

☒ **No.**

Part 7:   Sign here. You MUST complete both pages of this form and SIGN it.

Under penalties of perjury, I declare that I have examined this return, including accompanying schedules and statements, and to the best of my knowledge and belief, it is true, correct, and complete, and that no part of any payment made to a state unemployment fund claimed as a credit was, or is to be, deducted from the payments made to employees. Declaration of preparer (other than taxpayer) is based on all information of which preparer has any knowledge.

✗ **Sign your name here**   *Mickey Vixon*

Print your name here   Mickey Vixon

Print your title here   Vice President

Date   2 / 2 / 15

Best daytime phone   219-555-8310

Paid Preparer Use Only   Check if you are self-employed   . . . ☐

Preparer's name		PTIN	
Preparer's signature		Date	/ /
Firm's name (or yours if self-employed)		EIN	
Address		Phone	
City		State		ZIP code	

Page **2**   Form **940** (2012)

Source: Internal Revenue Service.

5–16A. Form 940 (Concluded)

Schedule A (Form 940) for 20--:

Multi-State Employer and Credit Reduction Information

Department of the Treasury — Internal Revenue Service

OMB No. 1545-0028

See the instructions on page 2. File this schedule with Form 940.

Employer identification number (EIN)   0 0 – 0 0 0 3 7 9 3

Name *(not your trade name)*   Runson Moving Company

Place an "X" in the box of EVERY state in which you were required to pay state unemployment tax this year. For states with a credit reduction rate greater than zero, enter the FUTA taxable wages, multiply by the reduction rate, and then enter the credit reduction amount for that state. If any states do not apply to you, leave them blank.

	Postal Abbreviation	FUTA Taxable Wages	Reduction Rate	Credit Reduction		Postal Abbreviation	FUTA Taxable Wages	Reduction Rate	Credit Reduction
	AK	.	× .000	.		NC	.	× .006	.
	AL	.	× .000	.		ND	.	× .000	.
	AR	.	× .006	.		NE	.	× .000	.
✖	AZ	7000.00*	× .003	21.00		NH	.	× .000	.
✖	CA	73800.00**	× .006	442.80		NJ	.	× .006	.
	CO	.	× .000	.		NM	.	× .000	.
	CT	.	× .006	.		NV	.	× .006	.
	DC	.	× .000	.		NY	.	× .006	.
	DE	.	× .003	.		OH	.	× .006	.
	FL	.	× .006	.		OK	.	× .000	.
	GA	.	× .006	.		OR	.	× .000	.
	HI	.	× .000	.		PA	.	× .000	.
	IA	.	× .000	.		RI	.	× .006	.
	ID	.	× .000	.		SC	.	× .000	.
	IL	.	× .000	.		SD	.	× .000	.
	IN	.	× .009	.		TN	.	× .000	.
	KS	.	× .000	.		TX	.	× .000	.
	KY	.	× .006	.		UT	.	× .000	.
	LA	.	× .000	.		VA	.	× .000	.
	MA	.	× .000	.		VT	.	× .003	.
	MD	.	× .000	.		WA	.	× .000	.
	ME	.	× .000	.		WI	.	× .006	.
	MI	.	× .000	.		WV	.	× .000	.
	MN	.	× .000	.		WY	.	× .000	.
	MO	.	× .006	.		PR	.	× .000	.
	MS	.	× .000	.		VI	.	× .015	.
	MT	.	× .000	.					

Total Credit Reduction. Add all amounts shown in the *Credit Reduction* boxes. Enter the total here and on Form 940, line 11 . . . .   463.80

For Privacy Act and Paperwork Reduction Act Notice, see the last page of Form 940.   Cat. No. 16997C   Schedule A (Form 940) 2012

Source: Internal Revenue Service.

*$18,490 – $11,490 (payments in excess of $7,000)

**$102,310 – $3,500 (Retirement Plan) – $25,010 (payments in excess of $7,000)

5–17A.

(a) Tax payments: 2/2/2015 $474.60

(b) Employer's Report for Unemployment Compensation—State D:

D State **Form UC-2 REV 1-12, Employer's Report for Unemployment Compensation**
QTR./YEAR 4/20--

Read Instructions – Answer Each Item

DUE DATE 1/31/20--

	1ST MONTH	2ND MONTH	3RD MONTH
INV. ☐ EXAMINED BY: ☐ 1. TOTAL COVERED EMPLOYEES IN PAY PERIOD INCL. 12TH OF MONTH	8	7	8

FOR DEPT. USE

Signature certifies that the information contained herein is true and correct to the best of the signer's knowledge.

Bertram A. Gompers

10. SIGN HERE-DO NOT PRINT

TITLE President DATE 1/13/14 PHONE # (613) 555-0029

11. FILED ☐ PAPER UC-2A ☐ INTERNET UC-2A ☐ MAGNETIC MEDIA UC-2A

12. FEDERAL IDENTIFICATION NUMBER _____

| EMPLOYER'S CONTRIBUTION RATE ▷ | 2.8% | EMPLOYER'S ACCT. NO. | 00 | 596 | CHECK DIGIT | 1 |

2. GROSS WAGES	98100.00	
3. EMPLOYEE CONTRIBUTIONS		
4. TAXABLE WAGES FOR EMPLOYER CONTRIBUTIONS	2100.00	
5. EMPLOYER CONTRIBUTIONS DUE (RATE X ITEM 4)	58.80	
6. TOTAL CONTRIBUTIONS DUE (ITEMS 3 + 5)	58.80	
7. INTEREST DUE SEE INSTRUCTIONS		
8. PENALTY DUE SEE INSTRUCTIONS		
9. TOTAL REMITTANCE (ITEMS 6 + 7 + 8)	$ 58.80	

LEMONICA COMPANY
123 SWAMP ROAD
PIKESVILLE, D STATE
10777-2017

MAKE CHECKS PAYABLE TO: D UC FUND

Employer name and address Make any corrections on Form UC-2B

DETACH HERE

State D UC-2A, Employer's Quarterly Report of Wages Paid to Each Employee

See instructions on separate sheet. Information MUST be typewritten or printed in BLACK ink. Do NOT use commas (,) or dollar signs ($).
If typed, disregard vertical bars and type a consecutive string of characters. If hand printed, print in CAPS and within the boxes as below:

| SAMPLE Typed: | 123456.00 . | SAMPLE Handwritten: | 1 2 3 4 5 6 . 0 0 | SAMPLE Filled-in: | → ● |

Employer name (make corrections on Form UC-2B)	Employer D UC account no.	Check digit	Quarter and year Q / YYYY	Quarter ending date M M / D D / Y Y Y Y
LEMONICA COMPANY	00596	1	4/20--	12/31/20--

1. Name and telephone number of preparer	2. Total number of pages in this report	3. Total number of employees listed in item 8 on all pages of Form UC-2A	4. Plant number (if approved)
BERTRAM A. GOMPERS (613) 555-0029	1	10	

5. Gross wages, MUST agree with item 2 on UC-2 and the sum of item 11 on all pages of Form UC-2A

98,100.00

6. Fill in this circle if you would like the Department to preprint your employee's names & SSNs on Form UC-2A next quarter → ○

7. Employee's Social Security Number	8. Employee's name FI	MI	LAST	9. Gross wages paid this qtr Example: 123456.00	10. Credit Weeks
000000001	R	G	CRAMER	5200.00	13
000000003	D	M	ENGLISH	13400.00	13
000001998	R	A	SMALL	2400.00	13
000007413	H	B	KLAUS	11700.00	13
000006523	K	N	GEORGE	15000.00	13
000001014	B	A	GOMPERS	26300.00	13
000007277	A	S	ROOKS	1700.00	8
000008111	M	R	BASTIAN	8200.00	13
000002623	K	C	WERNER	2500.00	13
000003534	K	T	TYLER	11700.00	9

List any additional employees on continuation sheets in the required format (see instructions).

11. Total gross wages for this page: → 98100.00
12. Total number of employees for this page ___10___

UC-2A REV 9-05   13. Page __1__ of __1__

This report is to be filed by February 2, 2015, and a check for $58.80 must accompany the tax report.

5–17A. (Continued)   (c) Form 940

Form **940 for 20--:** **Employer's Annual Federal Unemployment (FUTA) Tax Return**
Department of the Treasury — Internal Revenue Service

OMB No. 1545-0028

Employer identification number (EIN)   0 0 – 0 0 0 6 4 2 1

Name (not your trade name)   Lemonica Company

Trade name (if any)

Address   123 Swamp Road
Number   Street   Suite or room number

Pikesville   D   10777-2017
City   State   ZIP code

Type of Return
(Check all that apply.)

- a. Amended
- b. Successor employer
- c. No payments to employees in 20--
- d. Final: Business closed or stopped paying wages

Instructions and prior-year forms are available at *www.irs.gov/form940*.

Read the separate instructions before you complete this form. Please type or print within the boxes.

Part 1:   Tell us about your return. If any line does NOT apply, leave it blank.

1a   If you had to pay state unemployment tax in one state only, enter the state abbreviation .   **1a** | | D

1b   If you had to pay state unemployment tax in more than one state, you are a multi-state employer . . . .   **1b** ☐ Check here. Complete Schedule A (Form 940).

2   If you paid wages in a state that is subject to CREDIT REDUCTION . . . .   **2** ☐ Check here. Complete Schedule A (Form 940).

Part 2:   Determine your FUTA tax before adjustments for 20--. If any line does NOT apply, leave it blank.

3   Total payments to all employees . . . .   **3**   385600 • 00

4   Payments exempt from FUTA tax . . . . . .   **4** | •

Check all that apply: 4a ☐ Fringe benefits   4c ☐ Retirement/Pension   4e ☐ Other
4b ☐ Group-term life insurance   4d ☐ Dependent care

5   Total of payments made to each employee in excess of $7,000 . . . .   **5**   306500 • 00

6   Subtotal (line 4 + line 5 = line 6) . . . .   **6**   306500 • 00

7   Total taxable FUTA wages (line 3 – line 6 = line 7) (see instructions) . . . . . .   **7**   79100 • 00*

8   FUTA tax before adjustments (line 7 x .006 = line 8) . . . .   **8**   474 • 60

Part 3:   Determine your adjustments. If any line does NOT apply, leave it blank.

9   If ALL of the taxable FUTA wages you paid were excluded from state unemployment tax, multiply line 7 by .054 (line 7 x .054 = line 9). Go to line 12 . . . .   **9**   •

10   If SOME of the taxable FUTA wages you paid were excluded from state unemployment tax, OR you paid ANY state unemployment tax late (after the due date for filing Form 940), complete the worksheet in the instructions. Enter the amount from line 7 of the worksheet . .   **10**   •

11   If credit reduction applies, enter the total from Schedule A (Form 940) . . . .   **11**   •

Part 4:   Determine your FUTA tax and balance due or overpayment for 20--. If any line does NOT apply, leave it blank.

12   Total FUTA tax after adjustments (lines 8 + 9 + 10 + 11 = line 12) . . . .   **12**   474 • 60

13   FUTA tax deposited for the year, including any overpayment applied from a prior year .   **13**   474 • 60

14   Balance due (If line 12 is more than line 13, enter the excess on line 14.)
- If line 14 is more than $500, you must deposit your tax.
- If line 14 is $500 or less, you may pay with this return. (see instructions) . . . . . .   **14**   •

15   Overpayment (If line 13 is more than line 12, enter the excess on line 15 and check a box below.) . . . .   **15**   •

▶ You MUST complete both pages of this form and SIGN it.   Check one: ☐ Apply to next return.   ☐ Send a refund.

Next ▶

For Privacy Act and Paperwork Reduction Act Notice, see the back of Form 940-V, Payment Voucher.   Cat. No. 11234O   Form **940** (2012)

*FUTA taxable payrolls: 1st Quarter—$53,700; 2nd Quarter—$8,400; 3rd Quarter—$14,900; 4th Quarter—$2,100

5–17A. (Concluded)

(c) Form 940

Name *(not your trade name)*	Employer identification number (EIN)
Lemonica Company	00-0006421

Part 5: Report your FUTA tax liability by quarter only if line 12 is more than $500. If not, go to Part 6.

16 Report the amount of your FUTA tax liability for each quarter; do NOT enter the amount you deposited. If you had no liability for a quarter, leave the line blank.

16a 1st quarter (January 1 – March 31) **16a**	322 ▪ 20	
16b 2nd quarter (April 1 – June 30) **16b**	50 ▪ 40	
16c 3rd quarter (July 1 – September 30) **16c**	89 ▪ 40	
16d 4th quarter (October 1 – December 31) **16d**	12 ▪ 60	

17 Total tax liability for the year (lines 16a + 16b + 16c + 16d = line 17) **17** | 474 ▪ 60 | **Total must equal line 12.**

Part 6: May we speak with your third-party designee?

Do you want to allow an employee, a paid tax preparer, or another person to discuss this return with the IRS? See the instructions for details.

☐ **Yes.** Designee's name and phone number

Select a 5-digit Personal Identification Number (PIN) to use when talking to IRS

☒ **No.**

Part 7: Sign here. You MUST complete both pages of this form and SIGN it.

Under penalties of perjury, I declare that I have examined this return, including accompanying schedules and statements, and to the best of my knowledge and belief, it is true, correct, and complete, and that no part of any payment made to a state unemployment fund claimed as a credit was, or is to be, deducted from the payments made to employees. Declaration of preparer (other than taxpayer) is based on all information of which preparer has any knowledge.

X Sign your name here *Bertram A. Gompers*

Print your name here	Bertram A. Gompers
Print your title here	President

Date 2 / 2 / 15

Best daytime phone 613-555-0029

Paid Preparer Use Only

Check if you are self-employed . . . ☐

Preparer's name		PTIN	
Preparer's signature		Date	/ /
Firm's name (or yours if self-employed)		EIN	
Address		Phone	
City	State	ZIP code	

Form **940** (2012)

Source: Internal Revenue Service.

Solutions—Series B Problems

5–1B. (a)   Net FUTA tax ....$77,000 × 0.006   = $ 462.00
     (b)   Net SUTA tax..$77,000 × 0.063   =   4,851.00
     (c)   Total unemployment taxes $5,313.00

5–2B. Earnings subject to FUTA and SUTA:
       $593,150 − $211,630 = $381,520

     (a)   Net FUTA tax...$381,520 × 0.006   = $ 2,289.12
     (b)   Net SUTA tax...$381,520 × 0.029   =   11,064.08
     (c)   Total unemployment taxes $13,353.20

5–3B. (a)   Net FUTA tax...$77,900 × 0.006   = $ 467.40
     (b)   Net SUTA tax...$93,900 × 0.027   = $2,535.30

5–4B. (a)   SUTA taxes paid to New Mexico ....$28,000 × 0.039   = $1,092.00

     (b)   SUTA taxes paid to Colorado ....$23,000 × 0.0295   = $ 678.50

     (c)   SUTA taxes paid to Utah ....$65,000 × 0.041   = $2,665.00

     (d)   FUTA taxes paid..................................$94,500 × 0.006   = $ 567.00

5–5B. (a)   Yes. Cowen Company meets the test of having paid wages totaling more
       than $1,500 during any calendar quarter of the current year.

     (b)   Taxable wages ....$2,450 + $3,900   = $6,350.00
        Net FUTA tax..$6,350 × 0.006   = $ 38.10

5–6B. (a)   FUTA taxable wages:
       Total wages .... $ 212,640
       Less: Director's salary ....   (900)
       Less: Nontaxable portion of president's and vice
           president's salaries [($25,000 − $7,000) + ($15,000
           − $7,000)]...   (26,000)
       Less: Pretax cafeteria plan contributions.........................   (2,000)
       Taxable wages .... $ 183,740

       Net FUTA tax: $183,740 × 0.006.................................... $1,102.44

     (b)   SUTA taxable wages:
       Total wages .... $ 212,640
       Less: Director's salary ....   (900)
       Less: Nontaxable portion of president's and vice
           president's salaries [($25,000 − $7,000) + ($15,000
           − $7,000)]...   (26,000)
       Less: Pretax cafeteria plan contributions.........................   (2,000)
       Taxable wages .... $ 183,740

       SUTA tax: $183,740 × 0.041 .... $7,533.34

5–7B. (a) $4,950 × 0.032 = $158.40
(b) ($8,000 − $4,950) × 0.038 = $115.90
(c) ($7,000 × 0.006) + [($7,000 − $4,950) × 0.006] = $54.30

5–8B. (a)

FUTA tax	$7,000 × 0.006	=	$ 42.00
SUTA tax	$8,000 × 0.046	=	368.00
	Total	=	$ 410.00

(b)

FUTA tax	$7,000 × 0.006	=	$ 42.00
SUTA tax	$8,000 × 0.051	=	408.00
	Total	=	$450.00

5–9B. (a)

Gross payroll	$ 128,610
Less: Payroll to partners (nontaxable)	(71,000)
Less: Salaries beyond $7,000 limit	(18,710)
Taxable payroll	$ 38,900
FUTA tax rate	× 0.006
FUTA tax	$ 233.40

(b)

Gross payroll	$ 128,610
Less: Payroll to partners (nontaxable)	(71,000)
Less: Salaries beyond $9,000 limit	(8,800)
Taxable payroll	$ 48,810
SUTA tax rate	× 0.0295
SUTA tax	$ 1,439.90

5–10B. (a)

$193,900 × 0.043 × 90%	$ 7,503.93
$193,900 × 0.011 (additional credit to 5.4%)	2,132.90
Total FUTA tax credit	$ 9,636.83

(b)

$193,900 × 0.060	$11,634.00
Less: Credit against tax [see (a) above]	(9,636.83)
Net FUTA tax	$ 1,997.17

(c)

Net FUTA tax	$ 1,997.17
FUTA tax without penalty: $193,900 × 0.006	1,163.40
Penalty	$ 833.77

5–11B. (a) $194,300 × 0.051 = $9,909.30
(b) $ 93,400 × 0.006 = $560.40
(c) $194,300 × 0.0066 = $1,282.38

5–12B. (a) $21,560 ÷ $1,150,000 = 1.8748%

     (b)   5.2%

     (c)

Balance needed to qualify for 4.9% rate: $1,150,000 × 0.020	=	$23,000
Less: Actual balance		21,560
Contribution needed		$ 1,440

     (d)

Tax without voluntary contribution ......$1,295,000 × 0.052	=	$67,340
Tax with voluntary contribution ....$1,295,000 × 0.049	=	63,455
Tax decrease resulting from voluntary contribution		$ 3,885
Less: Amount of voluntary contribution............................		1,440
Tax savings realized...		$ 2,445

5–13B. (a) $1,015

     (b)

Tax without voluntary contribution ....$650,000 × 0.072	=	$46,800
Tax with voluntary contribution ....$650,000 × 0.067	=	43,550
Tax decrease resulting from voluntary contribution		$ 3,250
Less: Amount of voluntary contribution............................		1,015
Tax savings realized...		$ 2,235

5–14B. (a)

	Taxable Earnings	OASDI (6.2%)	HI (1.45%)
T. Binn	$715.38	$44.35	$10.37
W. Ashworth	576.92	35.77	8.37
K. Bitner......................................	280.00	17.36	4.06
J. Vern	350.00	21.70	5.08
A. Axel	240.00	14.88	3.48

        Givens and Moser (partners are not taxed under FICA)

     (b)   Taxable payroll: $2,162.30

OASDI ....$2,162.30 × 0.062	=	$134.06
HI...$2,162.30 × 0.0145	=	$ 31.35

     (c)   Taxable earnings:

A. Axel..	$240	
SUTA tax ....$240 × 0.0325	=	$7.80

     (d)   Taxable earnings:
         All employees are beyond the $7,000 limit; therefore, there is no FUTA
         tax on their salaries.

     (e)

FICA	$165.41
SUTA...	7.80
Net FUTA	0
Total payroll taxes	$173.21

5–15B. (a)   State contributions:

2000 to 2009 inclusive			$18,135.00
2010	$48,500 × 0.037	=	1,794.50
2011	$47,000 × 0.037	=	1,739.00
2012	$51,450 × 0.037	=	1,903.65
2013	$28,650 × 0.037	=	1,060.05
Total reserve 9/30/13			$24,632.20
Less: Benefits paid			23,194.15
Balance in reserve account 9/30/13			$ 1,438.05

Total annual payroll for last three years:

2011

$ 13,000	
11,000	
11,500	
12,750	
	$ 48,250

2012

$ 12,500	
13,000	
12,750	
12,200	
	50,450

2013

$ 14,000	
10,000	
9,300	
9,350	
	42,650
Total	$141,350

Average annual payroll:
Total payroll for last three years, $141,350, divided by 3 equals $47,116.67, the average annual payroll.

Computation of the rate for 2014:
Balance in reserve account, 9/30/13, $1,438.05, divided by the average annual payroll, $47,116.67, equals 3.1%.

Since the reserve is 3.1% of the average annual payroll, the rate for 2014 is 5.5%.

(b)   If $2,000 additional benefits had been charged against the account of Applebaum Security Company by mistake, the total reserve on 9/30/13 would be ($561.95). This converts to a negative reserve ratio, which yields a tax rate of 7.0%.

5–16B.   Form 940

Form **940 for 20--:**   **Employer's Annual Federal Unemployment (FUTA) Tax Return**
Department of the Treasury — Internal Revenue Service   OMB No. 1545-0028

Employer identification number (EIN)   0 0 – 0 0 0 3 7 9 3

Name (not your trade name)   Monroe Trucking Company

Trade name (if any)

Address   423 Bristol Pike
Number   Street   Suite or room number

Laredo   TX   78040-4523
City   State   ZIP code

Type of Return
(Check all that apply.)

☐ **a.** Amended
☐ **b.** Successor employer
☐ **c.** No payments to employees in 20--
☐ **d.** Final: Business closed or stopped paying wages

Instructions and prior-year forms are available at *www.irs.gov/form940.*

Read the separate instructions before you complete this form. Please type or print within the boxes.

Part 1:   **Tell us about your return. If any line does NOT apply, leave it blank.**

1a If you had to pay state unemployment tax in one state only, enter the state abbreviation .   **1a** ☐ ☐

1b If you had to pay state unemployment tax in more than one state, you are a multi-state employer . . . .   **1b** ☒   Check here. Complete Schedule A (Form 940).

2 If you paid wages in a state that is subject to **CREDIT REDUCTION** . . . . . .   **2** ☐   Check here. Complete Schedule A (Form 940).

Part 2:   **Determine your FUTA tax before adjustments for 20--. If any line does NOT apply, leave it blank.**

3 Total payments to all employees . . . .   **3**   75600 ∎ 00

4 Payments exempt from FUTA tax . . . . . .   **4**   1250 ∎ 00

   Check all that apply: **4a** ☐ Fringe benefits   **4c** ☒ Retirement/Pension   **4e** ☐ Other
                          4b ☐ Group-term life insurance   **4d** ☐ Dependent care

5 Total of payments made to each employee in excess of $7,000 . . . .   **5**   22150 ∎ 00

6 Subtotal (line 4 + line 5 = line 6) . . . .   **6**   23400 ∎ 00

7 Total taxable FUTA wages (line 3 – line 6 = line 7) (see instructions) . . . .   **7**   52200 ∎ 00

8 FUTA tax before adjustments (line 7 × .006 = line 8) . . . .   **8**   313 ∎ 20

Part 3:   **Determine your adjustments. If any line does NOT apply, leave it blank.**

9 If ALL of the taxable FUTA wages you paid were excluded from state unemployment tax, multiply line 7 by .054 (line 7 × .054 = line 9). Go to line 12 . . . .   **9**   ∎

10 If SOME of the taxable FUTA wages you paid were excluded from state unemployment tax, **OR you paid ANY state unemployment tax late** (after the due date for filing Form 940), complete the worksheet in the instructions. Enter the amount from line 7 of the worksheet . .   **10**   ∎

11 If credit reduction applies, enter the total from Schedule A (Form 940) . . . . . .   **11**   ∎

Part 4:   **Determine your FUTA tax and balance due or overpayment for 20--. If any line does NOT apply, leave it blank.**

12 Total FUTA tax after adjustments (lines 8 + 9 + 10 + 11 = line 12) . . . .   **12**   313 ∎ 20

13 FUTA tax deposited for the year, including any overpayment applied from a prior year .   **13**   313 ∎ 20

14 Balance due (If line 12 is more than line 13, enter the excess on line 14.)
• If line 14 is more than $500, you must deposit your tax.
• If line 14 is $500 or less, you may pay with this return. (see instructions) . . . . .   **14**   ∎

15 Overpayment (If line 13 is more than line 12, enter the excess on line 15 and check a box below.) . . . .   **15**   ∎

▶ You **MUST** complete both pages of this form and **SIGN** it.   Check one: ☐ Apply to next return.   ☐ Send a refund.

Next ▶

For Privacy Act and Paperwork Reduction Act Notice, see the back of Form 940-V, Payment Voucher.   Cat. No. 11234O   Form **940** (2012)

5–16B.   Form 940 (Continued)

Name (not your trade name)	Employer identification number (EIN)
Monroe Trucking Company	00-0003793

Part 5:   Report your FUTA tax liability by quarter only if line 12 is more than $500. If not, go to Part 6.

16 Report the amount of your FUTA tax liability for each quarter; do NOT enter the amount you deposited. If you had no liability for a quarter, leave the line blank.

16a **1st quarter** (January 1 – March 31) **16a**	97 ▪ 00	
16b **2nd quarter** (April 1 – June 30) **16b**	87 ▪ 00	
16c **3rd quarter** (July 1 – September 30) **16c**	69 ▪ 70	
16d **4th quarter** (October 1 – December 31) **16d**	59 ▪ 50	
17 **Total tax liability for the year** (lines 16a + 16b + 16c + 16d = line 17) **17**	313 ▪ 20	Total must equal line 12.

Part 6:   May we speak with your third-party designee?

Do you want to allow an employee, a paid tax preparer, or another person to discuss this return with the IRS? See the instructions for details.

☐ **Yes.**   Designee's name and phone number

Select a 5-digit Personal Identification Number (PIN) to use when talking to IRS

☒ **No.**

Part 7:   Sign here. You MUST complete both pages of this form and SIGN it.

Under penalties of perjury, I declare that I have examined this return, including accompanying schedules and statements, and to the best of my knowledge and belief, it is true, correct, and complete, and that no part of any payment made to a state unemployment fund claimed as a credit was, or is to be, deducted from the payments made to employees. Declaration of preparer (other than taxpayer) is based on all information of which preparer has any knowledge.

✗ Sign your name here   *Vernon Scott*

Print your name here   Vernon Scott

Print your title here   Vice President

Date   2 / 2 / 15

Best daytime phone   834-555-5551

Paid Preparer Use Only   Check if you are self-employed . . . ☐

Preparer's name		PTIN	
Preparer's signature		Date	/ /
Firm's name (or yours if self-employed)		EIN	
Address		Phone	
City	State	ZIP code	

Form **940** (2012)

Source: Internal Revenue Service.

5–16B. Form 940 (Concluded)

Schedule A (Form 940) for 20--:

Multi-State Employer and Credit Reduction Information
Department of the Treasury — Internal Revenue Service

OMB No. 1545-0028

See the instructions on page 2. File this schedule with Form 940.

Employer identification number (EIN) 0 0 – 0 0 0 3 7 9 3

Name *(not your trade name)* Monroe Trucking Company

Place an "X" in the box of EVERY state in which you were required to pay state unemployment tax this year. For states with a credit reduction rate greater than zero, enter the FUTA taxable wages, multiply by the reduction rate, and then enter the credit reduction amount for that state. If any states do not apply to you, leave them blank.

	Postal Abbreviation	FUTA Taxable Wages	Reduction Rate	Credit Reduction		Postal Abbreviation	FUTA Taxable Wages	Reduction Rate	Credit Reduction
	AK	.	× .000	.		NC	.	× .006	.
	AL	.	× .000	.		ND	.	× .000	.
	AR	.	× .006	.		NE	.	× .000	.
	AZ	.	× .003	.		NH	.	× .000	.
	CA	.	× .006	.		NJ	.	× .006	.
	CO	.	× .000	.		NM	.	× .000	.
	CT	.	× .006	.		NV	.	× .006	.
	DC	.	× .000	.		NY	.	× .006	.
	DE	.	× .003	.		OH	.	× .006	.
	FL	.	× .006	.		OK	.	× .000	.
	GA	.	× .006	.		OR	.	× .000	.
	HI	.	× .000	.		PA	.	× .000	.
	IA	.	× .000	.		RI	.	× .006	.
	ID	.	× .000	.		SC	.	× .000	.
	IL	.	× .000	.		SD	.	× .000	.
	IN	.	× .009	.		TN	.	× .000	.
	KS	.	× .000	.	✖	TX	.	× .000	.
	KY	.	× .006	.		UT	.	× .000	.
✖	LA	.	× .000	.		VA	.	× .000	.
	MA	.	× .000	.		VT	.	× .003	.
	MD	.	× .000	.		WA	.	× .000	.
	ME	.	× .000	.		WI	.	× .006	.
	MI	.	× .000	.		WV	.	× .000	.
	MN	.	× .000	.		WY	.	× .000	.
	MO	.	× .006	.		PR	.	× .000	.
	MS	.	× .000	.		VI	.	× .015	.
	MT	.	× .000	.					

Total Credit Reduction. Add all amounts shown in the *Credit Reduction* boxes. Enter the total here and on Form 940, line 11 . . . .

For Privacy Act and Paperwork Reduction Act Notice, see the last page of Form 940.   Cat. No. 16997C   Schedule A (Form 940) 2012

Source: Internal Revenue Service.

5–17B.

(a) Tax payment: <u>2/2/15</u>   <u>$1.80</u>

(b) Employer's Report for Unemployment Compensation—State D:

D State **Form UC-2 REV 1-12, Employer's Report for Unemployment Compensation**   QTR./YEAR   4 /20 – –

Read Instructions – Answer Each Item

DUE DATE   01/31/20–
1ST MONTH   2ND MONTH   3RD MONTH

INV. [ ]   EXAMINED BY: [ ]   1. TOTAL COVERED EMPLOYEES IN PAY PERIOD INCL. 12TH OF MONTH   1ST MONTH **10**   2ND MONTH **9**   3RD MONTH **8**

Signature certifies that the information contained herein is true and correct to the best of the signer's knowledge.

Terry M. Brennan

FOR DEPT. USE

2. GROSS WAGES   66800.00

10. SIGN HERE-DO NOT PRINT

TITLE **President**   DATE **1/31/14**   PHONE # **(613) 555-0029**

3. EMPLOYEE CONTRIBUTIONS (0 %)

11. FILED   ☐ PAPER UC-2A   ☐ INTERNET UC-2A   ☐ MAGNETIC MEDIA UC-2A

4. TAXABLE WAGES FOR EMPLOYER CONTRIBUTIONS   300.00

12. FEDERAL IDENTIFICATION NUMBER

EMPLOYER'S CONTRIBUTION RATE   EMPLOYER'S ACCT. NO.   CHECK DIGIT

5. EMPLOYER CONTRIBUTIONS DUE (RATE X ITEM 4)   10.80

EMPLOYER'S CONTRIBUTION RATE ▷ **3.6%**   **00 - 596 - 1**

6. TOTAL CONTRIBUTIONS DUE (ITEMS 3 + 5)   10.80

BRENNAN COMPANY
123 SWAMP ROAD
PIKESVILLE, D STATE
10777-2017

7. INTEREST DUE SEE INSTRUCTIONS

8. PENALTY DUE SEE INSTRUCTIONS

9. TOTAL REMITTANCE (ITEMS 6 + 7 + 8) $

MAKE CHECKS PAYABLE TO: D UC FUND

Employer name and address Make any corrections on Form UC-2B

State D UC-2A, Employer's Quarterly Report of Wages Paid to Each Employee

See instructions on separate sheet. Information MUST be typewritten or printed in BLACK ink. Do NOT use commas (,) or dollar signs ($). If typed, disregard vertical bars and type a consecutive string of characters. If hand printed, print in CAPS and within the boxes as below:

SAMPLE Typed: 123456.00   SAMPLE Handwritten: 1 2 3 4 5 6 . 0 0   SAMPLE Filled-in: ➡ ●

Employer name (make corrections on Form UC-2B)	Employer D UC account no.	Check digit	Quarter and year Q / YYYY	Quarter ending date MM / DD / YYYY
BRENNAN COMPANY	00596	1	4/20--	12/31/20--

1. Name and telephone number of preparer	2. Total number of pages in this report	3. Total number of employees listed in item 8 on all pages of Form UC-2A	4. Plant number (if approved)
TERRY M. BRENNAN (613) 555-0029	1	10	

5. Gross wages, MUST agree with item 2 on UC-2 and the sum of item 11 on all pages of Form UC-2A

67800.00

6. Fill in this circle if you would like the Department to preprint your employee's names & SSNs on Form UC-2A next quarter   ➡ ○

7. Employee's Social Security Number	8. Employee's name FI	MI	LAST	9. Gross wages paid this qtr Example: 123456.00	10. Credit Weeks
000000001	M	S	SUN	4100.00	8
000000003	D	R	MARO	4700.00	13
000001998	R	A	WADE	3200.00	13
000007413	H	B	CAHN	5500.00	13
000006523	P	C	MORSE	10000.00	13
000003334	K	K	WOODS	1800.00	13
000001014	T	M	BRENNAN	16900.00	13
000007277	A	A	MINTZ	9800.00	13
000002623	K	A	WEINER	8400.00	13
000003534	R	C	HARROW	2400.00	9

List any additional employees on continuation sheets in the required format (see instructions).

11. Total gross wages for this page: ➡   66800.00
12. Total number of employees for this page __10__

UC-2A REV 9-05   13. Page __1__ of __1__

This report is to be filed by February 2, 2015, and a check for $10.80 must accompany the tax report.

5–17B. (Continued) (c) Form 940

Form **940 for 20--:** Employer's Annual Federal Unemployment (FUTA) Tax Return
Department of the Treasury — Internal Revenue Service

OMB No. 1545-0028

Employer identification number (EIN) 0 0 – 0 0 0 6 4 2 1

Name (not your trade name) Brennan Company

Trade name (if any)

Address 123 Swamp Road
Number   Street   Suite or room number

Pikesville   D   10777-2017
City   State   ZIP code

Type of Return
(Check all that apply.)

- [ ] **a.** Amended
- [ ] **b.** Successor employer
- [ ] **c.** No payments to employees in 20--
- [ ] **d.** Final: Business closed or stopped paying wages

Instructions and prior-year forms are available at *www.irs.gov/form940*.

Read the separate instructions before you complete this form. Please type or print within the boxes.

Part 1: Tell us about your return. If any line does NOT apply, leave it blank.

1a If you had to pay state unemployment tax in one state only, enter the state abbreviation . **1a** [ ] D

1b If you had to pay state unemployment tax in more than one state, you are a multi-state employer . . . . **1b** [ ] Check here. Complete Schedule A (Form 940).

2 If you paid wages in a state that is subject to CREDIT REDUCTION . . . . **2** [ ] Check here. Complete Schedule A (Form 940).

Part 2: Determine your FUTA tax before adjustments for 20--. If any line does NOT apply, leave it blank.

3 Total payments to all employees . . . . **3** 267700 · 00

4 Payments exempt from FUTA tax . . . . . . **4** [·]

Check all that apply: **4a** [ ] Fringe benefits **4c** [ ] Retirement/Pension **4e** [ ] Other
4b [ ] Group-term life insurance **4d** [ ] Dependent care

5 Total of payments made to each employee in excess of $7,000 . . . . **5** 183700 · 00

6 Subtotal (line 4 + line 5 = line 6) . . . . **6** 183700 · 00

7 Total taxable FUTA wages (line 3 – line 6 = line 7) (see instructions) . . . . . . **7** 84000 · 00*

8 FUTA tax before adjustments (line 7 x .006 = line 8) . . . . **8** 504 · 00

Part 3: Determine your adjustments. If any line does NOT apply, leave it blank.

9 If ALL of the taxable FUTA wages you paid were excluded from state unemployment tax, multiply line 7 by .054 (line 7 x .054 = line 9). Go to line 12 . . . . **9** [·]

10 If SOME of the taxable FUTA wages you paid were excluded from state unemployment tax, OR you paid ANY state unemployment tax late (after the due date for filing Form 940), complete the worksheet in the instructions. Enter the amount from line 7 of the worksheet . . **10** [·]

11 If credit reduction applies, enter the total from Schedule A (Form 940) . . . . . . **11** [·]

Part 4: Determine your FUTA tax and balance due or overpayment for 20--. If any line does NOT apply, leave it blank.

12 Total FUTA tax after adjustments (lines 8 + 9 + 10 + 11 = line 12) . . . . **12** 504 · 00

13 FUTA tax deposited for the year, including any overpayment applied from a prior year . **13** 504 · 00

14 Balance due (If line 12 is more than line 13, enter the excess on line 14.)
- If line 14 is more than $500, you must deposit your tax.
- If line 14 is $500 or less, you may pay with this return. (see instructions) . . . . **14** [·]

15 Overpayment (If line 13 is more than line 12, enter the excess on line 15 and check a box below.) . . . . **15** [·]

▶ You **MUST** complete both pages of this form and **SIGN** it.   Check one: [ ] Apply to next return. [ ] Send a refund.

Next ▶

For Privacy Act and Paperwork Reduction Act Notice, see the back of Form 940-V, Payment Voucher.   Cat. No. 11234O   Form **940** (2012)

*FUTA taxable payrolls: 1st Quarter—$46,000; 2nd Quarter—$26,500; 3rd Quarter—$11,200; 4th Quarter—$300

5–17B. (Concluded)   (c) Form 940

Name *(not your trade name)*	Employer identification number (EIN)
Brennan Company	00-0006421

Part 5:   Report your FUTA tax liability by quarter only if line 12 is more than $500. If not, go to Part 6.

16 Report the amount of your FUTA tax liability for each quarter; do **NOT** enter the amount you deposited. If you had no liability for a quarter, leave the line blank.

16a 1st quarter (January 1 – March 31)	**16a**	276 ▪ 00
16b 2nd quarter (April 1 – June 30)	**16b**	159 ▪ 00
16c 3rd quarter (July 1 – September 30)	**16c**	67 ▪ 20
16d 4th quarter (October 1 – December 31)	**16d**	1 ▪ 80
17 Total tax liability for the year (lines 16a + 16b + 16c + 16d = line 17) **17**		504 ▪ 00 **Total must equal line 12.**

Part 6:   May we speak with your third-party designee?

Do you want to allow an employee, a paid tax preparer, or another person to discuss this return with the IRS? See the instructions for details.

☐ **Yes.**   Designee's name and phone number

Select a 5-digit Personal Identification Number (PIN) to use when talking to IRS

☒ **No.**

Part 7:   Sign here. You MUST complete both pages of this form and SIGN it.

Under penalties of perjury, I declare that I have examined this return, including accompanying schedules and statements, and to the best of my knowledge and belief, it is true, correct, and complete, and that no part of any payment made to a state unemployment fund claimed as a credit was, or is to be, deducted from the payments made to employees. Declaration of preparer (other than taxpayer) is based on all information of which preparer has any knowledge.

✗ Sign your name here   *Terry M. Brennan*

Print your name here   Terry M. Brennan

Print your title here   President

Date   2 / 2 / 15

Best daytime phone   613-555-0029

Paid Preparer Use Only

Check if you are self-employed . . . ☐

Preparer's name		PTIN
Preparer's signature		Date / /
Firm's name (or yours if self-employed)		EIN
Address		Phone
City	State	ZIP code

Form **940** (2012)

Source: Internal Revenue Service.

Continuing Payroll Problem A (p. 5–55)

See the completed payroll register on pages CPP-1 through CPP-3.

Continuing Payroll Problem B (p. 5–55)

See the completed payroll register on pages CPP-4 through CPP-6.

Case Problem (p. 5–55)

Case 5–1

The eligibility reports received from the state must be examined carefully before being signed and returned to the state. Someone in authority (in the Personnel Department) should have charge over these reports and be the only one who can sign them. This person should know the reasons for an employee's leaving the company. If this change is instituted, employees who quit voluntarily or who were discharged for misconduct would have this noted on their eligibility notices. This would disqualify them from collecting benefits.

Another way for the company to save taxes could be by voluntarily contributing to the state unemployment compensation fund. This would take some investigating. First, the company must learn if its state allows such contributions. Second, the method of calculating the tax rates must be known so that the company can determine the amount of the contribution needed in order to reduce its tax rate.

The program to cut unemployment tax costs should also involve the hiring office. One of the things that should be done when applicants are evaluated is to screen poor unemployment insurance risks. "Drifters" and "job-hoppers" can be very costly. They will deplete a company's unemployment reserve balance with the state and boost the company's tax rate.

During the employee's probationary period, the supervisors should make sure that expected performance is achieved. If new employees do not perform satisfactorily, they should be terminated before the end of three months. If the terminated employees cannot obtain other jobs, the former employer should suggest that they file for unemployment compensation benefits. Most states will not count the wages paid by the most recent employer since the employees did not work a full quarter on the firm's payroll. As a result, any benefits collected by discharged workers for the following 12 months will not be charged against the account of the last employer.

Alternatives to dismissing an employee should also be explored. For example, if there is a full-time worker about to be discharged, is there part-time work available for that person? If a full-time worker's skills are no longer required, can that person be retrained and retained on the payroll?

A company with many seasonal workers may consider the hiring of a data-processing firm to process and audit the unemployment claim forms. The company supplies the data-processing firm with a list of all its employees by social security number, including a work history showing where each employee works and what each worker earned in the last quarter. In exchange, the data-processing firm uses its computer system to process all claims and to keep the company informed of changes in unemployment compensation procedures.

The long-term solution must involve a reduction in the turnover rate among employees. Only by maintaining a low turnover can a company "earn" a minimum tax rate.

CHAPTER 6

Learning Objectives

After studying this chapter, students should be able to:

1. Record payrolls in payroll registers and post to employees' earnings records.

2. Understand the various deductions—both voluntary and involuntary (taxes and garnishments)—that are taken out of employees' gross pay.

3. Journalize the entries to record the payroll and payroll taxes.

4. Post to the various general ledger accounts that are used to accumulate information from the payroll entries.

5. Explain the recording of the payroll tax deposits.

6. Understand the need for end-of-period adjustments.

Contents

METHODS OF PAYING WAGES AND SALARIES
    Paying in Cash
    Paying by Check
    Paying by Electronic Transfer
    Pay Cards
    Electronic Paystub
    Final Pay
    Unclaimed Wages
RECORDING PAYROLL TAXES
    FICA Taxes—Employer
    SUTA Taxes
    FUTA Tax
    Entries to Record Wages and Payroll Taxes
RECORDING WORKERS' COMPENSATION INSURANCE EXPENSE
RECORDING THE DEPOSIT OR PAYMENT OF PAYROLL TAXES
    Depositing FICA Taxes and Federal Income Taxes Withheld
    Paying State or City Income Taxes
    Paying FUTA and SUTA Taxes
RECORDING END-OF-PERIOD ADJUSTMENTS
    Wages
    Vacation Pay
SUMMARY OF ACCOUNTS USED IN RECORDING PAYROLL TRANSACTIONS
ILLUSTRATIVE CASE
KEY TERMS
CHAPTER SUMMARY

Matching Quiz (p. 6–31)

1.	E	**6.**	I
2.	C	**7.**	J
3.	H	**8.**	F
4.	G	**9.**	D
5.	A	**10.**	B

Questions for Review (p. 6–32)

1. The main kinds of information contained in a payroll register include period covered by the payroll, name of each employee, marital status and number of withholding allowances for each employee, a record of time worked (regular hours and overtime hours), regular and overtime pay rates, total earnings, deductions from total earnings, net pay for each worker, and taxable earnings columns.

2. Distribution columns are sometimes provided in the payroll register in order to classify the wages and salaries according to the nature of the wage and salary expense, such as "Sales Salaries," "Office Salaries," and "Plant Wages." The total of each distribution column shows the total amount of wages or salaries for that particular operating expense.

3. The Cumulative column in the employee's earnings record is used to record the total amount of accumulated wages each pay period so that the cutoff point for each employee for FICA (OASDI), FUTA, and SUTA can be easily determined. When a worker's wages reach the cutoff point for a particular payroll tax, the wages are no longer subject to that tax.

4. No, a separate account should be kept in the general ledger for recording the employer's liability for each of the three kinds of income tax withheld. Thus, at the time of depositing the federal income taxes withheld and submitting to the state and the city the withheld amounts, the employer can easily determine the appropriate amount of each separate income tax by referring to the appropriate ledger account balance.

5. Garnishment refers to the legal or equitable procedure by means of which a portion of the wages of any person must be withheld for payment of a debt. Through the garnishment process, a creditor, with the aid of the courts, may require the employer to hold back a portion of the debtor's wages and pay that amount to the court or to the creditor.

6. In regard to wage attachments, the following priority withholding orders apply: (1) bankruptcy; (2) federal tax levies and child support orders, whichever is delivered first; and (3) creditor, student loan, or federal administrative wage garnishments.

7. The maximum amount of wages subject to a student loan garnishment is 15 percent of disposable earnings.

8. The only portions of an employee's wages exempt from a federal tax levy are the taxpayer's standard deduction and taxpayer's personal exemptions allowed for the tax year prorated over the total number of pays in a year.

9. The amounts withheld for employees' contributions into their 401(k) plans are recorded like any other liability. These amounts are credited to the appropriate liability account in the payroll entry. This liability account will later be debited when the funds are transferred into the designated investment fund.

10. These employees are given payroll cards that allow employers to deposit employees' pay directly into a prepaid card issued to the employee. The card can then be used like a debit or credit card to access cash at certain automated teller machines. These cards will then be "reloaded" each payday with the employee's net pay.

11. The information will be made available through a secure Web site, kiosk, or interactive voice response system.

12. The uniform law followed by most states provides that the holder of this unclaimed property must file a report after a specified statutory period and then surrender the money to the state as abandoned property.

13. Those special accounts that must usually be opened in the general ledger to record payroll tax entries include:

Payroll Taxes
FICA Taxes Payable—OASDI
FICA Taxes Payable—HI
FUTA Taxes Payable
SUTA Taxes Payable

14. No. Since FICA and FUTA taxes are social security taxes, they may be recorded in the same expense account. However, there is no objection to keeping separate expense accounts for these taxes if the employer so desires.

15. a. A debit to Wages increases operating expenses and decreases the cash account. The increase in operating expenses reduces owner's equity. Liabilities are not affected by the posting unless the total net pay is being accrued; in such a case, the asset account Cash is not decreased until the liability is removed.

   b. A credit to FICA Taxes Payable—HI increases liabilities. If the credit represents withholdings from the employees' gross earnings, the credit to the cash account in the payroll entry is reduced as a result of a lesser amount of net pay being paid the workers. If the credit represents the employer's contribution for FICA Taxes—HI, the expense account Payroll Taxes is being increased (debited), thus reducing the owner's equity.

   c. A debit to SUTA Taxes Payable decreases liabilities. The cash account is also decreased (credited) when this liability is being paid. Owner's equity is not affected by the debit.

   d. A credit to Cash decreases assets. If the credit represents the payment of a liability, the liabilities are being decreased (debited). If the credit represents the payment of an expense, the owner's equity is being decreased.

16. When computing the cost of workers' compensation insurance, employees should be classified by the kind of work performed, since the premium rate for workers' compensation insurance varies with the hazard involved in the work performed.

17. When the employer records the deposit of FICA taxes and federal income taxes withheld, the following entry is made:

FICA Taxes Payable—OASDI	XXX	
FICA Taxes Payable—HI	XXX	
Employees FIT Payable	XXX	
Cash		XXX

      To record payment of the FICA taxes and the federal income taxes withheld.

18. In order to save the time of accumulating timesheets for a portion of a week, the amount of the adjustment could be based on a percentage of the prior week's pay. This percentage would be based on the number of workdays to be accrued divided by the total number of workdays in a weekly payroll.

19. The expenses of these benefits are recorded in the periods when the employees earn them. The liability to the employer is created during the employees' working years and must be recorded over those years.

20. The expenses incurred include wages and salaries, payroll taxes, workers' compensation insurance, vacation benefits expense, and pension benefits.

Questions for Discussion (p. 6–32)

1. The CCPA protects employees with a garnishment for a single indebtedness from discharge and this would include any adverse action that interrupts employment to a degree that the employee would look for another job. A long suspension would be considered the equivalent of a termination of employment. A demotion and/or transfer is considered a constructive discharge in violation of the CCPA.[1]

2. Some of the costs that a company might incur as a result of its salary payments include:

    a. Wages and salary expense—gross wages and salaries.
    b. Payroll taxes—FICA taxes, FUTA tax, and SUTA tax.
    c. Workers' compensation insurance expense.
    d. Health insurance and dental insurance plans—wholly or partially employer financed.
    e. Pension plan—wholly or partially employer financed.
    f. Savings plan—employer's matching of the employees' deposits.

Other employee benefits that may be cited by students include: group life insurance, sick leave, maternity and paternity leave, disability income, profit-sharing plans, employee stock ownership plans, vacations, holidays, Christmas bonuses, food services, educational assistance, and prepaid legal service plans.

---

[1]*Payroll Currently*, January 9, 2009, Issue #1, p. 2.

3. Since an exempt employee must be paid a salary each payday, the company would not be allowed arbitrarily to take the salary back in subsequent pays. An arrangement could be made with the employee in which the employee voluntarily agrees to a pay-back plan and authorizes the company to take a certain amount out of subsequent paychecks. This arrangement should be in writing and signed by the employee.

Practical Problems (p. 6–33)

The principles and practices of payroll accounting discussed in Chapter 6 are applied in the Practical Problems as shown below.

Principle or Practice	**Practical Problem No. (A and B)**
1. Calculating garnishments.	6–1, 6–2
2. Recording payrolls and payroll tax entries.	6–3 through 6–16
3. Determining cash payments to employees.	6–5, 6–6
4. Calculating workers' compensation insurance expense.	6–13
5. Recording vacation benefit expense.	6–14
6. Calculating the taxes withheld from employees' pay and the employer's payroll taxes.	6–15
7. Journalizing and posting payroll, payroll taxes, and deposits for a quarter of a year.	6–16

Solutions—Series A Problems

6–1A.
Take-home pay		$1,020.00
Standard deduction	$12,200	
Personal exemptions ($3,900 × 3) =	11,700	
	$23,900 ÷ 52 =	459.62
Federal tax levy...		$ 560.38

6–2A. (a) Disposable earnings (exclude health insurance, credit union, United Fund) $553.04

(b) Pay subject to garnishment ($553.04 × 0.25)....... $138.26

6–3A. (a) Wages... 8,500.00

    FICA Taxes Payable—OASDI........................   527.00
    FICA Taxes Payable—HI 123.25
    Employees FIT Payable 1,040.00
    Cash 6,809.75

    Payroll Taxes 650.25

    FICA Taxes Payable—OASDI........................   527.00
    FICA Taxes Payable—HI 123.25

(b) FICA Taxes Payable—OASDI 1,054.00

    FICA Taxes Payable—HI..................................... 246.50
    Employees FIT Payable.................................... 1,040.00
    Cash 2,340.50

6–4A.   Wages... 4,690.00

    FICA Taxes Payable—OASDI........................   290.78
    FICA Taxes Payable—HI 68.01
    Employees FIT Payable 685.00
    Cash 3,646.21

    Payroll Taxes 555.77

    FICA Taxes Payable—OASDI........................   290.78
    FICA Taxes Payable—HI 68.01
    FUTA Taxes Payable 28.14
    SUTA Taxes Payable 168.84

6–5A. (a) Wages... 67,000.00

    FICA Taxes Payable—OASDI........................   3,958.70
    FICA Taxes Payable—HI 971.50
    Employees FIT Payable 9,911.00
    Employees SIT Payable 1,410.00
    Cash 50,748.80

    Payroll Taxes 5,414.30

    FICA Taxes Payable—OASDI........................   3,958.70
    FICA Taxes Payable—HI 971.50
    FUTA Taxes Payable 61.80
    SUTA Taxes Payable 422.30

(b) Wages... 67,000.00

    FICA Taxes Payable—OASDI........................   3,958.70
    FICA Taxes Payable—HI 971.50
    Employees Disability Contributions Payable 621.00
    Employees FIT Payable 9,911.00
    Employees SIT Payable 1,410.00
    Cash 50,127.80

6–6A. For Period Ending <u>August 15, 20--</u>

Employee	Net Amount Paid	Bills				Coins				
		$20	$10	$5	$1	50¢	25¢	10¢	5¢	1¢
Chad T. Biskis	$ 251.75	12	1		1	1	1			
Nicole A. Cibik	256.52	12	1	1	1	1				2
Domingo M. Diaz	384.94	19			4	1	1	1	1	4
Laura B. Elias	202.59	10			2	1			1	4
Ari M. Fleischer	253.64	12	1		3	1		1		4
Diane Y. Germano	296.50	14	1	1	1	1				
Arnold B. Herst	594.26	29	1		4		1			1
Edward C. Kenner	399.89	19	1	1	4	1	1	1		4
Kathleen J. Marfia	234.01	11	1		4					1
Kimberly A. Picket	595.80	29	1	1		1	1		1	
Total	$3,469.90	167	8	4	24	8	5	3	3	20

Table title: **PAULEY, INC.** / **Supplementary Payroll Sheet**

6–7A.

Wages	1,500.00	
FICA Taxes Payable—OASDI		93.00
FICA Taxes Payable—HI		21.75
Employees FIT Payable		232.00
Employees SIT Payable		51.04
Retirement Plan Contributions Payable		45.00
Garnishment Payable		100.00
Health Insurance Premiums Payable		95.00
Cash		862.21
Payroll Taxes	114.75	
FICA Taxes Payable—OASDI		93.00
FICA Taxes Payable—HI		21.75

6–8A.

Wages	12,000.00	
FICA Taxes Payable—OASDI		744.00
FICA Taxes Payable—HI		174.00
Employees FIT Payable		260.00
SUTA Taxes Payable		49.00
Cash		10,773.00
Payroll Taxes	1,261.00	
FICA Taxes Payable—OASDI		744.00
FICA Taxes Payable—HI		174.00
FUTA Taxes Payable		58.80
SUTA Taxes Payable		284.20

6–9A.   Wages 17,210.00
          FICA Taxes Payable—OASDI 1,067.02
          FICA Taxes Payable—HI..................................   249.55
          Employees FIT Payable....................................   1,890.00
          Employees SIT Payable 369.40
          Group Insurance Premiums Collected...............   193.00
          Cash..   13,441.03

        Payroll Taxes...   2,022.18
          FICA Taxes Payable—OASDI 1,067.02
          FICA Taxes Payable—HI..................................   249.55
          FUTA Taxes Payable.......................................   103.26
          SUTA Taxes Payable.......................................   602.35

6–10A.   FUTA Taxes Payable 98.75
          Cash..   98.75

6–11A.   Wages 13,060.00
          Wages Payable..   13,060.00

6–12A. (a) $1,104
    (b) <u>   92</u>
    (c) <u>$1,196</u>

    (d) Salary Expense   1,196
          Salaries Payable...   1,196

6–13A. (a) Full-time employee-hours...   8,270
        Part-time employee-hours ....   <u>1,950</u>
          Total...   10,220
        Contribution rate ....   <u>× 0.033</u>
        July withholding ....   <u>$337.26</u>

    (b) Workers Compensation Contributions Collected, Workers Compensation
        Payments Withheld, or Workers Compensation Contributions Payable[*]

    (c) Workers Compensation Insurance Expense...........   337.26
          Workers Compensation Contributions
          Payable..   337.26

        Full-time employee-hours.....................................   8,270
        Part-time employee-hours ....   <u>1,950</u>
          Total...   10,220
        Contribution rate ....   <u>× 0.033</u>
        Employer's liability for July ....   <u>$337.26</u>

    (d) *Workers Compensation Contributions Collected ...   337.26
        Workers Compensation Contributions Payable 337.26
          Cash..   674.52

---

*A company could also use the same account for both the employees' and employer's contribution.

6–14A.

| Vacation Benefits Expense | 740.00 | |
| Vacation Benefits Payable | | 740.00 |

6–15A.

1.

| | Taxes to Be Withheld from Employees' Earnings Under | | |
| | FICA | | |
Employee	OASDI	HI	SUTA
1. Weiser, Robert A.	$ 0.00	$11.46	....
2. Stankard, Laurie C.	18.29	4.28	....
3. Grow, Joan L.	14.88	3.48	$1.20
4. Rowe, Paul C.	14.57	3.41	....
5. McNamara, Joyce M.	12.09	2.83	0.98
6. O'Connor, Roger T.	17.98	11.75	....
7. Carson, Ronald B.	17.36	4.06	....
8. Kenny, Ginni C.	10.85	2.54	0.88
9. Devery, Virginia S.	36.58	8.56	....
10. Wilson, Joe W.	12.71	2.97	1.03
Total employee taxes	$155.31	$55.34	$4.09
	(a)	(b)	(c)

| | Employer Taxes: Portion of Employees' Earnings Taxable Under | | | |
| | FICA | | | |
Employee	OASDI	HI	FUTA	SUTA
1. Weiser, Robert A.	$	$ 790.00	....	....
2. Stankard, Laurie C.	295.00	295.00	....	....
3. Grow, Joan L.	240.00	240.00	$240.00	$240.00
4. Rowe, Paul C.	235.00	235.00	....	....
5. McNamara, Joyce M.	195.00	195.00	....	195.00
6. O'Connor, Roger T.	290.00	810.00	....	....
7. Carson, Ronald B.	280.00	280.00	....	....
8. Kenny, Ginni C.	175.00	175.00	175.00	175.00
9. Devery, Virginia S.	590.00	590.00	....	....
10. Wilson, Joe W.	205.00	205.00	205.00	205.00

2.

	FICA OASDI	FICA HI	FUTA	SUTA
Total taxable earnings	$2,505.00	$3,815.00	$620.00	$815.00
× Applicable tax rate	0.062	0.0145	0.006	0.018
Totals	$ 155.31	$ 55.32	$ 3.72	$ 14.67

| Total payroll taxes | $229.02 |

6–16A.   (a)

BROOKINS COMPANY JOURNAL

Page *19*

20--

Apr.	1	Union Dues Payable	28	100.00	
		Cash	11		100.00
	15	Wages and Salaries	51	6,105.00	
		FICA Taxes Payable—OASDI	20		378.51
		FICA Taxes Payable—HI	21		88.52
		Employees FIT Payable	25		565.00
		Employees SIT Payable	26		107.32
		Union Dues Payable	28		50.00
		Cash	11		4,915.65
	15	Payroll Taxes	55	644.08	
		FICA Taxes Payable—OASDI	20		378.51
		FICA Taxes Payable—HI	21		88.52
		FUTA Taxes Payable	22		36.63
		SUTA Taxes Payable	23		140.42
	15	Employees SIT Payable	26	546.92	
		Cash	11		546.92
	15	FICA Taxes Payable—OASDI	20	1,068.88	
		FICA Taxes Payable—HI	21	249.98	
		Employees FIT Payable	25	1,124.00	
		Cash	11		2,442.86
	29	Wages and Salaries	51	5,850.00	
		FICA Taxes Payable—OASDI	20		362.70
		FICA Taxes Payable—HI	21		84.83
		Employees FIT Payable	25		509.00
		Employees SIT Payable	26		128.90
		Union Dues Payable	28		55.00
		Cash	11		4,709.57
	29	Payroll Taxes	55	617.18	
		FICA Taxes Payable—OASDI	20		362.70
		FICA Taxes Payable—HI	21		84.83
		FUTA Taxes Payable	22		35.10
		SUTA Taxes Payable	23		134.55
	29	SUTA Taxes Payable	23	571.78	
		Cash	11		571.78

6–16A. (Continued)

JOURNAL   Page *20*

20--					
May	2	Union Dues Payable	28	105.00	
		Cash	11		105.00
	13	Wages and Salaries	51	5,810.00	
		FICA Taxes Payable—OASDI	20		360.22
		FICA Taxes Payable—HI..................	21		84.25
		Employees FIT Payable....................	25		507.00
		Employees SIT Payable....................	26		125.05
		Union Dues Payable	28		55.00
		Cash	11		4,678.48
	13	Payroll Taxes	55	612.96	
		FICA Taxes Payable—OASDI	20		360.22
		FICA Taxes Payable—HI..................	21		84.25
		FUTA Taxes Payable........................	22		34.86
		SUTA Taxes Payable........................	23		133.63
	16	FICA Taxes Payable—OASDI................	20	1,482.42	
		FICA Taxes Payable—HI	21	346.70	
		Employees FIT Payable	25	1,074.00	
		Cash	11		2,903.12
	31	Wages and Salaries	51	6,060.00	
		FICA Taxes Payable—OASDI	20		375.72
		FICA Taxes Payable—HI..................	21		87.87
		Employees FIT Payable....................	25		533.00
		Employees SIT Payable....................	26		119.00
		Union Dues Payable	28		50.00
		Cash	11		4,894.41
	31	Payroll Taxes	55	639.33	
		FICA Taxes Payable—OASDI	20		375.72
		FICA Taxes Payable—HI..................	21		87.87
		FUTA Taxes Payable........................	22		36.36
		SUTA Taxes Payable........................	23		139.38
June	3	Union Dues Payable	28	105.00	
		Cash	11		105.00

6–16A. (Continued)

JOURNAL   Page 21

20-- June 15	Wages and Salaries	51	6,380.00	
	FICA Taxes Payable—OASDI	20		395.56
	FICA Taxes Payable—HI	21		92.51
	Employees FIT Payable	25		549.00
	Employees SIT Payable	26		128.70
	Union Dues Payable	28		50.00
	Cash	11		5,164.23
15	Payroll Taxes	55	633.07	
	FICA Taxes Payable—OASDI	20		395.56
	FICA Taxes Payable—HI	21		92.51
	FUTA Taxes Payable	22		30.00
	SUTA Taxes Payable	23		115.00
15	FICA Taxes Payable—OASDI	20	1,471.88	
	FICA Taxes Payable—HI	21	344.24	
	Employees FIT Payable	25	1,040.00	
	Cash	11		2,856.12
30	Wages and Salaries	51	6,250.00	
	FICA Taxes Payable—OASDI	20		387.50
	FICA Taxes Payable—HI	21		90.63
	Employees FIT Payable	25		538.00
	Employees SIT Payable	26		127.60
	Union Dues Payable	28		50.00
	Cash	11		5,056.27
30	Payroll Taxes	55	616.46	
	FICA Taxes Payable—OASDI	20		387.50
	FICA Taxes Payable—HI	21		90.63
	FUTA Taxes Payable	22		28.62
	SUTA Taxes Payable	23		109.71

6–16A. (Continued)

GENERAL LEDGER

(b)

CASH   11

Date		Item	P.R.	Dr.	Cr.	Balance Dr.	Cr.
20--							
Apr.	1	Balance..........	✓	....	....	57,673.56	....
	1	....	J19	....	100.00	57,573.56	....
	15	....	J19	....	4,915.65	52,657.91	....
	15	....	J19	....	546.92	52,110.99	....
	15	....	J19	....	2,442.86	49,668.13	....
	29	....	J19	....	4,709.57	44,958.56	....
	29	....	J19	....	571.78	44,386.78	....
May	2	....	J20	....	105.00	44,281.78	....
	13	....	J20	....	4,678.48	39,603.30	....
	16	....	J20	....	2,903.12	36,700.18	....
	31	....	J20	....	4,894.41	31,805.77	....
June	3	....	J20	....	105.00	31,700.77	....
	15	....	J21	....	5,164.23	26,536.54	....
	15	....	J21	....	2,856.12	23,680.42	....
	30	....	J21	....	5,056.27	18,624.15	....

FICA TAXES PAYABLE—OASDI   20

Date		Item	P.R.	Dr.	Cr.	Balance Dr.	Cr.
20--							
Apr.	1	Balance	✓	....	....	....	1,068.88
	15	....	J19	....	378.51	....	1,447.39
	15	....	J19	....	378.51	....	1,825.90
	15	....	J19	1,068.88	....	....	757.02
	29	....	J19	....	362.70	....	1,119.72
	29	....	J19	....	362.70	....	1,482.42
May	13	....	J20	....	360.22	....	1,842.64
	13	....	J20	....	360.22	....	2,202.86
	16	....	J20	1,482.42	....	....	720.44
	31	....	J20	....	375.72	....	1,096.16
	31	....	J20	....	375.72	....	1,471.88
June	15	....	J21	....	395.56	....	1,867.44
	15	....	J21	....	395.56	....	2,263.00
	15	....	J21	1,471.88	....	....	791.12
	30	....	J21	....	387.50	....	1,178.62
	30	....	J21	....	387.50	....	1,566.12

6–16A. (Continued)

FICA TAXES PAYABLE—HI 21

Date		Item	P.R.	Dr.	Cr.	Balance Dr.	Cr.
20--							
Apr.	1	Balance	✓	....	....	....	249.98
	15	....	J19	....	88.52	....	338.50
	15	....	J19	....	88.52	....	427.02
	15	....	J19	249.98	....	....	177.04
	29	....	J19	....	84.83	....	261.87
	29	....	J19	....	84.83	....	346.70
May	13	....	J20	....	84.25	....	430.95
	13	....	J20	....	84.25	....	515.20
	16	....	J20	346.70	....	....	168.50
	31	....	J20	....	87.87	....	256.37
	31	....	J20	....	87.87	....	344.24
June	15	....	J21	....	92.51	....	436.75
	15	....	J21	....	92.51	....	529.26
	15	....	J21	344.24	....	....	185.02
	30	....	J21	....	90.63	....	275.65
	30	....	J21	....	90.63	....	366.28

FUTA TAXES PAYABLE 22

Date		Item	P.R.	Dr.	Cr.	Balance Dr.	Cr.
20--							
Apr.	1	Balance	✓	....	....	....	149.16
	15	....	J19	....	36.63	....	185.79
	29	....	J19	....	35.10	....	220.89
May	13	....	J20	....	34.86	....	255.75
	31	....	J20	....	36.36	....	292.11
June	15	....	J21	....	30.00	....	322.11
	30	....	J21	....	28.62	....	350.73

6–16A. (Continued)

SUTA TAXES PAYABLE 23

Date		Item	P.R.	Dr.	Cr.	Balance Dr.	Cr.
20--							
Apr.	1	Balance	✓	....	....	....	571.78
	15	....	J19	....	140.42	....	712.20
	29	....	J19	....	134.55	....	846.75
	29	....	J19	571.78	....	....	274.97
May	13	....	J20	....	133.63	....	408.60
	31	....	J20	....	139.38	....	547.98
June	15	....	J21	....	115.00	....	662.98
	30	....	J21	....	109.71	....	772.69

EMPLOYEES FIT PAYABLE 25

Date		Item	P.R.	Dr.	Cr.	Balance Dr.	Cr.
20--							
Apr.	1	Balance	✓	....	....	....	1,124.00
	15	....	J19	....	565.00	....	1,689.00
	15	....	J19	1,124.00	....	....	565.00
	29	....	J19	....	509.00	....	1,074.00
May	13	....	J20	....	507.00	....	1,581.00
	16	....	J20	1,074.00	....	....	507.00
	31	....	J20	....	533.00	....	1,040.00
June	15	....	J21	....	549.00	....	1,589.00
	15	....	J21	1,040.00	....	....	549.00
	30	....	J21	....	538.00	....	1,087.00

EMPLOYEES SIT PAYABLE 26

Date		Item	P.R.	Dr.	Cr.	Balance Dr.	Cr.
20--							
Apr.	1	Balance	✓	....	....	....	546.92
	15	....	J19	....	107.32	....	654.24
	15	....	J19	546.92	....	....	107.32
	29	....	J19	....	128.90	....	236.22
May	13	....	J20	....	125.05	....	361.27
	31	....	J20	....	119.00	....	480.27
June	15	....	J21	....	128.70	....	608.97
	30	....	J21	....	127.60	....	736.57

6–16A. (Continued)

UNION DUES PAYABLE 28

Date		Item	P.R.	Dr.	Cr.	Balance Dr.	Balance Cr.
20--							
Apr.	1	Balance	✓	....	....	....	100.00
	1	....	J19	100.00	....	—	—
	15	....	J19	....	50.00	....	50.00
	29	....	J19	....	55.00	....	105.00
May	2	....	J20	105.00	....	—	—
	13	....	J20	....	55.00	....	55.00
	31	....	J20	....	50.00	....	105.00
June	3	....	J20	105.00	....	—	—
	15	....	J21	....	50.00	....	50.00
	30	....	J21	....	50.00	....	100.00

WAGES AND SALARIES 51

Date		Item	P.R.	Dr.	Cr.	Balance Dr.	Balance Cr.
20--							
Apr.	1	Balance	✓	....	....	71,360.00	....
	15	....	J19	6,105.00	....	77,465.00	....
	29	....	J19	5,850.00	....	83,315.00	....
May	13	....	J20	5,810.00	....	89,125.00	....
	31	....	J20	6,060.00	....	95,185.00	....
June	15	....	J21	6,380.00	....	101,565.00	....
	30	....	J21	6,250.00	....	107,815.00	....

PAYROLL TAXES 55

Date		Item	P.R.	Dr.	Cr.	Balance Dr.	Balance Cr.
20--							
Apr.	1	Balance	✓	....	....	6,846.74	....
	15	....	J19	644.08	....	7,490.82	....
	29	....	J19	617.18	....	8,108.00	....
May	13	....	J20	612.96	....	8,720.96	....
	31	....	J20	639.33	....	9,360.29	....
June	15	....	J21	633.07	....	9,993.36	....
	30	....	J21	616.46	....	10,609.82	....

6–16A.   (Concluded)

(c) Questions

1. FICA Taxes Payable—OASDI $1,566.12
    FICA Taxes Payable—HI 366.28
    Employees FIT Payable 1,087.00
        Total liability $3,019.40

2. $736.57

3. $0

4. $772.69

5. $100

6. $107,815.00

7. $10,609.82

8. Vacation Benefits Expense 15,000.00
        Vacation Benefits Payable 15,000.00

Solutions—Series B Problems

6–1B.   Take-home pay $499.00
              Standard deduction $ 6,100
              Personal exemptions ($3,900 × 2) =   7,800
                                         $13,900 ÷ 52 =   267.31
              Federal tax levy $231.69

6–2B. (a) Disposable earnings (exclude health insurance,
              credit union, United Fund) $697.07

      (b) Pay subject to garnishment ($697.07 × 0.25) $174.27

6–3B. (a) Wages 16,900.00
              FICA Taxes Payable—OASDI 1,047.80
              FICA Taxes Payable—HI 245.05
              Employees FIT Payable 1,698.00
              Cash 13,909.15

              Payroll Taxes 1,292.85
              FICA Taxes Payable—OASDI 1,047.80
              FICA Taxes Payable—HI 245.05

      (b) FICA Taxes Payable—OASDI 2,095.60
          FICA Taxes Payable—HI 490.10
          Employees FIT Payable 1,698.00
              Cash 4,283.70

6–4B.   Wages..   7,780.00
                FICA Taxes Payable—OASDI.......................   482.36
                FICA Taxes Payable—HI 112.81
                Employees FIT Payable 998.00
                Cash...   6,186.83

                Payroll Taxes..   976.39
                FICA Taxes Payable—OASDI.......................   482.36
                FICA Taxes Payable—HI 112.81
                FUTA Taxes Payable 46.68
                SUTA Taxes Payable 334.54

6–5B. (a) Wages..   53,900.00
                FICA Taxes Payable—OASDI.......................   3,124.80
                FICA Taxes Payable—HI 781.55
                Employees FIT Payable 6,995.00
                Employees SIT Payable 1,010.00
                Cash...   41,988.65

                Payroll Taxes..   4,176.45
                FICA Taxes Payable—OASDI.......................   3,124.80
                FICA Taxes Payable—HI 781.55
                FUTA Taxes Payable 43.80
                SUTA Taxes Payable 226.30

         (b) Wages..   53,900.00
                FICA Taxes Payable—OASDI.......................   3,124.80
                FICA Taxes Payable—HI 781.55
                Employees Disability Contributions Payable ..   241.00
                Employees FIT Payable 6,995.00
                Employees SIT Payable 1,010.00
                Cash...   41,747.65

6–6B. **For Period Ending** <u>August 15, 20--</u>

Employee	Net Amount Paid	Bills				Coins				
		$20	$10	$5	$1	50¢	25¢	10¢	5¢	1¢
Ben Dowd	$ 639.57	31	1	1	4	1			1	2
Erin Martin	248.95	12		1	3	1	1	2		
Dot Ruiz	491.95	24	1		1	1	1	2		
Randi Heavner	832.14	41	1		2			1		4
Rex Sundry	710.15	35	1					1	1	
Hal Roach	709.13	35		1	4			1		3
Mandy Arnold	519.13	25	1	1	4			1		3
Faye Montgomery	227.24	11		1	2			2		4
Max Held	473.18	23	1		3			1	1	3
Pedro Rodries	590.90	29	1			1	1	1	1	
Total	$ 5,442.34	266	7	5	23	4	3	12	4	19

ADAMS, INC.
Supplementary Payroll Sheet

6–7B.

Wages	2,400.00	
FICA Taxes Payable—OASDI		148.80
FICA Taxes Payable—HI		34.80
Employees FIT Payable		532.00
Employees SIT Payable		117.04
Retirement Plan Contributions Payable		72.00
Garnishment Payable		125.00
Health Insurance Premiums Payable		110.00
Cash		1,260.36
Payroll Taxes	183.60	
FICA Taxes Payable—OASDI		148.80
FICA Taxes Payable—HI		34.80

6–8B.

Wages	15,600.00	
FICA Taxes Payable—OASDI		967.20
FICA Taxes Payable—HI		226.20
Employees FIT Payable		424.00
SUTA Taxes Payable		54.00
Cash		13,928.60
Payroll Taxes	1,679.40	
FICA Taxes Payable—OASDI		967.20
FICA Taxes Payable—HI		226.20
FUTA Taxes Payable		64.80
SUTA Taxes Payable		421.20

6–9B. Wages 2,910.00
    FICA Taxes Payable—OASDI 180.42
    FICA Taxes Payable—HI................................ 42.20
    Employees FIT Payable.................................. 491.00
    Employees SIT Payable 49.10
    Group Insurance Premiums Collected.............. 87.10
    Cash.. 2,060.18

    Payroll Taxes.. 349.21
    FICA Taxes Payable—OASDI 180.42
    FICA Taxes Payable—HI................................ 42.20
    FUTA Taxes Payable.................................... 17.46
    SUTA Taxes Payable.................................... 109.13

6–10B. FUTA Taxes Payable 619.24
    Cash.. 619.24

6–11B. Wages 17,922.00
    Wages Payable.. 17,922.00

6–12B. (a) $866.80
    (b)   39.40
    (c) $906.20

    (d) Salary Expense 906.20
        Salaries Payable 906.20

6–13B. (a) Full-time employee-hours 26,110
    Part-time employee-hours.. 3,490
      Total 29,600
    Contribution rate .... × 0.033
    July withholding $976.80

    (b) Workers Compensation Contributions Collected, Workers Compensation Payments Withheld, or Workers Compensation Contributions Payable[*]

    (c) Workers Compensation Insurance Expense........ 976.80
        Workers Compensation Contributions
        Payable 976.80

    Full-time employee-hours 26,110
    Part-time employee-hours.................................. 3,490
      Total 29,600
    Contribution rate .... × 0.033
    Employer's liability for July................................ $976.80

    (d) *Workers Compensation Contributions Collected... 976.80
        Workers Compensation Contributions Payable 976.80
        Cash... 1,953.60

*A company could also use the same account for both the employees' and employer's contribution.

6–14B.

Vacation Benefits Expense	620.00	
Vacation Benefits Payable		620.00

6–15B.

1.

	Taxes to Be Withheld from Employees' Earnings Under			Employer Taxes: Portion of Employees' Earnings Taxable Under			
	FICA			FICA			
Employee	OASDI	HI	SUTA	OASDI	HI	FUTA	SUTA
1. Watson, Ruth T.	$ 0.00	$ 27.41	....	$	$1,890.00	....	....
2. Kinder, Ralph A.	25.42	5.95	....	410.00	410.00	....	....
3. Sanchez, Robert T.	24.49	5.73	$1.98	395.00	395.00	$395.00	$395.00
4. Carey, Mary C.	18.29	4.28	....	295.00	295.00	....	....
5. Cox, Mason M.	26.35	6.16	2.13	425.00	425.00	425.00	425.00
6. Kenni, Jack T.	12.40	26.83	....	200.00	1,850.00	....	....
7. Britmayer, Tim A.	30.38	7.11	....	490.00	490.00	....	....
8. Candi, Mark B.	20.15	4.71	1.63	325.00	325.00	175.00	325.00
9. Boxer, Barbara C.	71.30	16.68	....	1,150.00	1,150.00	....	....
10. McBride, James W.	12.09	2.83	0.98	195.00	195.00	195.00	195.00
Total employee taxes	$240.87	$107.69	$6.72				
	(a)	(b)	(c)				

2.

	OASDI	HI	FUTA	SUTA
Total taxable earnings	$3,885.00	$7,425.00	$1,190.00	$1,340.00
× Applicable tax rate	0.062	0.0145	0.006	0.028
Totals	$ 240.87	$ 107.66	$ 7.14	$ 37.52

Total payroll taxes $393.19

6–16B. (a)

BROOKINS COMPANY JOURNAL

Page *19*

20--

Apr.	1	Union Dues Payable	28	100.00	
		Cash	11		100.00
	15	Wages and Salaries	51	8,310.00	
		FICA Taxes Payable—OASDI	20		515.22
		FICA Taxes Payable—HI	21		120.50
		Employees FIT Payable	25		890.00
		Employees SIT Payable	26		166.20
		Union Dues Payable	28		140.00
		Cash	11		6,478.08
	15	Payroll Taxes	55	876.71	
		FICA Taxes Payable—OASDI	20		515.22
		FICA Taxes Payable—HI	21		120.50
		FUTA Taxes Payable	22		49.86
		SUTA Taxes Payable	23		191.13
	15	Employees SIT Payable	26	546.92	
		Cash	11		546.92
	15	FICA Taxes Payable—OASDI	20	1,068.88	
		FICA Taxes Payable—HI	21	249.98	
		Employees FIT Payable	25	1,124.00	
		Cash	11		2,442.86
	29	Wages and Salaries	51	7,975.00	
		FICA Taxes Payable—OASDI	20		494.45
		FICA Taxes Payable—HI	21		115.64
		Employees FIT Payable	25		815.00
		Employees SIT Payable	26		151.50
		Union Dues Payable	28		135.00
		Cash	11		6,263.41
	29	Payroll Taxes	55	841.37	
		FICA Taxes Payable—OASDI	20		494.45
		FICA Taxes Payable—HI	21		115.64
		FUTA Taxes Payable	22		47.85
		SUTA Taxes Payable	23		183.43
	29	SUTA Taxes Payable	23	571.78	
		Cash	11		571.78

6–16B.   (Continued)

JOURNAL   Page *20*

20--					
May	2	Union Dues Payable	28	275.00	
		Cash	11		275.00
	13	Wages and Salaries	51	8,190.00	
		FICA Taxes Payable—OASDI	20		507.78
		FICA Taxes Payable—HI	21		118.76
		Employees FIT Payable	25		875.00
		Employees SIT Payable	26		160.05
		Union Dues Payable	28		135.00
		Cash	11		6,393.41
	13	Payroll Taxes	55	864.05	
		FICA Taxes Payable—OASDI	20		507.78
		FICA Taxes Payable—HI	21		118.76
		FUTA Taxes Payable	22		49.14
		SUTA Taxes Payable	23		188.37
	16	FICA Taxes Payable—OASDI	20	2,019.34	
		FICA Taxes Payable—HI	21	472.28	
		Employees FIT Payable	25	1,705.00	
		Cash	11		4,196.62
	31	Wages and Salaries	51	8,755.00	
		FICA Taxes Payable—OASDI	20		542.81
		FICA Taxes Payable—HI	21		126.95
		Employees FIT Payable	25		971.00
		Employees SIT Payable	26		174.05
		Union Dues Payable	28		140.00
		Cash	11		6,800.19
	31	Payroll Taxes	55	923.66	
		FICA Taxes Payable—OASDI	20		542.81
		FICA Taxes Payable—HI	21		126.95
		FUTA Taxes Payable	22		52.53
		SUTA Taxes Payable	23		201.37
June	3	Union Dues Payable	28	275.00	
		Cash	11		275.00

6–16B. (Continued)

JOURNAL   Page *21*

20--

June 15	Wages and Salaries	51	9,110.00	
	FICA Taxes Payable—OASDI	20		564.82
	FICA Taxes Payable—HI	21		132.10
	Employees FIT Payable	25		1,029.00
	Employees SIT Payable	26		187.15
	Union Dues Payable	28		145.00
	Cash	11		7,051.93
15	Payroll Taxes	55	819.01	
	FICA Taxes Payable—OASDI	20		564.82
	FICA Taxes Payable—HI	21		132.10
	FUTA Taxes Payable	22		25.26
	SUTA Taxes Payable	23		96.83
15	FICA Taxes Payable—OASDI	20	2,101.18	
	FICA Taxes Payable—HI	21	491.42	
	Employees FIT Payable	25	1,846.00	
	Cash	11		4,438.60
30	Wages and Salaries	51	8,960.00	
	FICA Taxes Payable—OASDI	20		555.52
	FICA Taxes Payable—HI	21		129.92
	Employees FIT Payable	25		988.00
	Employees SIT Payable	26		183.95
	Union Dues Payable	28		145.00
	Cash	11		6,957.61
30	Payroll Taxes	55	751.56	
	FICA Taxes Payable—OASDI	20		555.52
	FICA Taxes Payable—HI	21		129.92
	FUTA Taxes Payable	22		13.68
	SUTA Taxes Payable	23		52.44

6–16B. (Continued)

GENERAL LEDGER

(b)

CASH   11

Date		Item	P.R.	Dr.	Cr.	Balance Dr.	Balance Cr.
20--							
Apr.	1	Balance..........	✓	....	....	57,673.56	....
	1	....	J19	....	100.00	57,573.56	....
	15	....	J19	....	6,478.08	51,095.48	....
	15	....	J19	....	546.92	50,548.56	....
	15	....	J19	....	2,442.86	48,105.70	....
	29	....	J19	....	6,263.41	41,842.29	....
	29	....	J19	....	571.78	41,270.51	....
May	2	....	J20	....	275.00	40,995.51	....
	13	....	J20	....	6,393.41	34,602.10	....
	16	....	J20	....	4,196.62	30,405.48	....
	31	....	J20	....	6,800.19	23,605.29	....
June	3	....	J20	....	275.00	23,330.29	....
	15	....	J21	....	7,051.93	16,278.36	....
	15	....	J21	....	4,438.60	11,839.76	....
	30	....	J21	....	6,957.61	4,882.15	....

FICA TAXES PAYABLE—OASDI   20

Date		Item	P.R.	Dr.	Cr.	Balance Dr.	Balance Cr.
20--							
Apr.	1	Balance	✓	....	....	....	1,068.88
	15	....	J19	....	515.22	....	1,584.10
	15	....	J19	....	515.22	....	2,099.32
	15	....	J19	1,068.88	....	....	1,030.44
	29	....	J19	....	494.45	....	1,524.89
	29	....	J19	....	494.45	....	2,019.34
May	13	....	J20	....	507.78	....	2,527.12
	13	....	J20	....	507.78	....	3,034.90
	16	....	J20	2,019.34	....	....	1,015.56
	31	....	J20	....	542.81	....	1,558.37
	31	....	J20	....	542.81	....	2,101.18
June	15	....	J21	....	564.82	....	2,666.00
	15	....	J21	....	564.82	....	3,230.82
	15	....	J21	2,101.18	....	....	1,129.64
	30	....	J21	....	555.52	....	1,685.16
	30	....	J21	....	555.52	....	2,240.68

6–16B. (Continued)

FICA TAXES PAYABLE—HI 21

Date		Item	P.R.	Dr.	Cr.	Balance Dr.	Balance Cr.
20--							
Apr.	1	Balance	✓	....	....	....	249.98
	15	....	J19	....	120.50	....	370.48
	15	....	J19	....	120.50	....	490.98
	15	....	J19	249.98	....	....	241.00
	29	....	J19	....	115.64	....	356.64
	29	....	J19	....	115.64	....	472.28
May	13	....	J20	....	118.76	....	591.04
	13	....	J20	....	118.76	....	709.80
	16	....	J20	472.28	....	....	237.52
	31	....	J20	....	126.95	....	364.47
	31	....	J20	....	126.95	....	491.42
June	15	....	J21	....	132.10	....	623.52
	15	....	J21	....	132.10	....	755.62
	15	....	J21	491.42	....	....	264.20
	30	....	J21	....	129.92	....	394.12
	30	....	J21	....	129.92	....	524.04

FUTA TAXES PAYABLE 22

Date		Item	P.R.	Dr.	Cr.	Balance Dr.	Balance Cr.
20--							
Apr.	1	Balance	✓	....	....	....	149.16
	15	....	J19	....	49.86	....	199.02
	29	....	J19	....	47.85	....	246.87
May	13	....	J20	....	49.14	....	296.01
	31	....	J20	....	52.53	....	348.54
June	15	....	J21	....	25.26	....	373.80
	30	....	J21	....	13.68	....	387.48

6–16B. (Continued)

SUTA TAXES PAYABLE   23

Date		Item	P.R.	Dr.	Cr.	Balance Dr.	Cr.
20--							
Apr.	1	Balance	✓	....	....	....	571.78
	15	....	J19	....	191.13	....	762.91
	29	....	J19	....	183.43	....	946.34
	29	....	J19	571.78	....	....	374.56
May	13	....	J20	....	188.37	....	562.93
	31	....	J20	....	201.37	....	764.30
June	15	....	J21	....	96.83	....	861.13
	30	....	J21	....	52.44	....	913.57

EMPLOYEES FIT PAYABLE   25

Date		Item	P.R.	Dr.	Cr.	Balance Dr.	Cr.
20--							
Apr.	1	Balance	✓	....	....	....	1,124.00
	15	....	J19	....	890.00	....	2,014.00
	15	....	J19	1,124.00	....	....	890.00
	29	....	J19	....	815.00	....	1,705.00
May	13	....	J20	....	875.00	....	2,580.00
	16	....	J20	1,705.00	....	....	875.00
	31	....	J20	....	971.00	....	1,846.00
June	15	....	J21	....	1,029.00	....	2,875.00
	15	....	J21	1,846.00	....	....	1,029.00
	30	....	J21	....	988.00	....	2,017.00

EMPLOYEES SIT PAYABLE   26

Date		Item	P.R.	Dr.	Cr.	Balance Dr.	Cr.
20--							
Apr.	1	Balance	✓	....	....	....	546.92
	15	....	J19	....	166.20	....	713.12
	15	....	J19	546.92	....	....	166.20
	29	....	J19	....	151.50	....	317.70
May	13	....	J20	....	160.05	....	477.75
	31	....	J20	....	174.05	....	651.80
June	15	....	J21	....	187.15	....	838.95
	30	....	J21	....	183.95	....	1,022.90

6–16B. (Continued)

UNION DUES PAYABLE   28

Date	Item	P.R.	Dr.	Cr.	Balance Dr.	Balance Cr.
20--						
Apr. 1	Balance	✓				100.00
1		J19	100.00		—	—
15		J19		140.00		140.00
29		J19		135.00		275.00
May 2		J20	275.00		—	—
13		J20		135.00		135.00
31		J20		140.00		275.00
June 3		J20	275.00		—	—
15		J21		145.00		145.00
30		J21		145.00		290.00

WAGES AND SALARIES   51

Date	Item	P.R.	Dr.	Cr.	Balance Dr.	Balance Cr.
20--						
Apr. 1	Balance	✓			71,360.00	
15		J19	8,310.00		79,670.00	
29		J19	7,975.00		87,645.00	
May 13		J20	8,190.00		95,835.00	
31		J20	8,755.00		104,590.00	
June 15		J21	9,110.00		113,700.00	
30		J21	8,960.00		122,660.00	

PAYROLL TAXES   55

Date	Item	P.R.	Dr.	Cr.	Balance Dr.	Balance Cr.
20--						
Apr. 1	Balance	✓			6,846.74	
15		J19	876.71		7,723.45	
29		J19	841.37		8,564.82	
May 13		J20	864.05		9,428.87	
31		J20	923.66		10,352.53	
June 15		J21	819.01		11,171.54	
30		J21	751.56		11,923.10	

6–16B.   (Concluded)

(c) Questions

1. FICA Taxes Payable—OASDI $2,240.68
   FICA Taxes Payable—HI 524.04
   Employees FIT Payable 2,017.00
       Total liability $4,781.72

2. $1,022.90

3. $0

4. $913.57

5. $290.00

6. $122,660.00

7. $11,923.10

8. Vacation Benefits Expense 15,000.00
       Vacation Benefits Payable 15,000.00

Continuing Payroll Problem A (p. 6–80)

See the completed payroll register on pages CPP–1 through CPP–3.

Continuing Payroll Problem B (p. 6–80)

See the completed payroll register on pages CPP–4 through CPP–6.

Case Problem (p. 6–81)

Case 6–1

The additional payroll cost percentage would be calculated as follows:

FICA tax—OASDI	$24,000	×	0.062	=	$1,488.00
FICA tax—HI.......................................	$24,000	×	0.0145	=	348.00
FUTA tax...	$7,000	×	0.006	=	42.00
SUTA tax	$10,400	×	0.033	=	343.20
Workers' compensation costs	$24,000	×	$0.97/$100	=	232.80
Health insurance costs.........................	$ 75.15	×	12 months	=	901.80
Vacation pay	$24,000/52 weeks	×	2 weeks	=	923.08
Total additional cost...					$4,278.88

$$\text{Additional payroll cost percentage} = \frac{\$4,278.88}{\$24,000.00} = \underline{17.83\%}$$

CONTINUING PAYROLL PROBLEM • A
KIPLEY COMPANY, INC.

Payroll Register

1.

For Period Ending January 8, 20--

Time Card No.	Name	Marital Status	No. W/H Allow.	Regular Earnings			Overtime Earnings			Total Earnings
				Hours Worked	Rate per Hour	Amount	Hours Worked	Rate per Hour	Amount	
11	Carson, F.	S	1	40	7.50	300.00				300.00
12	Wilson, W.	S	0	40	7.25	290.00	8	10.88	87.04	377.04
13	Utley, H.	M	2	37 1/2	8.10	303.75				303.75
21	Fife, L.	M	4	40	7.90	316.00	6	11.85	71.10	387.10
22	Smith, L.	S	2	40	9.75	390.00				390.00
31	Fay, G.	M	3	40	......	515.00	1 1/4	19.32	24.15	539.15
32	Robey, G.	M	6	40	......	392.31				392.31
33	Schork, T.	S	1	40	......	542.31				542.31
51	Hardy, B.	M	5	40	......	348.46	4	13.07	52.28	400.74
99	Kipley, C.	M	7	40	......	1,000.00				1,000.00
	Totals			....		4,397.83	....	....	234.57	4,632.40

CPP–1

2.

CONTINUING PAYROLL PROBLEM • A
KIPLEY COMPANY, INC.
Payroll Register

| | DEDUCTIONS | | | | | | | | | NET PAID | | TAXABLE EARNINGS | | | |
OASDI TAX	HI TAX	FIT	SIT	SUTA	CIT	SIM-PLE DED.	GRP. INS.	HEALTH INS.	CK. NO.	AMT.	OASDI	HI	FUTA	SUTA
18.60	4.35	17.00	9.21	0.21	9.00	20.00	0.85	1.65	313	219.13	300.00	300.00	300.00	300.00
23.38	5.47	34.00	11.58	0.26	11.31	50.00	0.85	1.65	314	238.54	377.04	377.04	377.04	377.04
18.83	4.40	....	9.33	0.21	9.11	40.00	0.85	1.65	315	219.37	303.75	303.75	303.75	303.75
24.00	5.61	....	11.88	0.27	11.61	50.00	0.85	1.65	316	281.23	387.10	387.10	387.10	387.10
24.18	5.66	19.00	11.97	0.27	11.70	20.00	.....	1.65	317	295.57	390.00	390.00	390.00	390.00
33.43	7.82	11.00	16.55	0.38	16.17	40.00	0.85	1.65	318	411.30	539.15	539.15	539.15	539.15
24.32	5.69	....	12.04	0.27	11.77	50.00	0.85	1.65	319	285.72	392.31	392.31	392.31	392.31
33.62	7.86	47.00	16.65	0.38	16.27	60.00	.....	1.65	320	358.88	542.31	542.31	542.31	542.31
24.85	5.81	....	12.30	0.28	12.02	30.00	0.85	1.65	321	312.98	400.74	400.74	400.74	400.74
62.00	14.50	24.00	30.70	0.70	30.00	80.00	0.85	1.65	322	755.60	1,000.00	1,000.00	1,000.00	1,000.00
287.21	67.17	152.00	142.21	3.23	138.96	440.00	6.80	16.50	......	3,378.32	4,632.40	4,632.40	4,632.40	4,632.40

Continuing Payroll Problem • A (Concluded)

Questions from Chapter 5:

3. **(a)**   Net FUTA tax: $4,632.40 × 0.006 = $27.79

    (b)   SUTA tax: $4,632.40 × 0.036785 = $170.40

Questions from Chapter 6:

5.	Total net paid			$3,378.32
	Add deductions:			
		OASDI	$ 287.21	
		HI..	67.17	
		FIT	152.00	
		SIT	142.21	
		SUTA..	3.23	
		CIT..	138.96	
		Simple deductions	440.00	
		Group insurance...	6.80	
		Health insurance	16.50	1,254.08
	Total earnings			$4,632.40

6.	**(a)**		20--		
		Jan. 12	Wages and Salaries............................	4,632.40	
			FICA Taxes Payable—OASDI		287.21
			FICA Taxes Payable—HI.............		67.17
			Employees FIT Payable...............		152.00
			Employees SIT Payable		142.21
			Employees SUTA Payable		3.23
			Employees CIT Payable		138.96
			Simple Deductions Payable.........		440.00
			Group Insurance Premiums		
			Collected		6.80
			Health Insurance Premiums		
			Collected		16.50
			Salaries Payable.........................		3,378.32
		12	Payroll Taxes.....................................	552.57	
			FICA Taxes Payable—OASDI		287.21*
			FICA Taxes Payable—HI.............		67.17**
			FUTA Taxes Payable...................		27.79
			SUTA Taxes Payable		170.40
	(b)		20--		
		Jan. 14	Salaries Payable.................................	3,378.32	
			Cash		3,378.32

   *$4,632.40 × 0.062 = $287.21
 **$4,632.40 × 0.0145 = $67.17

CONTINUING PAYROLL PROBLEM • B
OLNEY COMPANY, INC.

Payroll Register

1.

For Period Ending January 8, 20--

Time Card No.	Name	Marital Status	No. W/H Allow.	Regular Earnings			Overtime Earnings			Total Earnings
				Hours Worked	Rate per Hour	Amount	Hours Worked	Rate per Hour	Amount	
11	Mangino, R.	S	1	40	8.50	340.00				340.00
12	Flores, I.	S	0	40	9.25	370.00	10	13.88	138.80	508.80
13	Palmetto, C.	M	2	38 1/2	7.80	300.30				300.30
21	Waters, R.	M	3	40	10.70	428.00	7	16.05	112.35	540.35
22	Kroll, C.	S	2	40	13.80	552.00				552.00
31	Ruppert, C.	M	3	40	......	800.00	1 1/4	30.00	37.50	837.50
32	Scott, W.	M	4	40	......	780.00				780.00
33	Wickman, S.	S	1	40	......	807.69				807.69
51	Foley, L.	M	5	40	......	1,038.46	5	38.94	194.70	1,233.16
99	Olney, M.	M	7	40	......	1,500.00				1,500.00
	Totals			......		6,916.45	......	......	483.35	7,399.80

CONTINUING PAYROLL PROBLEM • B
OLNEY COMPANY, INC.
Payroll Register

2.

			DEDUCTIONS						NET PAID		TAXABLE EARNINGS			
OASDI TAX	HI TAX	FIT	SIT	SUTA	CIT	SIM-PLE DED.	GRP. INS.	HEALTH INS.	CK. NO.	AMT.	OASDI	HI	FUTA	SUTA
21.08	4.93	23.00	10.44	0.24	4.59	20.00	0.85	1.65	313	253.22	340.00	340.00	340.00	340.00
31.55	7.38	53.00	15.62	0.36	6.87	50.00	0.85	1.65	314	341.52	508.80	508.80	508.80	508.80
18.62	4.35	....	9.22	0.21	4.05	40.00	......	1.65	315	222.20	300.30	300.30	300.30	300.30
33.50	7.84	10.00	16.59	0.38	7.29	60.00	0.85	1.65	316	402.25	540.35	540.35	540.35	540.35
34.22	8.00	43.00	16.95	0.39	7.45	20.00	0.85	1.65	317	419.49	552.00	552.00	552.00	552.00
51.93	12.14	44.00	25.71	0.59	11.31	40.00	0.85	1.65	318	649.32	837.50	837.50	837.50	837.50
48.36	11.31	28.00	23.95	0.55	10.53	50.00	0.85	1.65	319	604.80	780.00	780.00	780.00	780.00
50.08	11.71	87.00	24.80	0.57	10.90	50.00	......	1.65	320	570.98	807.69	807.69	807.69	807.69
76.46	17.88	83.00	37.86	0.86	16.65	30.00	0.85	1.65	321	967.95	1,233.16	1,233.16	1,233.16	1,233.16
93.00	21.75	93.10*	46.05	1.05	20.25	80.00	0.85	1.65	322	1,142.30	1,500.00	1,500.00	1,500.00	1,500.00
458.80	107.29	464.10	227.19	5.20	99.89	440.00	6.80	16.50	......	5,574.03	7,399.80	7,399.80	7,399.80	7,399.80

* $1,500.00 – $80.00 = $1,420.00 – 7($75.00) = $895.00 – $503.00 = $392.00 × 0.15 = $58.80 + $34.30 = $93.10

Continuing Payroll Problem • B (Concluded)

Questions from Chapter 5:

3. **(a)** Net FUTA tax: $7,399.80 × 0.006 = $44.40

   (b) SUTA tax: $7,399.80 × 0.036785 = $272.20

Questions from Chapter 6:

5. Total net paid... $5,574.03
   Add deductions:
OASDI...	$458.80	
HI	107.29	
FIT	464.10	
SIT	227.19	
SUTA	5.20	
CIT	99.89	
Simple deductions...	440.00	
Group insurance	6.80	
Health insurance..	16.50	1,825.77
Total earnings...		$7,399.80

6. **(a)**   20--
	Jan.	12	Wages and Salaries	7,399.80	
			FICA Taxes Payable—OASDI......		458.80
			FICA Taxes Payable—HI		107.29
			Employees FIT Payable		464.10
			Employees SIT Payable		227.19
			Employees SUTA Payable...........		5.20
			Employees CIT Payable...............		99.89
			Simple Deductions Payable		440.00
			Group Insurance Premiums		
			Collected...............................		6.80
			Health Insurance Premiums		
			Collected...............................		16.50
			Salaries Payable		5,574.03
		12	Payroll Taxes	882.69	
			FICA Taxes Payable—OASDI......		458.79*
			FICA Taxes Payable—HI		107.30**
			FUTA Taxes Payable		44.40
			SUTA Taxes Payable...................		272.20

   (b)   20--
	Jan.	14	Salaries Payable	5,574.03	
			Cash...		5,574.03

   *$7,399.80 × 0.062 = $458.79
   **$7,399.80 × 0.0145 = $107.30

CHAPTER 7

Note to Instructors

Depending upon the availability of time and your goals in teaching the payroll accounting course, you may use the Payroll Project in one of several ways:

1. Assign only the preparation of payroll registers and posting to employees' earnings records.

2. Assign (1) plus recording the entries in the general journal and posting to the general ledger.

3. Assign (1) and (2) plus completion of the quarterly tax reports.

4. Assign the complete project.

5. Appendix A uses the same practice set with the computer-assisted approach. If students are completing the project using Appendix A, it would be helpful to have them complete one of the payrolls manually. This would provide a better understanding of the operations that are being performed by the computer.

Chapter 7 consists of a simulation, or practice set, for payroll accounting. Students will apply the knowledge acquired in this course to practical payroll situations. This simulation is a culmination of the information presented in the textbook.

Learning Objectives

After completing the simulation, students should be able to:

1. Prepare payroll registers.

2. Maintain employees' earnings records.

3. Journalize and post payroll and payroll tax entries.

4. Complete federal, state, and city tax deposit forms and journalize the transactions.

5. Prepare various quarter-end and year-end payroll tax forms.

6. Make the accrual entries for the payroll at the end of a year.

Payroll Project Solution (p. 7–24)

JOURNAL

20--					
Oct.	9	Payroll Cash	12	11,097.25	
		Cash..	11		11,097.25

Oct.	9	Administrative Salaries	51	2,307.69	
		Office Salaries	52	3,353.08	
		Sales Salaries	53	3,600.00	
		Plant Wages	54	4,902.00	
		FICA Taxes Payable—OASDI	20.1		878.09
		FICA Taxes Payable—HI	20.2		205.37
		Employees FIT Payable	24		965.00
		Employees SIT Payable	25		434.82
		Employees SUTA Payable	25.1		9.94
		Employees CIT Payable	26		556.30
		Union Dues Payable	28		16.00
		Payroll Cash	12		11,097.25
	9	Payroll Taxes	56	1,231.14	
		FICA Taxes Payable—OASDI	20.1		878.09
		FICA Taxes Payable—HI	20.2		205.36
		FUTA Taxes Payable	21		19.68
		SUTA Taxes Payable—Employer	22		128.01
	20	Employees SIT Payable	25	434.82	
		Cash	11		434.82
	23	Payroll Cash	12	11,173.89	
		Cash	11		11,173.89
	23	Administrative Salaries	51	2,307.69	
		Office Salaries	52	3,353.08	
		Sales Salaries	53	3,600.00	
		Plant Wages	54	5,223.92	
		FICA Taxes Payable—OASDI	20.1		898.05
		FICA Taxes Payable—HI	20.2		210.04
		Employees FIT Payable	24		997.00
		Employees SIT Payable	25		444.70
		Employees SUTA Payable	25.1		10.16
		Employees CIT Payable	26		568.95
		Group Insurance Premiums Collected	27		165.90
		Union Dues Payable	28		16.00
		Payroll Cash	12		11,173.89
	23	Payroll Taxes	56	1,241.25	
		FICA Taxes Payable—OASDI	20.1		898.05
		FICA Taxes Payable—HI	20.2		210.03
		FUTA Taxes Payable	21		5.16
		SUTA Taxes Payable—Employer	22		128.01

Nov.	4	Employees SIT Payable	25	444.70	
		Cash	11		444.70
	6	Union Dues Payable	28	32.00	
		Cash	11		32.00
	6	Payroll Cash	12	10,937.71	
		Cash	11		10,937.71
	6	Administrative Salaries	51	2,307.69	
		Office Salaries	52	3,320.79	
		Sales Salaries	53	3,600.00	
		Plant Wages	54	4,902.00	
		FICA Taxes Payable—OASDI	20.1		876.09
		FICA Taxes Payable—HI	20.2		204.90
		Employees FIT Payable	24		1,097.00
		Employees SIT Payable	25		433.83
		Employees SUTA Payable	25.1		9.92
		Employees CIT Payable	26		555.03
		Union Dues Payable	28		16.00
		Payroll Cash	12		10,937.71
	6	Payroll Taxes	56	1,157.25	
		FICA Taxes Payable—OASDI	20.1		876.09
		FICA Taxes Payable—HI	20.2		204.89
		FUTA Taxes Payable	21		2.22
		SUTA Taxes Payable—Employer	22		74.05
	13	Payroll Cash	12	1,418.87	
		Cash	11		1,418.87
	13	Office Salaries	52	2,079.32	
		FICA Taxes Payable—OASDI	20.1		128.92
		FICA Taxes Payable—HI	20.2		30.15
		Employees FIT Payable	24		340.00
		Employees SIT Payable	25		63.84
		Employees SUTA Payable	25.1		1.46
		Employees CIT Payable	26		81.68
		Group Insurance Premiums Collected	27		14.40
		Payroll Cash	12		1,418.87
	13	Payroll Taxes	56	159.07	
		FICA Taxes Payable—OASDI	20.1		128.92
		FICA Taxes Payable—HI	20.2		30.15
	16	FICA Taxes Payable—OASDI	20.1	3,552.28	
		FICA Taxes Payable—HI	20.2	830.80	
		Employees FIT Payable	24	1,962.00	
		Cash	11		6,345.08

Nov. 16	Employees CIT Payable	26	1,125.25	
	Cash	11		1,125.25
18	Employees SIT Payable	25	497.67	
	Cash	11		497.67
20	Payroll Cash	12	8,281.28	
	Cash	11		8,281.28
20	Administrative Salaries	51	2,307.69	
	Office Salaries	52	2,112.94	
	Sales Salaries	53	3,600.00	
	Plant Wages	54	4,619.60	
	FICA Taxes Payable—OASDI	20.1		783.70
	FICA Taxes Payable—HI	20.2		183.30
	Employees FIT Payable	24		681.00
	Employees SIT Payable	25		388.08
	Employees SUTA Payable	25.1		8.87
	Employees CIT Payable	26		496.50
	Group Insurance Premiums Collected	27		151.50
	Union Dues Payable	28		16.00
	SIMPLE Contributions Payable	29		1,650.00
	Payroll Cash	12		8,281.28
20	Payroll Taxes	56	994.45	
	FICA Taxes Payable—OASDI	20.1		783.69
	FICA Taxes Payable—HI	20.2		183.28
	SUTA Taxes Payable—Employer	22		27.48
Dec. 3	Employees SIT Payable	25	388.08	
	Cash	11		388.08
4	Payroll Cash	12	9,771.04	
	Cash	11		9,771.04
4	Administrative Salaries	51	2,307.69	
	Office Salaries	52	3,330.00	
	Sales Salaries	53	3,600.00	
	Plant Wages	54	5,193.40	
	FICA Taxes Payable—OASDI	20.1		894.73
	FICA Taxes Payable—HI	20.2		209.27
	Employees FIT Payable	24		870.00
	Employees SIT Payable	25		443.06
	Employees SUTA Payable	25.1		10.13
	Employees CIT Payable	26		566.86
	Union Dues Payable	28		16.00
	SIMPLE Contributions Payable	29		1,650.00
	Payroll Cash	12		9,771.04

Dec.	4	Payroll Taxes	56	1,170.05	
		FICA Taxes Payable—OASDI	20.1		894.73
		FICA Taxes Payable—HI	20.2		209.25
		FUTA Taxes Payable	21		6.48
		SUTA Taxes Payable—Employer	22		59.59
	9	Union Dues Payable	28	32.00	
		Cash	11		32.00
	14	Payroll Cash	12	1,306.44	
		Cash	11		1,306.44
	14	Office Salaries	52	1,425.16	
		FICA Taxes Payable—OASDI	20.1		88.36
		FICA Taxes Payable—HI	20.2		20.66
		Employees SUTA Payable	25.1		1.00
		Group Insurance Premiums Collected	27		8.70
		Payroll Cash	12		1,306.44
	14	Payroll Taxes	56	109.02	
		FICA Taxes Payable—OASDI	20.1		88.36
		FICA Taxes Payable—HI	20.2		20.66
	15	FICA Taxes Payable—OASDI	20.1	3,577.41	
		FICA Taxes Payable—HI	20.2	836.67	
		Employees FIT Payable	24	2,118.00	
		Cash	11		6,532.08
	15	Employees CIT Payable	26	1,133.21	
		Cash	11		1,133.21
	18	Employees SIT Payable	25	443.06	
		Cash	11		443.06
	18	Group Insurance Premiums Collected	27	8.70	
		Cash	11		8.70
	18	Payroll Cash	12	37,381.42	
		Cash	11		37,381.42

Date		Account	Post Ref	Debit	Credit
Dec.	18	Administrative Salaries	51	62,307.69	
		Office Salaries	52	2,692.50	
		Sales Salaries	53	4,407.70	
		Plant Wages	54	5,514.60	
		FICA Taxes Payable—OASDI	20.1		4,469.21
		FICA Taxes Payable—HI	20.2		1,086.39
		Employees FIT Payable	24		21,554.20
		Employees SIT Payable	25		2,300.14
		Employees SUTA Payable	25.1		52.46
		Employees CIT Payable	26		2,942.97
		Group Insurance Premiums Collected	27		167.70
		Union Dues Payable	28		18.00
		SIMPLE Contributions Payable	29		4,950.00
		Payroll Cash	12		37,381.42
	18	Payroll Taxes	56	5,650.69	
		FICA Taxes Payable—OASDI	20.1		4,469.21
		FICA Taxes Payable—HI	20.2		1,086.38
		FUTA Taxes Payable	21		12.05
		SUTA Taxes Payable—Employer	22		83.05
20--					
Jan.	6	Employees SIT Payable		2,300.14	
		Cash			2,300.14
	8	Union Dues Payable		34.00	
		Cash			34.00
	15	FICA Taxes Payable—OASDI		10,904.60	
		FICA Taxes Payable—HI		2,632.61	
		Employees FIT Payable		22,424.20	
		Cash			35,961.41
	15	Employees CIT Payable		3,509.83	
		Cash			3,509.83
Feb.	1	FUTA Taxes Payable		438.53	
		Cash			438.53
	1	SUTA Taxes Payable—Employer		500.19	
		Employees SUTA Taxes Payable		103.94	
		Cash			604.13

GENERAL LEDGER

Date		Item	P.R.	Dr.	Cr.	Balance Dr.	Cr.
CASH						Account No. 11	
20--							
Oct.	1	Bal.	✓	....	....	199,846.33	....
	9	....	J41	....	11,097.25	188,749.08	....
	20	....	J41	....	434.82	188,314.26	....
	23	....	J41	....	11,173.89	177,140.37	....
Nov.	4	....	J42	....	444.70	176,695.67	....
	6	....	J42	....	32.00	176,663.67	....
	6	....	J43	....	10,937.71	165,725.96	....
	13	....	J43	....	1,418.87	164,307.09	....
	16	....	J44	....	6,345.08	157,962.01	....
	16	....	J44	....	1,125.25	156,836.76	....
	18	....	J44	....	497.67	156,339.09	....
	20	....	J44	....	8,281.28	148,057.81	....
Dec.	3	....	J45	....	388.08	147,669.73	....
	4	....	J45	....	9,771.04	137,898.69	....
	9	....	J46	....	32.00	137,866.69	....
	14	....	J46	....	1,306.44	136,560.25	....
	15	....	J46	....	6,532.08	130,028.17	....
	15	....	J46	....	1,133.21	128,894.96	....
	18	....	J46	....	443.06	128,451.90	....
	18	....	J46	....	8.70	128,443.20	....
	18	....	J46	....	37,381.42	91,061.78	....

PAYROLL CASH — Account No. 12

Date		Item	P.R.	Dr.	Cr.	Balance Dr.	Balance Cr.
20--							
Oct.	9	....	J41	11,097.25	....	11,097.25	....
	9	....	J41	....	11,097.25	....	....
	23	....	J41	11,173.89	....	11,173.89	....
	23	....	J42	....	11,173.89	....	....
Nov.	6	....	J43	10,937.71	....	10,937.71	....
	6	....	J43	....	10,937.71	....	....
	13	....	J43	1,418.87	....	1,418.87	....
	13	....	J44	....	1,418.87	....	....
	20	....	J44	8,281.28	....	8,281.28	....
	20	....	J44	....	8,281.28	....	....
Dec.	4	....	J45	9,771.04	....	9,771.04	....
	4	....	J45	....	9,771.04	....	....
	14	....	J46	1,306.44	....	1,306.44	....
	14	....	J46	....	1,306.44	....	....
	18	....	J46	37,381.42	....	37,381.42	....
	18	....	J47	....	37,381.42	....	....

FICA TAXES PAYABLE—OASDI — Account No. 20.1

Date		Item	P.R.	Dr.	Cr.	Balance Dr.	Balance Cr.
20--							
Oct.	9	....	J41	....	878.09	....	878.09
	9	....	J41	....	878.09	....	1,756.18
	23	....	J42	....	898.05	....	2,654.23
	23	....	J42	....	898.05	....	3,552.28
Nov.	6	....	J43	....	876.09	....	4,428.37
	6	....	J43	....	876.09	....	5,304.46
	13	....	J44	....	128.92	....	5,433.38
	13	....	J44	....	128.92	....	5,562.30
	16	....	J44	3,552.28	....	....	2,010.02
	20	....	J44	....	783.70	....	2,793.72
	20	....	J45	....	783.69	....	3,577.41
Dec.	4	....	J45	....	894.73	....	4,472.14
	4	....	J46	....	894.73	....	5,366.87
	14	....	J46	....	88.36	....	5,455.23
	14	....	J46	....	88.36	....	5,543.59
	15	....	J46	3,577.41	....	....	1,966.18
	18	....	J47	....	4,469.21	....	6,435.39
	18	....	J47	....	4,469.21	....	10,904.60

FICA TAXES PAYABLE—HI   Account No. 20.2

Date		Item	P.R.	Dr.	Cr.	Balance Dr.	Balance Cr.
20--							
Oct.	9	....	J41	....	205.37	....	205.37
	9	....	J41	....	205.36	....	410.73
	23	....	J42	....	210.04	....	620.77
	23	....	J42	....	210.03	....	830.80
Nov.	6	....	J43	....	204.90	....	1,035.70
	6	....	J43	....	204.89	....	1,240.59
	13	....	J44	....	30.15	....	1,270.74
	13	....	J44	....	30.15	....	1,300.89
	16	....	J44	830.80	....	....	470.09
	20	....	J44	....	183.30	....	653.39
	20	....	J45	....	183.28	....	836.67
Dec.	4	....	J45	....	209.27	....	1,045.94
	4	....	J46	....	209.25	....	1,255.19
	14	....	J46	....	20.66	....	1,275.85
	14	....	J46	....	20.66	....	1,296.51
	15	....	J46	836.67	....	....	459.84
	18	....	J47	....	1,086.39	....	1,546.23
	18	....	J47	....	1,086.38	....	2,632.61

FUTA TAXES PAYABLE   Account No. 21

Date		Item	P.R.	Dr.	Cr.	Balance Dr.	Balance Cr.
20--							
Oct.	1	Bal.	✓	....	....	....	392.94
	9	....	J41	....	19.68	....	412.62
	23	....	J42	....	5.16	....	417.78
Nov.	6	....	J43	....	2.22	....	420.00
Dec.	4	....	J46	....	6.48	....	426.48
	18	....	J47	....	12.05	....	438.53

SUTA TAXES PAYABLE—EMPLOYER   Account No. 22

Date		Item	P.R.	Dr.	Cr.	Balance Dr.	Balance Cr.
20--							
Oct.	9	....	J41	....	128.01	....	128.01
	23	....	J42	....	128.01	....	256.02
Nov.	6	....	J43	....	74.05	....	330.07
	20	....	J45	....	27.48	....	357.55
Dec.	4	....	J46	....	59.59	....	417.14
	18	....	J47	....	83.05	....	500.19

EMPLOYEES FIT PAYABLE   Account No.   24

Date		Item	P.R.	Dr.	Cr.	Balance Dr.	Balance Cr.
20--							
Oct.	9		J41	....	965.00	....	965.00
	23		J42	....	997.00	....	1,962.00
Nov.	6		J43	....	1,097.00	....	3,059.00
	13		J44	....	340.00	....	3,399.00
	16		J44	1,962.00	....	....	1,437.00
	20		J44	....	681.00	....	2,118.00
Dec.	4		J45	....	870.00	....	2,988.00
	15		J46	2,118.00	....	....	870.00
	18		J47	....	21,554.20	....	22,424.20

EMPLOYEES SIT PAYABLE   Account No.   25

Date		Item	P.R.	Dr.	Cr.	Balance Dr.	Balance Cr.
20--							
Oct.	9		J41	....	434.82	....	434.82
	20		J41	434.82	....	....	....
	23		J42	....	444.70	....	444.70
Nov.	4		J42	444.70	....	....	....
	6		J43	....	433.83	....	433.83
	13		J44	....	63.84	....	497.67
	18		J44	497.67	....	....	....
	20		J44	....	388.08	....	388.08
Dec.	3		J45	388.08	....	....	....
	4		J45	....	443.06	....	443.06
	18		J46	443.06	....	....	....
	18		J47	....	2,300.14	....	2,300.14

EMPLOYEES SUTA PAYABLE   Account No. 25.1

Date		Item	P.R.	Dr.	Cr.	Balance Dr.	Balance Cr.
20--							
Oct.	9		J41	....	9.94	....	9.94
	23		J42	....	10.16	....	20.10
Nov.	6		J43	....	9.92	....	30.02
	13		J44	....	1.46	....	31.48
	20		J44	....	8.87	....	40.35
Dec.	4		J45	....	10.13	....	50.48
	14		J46	....	1.00	....	51.48
	18		J47	....	52.46	....	103.94

EMPLOYEES CIT PAYABLE   Account No.   26

Date	Item	P.R.	Dr.	Cr.	Balance Dr.	Balance Cr.
20--						
Oct. 9	....	J41	....	556.30	....	556.30
23	....	J42	....	568.95	....	1,125.25
Nov. 6	....	J43	....	555.03	....	1,680.28
13	....	J44	....	81.68	....	1,761.96
16	....	J44	1,125.25	....	....	636.71
20	....	J44	....	496.50	....	1,133.21
Dec. 4	....	J45	....	566.86	....	1,700.07
15	....	J46	1,133.21	....	....	566.86
18	....	J47	....	2,942.97	....	3,509.83

GROUP INSURANCE PREMIUMS COLLECTED Account No.   27

Date	Item	P.R.	Dr.	Cr.	Balance Dr.	Balance Cr.
20--						
Oct. 23	....	J42	....	165.90	....	165.90
Nov. 13	....	J44	....	14.40	....	180.30
20	....	J44	....	151.50	....	331.80
Dec. 14	....	J46	....	8.70	....	340.50
18	....	J46	8.70	....	....	331.80
18	....	J47	....	167.70	....	499.50

UNION DUES PAYABLE   Account No.   28

Date	Item	P.R.	Dr.	Cr.	Balance Dr.	Balance Cr.
20--						
Oct. 9	....	J41	....	16.00	....	16.00
23	....	J42	....	16.00	....	32.00
Nov. 6	....	J42	32.00	....	....	....
6	....	J43	....	16.00	....	16.00
20	....	J44	....	16.00	....	32.00
Dec. 4	....	J45	....	16.00	....	48.00
9	....	J46	32.00	....	....	16.00
18	....	J47	....	18.00	....	34.00

SIMPLE CONTRIBUTIONS PAYABLE   Account No. 29

Date	Item	P.R.	Dr.	Cr.	Balance Dr.	Balance Cr.
20--						
Nov. 20	....	J44	....	1,650.00	....	1,650.00
Dec. 4	....	J45	....	1,650.00	....	3,300.00
18	....	J47	....	4,950.00	....	8,250.00

ADMINISTRATIVE SALARIES   Account No. 51

Date	Item	P.R.	Dr.	Cr.	Balance Dr.	Balance Cr.
20--						
Oct. 1	Bal.............	✓	....	....	42,692.27	....
9	....	J41	2,307.69	....	44,999.96	....
23	....	J42	2,307.69	....	47,307.65	....
Nov. 6	....	J43	2,307.69	....	49,615.34	....
20	....	J44	2,307.69	....	51,923.03	....
Dec. 4	....	J45	2,307.69	....	54,230.72	....
18	....	J47	62,307.69	....	116,538.41	....

OFFICE SALARIES   Account No. 52

Date	Item	P.R.	Dr.	Cr.	Balance Dr.	Balance Cr.
20--						
Oct. 1	Bal.............	✓	....	....	28,350.00	....
9	....	J41	3,353.08	....	31,703.08	....
23	....	J42	3,353.08	....	35,056.16	....
Nov. 6	....	J43	3,320.79	....	38,376.95	....
13	....	J44	2,079.32	....	40,456.27	....
20	....	J44	2,112.94	....	42,569.21	....
Dec. 4	....	J45	3,330.00	....	45,899.21	....
14	....	J46	1,425.16	....	47,324.37	....
18	....	J47	2,692.50	....	50,016.87	....

SALES SALARIES   Account No.   53

Date	Item	P.R.	Dr.	Cr.	Balance Dr.	Balance Cr.
20--						
Oct. 1	Bal.	✓	....	....	28,525.00	....
9	....	J41	3,600.00	....	32,125.00	....
23	....	J42	3,600.00	....	35,725.00	....
Nov. 6	....	J43	3,600.00	....	39,325.00	....
20	....	J44	3,600.00	....	42,925.00	....
Dec. 4	....	J45	3,600.00	....	46,525.00	....
18	....	J47	4,407.70	....	50,932.70	....

PLANT WAGES   Account No.   54

Date	Item	P.R.	Dr.	Cr.	Balance Dr.	Balance Cr.
20--						
Oct. 1	Bal.	✓	....	....	42,657.30	....
9	....	J41	4,902.00	....	47,559.30	....
23	....	J42	5,223.92	....	52,783.22	....
Nov. 6	....	J43	4,902.00	....	57,685.22	....
20	....	J44	4,619.60	....	62,304.82	....
Dec. 4	....	J45	5,193.40	....	67,498.22	....
18	....	J47	5,514.60	....	73,012.82	....

PAYROLL TAXES   Account No.   56

Date	Item	P.R.	Dr.	Cr.	Balance Dr.	Balance Cr.
20--						
Oct. 1	Bal.	✓	....	....	14,013.23	....
9	....	J41	1,231.14	....	15,244.37	....
23	....	J42	1,241.25	....	16,485.62	....
Nov. 6	....	J43	1,157.25	....	17,642.87	....
13	....	J44	159.07	....	17,801.94	....
20	....	J45	994.45	....	18,796.39	....
Dec. 4	....	J46	1,170.05	....	19,966.44	....
14	....	J46	109.02	....	20,075.46	....
18	....	J47	5,650.69	....	25,726.15	....

PAYROLL REGISTER (left-hand page)

Name	Marital Status	No. W/H Allow.	Regular Earnings			Overtime Earnings			Total Earnings	Deductions				
			Hrs.	Rate Per Hour	Amount	Hrs.	Rate Per Hour	Amount		OASDI	HI	FIT	SIT	SUTA
Payday, October 9, 20-- For Period Ending October 3, 20--														
Bonno, A.	M	4	80	17.65	1,412.00	....	....	....	1,412.00	87.54	20.47	49.00	43.35	0.99
Ferguson, J.	M	5	80	....	2,250.00	....	....	....	2,250.00	139.50	32.63	143.00	69.08	1.58
Ford, C.	S	2	80	....	900.00	....	....	....	900.00	55.80	13.05	62.00	27.63	0.63
Mann, D.	M	4	80	....	1,350.00	....	....	....	1,350.00	83.70	19.58	43.00	41.45	0.95
O'Neill, J.	M	3	80	....	2,307.69	....	....	....	2,307.69	143.08	33.46	197.00	70.85	1.62
Russell, V.	S	1	80	....	690.00	....	....	....	690.00	42.78	10.01	51.00	21.18	0.48
Ryan, N.	M	4	80	18.00	1,440.00	....	....	....	1,440.00	89.28	20.88	53.00	44.21	1.01
Sokowski, T.	M	2	80	....	2,050.00	....	....	....	2,050.00	127.10	29.73	180.00	62.94	1.44
Student	S	1	72	7.50	540.00	....	....	....	540.00	33.48	7.83	32.00	16.58	0.38
Williams, R.	S	0	80	....	1,223.08	....	....	....	1,223.08	75.83	17.73	155.00	37.55	0.86
Totals					14,162.77	....	....	....	14,162.77	878.09	205.37	965.00	434.82	9.94
Payday, October 23, 20-- For Period Ending October 17, 20--														
Bonno, A.	M	4	80	17.65	1,412.00	4	26.48	105.92	1,517.92	94.11	22.01	59.00	46.60	1.06
Ferguson, J.	M	5	80	....	2,250.00	....	....	....	2,250.00	139.50	32.63	143.00	69.08	1.58
Ford, C.	S	2	80	....	900.00	....	....	....	900.00	55.80	13.05	62.00	27.63	0.63
Mann, D.	M	4	80	....	1,350.00	....	....	....	1,350.00	83.70	19.58	43.00	41.45	0.95
O'Neill, J.	M	3	80	....	2,307.69	....	....	....	2,307.69	143.08	33.46	197.00	70.85	1.62
Russell, V.	S	1	80	....	690.00	....	....	....	690.00	42.78	10.01	51.00	21.18	0.48
Ryan, N.	M	4	80	18.00	1,440.00	8	27.00	216.00	1,656.00	102.67	24.01	75.00	50.84	1.16
Sokowski, T.	M	2	80	....	2,050.00	....	....	....	2,050.00	127.10	29.73	180.00	62.94	1.44
Student	S	1	72	7.50	540.00	....	....	....	540.00	33.48	7.83	32.00	16.58	0.38
Williams, R.	S	0	80	....	1,223.08	....	....	....	1,223.08	75.83	17.73	155.00	37.55	0.86
Totals					14,162.77	....	....	321.92	14,484.69	898.05	210.04	997.00	444.70	10.16
Payday, November 6, 20-- For Period Ending October 31, 20--														
Bonno, A.	M	4	80	17.65	1,412.00	....	....	....	1,412.00	87.54	20.47	49.00	43.35	0.99
Ferguson, J.	M	5	80	....	2,250.00	....	....	....	2,250.00	139.50	32.63	143.00	69.08	1.58
Ford, C.	S	2	80	....	900.00	....	....	....	900.00	55.80	13.05	62.00	27.63	0.63
Mann, D.	M	0	80	....	1,350.00	....	....	....	1,350.00	83.70	19.58	120.00	41.45	0.95
O'Neill, J.	M	3	80	....	2,307.69	....	....	....	2,307.69	143.08	33.46	197.00	70.85	1.62
Russell, V.	S	2	78	....	672.94*	....	....	....	672.94	41.72	9.76	29.00	20.66	0.47
Ryan, N.	M	4	80	18.00	1,440.00	....	....	....	1,440.00	89.28	20.88	53.00	44.21	1.01
Sokowski, T.	S	2	80	....	2,050.00	....	....	....	2,050.00	127.10	29.73	260.00	62.94	1.44
Student	S	1	72	7.50	540.00	....	....	....	540.00	33.48	7.83	32.00	16.58	0.38
Williams, R.	S	0	79	....	1,207.85†	....	....	....	1,207.85	74.89	17.51	152.00	37.08	0.85
Totals					14,130.48	....	....	....	14,130.48	876.09	204.90	1,097.00	433.83	9.92

*$345 + (38 × $8.63)
†$611.54 + (39 × $15.29)

Name	Marital Status	No. W/H Allow.	Regular Earnings			Overtime Earnings			Total Earnings	Deductions				
Payday, November 13, 20-- For Period Ending November 14, 20--														
Williams, R.	S	0	136	....	2,079.32	....	....	....	2,079.32	128.92	30.15	340.00	63.84	1.46

(Discharged November 13, 20--)

Name	Marital Status	No. W/H Allow.	Regular Earnings			Overtime Earnings			Total Earnings	Deductions				
Payday, November 20, 20-- For Period Ending November 14, 20--														
Bonno, A.	M	4	64	17.65	1,129.60	....	....	....	1,129.60	70.04	16.38	21.00	34.68	0.79
Ferguson, J.	M	5	80	....	2,250.00	....	....	....	2,250.00	139.50	32.63	68.00	69.08	1.58
Ford, C.	S	2	80	....	900.00	....	....	....	900.00	55.80	13.05	62.00	27.63	0.63
Mann, D.	M	0	80	....	1,350.00	....	....	....	1,350.00	83.70	19.58	84.00	41.45	0.95
O'Neill, J.	M	3	80	....	2,307.69	....	....	....	2,307.69	143.08	33.46	92.00	70.85	1.62
Russell, V.	S	2	78	....	672.94	....	....	....	672.94	41.72	9.76	29.00	20.66	0.47
Ryan, N.	M	4	80	18.00	1,440.00	....	....	....	1,440.00	89.28	20.88	33.00	44.21	1.01
Sokowski, T.	S	2	80	....	2,050.00	....	....	....	2,050.00	127.10	29.73	260.00	62.94	1.44
Student	S	1	72	7.50	540.00	....	....	....	540.00	33.48	7.83	32.00	16.58	0.38
Totals					12,640.23	....	....	....	12,640.23	783.70	183.30	681.00	388.08	8.87

PAYROLL REGISTER   (right-hand page)

	Deductions			Net Paid		Taxable Earnings				Labor Cost Distribution			
CIT	Group Ins.	Union Dues	SIMPLE	Ck. No.	Amount	OASDI	HI	FUTA	SUTA	Admin.	Office	Sales	Plant
Payday, October 9, 20-- For Period Ending October 3, 20--													
55.46		8.00		672	1,147.19	1,412.00	1,412.00						1,412.00
88.38				673	1,775.83	2,250.00	2,250.00					2,250.00	
35.35				674	705.54	900.00	900.00	700.00	900.00		900.00		
53.03				675	1,108.29	1,350.00	1,350.00	1,350.00	1,350.00			1,350.00	
90.65				676	1,771.03	2,307.69	2,307.69			2,307.69			
27.10				677	537.45	690.00	690.00	690.00	690.00		690.00		
56.56		8.00		678	1,167.06	1,440.00	1,440.00						1,440.00
80.52				679	1,568.27	2,050.00	2,050.00						2,050.00
21.21				680	428.52	540.00	540.00	540.00	540.00		540.00		
48.04				681	888.07	1,223.08	1,223.08				1,223.08		
556.30		16.00			11,097.25	14,162.77	14,162.77	3,280.00	3,480.00	2,307.69	3,353.08	3,600.00	4,902.00
Payday, October 23, 20-- For Period Ending October 17, 20--													
59.62	16.50	8.00		682	1,211.02	1,517.92	1,517.92						1,517.92
88.38	26.40			683	1,749.43	2,250.00	2,250.00					2,250.00	
35.35	10.50			684	695.04	900.00	900.00		900.00		900.00		
53.03	15.90			685	1,092.39	1,350.00	1,350.00	250.00	1,350.00			1,350.00	
90.65	27.00			686	1,744.03	2,307.69	2,307.69			2,307.69			
27.10	8.10			687	529.35	690.00	690.00	70.00	690.00		690.00		
65.05	16.80	8.00		688	1,312.47	1,656.00	1,656.00						1,656.00
80.52	24.00			689	1,544.27	2,050.00	2,050.00						2,050.00
21.21	6.30			690	422.22	540.00	540.00	540.00	540.00		540.00		
48.04	14.40			691	873.67	1,223.08	1,223.08				1,223.08		
568.95	165.90	16.00			11,173.89	14,484.69	14,484.69	860.00	3,480.00	2,307.69	3,353.08	3,600.00	5,223.92
Payday, November 6, 20-- For Period Ending October 31, 20--													
55.46		8.00		692	1,147.19	1,412.00	1,412.00						1,412.00
88.38				693	1,775.83	2,250.00	2,250.00					2,250.00	
35.35				694	705.54	900.00	900.00		400.00		900.00		
53.03				695	1,031.29	1,350.00	1,350.00		400.00			1,350.00	
90.65				696	1,771.03	2,307.69	2,307.69			2,307.69			
26.43				697	544.90	672.94	672.94		672.94		672.94		
56.56		8.00		698	1,167.06	1,440.00	1,440.00						1,440.00
80.52				699	1,488.27	2,050.00	2,050.00						2,050.00
21.21				700	428.52	540.00	540.00	370.00	540.00		540.00		
47.44				701	878.08	1,207.85	1,207.85				1,207.85		
555.03		16.00			10,937.71	14,130.48	14,130.48	370.00	2,012.94	2,307.69	3,320.79	3,600.00	4,902.00
Payday, November 13, 20-- For Period Ending November 14, 20--													
81.68	14.40			702	1,418.87	2,079.32	2,079.32				2,079.32		
Payday, November 20, 20-- For Period Ending November 14, 20--													
44.37	16.50	8.00		703	917.84	1,129.60	1,129.60						1,129.60
88.38	26.40		500.00	704	1,324.43	2,250.00	2,250.00					2,250.00	
35.35	10.50			705	695.04	900.00	900.00				900.00		
53.03	15.90		250.00	706	801.39	1,350.00	1,350.00					1,350.00	
90.65	27.00		700.00	707	1,149.03	2,307.69	2,307.69			2,307.69			
26.43	8.10			708	536.80	672.94	672.94			207.06	672.94		
56.56	16.80	8.00	200.00	709	970.26	1,440.00	1,440.00						1,440.00
80.52	24.00			710	1,464.27	2,050.00	2,050.00						2,050.00
21.21	6.30			711	422.22	540.00	540.00		540.00		540.00		
496.50	151.50	16.00	1,650.00		8,281.28	12,640.23	12,640.23		747.06	2,307.69	2,112.94	3,600.00	4,619.60

PAYROLL REGISTER   (left-hand page)

Name	Marital Status	No. W/H Allw.	Regular Earnings Hrs.	Regular Earnings Rate Per Hour	Regular Earnings Amount	Overtime Earnings Hrs.	Overtime Earnings Rate Per Hour	Overtime Earnings Amount	Total Earnings	Deductions OASDI	HI	FIT	SIT	SUTA
Payday, December 4, 20-- For Period Ending November 28, 20--														
Bonno, A.	M	4	80	17.65	1,412.00	8	35.30	282.40	1,694.40	105.05	24.57	81.00	52.02	1.19
Ferguson, J.	M	5	80	....	2,250.00	......	....	....	2,250.00	139.50	32.63	68.00	69.08	1.58
Ford, C.	S	2	80	....	960.00	......	....	....	960.00	59.52	13.92	71.00	29.47	0.67
Mann, D.	M	0	80	....	1,350.00	......	....	....	1,350.00	83.70	19.58	84.00	41.45	0.95
O'Neill, J.	M	3	80	....	2,307.69	......	....	....	2,307.69	143.08	33.46	92.00	70.85	1.62
Russell, V.	S	2	80	....	750.00	......	....	....	750.00	46.50	10.88	38.00	23.03	0.53
Ryan, N.	M	4	76	18.00	1,368.00	3	27.00	81.00	1,449.00	89.84	21.01	33.00	44.48	1.01
Sokowski, T.	S	2	80	....	2,050.00	......	....	....	2,050.00	127.10	29.73	260.00	62.94	1.44
Student	S	1	72	7.50	540.00	......	....	....	540.00	33.48	7.83	32.00	16.58	0.38
Woods, B.	S	1	72	....	1,080.00	......	....	....	1,080.00	66.96	15.66	111.00	33.16	0.76
Totals					14,067.69	......	....	363.40	14,431.09	894.73	209.27	870.00	443.06	10.13
Payday, December 14, 20-- For Period Ending December 12, 20--														
Estate of Virginia A. Russell	S	2	152	....	1,425.16*	......	....	....	1,425.16	88.36	20.66	....	....	1.00

(Virginia A. Russell died December 10, 20--) *$750 + $375 + (32 × $9.38)

Name	Marital Status	No. W/H Allw.	Regular Earnings Hrs.	Regular Earnings Rate Per Hour	Regular Earnings Amount	Overtime Earnings Hrs.	Overtime Earnings Rate Per Hour	Overtime Earnings Amount	Total Earnings	Deductions OASDI	HI	FIT	SIT	SUTA
Payday, December 18, 20-- For Period Ending December 12, 20--														
Bonno, A.	M	5	80	17.65	1,412.00	12	35.30	423.60	1,835.60	113.81	26.62	80.00	56.35	1.28
Ferguson, J.	M	5	80	....	2,250.00	......	....	....	2,250.00	139.50	32.63	68.00	69.08	1.58
Ford, C.	S	2	80	....	960.00	......	....	....	960.00	59.52	13.92	71.00	29.47	0.67
Mann, D.	M	0	80	....	1,350.00	......	....	....	1,350.00	83.70	19.58	84.00	41.45	0.95
O'Neill, J.	M	4	80	....	62,307.69	......	....	....	62,307.69	3,687.08*	903.46	20,712.20**	1,912.85	43.62
Ryan, N.	M	4	80	18.00	1,440.00	7	27.00	189.00	1,629.00	101.00	23.62	51.00	50.01	1.14
Sokowski, T.	S	2	80	....	2,050.00	......	....	....	2,050.00	127.10	29.73	260.00	62.94	1.44
Student	S	1	71	7.50	532.50	......	....	....	532.50	33.02	7.72	30.00	16.35	0.37
Woods, B.	S	1	80	....	1,200.00	......	....	....	1,200.00	74.40	17.40	129.00	36.84	0.84
Young, P.	S	1	80	....	807.70	......	....	....	807.70	50.08	11.71	69.00	24.80	0.57
Totals					74,309.89	......	....	612.60	74,922.49	4,469.21	1,086.39	21,554.20	2,300.14	52.46

*$59,469.28 of O'Neill's earnings this pay is taxable for OASDI. This amount brings his earnings up to the $113,700 taxable limit.
$113,700 × 0.062 – $3,362.32 (O'Neill's ytd OASDI withheld) = $3,687.08
**[($62,307.69 – $4,000.00 – $600.00 – $17,627.00) × 0.396] + $4,840.25 = $20,712.20

PAYROLL REGISTER (right-hand page)

		Deductions			Net Paid		Taxable Earnings				Labor Cost Distributions			
CIT	Group Ins.	Un-ion Dues	SIMPLE	Ck. No.	Amount	OASDI	HI	FUTA	SUTA	Admin.	Office	Sales	Plant	

Payday, December 4, 20-- For Period Ending November 28, 20--

CIT	Group Ins.	Union Dues	SIMPLE	Ck. No.	Amount	OASDI	HI	FUTA	SUTA	Admin.	Office	Sales	Plant
66.56		8.00		712	1,356.01	1,694.40	1,694.40						1,694.40
88.38			500.00	713	1,350.83	2,250.00	2,250.00					2,250.00	
37.71				714	747.71	960.00	960.00				960.00		
53.03			250.00	715	817.29	1,350.00	1,350.00					1,350.00	
90.65			700.00	716	1,176.03	2,307.69	2,307.69			2,307.69			
29.46				717	601.60	750.00	750.00				750.00		
56.92		8.00	200.00	718	994.74	1,449.00	1,449.00						1,449.00
80.52				719	1,488.27	2,050.00	2,050.00						2,050.00
21.21				720	428.52	540.00	540.00		540.00		540.00		
42.42				721	810.04	1,080.00	1,080.00	1,080.00	1,080.00		1,080.00		
566.86		16.00	1,650.00		9,771.04	14,431.09	14,431.09	1,080.00	1,620.00	2,307.69	3,330.00	3,600.00	5,193.40

Payday, December 14, 20-- For Period Ending December 12, 20--

CIT	Group Ins.	Union Dues	SIMPLE	Ck. No.	Amount	OASDI	HI	FUTA	SUTA	Admin.	Office	Sales	Plant
	8.70			722	1,306.44	1,425.16	1,425.16				1,425.16		

Payday, December 18, 20-- For Period Ending December 12, 20--

CIT	Group Ins.	Union Dues	SIMPLE	Ck. No.	Amount	OASDI	HI	FUTA	SUTA	Admin.	Office	Sales	Plant
72.10	16.50	9.00		723	1,459.94	1,835.60	1,835.60						1,835.60
88.38	26.40		500.00	724	1,324.43	2,250.00	2,250.00					2,250.00	
37.71	11.10			725	736.61	960.00	960.00				960.00		
53.03	15.90		250.00	726	801.39	1,350.00	1,350.00					1,350.00	
2,447.45	27.00		4,000.00	727	28,574.03	59,469.28	62,307.69			62,307.69			
63.99	16.80	9.00	200.00	728	1,112.44	1,629.00	1,629.00						1,629.00
80.52	24.00			729	1,464.27	2,050.00	2,050.00						2,050.00
20.92	6.30			730	417.82	532.50	532.50			250.00	532.50		
47.14	14.10			731	880.28	1,200.00	1,200.00	1,200.00	1,200.00	1,200.00			
31.73	9.60			732	610.21	807.70	807.70	807.70	807.70			807.70	
2,942.97	167.70	18.00	4,950.00		37,381.42	72,084.08	74,922.49	2,007.70	2,257.70	62,307.69	2,692.50	4,407.70	5,514.60

EMPLOYEES' EARNINGS RECORD

Payday	Reg Hrs	Reg Rate	Reg Amount	OT Hrs	OT Rate	OT Amount	Cumulative Earnings	OASDI	HI	FIT	SIT	SUTA	CIT	SIMPLE	Other Deduct.	Ck. No.	Net Amount
BONNO, Anthony V.																	
Year-to-Date																	
Total			10,293.40			1,028.60	11,322.00	701.96	164.17	810.00	347.59	7.93	444.73		216.80		8,628.82
10/9	80	17.65	1,412.00				12,734.00	87.54	20.47	49.00	43.35	0.99	55.46		8.00	672	1,147.19
10/23	80	17.65	1,412.00	4	26.48	105.92	14,251.92	94.11	22.01	59.00	46.60	1.06	59.62		24.50	682	1,211.02
11/6	80	17.65	1,412.00				15,663.92	87.54	20.47	49.00	43.35	0.99	55.46		8.00	692	1,147.19
11/20	64	17.65	1,129.60				16,793.52	70.04	16.38	21.00	34.68	0.79	44.37		24.50	703	917.84
12/4	80	17.65	1,412.00	8	35.30	282.40	18,487.92	105.05	24.57	81.00	52.02	1.19	66.56		8.00	712	1,356.01
12/18	80	17.65	1,412.00	12	35.30	423.60	20,323.52	113.81	26.62	80.00	56.35	1.28	72.10		25.50	723	1,459.94
Qtr. Tot.	464		8,189.60			811.92	9,001.52	558.09	130.52	339.00	276.35	6.30	353.57		98.50		7,239.19
Yr. Tot.			18,483.00			1,840.52	20,323.52	1,260.05	294.69	1,149.00	623.94	14.23	798.30		315.30		15,868.01
FERGUSON, James C.																	
Year-to-Date																	
Total			23,125.00				23,125.00	1,433.75	335.31	2,291.00	709.94	16.19	908.35		132.30		17,298.16
10/9	80		2,250.00				25,375.00	139.50	32.63	143.00	69.08	1.58	88.38			673	1,775.83
10/23	80		2,250.00				27,625.00	139.50	32.63	143.00	69.08	1.58	88.38		26.40	683	1,749.43
11/6	80		2,250.00				29,875.00	139.50	32.63	143.00	69.08	1.58	88.38			693	1,775.83
11/20	80		2,250.00				32,125.00	139.50	32.63	68.00	69.08	1.58	88.38	500.00	26.40	704	1,324.43
12/4	80		2,250.00				34,375.00	139.50	32.63	68.00	69.08	1.58	88.38	500.00		713	1,350.83
12/18	80		2,250.00				36,625.00	139.50	32.63	68.00	69.08	1.58	88.38	500.00	26.40	724	1,324.43
Qtr. Tot.	480		13,500.00				13,500.00	837.00	195.78	633.00	414.48	9.48	530.28	1,500.00	79.20		9,300.78
Yr. Tot.			36,625.00				36,625.00	2,270.75	531.09	2,924.00	1,124.42	25.67	1,438.63	1,500.00	211.50		26,598.94
FORD, Catherine L.																	
Year-to-Date																	
Total			6,300.00				6,300.00	390.60	91.35	639.00	193.41	4.41	247.46		37.80		4,695.97
10/9	80		900.00				7,200.00	55.80	13.05	62.00	27.63	0.63	35.35			674	705.54
10/23	80		900.00				8,100.00	55.80	13.05	62.00	27.63	0.63	35.35		10.50	684	695.04
11/6	80		900.00				9,000.00	55.80	13.05	62.00	27.63	0.63	35.35			694	705.54
11/20	80		900.00				9,900.00	55.80	13.05	62.00	27.63	0.63	35.35		10.50	705	695.04
12/4	80		960.00				10,860.00	59.52	13.92	71.00	29.47	0.67	37.71			714	747.71
12/18	80		960.00				11,820.00	59.52	13.92	71.00	29.47	0.67	37.71		11.10	725	736.61
Qtr. Tot.	480		5,520.00				5,520.00	342.24	80.04	390.00	169.46	3.86	216.82		32.10		4,285.48
Yr. Tot.			11,820.00				11,820.00	732.84	171.39	1,029.00	362.87	8.27	464.28		69.90		8,981.45

EMPLOYEES' EARNINGS RECORD

Payday	Reg. Hrs.	Reg. Rate	Reg. Amount	OT Hrs.	OT Rate	OT Amount	Cumulative Earnings	OASDI	HI	FIT	SIT	SUTA	CIT	SIMPLE	Other Deduct.	Ck. No.	Net Amount
MANN, Dewey W.																	
Year-to-Date																	
Total			5,400.00				5,400.00	334.80	78.30	332.00	165.78	3.78	212.11		31.50		4,241.73
10/9	80		1,350.00				6,750.00	83.70	19.58	43.00	41.45	0.95	53.03			675	1,108.29
10/23	80		1,350.00				8,100.00	83.70	19.58	43.00	41.45	0.95	53.03		15.90	685	1,092.39
11/6	80		1,350.00				9,450.00	83.70	19.58	120.00	41.45	0.95	53.03			695	1,031.29
11/20	80		1,350.00				10,800.00	83.70	19.58	84.00	41.45	0.95	53.03	250.00	15.90	706	801.39
12/4	80		1,350.00				12,150.00	83.70	19.58	84.00	41.45	0.95	53.03	250.00		715	817.29
12/18	80		1,350.00				13,500.00	83.70	19.58	84.00	41.45	0.95	53.03	250.00	15.90	726	801.39
Qtr. Tot.	480		8,100.00				8,100.00	502.20	117.48	458.00	248.70	5.70	318.18	750.00	47.70		5,652.04
Yr. Tot.			13,500.00				13,500.00	837.00	195.78	790.00	414.48	9.48	530.29	750.00	79.20		9,893.77
O'NEILL, Joseph T.																	
Year-to-Date																	
Total			42,692.27				42,692.27	2,646.92	619.04	6,116.00	1,310.65	29.88	1,676.95		202.50		30,090.33
10/9	80		2,307.69				44,999.96	143.08	33.46	197.00	70.85	1.62	90.65			676	1,771.03
10/23	80		2,307.69				47,307.65	143.08	33.46	197.00	70.85	1.62	90.65		27.00	686	1,744.03
11/6	80		2,307.69				49,615.34	143.08	33.46	197.00	70.85	1.62	90.65			696	1,771.03
11/20	80		2,307.69				51,923.03	143.08	33.46	92.00	70.85	1.62	90.65	700.00	27.00	707	1,149.03
12/4	80		2,307.69				54,230.72	143.08	33.46	92.00	70.85	1.62	90.65	700.00		716	1,176.03
12/18	80		62,307.69				116,538.41	3,687.08	903.46	20,712.20	1,912.85	43.62	2,447.45	4,000.00	27.00	727	28,574.03
Qtr. Tot.	480		73,846.14				73,846.14	4,402.48	1,070.76	21,487.20	2,267.10	51.72	2,900.70	5,400.00	81.00		36,185.18
Yr. Tot.			116,538.41				116,538.41	7,049.40	1,689.80	27,603.20	3,577.75	81.60	4,577.65	5,400.00	283.50		66,275.51
RUSSELL, Virginia A.																	
Year-to-Date																	
Total			6,240.00				6,240.00	386.88	90.48	642.00	191.56	4.37	245.11		31.50		4,648.10
10/9	80		690.00				6,930.00	42.78	10.01	51.00	21.18	0.48	27.10			677	537.45
10/23	80		690.00				7,620.00	42.78	10.01	51.00	21.18	0.48	27.10		8.10	687	529.35
11/6	78		672.94				8,292.94	41.72	9.76	29.00	20.66	0.47	26.43			697	544.90
11/20	78		672.94				8,965.88	41.72	9.76	29.00	20.66	0.47	26.43		8.10	708	536.80
12/4	80		750.00				9,715.88	46.50	10.88	38.00	23.03	0.53	29.46			717	601.60
12/14	152		1,425.16				11,141.04	88.36	20.66			1.00			8.70	722	1,306.44
Deceased December 10, 20--																	
Qtr. Tot.	548		4,901.04				4,901.04	303.86	71.08	198.00	106.71	3.43	136.52		24.90		4,056.54
Yr. Tot.			11,141.04				11,141.04	690.74	161.56	840.00	298.27	7.80	381.63		56.40		8,704.64

EMPLOYEES' EARNINGS RECORD

Payday	Regular Earnings			Overtime Earnings			Cumulative Earnings	Deductions								Net Paid	
	Hrs.	Rate	Amount	Hrs.	Rate	Amount		OASDI	HI	FIT	SIT	SUTA	CIT	SIMPLE	Other Deduct.	Ck. No.	Amount
RYAN, Norman A.																	
Year-to-Date																	
Total			13,287.50			1,397.80	14,685.30	910.49	212.94	1,070.00	450.84	10.28	576.84		235.70		11,218.21
10/9	80	18.00	1,440.00				16,125.30	89.28	20.88	53.00	44.21	1.01	56.56		8.00	678	1,167.06
10/23	80	18.00	1,440.00	8	27.00	216.00	17,781.30	102.67	24.01	75.00	50.84	1.16	65.05		24.80	688	1,312.47
11/6	80	18.00	1,440.00				19,221.30	89.28	20.88	53.00	44.21	1.01	56.56		8.00	698	1,167.06
11/20	80	18.00	1,440.00				20,661.30	89.28	20.88	33.00	44.21	1.01	56.56		24.80	709	970.26
12/4	76	18.00	1,368.00	3	27.00	81.00	22,110.30	89.84	21.01	33.00	44.48	1.01	56.92		8.00	718	994.74
12/18	80	18.00	1,440.00	7	27.00	189.00	23,739.30	101.00	23.62	51.00	50.01	1.14	63.99		25.80	728	1,112.44
Qtr. Tot.	476		8,568.00			486.00	9,054.00	561.35	131.28	298.00	277.96	6.34	355.64	600.00	99.40		6,724.03
Yr. Tot.			21,855.50			1,883.80	23,739.30	1,471.84	344.22	1,368.00	728.80	16.62	932.48	600.00	335.10		17,942.24
SOKOWSKI, Thomas J.																	
Year-to-Date																	
Total			16,650.00				16,650.00	1,032.30	241.43	2,002.00	511.16	11.66	654.01		94.50		12,102.94
10/9	80		2,050.00				18,700.00	127.10	29.73	180.00	62.94	1.44	80.52			679	1,568.27
10/23	80		2,050.00				20,750.00	127.10	29.73	180.00	62.94	1.44	80.52		24.00	689	1,544.27
11/6	80		2,050.00				22,800.00	127.10	29.73	260.00	62.94	1.44	80.52			699	1,488.27
11/20	80		2,050.00				24,850.00	127.10	29.73	260.00	62.94	1.44	80.52	200.00	24.00	710	1,464.27
12/4	80		2,050.00				26,900.00	127.10	29.73	260.00	62.94	1.44	80.52	200.00		719	1,488.27
12/18	80		2,050.00				28,950.00	127.10	29.73	260.00	62.94	1.44	80.52	200.00	24.00	729	1,464.27
Qtr. Tot.	480		12,300.00				12,300.00	762.60	178.38	1,400.00	377.64	8.64	483.12	600.00	72.00		9,017.62
Yr. Tot.			28,950.00				28,950.00	1,794.90	419.81	3,402.00	888.80	20.30	1,137.13	600.00	166.50		21,120.56
STUDENT																	
Year-to-Date																	
Total			5,550.00				5,550.00	344.10	80.48	409.00	170.38	3.89	218.00		32.40		4,291.75
10/9	72	7.50	540.00				6,090.00	33.48	7.83	32.00	16.58	0.38	21.21			680	428.52
10/23	72	7.50	540.00				6,630.00	33.48	7.83	32.00	16.58	0.38	21.21		6.30	690	422.22
11/6	72	7.50	540.00				7,170.00	33.48	7.83	32.00	16.58	0.38	21.21			700	428.52
11/20	72	7.50	540.00				7,710.00	33.48	7.83	32.00	16.58	0.38	21.21		6.30	711	422.22
12/4	72	7.50	540.00				8,250.00	33.48	7.83	32.00	16.58	0.38	21.21			720	428.52
12/18	71	7.50	532.50				8,782.50	33.02	7.72	30.00	16.35	0.37	20.92		6.30	730	417.82
Qtr. Tot.	431		3,232.50				3,232.50	200.42	46.87	190.00	99.25	2.27	126.97		18.90		2,547.82
Yr. Tot.			8,782.50				8,782.50	544.52	127.35	599.00	269.63	6.16	344.97		51.30		6,839.57

EMPLOYEES' EARNINGS RECORD

Payday	Regular Earnings Hrs.	Rate	Amount	Overtime Earnings Hrs.	Rate	Amount	Cumulative Earnings	OASDI	HI	FIT	SIT	SUTA	CIT	SIMPLE	Other Deduct.	Ck. No.	Net Paid Amount
WILLIAMS, Ruth V.																	
Year-to-Date																	
Total			10,260.00				10,260.00	636.12	148.77	1,606.00	314.98	7.18	403.01		59.40		7,084.54
10/9	80		1,223.08				11,483.08	75.83	17.73	155.00	37.55	0.86	48.04			681	888.07
10/23	80		1,223.08				12,706.16	75.83	17.73	155.00	37.55	0.86	48.04		14.40	691	873.67
11/6	79		1,207.85				13,914.01	74.89	17.51	152.00	37.08	0.85	47.44			701	878.08
11/13	136		2,079.32		Discharged November 13		15,993.33	128.92	30.15	340.00	63.84	1.46	81.68		14.40	702	1,418.87
Qtr. Tot.	375		5,733.33				5,733.33	355.47	83.12	802.00	176.02	4.03	225.20		28.80		4,058.69
Yr. Tot.			15,993.33				15,993.33	991.59	231.89	2,408.00	491.00	11.21	628.21		88.20		11,143.23
WOODS, Beth A.																	
12/4	72		1,080.00				1,080.00	66.96	15.66	111.00	33.16	0.76	42.42			721	810.04
12/18	80		1,200.00				2,280.00	74.40	17.40	129.00	36.84	0.84	47.14		14.10	731	880.28
Qtr. Tot.	152		2,280.00				2,280.00	141.36	33.06	240.00	70.00	1.60	89.56		14.10		1,690.32
Yr. Tot.			2,280.00				2,280.00	141.36	33.06	240.00	70.00	1.60	89.56		14.10		1,690.32
YOUNG, Paul W.																	
12/18	80		807.70				807.70	50.08	11.71	69.00	24.80	0.57	31.73		9.60	732	610.21
Qtr. Tot.	80		807.70				807.70	50.08	11.71	69.00	24.80	0.57	31.73		9.60		610.21
Yr. Tot.			807.70				807.70	50.08	11.71	69.00	24.80	0.57	31.73		9.60		610.21

Transaction No. 11

FEDERAL DEPOSIT INFORMATION WORKSHEET	
Employer Identification Number 00-0000660	Name Glo-Brite Paint Company
Month Tax Year Ends 12	Amount of Deposit 6,345.08
Type of Tax (Form) 941	Tax Period 4th Qtr
Address 2215 Salvador St.	Phone Number (215) 555-9559
City, State, Zip Philadelphia, PA 19175-0682	

Transaction No. 25

FEDERAL DEPOSIT INFORMATION WORKSHEET	
Employer Identification Number 00-0000660	Name Glo-Brite Paint Company
Month Tax Year Ends 12	Amount of Deposit 6,532.08
Type of Tax (Form) 941	Tax Period 4th Qtr
Address 2215 Salvador St.	Phone Number (215) 555-9559
City, State, Zip Philadelphia, PA 19175-0682	

Transaction No. 33

FEDERAL DEPOSIT INFORMATION WORKSHEET

Employer
Identification Number <u>00-0000660</u> Name <u>Glo-Brite Paint Company</u>

Month Tax Year Ends <u>12</u> Amount of Deposit <u>35,961.41</u>

Type of Tax (Form) <u>941</u> Tax Period <u>4th Qtr</u>

Address <u>2215 Salvador St.</u> Phone Number <u>(215) 555-9559</u>

City, State, Zip <u>Philadelphia, PA 19175-0682</u>

Transaction No. 36

FEDERAL DEPOSIT INFORMATION WORKSHEET

Employer
Identification Number <u>00-0000660</u> Name <u>Glo-Brite Paint Company</u>

Month Tax Year Ends <u>12</u> Amount of Deposit <u>438.53</u>

Type of Tax (Form) <u>940</u> Tax Period <u>20--</u>

Address <u>2215 Salvador St.</u> Phone Number <u>(215) 555-9559</u>

City, State, Zip <u>Philadelphia, PA 19175-0682</u>

Transaction No. 2

STATE FILING INFORMATION WORKSHEET

Company Name	**Glo-Brite Paint Co.**	Payment Frequency	**Semimonthly**
Employer Account #	**00003300**	Gross Compensation	**14,162.77**
Employer ID #	**00-0000660**	PA Withholding Tax	**434.82**
Employer Password	**GBPCOM**	Credits	
Quarter Ending Date	**12/31/--**	Interest	
Telephone Number	**(215) 555-9559**	Payment	**434.82**

Transaction No. 4

STATE FILING INFORMATION WORKSHEET

Company Name	**Glo-Brite Paint Co.**	Payment Frequency	**Semimonthly**
Employer Account #	**00003300**	Gross Compensation	**14,484.69**
Employer ID #	**00-0000660**	PA Withholding Tax	**444.70**
Employer Password	**GBPCOM**	Credits	
Quarter Ending Date	**12/31/--**	Interest	
Telephone Number	**(215) 555-9559**	Payment	**444.70**

Transaction No. 14

STATE FILING INFORMATION WORKSHEET

Company Name	**Glo-Brite Paint Co.**	Payment Frequency	**Semimonthly**
Employer Account #	**00003300**	Gross Compensation	**16,209.80**
Employer ID #	**00-0000660**	PA Withholding Tax	**497.67**
Employer Password	**GBPCOM**	Credits	
Quarter Ending Date	**12/31/--**	Interest	
Telephone Number	**(215) 555-9559**	Payment	**497.67**

Transaction No. 18

STATE FILING INFORMATION WORKSHEET

Company Name	**Glo-Brite Paint Co.**	Payment Frequency	**Semimonthly**
Employer Account #	**00003300**	Gross Compensation	**12,640.23**
Employer ID #	**00-0000660**	PA Withholding Tax	**388.08**
Employer Password	**GBPCOM**	Credits	
Quarter Ending Date	**12/31/--**	Interest	
Telephone Number	**(215) 555-9559**	Payment	**388.08**

Transaction No. 27

STATE FILING INFORMATION WORKSHEET

Company Name	**Glo-Brite Paint Co.**	Payment Frequency	**Semimonthly**
Employer Account #	**00003300**	Gross Compensation	**14,431.09**
Employer ID #	**00-0000660**	PA Withholding Tax	**443.06**
Employer Password	**GBPCOM**	Credits	
Quarter Ending Date	**12/31/--**	Interest	
Telephone Number	**(215) 555-9559**	Payment	**443.06**

Transaction No. 31

STATE FILING INFORMATION WORKSHEET

Company Name	**Glo-Brite Paint Co.**	Payment Frequency	**Semimonthly**
Employer Account #	**00003300**	Gross Compensation	**74,922.49**
Employer ID #	**00-0000660**	PA Withholding Tax	**2,300.14**
Employer Password	**GBPCOM**	Credits	
Quarter Ending Date	**12/31/--**	Interest	
Telephone Number	**(215) 555-9559**	Payment	**2,300.14**

Transaction No. 12

Monthly Wage Tax

Glo-Brite Paint Company
2215 Salvador Street
Philadelphia, PA 19175-0682

Account #: 0001855   From: 10/1

Tax Type: 01   To: 10/31

Period/Yr: 10/—   Due Date:
                     11/16

1. TAX DUE PER WORKSHEET, *Line 8*	
	1,125	25

2. INTEREST AND PENALTY	
	—0—	

3. TOTAL DUE (LINES 1 & 2)	
	1,125	25

Signature: *Joseph T. O'Neill*

I hereby certify that I have examined this return and that it is correct to the best of my knowledge.
Phone #:   **(215) 555-9559**

Philadelphia Revenue Department

P.O. Box 8040
Philadelphia, PA 19101-8040

Make checks payable to:

CITY OF PHILADELPHIA

Transaction No. 26

Monthly Wage Tax

Glo-Brite Paint Company
2215 Salvador Street
Philadelphia, PA 19175-0682

Account #: 0001855   From: 11/1

Tax Type: 01   To: 11/30

Period/Yr: 11/—   Due Date:
                     12/15

1. TAX DUE PER WORKSHEET, *Line 8*	
	1,133	21

2. INTEREST AND PENALTY	
	—0—	

3. TOTAL DUE (LINES 1 & 2)	
	1,133	21

Signature: *Joseph T. O'Neill*

I hereby certify that I have examined this return and that it is correct to the best of my knowledge.
Phone #:   **(215) 555-9559**

Philadelphia Revenue Department

P.O. Box 8040
Philadelphia, PA 19101-8040

Make checks payable to:

CITY OF PHILADELPHIA

Transaction No. 34

Monthly Wage Tax

Glo-Brite Paint Company
2215 Salvador Street
Philadelphia, PA 19175-0682

Account #: 0001855   From: 12/1

Tax Type: 01   To: 12/31

Period/Yr: 12/—   Due Date:
                     1/15

1. TAX DUE PER WORKSHEET, *Line 8*	
	3,509	83

2. INTEREST AND PENALTY	
	—0—	

3. TOTAL DUE (LINES 1 & 2)	
	3,509	83

Signature: *Joseph T. O'Neill*

I hereby certify that I have examined this return and that it is correct to the best of my knowledge.
Phone #:   **(215) 555-9559**

Philadelphia Revenue Department

P.O. Box 8040
Philadelphia, PA 19101-8040

Make checks payable to:

CITY OF PHILADELPHIA

Source: Philadelphia Revenue Department

Transaction No. 43

PA Employer's Quarterly Reconciliation Worksheet

Company Name	**Glo-Brite Paint Co.**
Account Number	**00003300**
ID #	**00-0000660**
Telephone #	**(215) 555-9559**
Quarter Ending Date	**12/31/--**

Record of PA Withholding Tax:

1st half of month	**434.82**	1.	Total Compensation	**146,851.07***
2nd half of month	**444.70**	2.	Total PA W/H Tax	**4,508.47**
1st half of month	**497.67**	3.	Total Deposits/Quarter	**4,508.47**
2nd half of month	**388.08**	4.	Tax Due	**—**
1st half of month	**443.06**			
2nd half of month	**2,300.14**			
TOTAL	**4,508.47**			

*$148,276.23 less exempt wages paid Russell on December 14 ($1,425.16).

Transaction No. 44

CITY OF PHILADELPHIA
ANNUAL RECONCILIATION OF
20-- EMPLOYER WAGE TAX
DUE DATE: FEBRUARY 28, 20--

5 0 1 1

City Account Number
0 0 0 1 8 5 5

Federal Identification Number
0 0 - 0 0 0 0 6 6 0

Name and Address
Glo-Brite Paint Company

2215 Salvador Street

Philadelphia, PA 19175-0682

To file online, click on "Online Services" at
www.phila.gov/revenue.

If your business terminated in 20--, enter the termination date **AND** file a CHANGE FORM.

<u>YOU MUST USE THE CHANGE FORM TO REPORT A CHANGE OF ADDRESS.</u>   *If this is an amended return place an "X" here:*

A. Enter the number of Philadelphia Residents for whom wage tax was remitted for the pay period including
March 12, 20-- ....A.   **1 0**

B. Enter the number of **nonresidents** (employees living outside Philadelphia city limits) for whom wage tax
was remitted for the pay period including March 12, 20-- ....B.

C. Total number of employees **for all company locations** reported on the Employer's Federal Quarterly
Tax Return for the first quarter of 20-- (for the pay period including March 12, 20--) ....C.   **1 0**

D. Number of employees working **at company locations within Philadelphia city limits**, for the pay period
including March 12, 20--...D.   **1 0**

1. Gross Compensation per W-2 forms for all employees.................1. , 2 8 9 , 0 7 6 . 0 0 *

2. Non-Taxable Gross Compensation included in Line 1.
(Paid to nonresidents working outside of Philadelphia).................2. , , . 0 0

3. Gross Compensation per W-2 forms on which Philadelphia Wage Tax was
withheld or due (Line 1 minus Line 2)..................3. , 2 8 9 , 0 7 6 . 0 0

4. Total Taxable Gross Compensation paid to **residents** of Philadelphia in 20-- ......4. , 2 8 9 , 0 7 6 . 0 0

5. Tax Due (Line 4 times .03928)..................5. , 1 1 , 3 5 5 . 0 0

6. Total Taxable Gross Compensation paid to **nonresidents** of Philadelphia in 20-- ......6. , , . 0 0

7. Tax Due (Line 6 times .034985)..................7. , , . 0 0

8. **Total Tax Due** (Line 5 plus Line 7)..................8. , 1 1 , 3 5 5 . 0 0

9. **Tax previously paid for 20--** ....9. , 1 1 , 3 5 5 . 0 0

10. **ADDITIONAL TAX DUE** If Line 8 is greater than Line 9, enter the amount here.........10. , , . 0 0

11. **TAX OVERPAID** If Line 9 is greater than Line 8, enter the amount here.
See instructions for filing a Refund Petition..................11. , , . 0 0

Under penalties of perjury, as set forth in 18 PA C.S. §§ 4902-4903 as amended, I swear that I have reviewed this return
and accompanying statements and schedules, and to the best of my knowledge and belief, they are true and complete.

Taxpayer Signature *Joseph T. O'Neill*   Date *2/1/--*   Phone # *(215) 555-9559*

Preparer Signature_____ Date_____ Phone #_____

2011 Wage Internet 6-28-2011 Ver 1.0

Source: Philadelphia Revenue Department.

*$290,500.80 less exempt wages paid to Russell on December 14 ($1,425.16).

Transaction No. 35

Form 941 for 20--: **Employer's QUARTERLY Federal Tax Return**
(Rev. January 2013)   Department of the Treasury — Internal Revenue Service

OMB No. 1545-0029

Employer identification number (EIN) 0 0 — 0 0 0 0 6 6 0

Name (not your trade name) Glo-Brite Paint Company

Trade name (if any)

Address 2215 Salvador Street
         Number   Street   Suite or room number

Philadelphia   PA   19175-0682
City   State   ZIP code

Report for this Quarter of 20--
(Check one.)

☐ 1: January, February, March

☐ 2: April, May, June

☐ 3: July, August, September

☒ 4: October, November, December

Instructions and prior year forms are available at www.irs.gov/form941.

Read the separate instructions before you complete Form 941. Type or print within the boxes.

Part 1: Answer these questions for this quarter.

1	Number of employees who received wages, tips, or other compensation for the pay period including: *Mar. 12* (Quarter 1), *June 12* (Quarter 2), *Sept. 12* (Quarter 3), or *Dec. 12* (Quarter 4)	1	10
2	Wages, tips, and other compensation	2	138601 ▪ 07*
3	Income tax withheld from wages, tips, and other compensation	3	26504 ▪ 20
4	If no wages, tips, and other compensation are subject to social security or Medicare tax	☐ Check and go to line 6.	

		Column 1		Column 2
5a	Taxable social security wages	145437 ▪ 82**	× .124 =	18034 ▪ 29
5b	Taxable social security tips	▪	× .124 =	▪
5c	Taxable Medicare wages & tips	148276 ▪ 23	× .029 =	4300 ▪ 01
5d	Taxable wages & tips subject to Additional Medicare Tax withholding	▪	× .009 =	▪

5e	Add Column 2 from lines 5a, 5b, 5c, and 5d	5e	22334 ▪ 30
5f	Section 3121(q) Notice and Demand—Tax due on unreported tips (see instructions)	5f	▪
6	Total taxes before adjustments (add lines 3, 5e, and 5f)	6	48838 ▪ 50
7	Current quarter's adjustment for fractions of cents	7	▪ 07
8	Current quarter's adjustment for sick pay	8	▪
9	Current quarter's adjustments for tips and group-term life insurance	9	▪
10	Total taxes after adjustments. Combine lines 6 through 9	10	48838 ▪ 57
11	Total deposits for this quarter, including overpayment applied from a prior quarter and overpayment applied from Form 941-X or Form 944-X filed in the current quarter	11	48838 ▪ 57
12a	COBRA premium assistance payments (see instructions)	12a	▪
12b	Number of individuals provided COBRA premium assistance		
13	Add lines 11 and 12a	13	48838 ▪ 57
14	Balance due. If line 10 is more than line 13, enter the difference and see instructions	14	▪
15	Overpayment. If line 13 is more than line 10, enter the difference [▪] Check one: ☐ Apply to next return. ☐ Send a refund.		

▶ **You MUST complete both pages of Form 941 and SIGN it.**   Next ▶

For Privacy Act and Paperwork Reduction Act Notice, see the back of the Payment Voucher.   Cat. No. 17001Z   Form **941** (Rev. 1-2013)

*Total wages paid, $148,276.23 less earnings paid Russell on 12/14 ($1,425.16), less SIMPLE deductions, $8,250.00.

**Total wages paid, $148,276.23 less O'Neill's nontaxable wages of $2,838.41 (in excess of $113,700).

Transaction No. 35   (Concluded)

Name *(not your trade name)*	**Employer identification number (EIN)**
Glo-Brite Paint Company	00-0000660

Part 2:   **Tell us about your deposit schedule and tax liability for this quarter.**

If you are unsure about whether you are a monthly schedule depositor or a semiweekly schedule depositor, see Pub. 15 (Circular E), section 11.

16   Check one: ☐   **Line 10 on this return is less than $2,500 or line 10 on the return for the prior quarter was less than $2,500, and you did not incur a $100,000 next-day deposit obligation during the current quarter.** If line 10 for the prior quarter was less than $2,500 but line 10 on this return is $100,000 or more, you must provide a record of your federal tax liability. If you are a monthly schedule depositor, complete the deposit schedule below; if you are a semiweekly schedule depositor, attach Schedule B (Form 941). Go to Part 3.

☒   **You were a monthly schedule depositor for the entire quarter.** Enter your tax liability for each month and total liability for the quarter, then go to Part 3.

	Tax liability:	Month 1	6345 ▪ 08
		Month 2	6532 ▪ 08
		Month 3	35961 ▪ 41
	Total liability for quarter		48838 ▪ 57 **Total must equal line 10.**

☐   **You were a semiweekly schedule depositor for any part of this quarter.** Complete Schedule B (Form 941), Report of Tax Liability for Semiweekly Schedule Depositors, and attach it to Form 941.

Part 3:   **Tell us about your business. If a question does NOT apply to your business, leave it blank.**

17   **If your business has closed or you stopped paying wages** . . . .   ☐ Check here, and

enter the final date you paid wages   [/ /] .

18   **If you are a seasonal employer and you do not have to file a return for every quarter of the year** . .   ☐ Check here.

Part 4:   **May we speak with your third-party designee?**

Do you want to allow an employee, a paid tax preparer, or another person to discuss this return with the IRS? See the instructions for details.

☐ Yes.   Designee's name and phone number   [   ]   [   ]

Select a 5-digit Personal Identification Number (PIN) to use when talking to the IRS.   ☐ ☐ ☐ ☐ ☐

☒ No.

Part 5:   **Sign here. You MUST complete both pages of Form 941 and SIGN it.**

Under penalties of perjury, I declare that I have examined this return, including accompanying schedules and statements, and to the best of my knowledge and belief, it is true, correct, and complete. Declaration of preparer (other than taxpayer) is based on all information of which preparer has any knowledge.

X **Sign your name here**	*Joseph T. O'Neill*	Print your name here	Joseph T. O'Neill
		Print your title here	President
Date	02 / 01 / --	Best daytime phone	215-555-9559

Paid Preparer Use Only   Check if you are self-employed . . . ☐

Preparer's name		PTIN	
Preparer's signature		Date	/ /
Firm's name (or yours if self-employed)		EIN	
Address		Phone	
City		State	ZIP code	

Page **2**   Form **941** (Rev. 1-2013)

Source: Internal Revenue Service.

*Total wages paid, $148,276.23 less earnings paid Russell on 12/14 ($1,425.16), less SIMPLE deductions $8,250.00.

**Total wages paid, $148,276.23 less O'Neill's nontaxable wages of $2,838.41(in excess of $113,700).

Transaction No. 36

Form **940 for 20--:** **Employer's Annual Federal Unemployment (FUTA) Tax Return**

Department of the Treasury — Internal Revenue Service

OMB No. 1545-0028

Employer identification number (EIN)	0 0 – 0 0 0 0 0 6 6 0

Name (not your trade name) GLO-BRITE PAINT COMPANY

Trade name (if any)

Address 2215 SALVADOR ST

Number   Street   Suite or room number

PHILADELPHIA   PA   19175-0682

City   State   ZIP code

Type of Return
(Check all that apply.)

☐ **a.** Amended
☐ **b.** Successor employer
☐ **c.** No payments to employees in 20--
☐ **d.** Final: Business closed or stopped paying wages

Instructions and prior-year forms are available at *www.irs.gov/form940.*

Read the separate instructions before you complete this form. Please type or print within the boxes.

Part 1: Tell us about your return. If any line does NOT apply, leave it blank.

1a If you had to pay state unemployment tax in one state only, enter the state abbreviation . **1a** P   A

1b If you had to pay state unemployment tax in more than one state, you are a multi-state employer . . . . **1b** ☐ Check here. Complete Schedule A (Form 940).

2 If you paid wages in a state that is subject to **CREDIT REDUCTION** . . . . **2** ☐ Check here. Complete Schedule A (Form 940).

Part 2: Determine your FUTA tax before adjustments for 20--. If any line does NOT apply, leave it blank.

3 Total payments to all employees **3** 290500.80

4 Payments exempt from FUTA tax . . . . . **4** .

Check all that apply: **4a** ☐ Fringe benefits   **4c** ☐ Retirement/Pension   **4e** ☐ Other
                        4b ☐ Group-term life insurance **4d** ☐ Dependent care

5 Total of payments made to each employee in excess of $7,000 . . . . **5** 217413.10

6 **Subtotal** (line 4 + line 5 = line 6) **6** 217413.10

7 Total taxable **FUTA wages** (line 3 – line 6 = line 7) (see instructions) **7** 73087.70

8 FUTA tax before adjustments (line 7 x .006 = line 8) **8** 438.53

Part 3: Determine your adjustments. If any line does NOT apply, leave it blank.

9 If ALL of the taxable FUTA wages you paid were excluded from state unemployment tax, multiply line 7 by **.054** (line 7 × .054 = line 9). Go to line 12 . . . . **9** .

10 If SOME of the taxable FUTA wages you paid were excluded from state unemployment tax, **OR** you paid **ANY** state unemployment tax late (after the due date for filing Form 940), complete the worksheet in the instructions. Enter the amount from line 7 of the worksheet . . **10** .

11 If credit reduction applies, enter the total from Schedule A (Form 940) . . . . . **11** .

Part 4: Determine your FUTA tax and balance due or overpayment for 20--. If any line does NOT apply, leave it blank.

12 Total FUTA tax after adjustments (lines 8 + 9 + 10 + 11 = line 12) **12** 438.53

13 FUTA tax deposited for the year, including any overpayment applied from a prior year . **13** 438.53

14 **Balance due** (If line 12 is more than line 13, enter the excess on line 14.)
• If line 14 is more than $500, you must deposit your tax.
• If line 14 is $500 or less, you may pay with this return. (see instructions) . . . . . . **14** .

15 **Overpayment** (If line 13 is more than line 12, enter the excess on line 15 and check a box below.) . . . . **15** .

▶ You **MUST** complete both pages of this form and **SIGN** it.   Check one: ☐ Apply to next return. ☐ Send a refund.

Next ▶

For Privacy Act and Paperwork Reduction Act Notice, see the back of Form 940-V, Payment Voucher.   Cat. No. 11234O   Form **940** (2012)

Transaction No. 36   (Concluded)

Name (not your trade name)	**Employer identification number (EIN)**
GLO-BRITE PAINT COMPANY	00-0000660

Part 5:   Report your FUTA tax liability by quarter only if line 12 is more than $500. If not, go to Part 6.

16   Report the amount of your FUTA tax liability for each quarter; do NOT enter the amount you deposited. If you had no liability for a quarter, leave the line blank.

16a **1st quarter** (January 1 – March 31)	**16a**	204.53
16b **2nd quarter** (April 1 – June 30)	**16b**	105.25
16c **3rd quarter** (July 1 – September 30)	**16c**	83.16
16d **4th quarter** (October 1 – December 31)	**16d**	45.59

17   Total tax liability for the year (lines 16a + 16b + 16c + 16d = line 17) **17**   438.53   Total must equal line 12.

Part 6:   May we speak with your third-party designee?

Do you want to allow an employee, a paid tax preparer, or another person to discuss this return with the IRS? See the instructions for details.

☐ **Yes.**   Designee's name and phone number

             Select a 5-digit Personal Identification Number (PIN) to use when talking to IRS

☑ **No.**

Part 7:   Sign here. You MUST complete both pages of this form and SIGN it.

Under penalties of perjury, I declare that I have examined this return, including accompanying schedules and statements, and to the best of my knowledge and belief, it is true, correct, and complete, and that no part of any payment made to a state unemployment fund claimed as a credit was, or is to be, deducted from the payments made to employees. Declaration of preparer (other than taxpayer) is based on all information of which preparer has any knowledge.

X **Sign your name here**   *Joseph T. O'Neill*

Print your name here	Joseph T. O'Neill
Print your title here	President
Best daytime phone	215-555-9559

Date   02 / 01 /--

Paid Preparer Use Only   Check if you are self-employed . . . ☐

Preparer's name		PTIN	
Preparer's signature		Date	/ /
Firm's name (or yours if self-employed)		EIN	
Address		Phone	
City		State	ZIP code

Page **2**   Form **940** (2012)

Source: Internal Revenue Service.

Transaction No. 37

PA Form UC-2 REV 1-12 Employer's Report for Unemployment Compensation

Read Instructions – Answer Each Item

QTR./YEAR 4/20--

DUE DATE 01/31/20--

1ST MONTH   2ND MONTH   3RD MONTH

W   INV. ☐   EXAMINED BY: ☐

1. TOTAL COVERED EMPLOYEES IN PAY PERIOD INCL. 12TH OF MONTH

Signature certifies that the information contained herein is true and correct to the best of the signer's knowledge.

2. GROSS WAGES	148276.23
3. EMPLOYEE CONTRIBUTIONS	103.94
4. TAXABLE WAGES FOR EMPLOYER CONTRIBUTIONS	13597.70
5. EMPLOYER CONTRIBUTIONS DUE (RATE X ITEM 4)	500.19
6. TOTAL CONTRIBUTIONS DUE (ITEMS 3 + 5)	604.13
7. INTEREST DUE SEE INSTRUCTIONS	
8. PENALTY DUE SEE INSTRUCTIONS	$
9. TOTAL REMITTANCE (ITEMS 6 + 7 + 8)	604.13

FOR DEPT. USE

10. SIGN HERE-DO NOT PRINT

TITLE ___ DATE ___ PHONE # ___

11. FILED ☐ PAPER UC-2A ☐ INTERNET UC-2A ☐ MAGNETIC MEDIA UC-2A

12. FEDERAL IDENTIFICATION NUMBER

EMPLOYER'S CONTRIBUTION RATE ▷ .036785   EMPLOYER'S ACCT. NO. 000-0-3300 CHECK DIGIT 1

GLO-BRITE PAINT COMPANY
2215 SALVADOR STREET
PHILADELPHIA, PA 19175-0682

MAKE CHECKS PAYABLE TO: PA UC FUND
SUBJECTIVITY DATE   REPORT DELINQUENT DATE

PA Form UC-2A, Employer's Quarterly Report of Wages Paid to Each Employee

See instructions on separate sheet. Information MUST be typewritten or printed in BLACK ink. Do NOT use commas (,) or dollar singns ($). If typed, disregard vertical bars and type a consecutive string of characters. If hand printed, print in CAPS and within the boxes as below:

SAMPLE Typed: 123456.00   SAMPLE Handwritten: 123456.00   SAMPLE Filled-in: →

Employer name: Glo-Brite Paint Company   Employer PA UC account no.: 000-0-3300   Check digit: 1   Quarter and year Q/YYYY: 4/20--   Quarter ending date MM/DD/YYYY: 12/31/20--

1. Name and telephone number of preparer
2. Total number of pages in this report
3. Total number of employees listed in item 8 on all pages of Form UC-2A
4. Plant number (if approved)

5. Gross wages, MUST agree with item 2 on UC-2 and the sum of item 11 on all pages of Form UC-2A

6. Fill in this circle if you would like the Department to preprint your employees' names & SSNs on Form UC-2A next quarter

7. Employee's social security number	8. Employee's name FI MI LAST	9. Gross wages paid this qtr	10. Credit weeks
000003481	A V BONNO	9001.52	13
000008645	J C FERGUSON	13500.00	13
000004567	C L FORD	5520.00	13
000009352	D W MANN	8100.00	13
000001534	J T ONEILL	73846.14	13
000006337	V A RUSSELL	4901.04	11
000001223	N A RYAN	9054.00	13
000008832	T J SOKOWSKI	12300.00	13
	STUDENT	3232.50	13
000006741	R V WILLIAMS	5733.33	7
000001587	B A WOODS	2280.00	6
000006057	P W YOUNG	807.70	4

List any additional employees on continuation sheets in the required format (see instructions).

11. Total gross wages for this page: → 148276.23
12. Total number of employees for this page: 12

UC-2A REV 9-05   13. Page 1 of 1

Source: PA Department of Labor & Industry.

Transaction No. 10

22222 Void ☐	a Employee's social security number 000-00-6741	For Official Use Only OMB No. 1 545-0008		
b Employer identification number (EIN) 00-0000660		1 Wages, tips, other compensation 15993.33	2 Federal income tax withheld 2408.00	
c Employer's name, address, and ZIP code		3 Social security wages 15993.33	4 Social security tax withheld 991.59	
Glo-Brite Paint Company 2215 Salvador Street Philadelphia, PA 19175-0682		5 Medicare wages and tips 15993.33	6 Medicare tax withheld 231.89	
		7 Social security tips	8 Allocated tips	
d Control number		9	10 Dependent care benefits	
e Employee's first name and initial Ruth V.	Last name Williams	Suff.	11 Nonqualified plans	12a See instructions for box 12 Code
			13 Statutory employee ☐ Retirement plan ☐ Third-party sick pay ☐	12b Code
9433 STATE STREET PHILADELPHIA, PA 19149-0819		14 Other	12c Code
f Employee's address and ZIP code				12d Code

15 State PA	Employer's state ID number 000-0-3300	16 State wages, tips, etc. 15993.33	17 State income tax 491.00	18 Local wages, tips, etc. 15993.33	19 Local income tax 628.21	20 Locality name PHILA.

Form **W-2** Wage and Tax Statement   **20--**

Department of the Treasury—Internal Revenue Service
For Privacy Act and Paperwork
Reduction Act Notice, see back of Copy D.

Transaction No. 24

22222 Void ☐	a Employee's social security number 000-00-6337	For Official Use Only OMB No. 1 545-0008		
b Employer identification number (EIN) 00-0000660		1 Wages, tips, other compensation 9715.88*	2 Federal income tax withheld 840.00	
c Employer's name, address, and ZIP code		3 Social security wages 11141.04	4 Social security tax withheld 690.74	
Glo-Brite Paint Company 2215 Salvador Street Philadelphia, PA 19175-0682		5 Medicare wages and tips 11141.04	6 Medicare tax withheld 161.56	
		7 Social security tips	8 Allocated tips	
d Control number		9	10 Dependent care benefits	
e Employee's first name and initial Virginia A.	Last name Russell	Suff.	11 Nonqualified plans	12a See instructions for box 12 Code
			13 Statutory employee ☐ Retirement plan ☐ Third-party sick pay ☐	12b Code
8004 DOWLING ROAD PHILADELPHIA, PA 19135-9001		14 Other	12c Code
f Employee's address and ZIP code				12d Code

15 State PA	Employer's state ID number 000-0-3300	16 State wages, tips, etc. 9715.88*	17 State income tax 298.27	18 Local wages, tips, etc. 9715.88*	19 Local income tax 381.63	20 Locality name PHILA.

Form **W-2** Wage and Tax Statement   **20--**

Department of the Treasury—Internal Revenue Service
For Privacy Act and Paperwork
Reduction Act Notice, see back of Copy D.

Source: Internal Revenue Service.

*$11,141.04 – $1,425.16 (not considered wages for purposes of FIT, SIT, and CIT).

Transaction No. 38

22222	Void ☐	a Employee's social security number 000-00-3481	For Official Use Only OMB No. 1 545-0008		
b	Employer identification number (EIN) 00-0000660		1 Wages, tips, other compensation 20323.52	2 Federal income tax withheld 1149.00	
c	Employer's name, address, and ZIP code		3 Social security wages 20323.52	4 Social security tax withheld 1260.05	

Glo-Brite Paint Company
2215 Salvador Street
Philadelphia, PA 19175-0682

5 Medicare wages and tips 20323.52	6 Medicare tax withheld 294.69
7 Social security tips	8 Allocated tips

d	Control number	9	10 Dependent care benefits

e Employee's first name and initial Anthony V.	Last name Bonno	Suff.	11 Nonqualified plans	12a See instructions for box 12 Code

13 Statutory employee ☐	Retirement plan ☐	Third-party sick pay ☐	12b Code

694 BRISTOL AVENUE
PHILADELPHIA, PA 19135-0617

14 Other Union Dues 121.00	12c Code
	12d Code

f	Employee's address and ZIP code

15 State PA	Employer's state ID number 000-0-3300	16 State wages, tips, etc. 20323.52	17 State income tax 623.94	18 Local wages, tips, etc. 20323.52	19 Local income tax 798.30	20 Locality name PHILA.

Form **W-2** Wage and Tax Statement **20--**

Department of the Treasury—Internal Revenue Service
For Privacy Act and Paperwork
Reduction Act Notice, see back of Copy D.

22222	Void ☐	a Employee's social security number 000-00-8645	For Official Use Only OMB No. 1 545-0008		
b	Employer identification number (EIN) 00-0000660		1 Wages, tips, other compensation 35125.00	2 Federal income tax withheld 2924.00	
c	Employer's name, address, and ZIP code		3 Social security wages 36625.00	4 Social security tax withheld 2270.75	

Glo-Brite Paint Company
2215 Salvador Street
Philadelphia, PA 19175-0682

5 Medicare wages and tips 36625.00	6 Medicare tax withheld 531.09
7 Social security tips	8 Allocated tips

d	Control number	9	10 Dependent care benefits

e Employee's first name and initial James C.	Last name Ferguson	Suff.	11 Nonqualified plans	12a See instructions for box 12 Code S 1500.00

13 Statutory employee ☐	Retirement plan ☒	Third-party sick pay ☐	12b Code

808 SIXTH STREET
PHILADELPHIA, PA 19106-0995

14 Other	12c Code
	12d Code

f	Employee's address and ZIP code

15 State PA	Employer's state ID number 000-0-3300	16 State wages, tips, etc. 36625.00	17 State income tax 1124.42	18 Local wages, tips, etc. 36625.00	19 Local income tax 1438.63	20 Locality name PHILA.

Form **W-2** Wage and Tax Statement **20--**

Department of the Treasury—Internal Revenue Service
For Privacy Act and Paperwork
Reduction Act Notice, see back of Copy D.

Source: Internal Revenue Service.

Transaction No. 38   (Continued)

22222	Void ☐	a Employee's social security number 000-00-4567	For Official Use Only OMB No. 1 545-0008		

b Employer identification number (EIN) 00-0000660	**1** Wages, tips, other compensation 11820.00	**2** Federal income tax withheld 1029.00

c Employer's name, address, and ZIP code	**3** Social security wages 11820.00	**4** Social security tax withheld 732.84

Glo-Brite Paint Company
2215 Salvador Street
Philadelphia, PA 19175-0682

	5 Medicare wages and tips 11820.00	**6** Medicare tax withheld 171.39
	7 Social security tips	**8** Allocated tips

d Control number	**9**	**10** Dependent care benefits

e Employee's first name and initial Catherine L.	Last name Ford	Suff.	**11** Nonqualified plans	**12a** See instructions for box 12 Code

13 Statutory employee ☐ Retirement plan ☐ Third-party sick pay ☐	**12b** Code

18 DUNDEE AVENUE
PHILADELPHIA, PA 19151-1919

	12c Code
14 Other	**12d** Code

f Employee's address and ZIP code						
15 State PA	Employer's state ID number 000-0-3300	**16** State wages, tips, etc. 11820.00	**17** State income tax 362.87	**18** Local wages, tips, etc. 11820.00	**19** Local income tax 464.28	**20** Locality name PHILA.

Form **W-2** **Wage and Tax Statement**   **20--**

Department of the Treasury—Internal Revenue Service
For Privacy Act and Paperwork
Reduction Act Notice, see back of Copy D.

22222	Void ☐	a Employee's social security number 000-00-9352	For Official Use Only OMB No. 1 545-0008		

b Employer identification number (EIN) 00-0000660	**1** Wages, tips, other compensation 12750.00	**2** Federal income tax withheld 790.00

c Employer's name, address, and ZIP code	**3** Social security wages 13500.00	**4** Social security tax withheld 837.00

Glo-Brite Paint Company
2215 Salvador Street
Philadelphia, PA 19175-0682

	5 Medicare wages and tips 13500.00	**6** Medicare tax withheld 195.78
	7 Social security tips	**8** Allocated tips

d Control number	**9**	**10** Dependent care benefits

e Employee's first name and initial Dewey W.	Last name Mann	Suff.	**11** Nonqualified plans	**12a** See instructions for box 12 Code S 750.00

13 Statutory employee ☐ Retirement plan ☒ Third-party sick pay ☐	**12b** Code

3007 BISQUE DRIVE
PHILADELPHIA, PA 19199-0718

	12c Code
14 Other	**12d** Code

f Employee's address and ZIP code						
15 State PA	Employer's state ID number 000-0-3300	**16** State wages, tips, etc. 13500.00	**17** State income tax 414.48	**18** Local wages, tips, etc. 13500.00	**19** Local income tax 530.29	**20** Locality name PHILA.

Form **W-2** **Wage and Tax Statement**   **20--**

Department of the Treasury—Internal Revenue Service
For Privacy Act and Paperwork
Reduction Act Notice, see back of Copy D.

Source: Internal Revenue Service.

Transaction No. 38   (Continued)

22222	Void ☐	a Employee's social security number 000-00-1534	For Official Use Only OMB No. 1 545-0008			
b	Employer identification number (EIN) 00-0000660		1 Wages, tips, other compensation 111138.41		2 Federal income tax withheld 27603.20	
c	Employer's name, address, and ZIP code *Glo-Brite Paint Company* *2215 Salvador Street* *Philadelphia, PA 19175-0682*		3 Social security wages 113700.00		4 Social security tax withheld 7049.40	
			5 Medicare wages and tips 116538.41		6 Medicare tax withheld 1689.80	
			7 Social security tips		8 Allocated tips	
d	Control number		9		10 Dependent care benefits	
e	Employee's first name and initial Joseph T. Last name O'Neill Suff.		11 Nonqualified plans		12a See instructions for box 12 Code **S** 5400.00	
			13 Statutory employee ☐ Retirement plan ☒ Third-party sick pay ☐		12b Code	
	2100 BROAD STREET PHILADELPHIA, PA 19121-7189		14 Other		12c Code	
					12d Code	
f	Employee's address and ZIP code					

| 15 State
PA | Employer's state ID number
000-0-3300 | 16   State wages, tips, etc.
116538.41 | 17   State income tax
3577.75 | 18   Local wages, tips, etc.
116538.41 | 19   Local income tax
4577.65 | 20   Locality name
PHILA. |

Form **W-2**   Wage and Tax Statement   **20--**

Department of the Treasury—Internal Revenue Service
For Privacy Act and Paperwork
Reduction Act Notice, see back of Copy D.

22222	Void ☐	a Employee's social security number 000-00-1223	For Official Use Only OMB No. 1 545-0008			
b	Employer identification number (EIN) 00-0000660		1 Wages, tips, other compensation 23139.30		2 Federal income tax withheld 1368.00	
c	Employer's name, address, and ZIP code *Glo-Brite Paint Company* *2215 Salvador Street* *Philadelphia, PA 19175-0682*		3 Social security wages 23739.30		4 Social security tax withheld 1471.84	
			5 Medicare wages and tips 23739.30		6 Medicare tax withheld 344.22	
			7 Social security tips		8 Allocated tips	
d	Control number		9		10 Dependent care benefits	
e	Employee's first name and initial Norman A. Last name Ryan Suff.		11 Nonqualified plans		12a See instructions for box 12 Code **S** 600.00	
			13 Statutory employee ☐ Retirement plan ☒ Third-party sick pay ☐		12b Code	
	7300 HARRISON STREET PHILADELPHIA, PA 19124-6699		14 Other Union Dues 121.00		12c Code	
					12d Code	
f	Employee's address and ZIP code					

| 15 State
PA | Employer's state ID number
000-0-3300 | 16   State wages, tips, etc.
23739.30 | 17   State income tax
728.80 | 18   Local wages, tips, etc.
23739.30 | 19   Local income tax
932.48 | 20   Locality name
PHILA. |

Form **W-2**   Wage and Tax Statement   **20--**

Department of the Treasury—Internal Revenue Service
For Privacy Act and Paperwork
Reduction Act Notice, see back of Copy D.

Source: Internal Revenue Service.

Transaction No. 38   (Continued)

22222	Void ☐	a Employee's social security number 000-00-8832	For Official Use Only OMB No. 1 545-0008		
b	Employer identification number (EIN) 00-0000660		1 Wages, tips, other compensation 28950.00		2 Federal income tax withheld 3402.00
c	Employer's name, address, and ZIP code		3 Social security wages 28950.00		4 Social security tax withheld 1794.90
	Glo-Brite Paint Company 2215 Salvador Street Philadelphia, PA 19175-0682		5 Medicare wages and tips 28950.00		6 Medicare tax withheld 419.81
			7 Social security tips		8 Allocated tips
d	Control number		9		10 Dependent care benefits
e	Employee's first name and initial Thomas J.	Last name Sokowski	Suff.	11 Nonqualified plans	12a Code
			13 Statutory employee ☐ Retirement plan ☐ Third-party sick pay ☐	12b Code
	133 CORNWELLS STREET PHILADELPHIA, PA 19171-5718		14 Other	12c Code
				12d Code
f	Employee's address and ZIP code				

15 State PA	Employer's state ID number 000-0-3300	16 State wages, tips, etc. 28950.00	17 State income tax 888.80	18 Local wages, tips, etc. 28950.00	19 Local income tax 1137.13	20 Locality name PHILA.

Form **W-2** Wage and Tax Statement   **20--**

Department of the Treasury—Internal Revenue Service
For Privacy Act and Paperwork Reduction Act Notice, see back of Copy D.

22222	Void ☐	a Employee's social security number	For Official Use Only OMB No. 1 545-0008		
b	Employer identification number (EIN) 00-0000660		1 Wages, tips, other compensation 8782.50		2 Federal income tax withheld 599.00
c	Employer's name, address, and ZIP code		3 Social security wages 8782.50		4 Social security tax withheld 544.52
	Glo-Brite Paint Company 2215 Salvador Street Philadelphia, PA 19175-0682		5 Medicare wages and tips 8782.50		6 Medicare tax withheld 127.35
			7 Social security tips		8 Allocated tips
d	Control number		9		10 Dependent care benefits
e	Employee's first name and initial STUDENT	Last name	Suff.	11 Nonqualified plans	12a Code
			13 Statutory employee ☐ Retirement plan ☐ Third-party sick pay ☐	12b Code
	7018 ERDRICK STREET PHILADELPHIA, PA 19135-8517		14 Other	12c Code
				12d Code
f	Employee's address and ZIP code				

15 State PA	Employer's state ID number 000-0-3300	16 State wages, tips, etc. 8782.50	17 State income tax 269.63	18 Local wages, tips, etc. 8782.50	19 Local income tax 344.97	20 Locality name PHILA.

Form **W-2** Wage and Tax Statement   **20--**

Department of the Treasury—Internal Revenue Service
For Privacy Act and Paperwork Reduction Act Notice, see back of Copy D.

Source: Internal Revenue Service.

Transaction No. 38   (Concluded)

22222	Void ☐	a Employee's social security number 000-00-1587	For Official Use Only OMB No. 1 545-0008		
b Employer identification number (EIN) 00-0000660			**1** Wages, tips, other compensation 2280.00	**2** Federal income tax withheld 240.00	
c Employer's name, address, and ZIP code			**3** Social security wages 2280.00	**4** Social security tax withheld 141.36	
Glo-Brite Paint Company *2215 Salvador Street* *Philadelphia, PA 19175-0682*			**5** Medicare wages and tips 2280.00	**6** Medicare tax withheld 33.06	
			7 Social security tips	**8** Allocated tips	
d Control number			**9**	**10** Dependent care benefits	
e Employee's first name and initial Beth A.	Last name Woods	Suff.	**11** Nonqualified plans	**12a** See instructions for box 12 Code	
			13 Statutory employee ☐ Retirement plan ☐ Third-party sick pay ☐	**12b** Code	
8102 FRANKLIN COURT PHILADELPHIA, PA 19105-0915			**14** Other	**12c** Code	
				12d Code	
f Employee's address and ZIP code					

15 State PA	Employer's state ID number 000-0-3300	**16** State wages, tips, etc. 2280.00	**17** State income tax 70.00	**18** Local wages, tips, etc. 2280.00	**19** Local income tax 89.56	**20** Locality name PHILA.

Form **W-2** Wage and Tax Statement   **20--**

Department of the Treasury—Internal Revenue Service
For Privacy Act and Paperwork
Reduction Act Notice, see back of Copy D.

22222	Void ☐	a Employee's social security number 000-00-6057	For Official Use Only OMB No. 1 545-0008		
b Employer identification number (EIN) 00-0000660			**1** Wages, tips, other compensation 807.70	**2** Federal income tax withheld 69.00	
c Employer's name, address, and ZIP code			**3** Social security wages 807.70	**4** Social security tax withheld 50.08	
Glo-Brite Paint Company *2215 Salvador Street* *Philadelphia, PA 19175-0682*			**5** Medicare wages and tips 807.70	**6** Medicare tax withheld 11.71	
			7 Social security tips	**8** Allocated tips	
d Control number			**9**	**10** Dependent care benefits	
e Employee's first name and initial Paul W.	Last name Young	Suff.	**11** Nonqualified plans	**12a** See instructions for box 12 Code	
			13 Statutory employee ☐ Retirement plan ☐ Third-party sick pay ☐	**12b** Code	
7936 HOLMES DRIVE PHILADELPHIA, PA 19107-6107			**14** Other	**12c** Code	
				12d Code	
f Employee's address and ZIP code					

15 State PA	Employer's state ID number 000-0-3300	**16** State wages, tips, etc. 807.70	**17** State income tax 24.80	**18** Local wages, tips, etc. 807.70	**19** Local income tax 31.73	**20** Locality name PHILA.

Form **W-2** Wage and Tax Statement   **20--**

Department of the Treasury—Internal Revenue Service
For Privacy Act and Paperwork
Reduction Act Notice, see back of Copy D.

Source: Internal Revenue Service.

Transaction No. 39

DO NOT STAPLE

33333	a Control number	For Official Use Only ▶ OMB No. 1545-0008		

b Kind of Payer (Check one): 941 [X] Military [ ] 943 [ ] 944 [ ] CT-1 [ ] Hshld. emp. [ ] Medicare govt. emp. [ ]

Kind of Employer (Check one): None apply [X] 501c non-govt. [ ] State/local non-501c [ ] State/local 501c [ ] Federal govt. [ ] Third-party sick pay (Check if applicable) [ ]

c Total number of Forms W-2	d Establishment number	1 Wages, tips, other compensation	2 Federal income tax withheld
12		280825.64*	42421.20

e Employer identification number (EIN)	3 Social security wages	4 Social security tax withheld
	287662.39**	17835.07

f Employer's name	5 Medicare wages and tips	6 Medicare tax withheld
GLO-BRITE PAINT COMPANY	290500.80	4212.35

	7 Social security tips	8 Allocated tips
2215 SALVADOR STREET PHILADELPHIA, PA 19175-0682	9	10 Dependent care benefits
	11 Nonqualified plans	12a Deferred compensation 8250.00
g Employer's address and ZIP code		
h Other EIN used this year	13 For third-party sick pay use only	12b

15 State	Employer's state ID number	14 Income tax withheld by payer of third-party sick pay
PA	000-0-3300	

16 State wages, tips, etc.	17 State income tax	18 Local wages, tips, etc.	19 Local income tax
289075.64***	8874.76	289075.64	11354.86

Contact person	Telephone number	For Official Use Only
Student		
Email address	Fax number	

Under penalties of perjury, I declare that I have examined this return and accompanying documents and, to the best of my knowledge and belief, they are true, correct, and complete.

Signature ▶ *Joseph T. O'Neill*   Title ▶ **President**   Date ▶ 2/1/--

Form **W-3** **Transmittal of Wage and Tax Statements**   **20 - -**   Department of the Treasury Internal Revenue Service

*$290,500.80 – $1,425.16 (Russell's earnings on December 14) – $8,250.00 (SIMPLE Contributions).

**$290,500.80 – $2,838.41 (O'Neill's nontaxable wages for OASDI).

***$290,500.80 – $1,425.16.

Transaction No. 40

pennsylvania DEPARTMENT OF REVENUE REV-1667 R AS (08-10) (I)

W-2 TRANSMITTAL DUE DATE JANUARY 31

ENTITY ID (EIN)

0 0 0 0 0 0 6 6 0

EMPLOYER ACCOUNT ID

0 0 0 0 3 3 0 0

YEAR 2 0 - -

Part I W-2 RECONCILIATION

1a	Number of W-2 forms attached	12
1b	Number of 1099 forms with PA withholding tax	
1c	Number of W-2s reported on magnetic tape(s)	
1d	Number of W-2s reported on compact discs	
2	Total compensation subject to PA withholding tax	$ 2 8 9 0 7 5 . 6 4
3	PA INCOME TAX WITHHELD	$ 8 8 7 4 . 7 6

Part II ANNUAL RECONCILIATION

	Wages paid subject to PA withholding tax	PA tax withheld
1st Quarter	34088.75	1046.52
2nd Quarter	45535.62	1397.94
3rd Quarter	62600.20	1921.83
4th Quarter	146851.07*	4508.47
TOTAL	289075.64	8874.76

DATE 2/1/- -	DAYTIME TELEPHONE # (215) 555-9559	EXT.	TITLE President

Part III FOR MEDIA REPORTING

NUMBER OF TAPES NUMBER OF CD's

BUSINESS NAME AND ADDRESS

LEGAL NAME Glo-Brite Paint Company

TRADE NAME

ADDRESS 2215 Salvador Street

CITY, STATE, ZIP Philadelphia, PA 19175-0682

DO NOT SEND PAYMENT WITH THIS FORM.

Attach adding machine tape(s) or some acceptable listing of tax withheld as reported on accompanying W-2 form(s) to substantiate reported PA withholding tax. This tape or listing applies only to paper W-2s, not media reporting.

SIGNATURE *Joseph T. O'Neill*

Source: PA Department of Revenue.

*$148,276.23 – $1,425.16 (Russell's earnings on December 14).

Transaction No. 41

9595   ☐ VOID   ☐ CORRECTED

PAYER'S name, street address, city or town, province or state, country, ZIP or foreign postal code, and telephone no.	1 Rents $	OMB No. 1545-0115	**Miscellaneous Income**
GLO-BRITE PAINT COMPANY 2215 SALVADOR ST PHILADELPHIA, PA 19175-0682	2 Royalties $	20-- / Form **1099-MISC**	
	3 Other income $ 1425.16	4 Federal income tax withheld $	Copy A For **Internal Revenue Service Center**

PAYER'S federal identification number	RECIPIENT'S identification number	5 Fishing boat proceeds $	6 Medical and health care payments $	File with Form 1096.
00-0000660	00-00-6637			

RECIPIENT'S name The Estate of Virginia Aloise Russell	7 Nonemployee compensation $	8 Substitute payments in lieu of dividends or interest $	For Privacy Act and Paperwork Reduction Act Notice, see the
Street address (including apt. no.) 8004 Dowling Road	9 Payer made direct sales of $5,000 or more of consumer products to a buyer (recipient) for resale ▶ ☐	10 Crop insurance proceeds $	**20-- General Instructions for Certain**
City or town, province or state, country, and ZIP or foreign postal code PHILADELPHIA, PA 19135-9001	11 Foreign tax paid $	12 Foreign country or U.S. possession	**Information Returns.**
Account number (see instructions) 2nd TIN not. ☐	13 Excess golden parachute payments $	14 Gross proceeds paid to an attorney $	

15a Section 409A deferrals $	15b Section 409A income $	16 State tax withheld $	17 State/Payer's state no.	18 State income $

Form **1099-MISC**   Cat. No. 14425J   www.irs.gov/form1099misc   Department of the Treasury - Internal Revenue Service

Do Not Cut or Separate Forms on This Page — Do Not Cut or Separate Forms on This Page

Source: Internal Revenue Service.

Transaction No. 42

Do Not Staple   6969

Form **1096**	Annual Summary and Transmittal of U.S. Information Returns	OMB No. 1545-0108
Department of the Treasury Internal Revenue Service		20--

FILER'S name

GLO-BRITE PAINT COMPANY

Street address (including room or suite number)

2215 SALVADOR ST

City or town, province or state, country, and ZIP or foreign postal code

PHILADELPHIA, PA 19175-0682

Name of person to contact	Telephone number	**For Official Use Only**
Student	(215) 555-9559	
Email address	Fax number	

1 Employer identification number	2 Social security number	3 Total number of forms	4 Federal income tax withheld	5 Total amount reported with this Form 1096
00-0000660		1	$ 0	$ 1425.16

6 Enter an "X" in only one box below to indicate the type of form being filed.

7 If this is your **final return**, enter an "X" here . . . . . . ▶ ☐

W-2G 32	1097-BTC 50	1098 81	1098-C 78	1098-E 84	1098-T 83	1099-A 80	1099-B 79	1099-C 85	1099-CAP 73	1099-DIV 91	1099-G 86	1099-H 71	1099-INT 92	1099-K 10	1099-LTC 93	1099-MISC 95	1099-OID 96
☐	☐	☐	☐	☐	☐	☐	☐	☐	☐	☐	☐	☐	☐	☐	☐	☒	☐

1099-PATR 97	1099-Q 31	1099-R 98	1099-S 75	1099-SA 94	3921 25	3922 26	5498 28	5498-ESA 72	5498-SA 27
☐	☐	☐	☐	☐	☐	☐	☐	☐	☐

Return this entire page to the Internal Revenue Service. Photocopies are not acceptable.

Under penalties of perjury, I declare that I have examined this return and accompanying documents, and, to the best of my knowledge and belief, they are true, correct, and complete.

Signature ▶ *Joseph T. O'Neill*   Title ▶ President   Date ▶ 2/1/--

Source: Internal Revenue Service.

Questions on the Payroll Project (p. 7–21)

1. Total of employer's FICA tax entries $11,167.14
   FUTA tax 45.59
   SUTA tax 500.19
   Total payroll tax expense $11,712.92*
      *Debits into Payroll Taxes (Account No. 56) during fourth quarter.

2. O'Neill's total earnings from the six payrolls in the fourth quarter were $73,846.14. This total amount was taxable for the HI part of the social security tax. However, since O'Neill passed the $113,700 ceiling during the fourth quarter, only $71,007.73 was taxable for the OASDI part of the social security tax. No FUTA or SUTA taxes were incurred because O'Neill's earnings had already surpassed the taxable bases.

   Payroll taxes—O'Neill:

OASDI—$71,007.73 × 0.062	=	$4,402.48
HI—$73,846.14 × 0.0145	=	1,070.77
Total		$5,473.25

3. $499.50

4.
Bonno	$1,016.18
Ferguson	1,831.25
Ford	591.00
Mann	675.00
Ryan	1,186.97
Sokowski	1,447.50
Student	439.13
Woods	114.00
Young	40.39
Total	$7,341.42

5. Calculation of accrued salaries and wages:

Administrative Salaries	Biweekly Gross Earnings	14 Days' Accrual
O'Neill	$2,307.69	$3,230.77*

   *($2,307.69 × 26 ÷ 260 × 14 = $3,230.77)

Office Salaries		
Ford	$ 960.00	$1,344.00
Student (104* hrs. × $7.50)	540.00	780.00
Woods	1,200.00	1,680.00
Zimmerman	660.00	660.00
		$4,464.00

   *(36 hours/wk × 2 + 32 hours)

Sales Salaries	Gross Earnings	Biweekly 14 Days' Accrual
Ferguson...	$2,250.00	$3,150.00
Mann..	1,350.00	1,890.00
Young	807.70	1,130.78
		$6,170.78

Plant Wages

Bonno	112 hrs. × $17.65	$1,976.80
Ryan	112 hrs. × $18.00	2,016.00
Sokowski...	$2,050.00	2,870.00
		$6,862.80

Adjusting Entry

20--				
Dec.	31	Administrative Salaries	3,230.77	
		Office Salaries	4,464.00	
		Sales Salaries	6,170.78	
		Plant Wages	6,862.80	
		Salaries and Wages Payable		20,728.35

6.	Bonno...	$ 1,412.00
	Ferguson...	3,375.00
	Ford..	960.00
	Mann...	675.00
	O'Neill	4,615.38
	Ryan..	1,440.00
	Sokowski...	2,050.00
	Student..	540.00
	Total..	$15,067.38

Adjusting Entry

20--				
Dec.	31	Vacation Benefits Expense..................	15,067.38	
		Vacation Benefits Payable		15,067.38

APPENDIX A

PAYROLL PROJECT SOLUTION

NOTES TO THE INSTRUCTOR

This edition of *Payroll Accounting* contains two different options for student solution: the complete, full version of the payroll project and a short version. Both versions are identical except the short version requires only the completion of the December payrolls (as well as the last quarter and annual tax reports and forms). Be sure to instruct your students as to which of the two versions you want them to complete.

To protect the short version's beginning balance data from use by students required to complete the full version, the following changes have been included in this version of *Payroll Accounting*: (1) The short version's beginning balance file (which is the solution file from the last pay period in November) has been given a special code to indicate that this is the "short version" beginning balance file; (2) the computer software looks for this special code in the file—if it finds it, it appends "Short Version" to the Problem Name field; and (3) the software includes this special code and the appended Problem Name in each of the student's saved files.

If your students save their files to be checked by the Inspector software, the Inspector's reports that are displayed/printed will show "Payroll Project Short Version" as the problem name and "Short Version" appended to the student's file name in the report headings. Likewise, if the students print hard copies of their reports from the *Payroll Accounting 2014* software, they will also show "Payroll Project Short Version." Therefore, you can easily tell if any student attempts to use the short version beginning balance file and/or any of their solution files instead of the beginning balance file required to solve the complete, full version of the payroll project.

Note: If your students are using this product as a distance or online course, and you wish to have them send you their completed solution files for electronic checking with the *Payroll 2014 Inspector* software, simply provide them with your e-mail address. The students will send you their completed solution files as an e-mail attachment. Save these file(s) attachments (by clicking on the attachment with the right mouse button and choosing the Save As menu item) to a folder on your hard drive that you have created for the class. Use the *Payroll 2014 Inspector* software to electronically check these files. When the detailed report of the students' results appears:

1. Click on the Copy command button.
2. When the Copy Report to Clipboard dialog box appears, select the Word Processor option, and click on OK.
3. A dialog box will appear indicating that the copy was successful; click on OK.
4. Switch to your e-mail application, position the insertion point at the location where you would like the data to appear, and choose Paste from the Edit menu.
5. Complete your e-mail by entering the appropriate student's e-mail address, a subject line, and any other information (or paste the report into the student's original e-mail and return the results as a reply).

OCTOBER 9 PAYROLL

Glo-Brite Paint Company
Employee List
10/09/--

Emp. No.	Employee Name/Address	Soc. Sec./ Mar. Stat.	# Pay Periods	G.L. Acct.	Salary/ Rate
100	BONNO, Anthony Victor 694 Bristol Avenue Philadelphia, PA 19135-0617	000-00-3481 Married W/H 4	26	54	17.65
110	FERGUSON, James Claude 808 Sixth Street Philadelphia, PA 19106-0995	000-00-8645 Married W/H 5	26	53	2,250.00
120	FORD, Catherine Louise 18 Dundee Avenue Philadelphia, PA 19151-1919	000-00-4567 Single W/H 2	26	52	900.00
130	MANN, Dewey Wilson 3007 Bisque Drive Philadelphia, PA 19199-0718	000-00-9352 Married W/H 4	26	53	1,350.00
140	O'NEILL, Joseph Tyler 2100 Broad Street Philadelphia, PA 19121-7189	000-00-1534 Married W/H 3	26	51	2,307.69
150	RUSSELL, Virginia Aloise 8004 Dowling Road Philadelphia, PA 19135-9001	000-00-6337 Single W/H 1	26	52	690.00
160	RYAN, Norman Allen 7300 Harrison Street Philadelphia, PA 19124-6699	000-00-1233 Married W/H 4	26	54	18.00
170	SOKOWSKI, Thomas James 133 Cornwells Street Philadelphia, PA 19171-5718	000-00-8832 Married W/H 2	26	54	2,050.00
180	STUDENT 7018 Erdrick Street Philadelphia, PA 19135-8517	000-00-5555 Single W/H 1	26	52	7.50
190	WILLIAMS, Ruth Virginia 9433 State Street Philadelphia, PA 19149-0819	000-00-6741 Single W/H 0	26	52	1,223.08

Glo-Brite Paint Company
Payroll Report
10/09/--

		Current	Quarterly	Yearly
100-BONNO, Anthony Victor	Gross Pay	1,412.00	1,412.00	12,733.95
54-Plant	FIT	52.35	52.35	862.35
Married Acct. 54	SIT	43.35	43.35	390.94
W/H 4 000-00-3481	Soc. Sec.—OASDI	87.54	87.54	789.50
Pay Periods 26	Medicare—HI	20.47	20.47	184.64
Salary	CIT	55.46	55.46	500.19
Hourly Rate 17.65	Group Ins.			144.80
Reg. Hours 80.00	Union Dues	8.00	8.00	80.00
O.T. Hours	Simple Plan			
Check Number 672	Employee SUTA	0.99	0.99	8.92
Check Date 10/09/--	Net Pay	1,143.84	1,143.84	9,772.61
110-FERGUSON, James Claude	Gross Pay	2,250.00	2,250.00	25,375.00
53-Sales	FIT	148.56	148.56	2,439.56
Married Acct. 53	SIT	69.08	69.08	779.02
W/H 5 000-00-8645	Soc. Sec.—OASDI	139.50	139.50	1,573.25
Pay Periods 26	Medicare—HI	32.63	32.63	367.94
Salary 2,250.00	CIT	88.38	88.38	996.73
Hourly Rate	Group Ins.			132.30
Reg. Hours	Union Dues			
O.T. Hours	Simple Plan			
Check Number 673	Employee SUTA	1.58	1.58	17.77
Check Date 10/09/--	Net Pay	1,770.27	1,770.27	19,068.43
120-FORD, Catherine Louise	Gross Pay	900.00	900.00	7,200.00
52-Office	FIT	62.45	62.45	701.45
Single Acct. 52	SIT	27.63	27.63	221.04
W/H 2 000-00-4567	Soc. Sec.—OASDI	55.80	55.80	446.40
Pay Periods 26	Medicare—HI	13.05	13.05	104.40
Salary 900.00	CIT	35.35	35.35	282.81
Hourly Rate	Group Ins.			37.80
Reg. Hours	Union Dues			
O.T. Hours	Simple Plan			
Check Number 674	Employee SUTA	0.63	0.63	5.04
Check Date 10/09/--	Net Pay	705.09	705.09	5,401.06
130-MANN, Dewey Wilson	Gross Pay	1,350.00	1,350.00	6,750.00
53-Sales	FIT	46.15	46.15	378.15
Married Acct. 53	SIT	41.45	41.45	207.23
W/H 4 000-00-9352	Soc. Sec.—OASDI	83.70	83.70	418.50
Pay Periods 26	Medicare—HI	19.58	19.58	97.88
Salary 1,350.00	CIT	53.03	53.03	265.14
Hourly Rate	Group Ins.			31.50
Reg. Hours	Union Dues			
O.T. Hours	Simple Plan			
Check Number 675	Employee SUTA	0.95	0.95	4.73
Check Date 10/09/--	Net Pay	1,105.14	1,105.14	5,346.87

		Current	Quarterly	Yearly
140-O'NEILL, Joseph Tyler	Gross Pay	2,307.69	2,307.69	44,999.96
51-Administrative	FIT	199.90	199.90	6,315.90
Married Acct. 51	SIT	70.85	70.85	1,381.50
W/H 3 000-00-1534	Soc. Sec.—OASDI	143.08	143.08	2,790.00
Pay Periods 26	Medicare—HI	33.46	33.46	652.50
Salary 2,307.69	CIT	90.65	90.65	1,767.60
Hourly Rate	Group Ins.			202.50
Reg. Hours	Union Dues			
O.T. Hours	Simple Plan			
Check Number 676	Employee SUTA	1.62	1.62	31.50
Check Date 10/09/--	Net Pay	1,768.13	1,768.13	31,858.46
150-RUSSELL, Virginia Aloise	Gross Pay	690.00	690.00	6,930.00
52-Office	FIT	52.30	52.30	694.30
Single Acct. 52	SIT	21.18	21.18	212.74
W/H 1 000-00-6337	Soc. Sec.—OASDI	42.78	42.78	429.66
Pay Periods 26	Medicare—HI	10.01	10.01	100.49
Salary 690.00	CIT	27.10	27.10	272.21
Hourly Rate	Group Ins.			31.50
Reg. Hours	Union Dues			
O.T. Hours	Simple Plan			
Check Number 677	Employee SUTA	0.48	0.48	4.85
Check Date 10/09/--	Net Pay	536.15	536.15	5,184.25
160-RYAN, Norman Allen	Gross Pay	1,440.00	1,440.00	16,125.30
54-Plant	FIT	55.15	55.15	1,125.15
Married Acct. 54	SIT	44.21	44.21	495.05
W/H 4 000-00-1233	Soc. Sec.—OASDI	89.28	89.28	999.77
Pay Periods 26	Medicare—HI	20.88	20.88	233.82
Salary	CIT	56.56	56.56	633.40
Hourly Rate 18.00	Group Ins.			163.70
Reg. Hours 80.00	Union Dues	8.00	8.00	80.00
O.T. Hours	Simple Plan			
Check Number 678	Employee SUTA	1.01	1.01	11.29
Check Date 10/09/--	Net Pay	1,164.91	1,164.91	12,383.12
170-SOKOWSKI, Thomas James	Gross Pay	2,050.00	2,050.00	18,700.00
54-Plant	FIT	182.60	182.60	2,184.60
Married Acct. 54	SIT	62.94	62.94	574.10
W/H 2 000-00-8832	Soc. Sec.—OASDI	127.10	127.10	1,159.40
Pay Periods 26	Medicare—HI	29.73	29.73	271.16
Salary 2,050.00	CIT	80.52	80.52	734.53
Hourly Rate	Group Ins.			94.50
Reg. Hours	Union Dues			
O.T. Hours	Simple Plan			
Check Number 679	Employee SUTA	1.44	1.44	13.10
Check Date 10/09/--	Net Pay	1,565.67	1,565.67	13,668.61
180-STUDENT	Gross Pay	540.00	540.00	6,090.00
52-Office	FIT	31.31	31.31	440.31
Single Acct. 52	SIT	16.58	16.58	186.96
W/H 1 000-00-5555	Soc. Sec.—OASDI	33.48	33.48	377.58
Pay Periods 26	Medicare—HI	7.83	7.83	88.31
Salary	CIT	21.21	21.21	239.21
Hourly Rate 7.50	Group Ins.			32.40
Reg. Hours 72.00	Union Dues			
O.T. Hours	Simple Plan			
Check Number 680	Employee SUTA	0.38	0.38	4.27
Check Date 10/09/--	Net Pay	429.21	429.21	4,720.96

		Current	Quarterly	Yearly
190-WILLIAMS, Ruth Virginia	Gross Pay	1,223.08	1,223.08	11,483.08
52-Office	FIT	153.61	153.61	1,759.61
Single Acct. 52	SIT	37.55	37.55	352.53
W/H 0 000-00-6741	Soc. Sec.—OASDI	75.83	75.83	711.95
Pay Periods 26	Medicare—HI	17.73	17.73	166.50
Salary 1,223.08	CIT	48.04	48.04	451.05
Hourly Rate	Group Ins.			59.40
Reg. Hours	Union Dues			
O.T. Hours	Simple Plan			
Check Number 681	Employee SUTA	0.86	0.86	8.04
Check Date 10/09/--	Net Pay	889.46	889.46	7,974.00
Payroll Summary	Gross Pay	14,162.77	14,162.77	156,387.29
	FIT	984.38	984.38	16,901.38
	SIT	434.82	434.82	4,801.11
	Soc. Sec.—OASDI	878.09	878.09	9,696.01
	Medicare—HI	205.37	205.37	2,267.64
	CIT	556.30	556.30	6,142.87
	Group Ins.			930.40
	Union Dues	16.00	16.00	160.00
	Simple Plan			
	Employee SUTA	9.94	9.94	109.51
	Net Pay	11,077.87	11,077.87	115,378.37

Glo-Brite Paint Company
General Journal
10/09/--

Date	Refer.	Acct.	Title	Debit	Credit
10/09	Payroll	54	Plant Wages	4,902.00	
10/09	Payroll	53	Sales Salaries	3,600.00	
10/09	Payroll	52	Office Salaries	3,353.08	
10/09	Payroll	51	Administrative Salaries	2,307.69	
10/09	Payroll	24	Employees FIT Payable		984.38
10/09	Payroll	25	Employees SIT Payable		434.82
10/09	Payroll	20.1	FICA Taxes Payable—OASDI		878.09
10/09	Payroll	20.2	FICA Taxes Payable—HI		205.37
10/09	Payroll	26	Employees CIT Payable		556.30
10/09	Payroll	28	Union Dues Payable		16.00
10/09	Payroll	25.1	Employees SUTA Payable		9.94
10/09	Payroll	12	Payroll Cash		11,077.87
10/09	Pay. Tax	56	Payroll Taxes	1,231.14	
10/09	Pay. Tax	20.1	FICA Taxes Payable—OASDI		878.09
10/09	Pay. Tax	20.2	FICA Taxes Payable—HI		205.36
10/09	Pay. Tax	22	SUTA Taxes Payable		128.01
10/09	Pay. Tax	21	FUTA Taxes Payable		19.68
10/09	General	12	Payroll Cash	11,077.87	
10/09	General	11	Cash		11,077.87
	Totals			26,471.78	26,471.78

Glo-Brite Paint Company
General Ledger
10/09/--

Account	Journal	Date	Refer.	Debit	Credit	Balance	
11-Cash							
	Balance Forward					199,846.33	Dr
	General	10/09	General		11,077.87	188,768.46	Dr
12-Payroll Cash							
	General	10/09	Payroll		11,077.87	11,077.87	Cr
	General	10/09	General	11,077.87		.00	
20.1-FICA Taxes Payable—OASDI							
	General	10/09	Payroll		878.09	878.09	Cr
	General	10/09	Pay. Tax		878.09	1,756.18	Cr

Account Journal	Date	Refer.	Debit	Credit	Balance	
20.2-FICA Taxes Payable—HI						
General	10/09	Payroll		205.37	205.37	Cr
General	10/09	Pay. Tax		205.36	410.73	Cr
21-FUTA Taxes Payable						
Balance Forward					392.94	Cr
General	10/09	Pay. Tax		19.68	412.62	Cr
22-SUTA Taxes Payable						
General	10/09	Pay. Tax		128.01	128.01	Cr
24-Employees FIT Payable						
General	10/09	Payroll		984.38	984.38	Cr
25-Employees SIT Payable						
General	10/09	Payroll		434.82	434.82	Cr
25.1-Employees SUTA Payable						
General	10/09	Payroll		9.94	9.94	Cr
26-Employees CIT Payable						
General	10/09	Payroll		556.30	556.30	Cr
27-Grp. Ins. Prem. Collected						
*** No Activity **					.00	
28-Union Dues Payable						
General	10/09	Payroll		16.00	16.00	Cr
29-Simple Contrib. Payable						
*** No Activity **					.00	
51-Administrative Salaries						
Balance Forward					42,692.27	Dr
General	10/09	Payroll	2,307.69		44,999.96	Dr
52-Office Salaries						
Balance Forward					28,350.00	Dr
General	10/09	Payroll	3,353.08		31,703.08	Dr
53-Sales Salaries						
Balance Forward					28,525.00	Dr
General	10/09	Payroll	3,600.00		32,125.00	Dr

Account	Journal	Date	Refer.	Debit	Credit	Balance	
54-Plant Wages							
	Balance Forward					42,657.30	Dr
	General	10/09	Payroll	4,902.00		47,559.30	Dr
56-Payroll Taxes							
	Balance Forward					14,013.23	Dr
	General	10/09	Pay. Tax	1,231.14		15,244.37	Dr

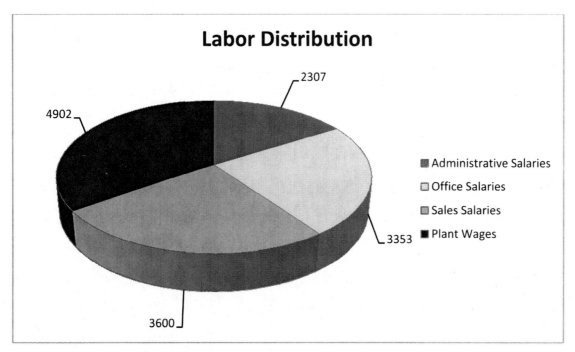

Student Audit Test: October 9 Payroll

Payroll Report
1. 5
2. $1,440.00
3. $17.73
4. $11,077.87
5. $4,801.11

Journal Entries Report
6. $3,353.08
7. $1,231.14
8. $11,077.87

General Ledger
9. $188,768.46
10. $44,999.96

OCTOBER 23 PAYROLL

Glo-Brite Paint Company
Payroll Report
10/23/--

		Current	Quarterly	Yearly
100-BONNO, Anthony Victor	Gross Pay	1,517.90	2,929.90	14,251.85
54-Plant	FIT	62.94	115.29	925.29
Married Acct. 54	SIT	46.60	89.95	437.54
W/H 4 000-00-3481	Soc. Sec.—OASDI	94.11	181.65	883.61
Pay Periods 26	Medicare—HI	22.01	42.48	206.65
Salary	CIT	59.62	115.08	559.81
Hourly Rate 17.65	Group Ins.	16.50	16.50	161.30
Reg. Hours 80.00	Union Dues	8.00	16.00	88.00
O.T. Hours 4.00	Simple Plan			
Check Number 682	Employee SUTA	1.06	2.05	9.98
Check Date 10/23/--	Net Pay	1,207.06	2,350.90	10,979.67
110-FERGUSON, James Claude	Gross Pay	2,250.00	4,500.00	27,625.00
53-Sales	FIT	148.56	297.12	2,588.12
Married Acct. 53	SIT	69.08	138.16	848.10
W/H 5 000-00-8645	Soc. Sec.—OASDI	139.50	279.00	1,712.75
Pay Periods 26	Medicare—HI	32.63	65.26	400.57
Salary 2,250.00	CIT	88.38	176.76	1,085.11
Hourly Rate	Group Ins.	26.40	26.40	158.70
Reg. Hours	Union Dues			
O.T. Hours	Simple Plan			
Check Number 683	Employee SUTA	1.58	3.16	19.35
Check Date 10/23/--	Net Pay	1,743.87	3,514.14	20,812.30
120-FORD, Catherine Louise	Gross Pay	900.00	1,800.00	8,100.00
52-Office	FIT	62.45	124.90	763.90
Single Acct. 52	SIT	27.63	55.26	248.67
W/H 2 000-00-4567	Soc. Sec.—OASDI	55.80	111.60	502.20
Pay Periods 26	Medicare—HI	13.05	26.10	117.45
Salary 900.00	CIT	35.35	70.70	318.16
Hourly Rate	Group Ins.	10.50	10.50	48.30
Reg. Hours	Union Dues			
O.T. Hours	Simple Plan			
Check Number 684	Employee SUTA	0.63	1.26	5.67
Check Date 10/23/--	Net Pay	694.59	1,399.68	6,095.65
130-MANN, Dewey Wilson	Gross Pay	1,350.00	2,700.00	8,100.00
53-Sales	FIT	46.15	92.30	424.30
Married Acct. 53	SIT	41.45	82.90	248.68
W/H 4 000-00-9352	Soc. Sec.—OASDI	83.70	167.40	502.20
Pay Periods 26	Medicare—HI	19.58	39.16	117.46
Salary 1,350.00	CIT	53.03	106.06	318.17
Hourly Rate	Group Ins.	15.90	15.90	47.40
Reg. Hours	Union Dues			
O.T. Hours	Simple Plan			
Check Number 685	Employee SUTA	0.95	1.90	5.68
Check Date 10/23/--	Net Pay	1,089.24	2,194.38	6,436.11

		Current	Quarterly	Yearly
140-O'NEILL, Joseph Tyler	Gross Pay	2,307.69	4,615.38	47,307.65
51-Administrative	FIT	199.90	399.80	6,515.80
Married Acct. 51	SIT	70.85	141.70	1,452.35
W/H 3 000-00-1534	Soc. Sec.—OASDI	143.08	286.16	2,933.08
Pay Periods 26	Medicare—HI	33.46	66.92	685.96
Salary 2,307.69	CIT	90.65	181.30	1,858.25
Hourly Rate	Group Ins.	27.00	27.00	229.50
Reg. Hours	Union Dues			
O.T. Hours	Simple Plan			
Check Number 686	Employee SUTA	1.62	3.24	33.12
Check Date 10/23/--	Net Pay	1,741.13	3,509.26	33,599.59
150-RUSSELL, Virginia Aloise	Gross Pay	690.00	1,380.00	7,620.00
52-Office	FIT	52.30	104.60	746.60
Single Acct. 52	SIT	21.18	42.36	233.92
W/H 1 000-00-6337	Soc. Sec.—OASDI	42.78	85.56	472.44
Pay Periods 26	Medicare—HI	10.01	20.02	110.50
Salary 690.00	CIT	27.10	54.20	299.31
Hourly Rate	Group Ins.	8.10	8.10	39.60
Reg. Hours	Union Dues			
O.T. Hours	Simple Plan			
Check Number 687	Employee SUTA	0.48	0.96	5.33
Check Date 10/23/--	Net Pay	528.05	1,064.20	5,712.30
160-RYAN, Norman Allen	Gross Pay	1,656.00	3,096.00	17,781.30
54-Plant	FIT	80.80	135.95	1,205.95
Married Acct. 54	SIT	50.84	95.05	545.89
W/H 4 000-00-1233	Soc. Sec.—OASDI	102.67	191.95	1,102.44
Pay Periods 26	Medicare—HI	24.01	44.89	257.83
Salary	CIT	65.05	121.61	698.45
Hourly Rate 18.00	Group Ins.	16.80	16.80	180.50
Reg. Hours 80.00	Union Dues	8.00	16.00	88.00
O.T. Hours 8.00	Simple Plan			
Check Number 688	Employee SUTA	1.16	2.17	12.45
Check Date 10/23/--	Net Pay	1,306.67	2,471.58	13,689.79
170-SOKOWSKI, Thomas James	Gross Pay	2,050.00	4,100.00	20,750.00
54-Plant	FIT	182.60	365.20	2,367.20
Married Acct. 54	SIT	62.94	125.88	637.04
W/H 2 000-00-8832	Soc. Sec.—OASDI	127.10	254.20	1,286.50
Pay Periods 26	Medicare—HI	29.73	59.46	300.89
Salary 2,050.00	CIT	80.52	161.04	815.05
Hourly Rate	Group Ins.	24.00	24.00	118.50
Reg. Hours	Union Dues			
O.T. Hours	Simple Plan			
Check Number 689	Employee SUTA	1.44	2.88	14.54
Check Date 10/23/--	Net Pay	1,541.67	3,107.34	15,210.28
180-STUDENT	Gross Pay	540.00	1,080.00	6,630.00
52-Office	FIT	31.31	62.62	471.62
Single Acct. 52	SIT	16.58	33.16	203.54
W/H 1 000-00-5555	Soc. Sec.—OASDI	33.48	66.96	411.06
Pay Periods 26	Medicare—HI	7.83	15.66	96.14
Salary	CIT	21.21	42.42	260.42
Hourly Rate 7.50	Group Ins.	6.30	6.30	38.70
Reg. Hours 72.00	Union Dues			
O.T. Hours	Simple Plan			
Check Number 690	Employee SUTA	0.38	0.76	4.65
Check Date 10/23/--	Net Pay	422.91	852.12	5,143.87

		Current	Quarterly	Yearly
190-WILLIAMS, Ruth Virginia	Gross Pay	1,223.08	2,446.16	12,706.16
52-Office	FIT	153.61	307.22	1,913.22
Single Acct. 52	SIT	37.55	75.10	390.08
W/H 0 000-00-6741	Soc. Sec.—OASDI	75.83	151.66	787.78
Pay Periods 26	Medicare—HI	17.73	35.46	184.23
Salary 1,223.08	CIT	48.04	96.08	499.09
Hourly Rate	Group Ins.	14.40	14.40	73.80
Reg. Hours	Union Dues			
O.T. Hours	Simple Plan			
Check Number 691	Employee SUTA	0.86	1.72	8.90
Check Date 10/23/--	Net Pay	875.06	1,764.52	8,849.06
Payroll Summary	Gross Pay	14,484.67	28,647.44	170,871.96
	FIT	1,020.62	2,005.00	17,922.00
	SIT	444.70	879.52	5,245.81
	Soc. Sec.—OASDI	898.05	1,776.14	10,594.06
	Medicare—HI	210.04	415.41	2,477.68
	CIT	568.95	1,125.25	6,711.82
	Group Ins.	165.90	165.90	1,096.30
	Union Dues	16.00	32.00	176.00
	Simple Plan			
	Employee SUTA	10.16	20.10	119.67
	Net Pay	11,150.25	22,228.12	126,528.62

Glo-Brite Paint Company
General Journal
10/23/--

Date	Refer.	Acct.	Title	Debit	Credit
10/20	General	25	Employees SIT Payable	434.82	
10/20	General	11	Cash		434.82
10/23	Payroll	54	Plant Wages	5,223.90	
10/23	Payroll	53	Sales Salaries	3,600.00	
10/23	Payroll	52	Office Salaries	3,353.08	
10/23	Payroll	51	Administrative Salaries	2,307.69	
10/23	Payroll	24	Employees FIT Payable		1,020.62
10/23	Payroll	25	Employees SIT Payable		444.70
10/23	Payroll	20.1	FICA Taxes Payable—OASDI		898.05
10/23	Payroll	20.2	FICA Taxes Payable—HI		210.04
10/23	Payroll	26	Employees CIT Payable		568.95
10/23	Payroll	27	Grp. Ins. Prem. Collected		165.90
10/23	Payroll	28	Union Dues Payable		16.00
10/23	Payroll	25.1	Employees SUTA Payable		10.16
10/23	Payroll	12	Payroll Cash		11,150.25
10/23	Pay. Tax	56	Payroll Taxes	1,241.25	
10/23	Pay. Tax	20.1	FICA Taxes Payable—OASDI		898.05
10/23	Pay. Tax	20.2	FICA Taxes Payable—HI		210.03
10/23	Pay. Tax	22	SUTA Taxes Payable		128.01
10/23	Pay. Tax	21	FUTA Taxes Payable		5.16
10/23	General	12	Payroll Cash	11,150.25	
10/23	General	11	Cash		11,150.25
		Totals		27,310.99	27,310.99

Glo-Brite Paint Company
General Ledger
10/23/--

Account	Journal	Date	Refer.	Debit	Credit	Balance	
11-Cash							
	Balance Forward					199,846.33	Dr
	General	10/09	General		11,077.87	188,768.46	Dr
	General	10/20	General		434.82	188,333.64	Dr
	General	10/23	General		11,150.25	177,183.39	Dr
12-Payroll Cash							
	General	10/09	Payroll		11,077.87	11,077.87	Cr
	General	10/09	General	11,077.87		.00	
	General	10/23	Payroll		11,150.25	11,150.25	Cr
	General	10/23	General	11,150.25		.00	

Account	Journal	Date	Refer.	Debit	Credit	Balance	
20.1-FICA Taxes Payable—OASDI							
	General	10/09	Payroll		878.09	878.09	Cr
	General	10/09	Pay. Tax		878.09	1,756.18	Cr
	General	10/23	Payroll		898.05	2,654.23	Cr
	General	10/23	Pay. Tax		898.05	3,552.28	Cr
20.2-FICA Taxes Payable—HI							
	General	10/09	Payroll		205.37	205.37	Cr
	General	10/09	Pay. Tax		205.36	410.73	Cr
	General	10/23	Payroll		210.04	620.77	Cr
	General	10/23	Pay. Tax		210.03	830.80	Cr
21-FUTA Taxes Payable							
	Balance Forward					392.94	Cr
	General	10/09	Pay. Tax		19.68	412.62	Cr
	General	10/23	Pay. Tax		5.16	417.78	Cr
22-SUTA Taxes Payable							
	General	10/09	Pay. Tax		128.01	128.01	Cr
	General	10/23	Pay. Tax		128.01	256.02	Cr
24-Employees FIT Payable							
	General	10/09	Payroll		984.38	984.38	Cr
	General	10/23	Payroll		1,020.62	2,005.00	Cr
25-Employees SIT Payable							
	General	10/09	Payroll		434.82	434.82	Cr
	General	10/20	General	434.82		.00	
	General	10/23	Payroll		444.70	444.70	Cr
25.1-Employees SUTA Payable							
	General	10/09	Payroll		9.94	9.94	Cr
	General	10/23	Payroll		10.16	20.10	Cr
26-Employees CIT Payable							
	General	10/09	Payroll		556.30	556.30	Cr
	General	10/23	Payroll		568.95	1,125.25	Cr
27-Grp. Ins. Prem. Collected							
	General	10/23	Payroll		165.90	165.90	Cr
28-Union Dues Payable							
	General	10/09	Payroll		16.00	16.00	Cr
	General	10/23	Payroll		16.00	32.00	Cr

Account	Journal	Date	Refer.	Debit	Credit	Balance	
29-Simple Contrib. Payable							
	*** No Activity **					.00	
51-Administrative Salaries							
	Balance Forward					42,692.27	Dr
	General	10/09	Payroll	2,307.69		44,999.96	Dr
	General	10/23	Payroll	2,307.69		47,307.65	Dr
52-Office Salaries							
	Balance Forward					28,350.00	Dr
	General	10/09	Payroll	3,353.08		31,703.08	Dr
	General	10/23	Payroll	3,353.08		35,056.16	Dr
53-Sales Salaries							
	Balance Forward					28,525.00	Dr
	General	10/09	Payroll	3,600.00		32,125.00	Dr
	General	10/23	Payroll	3,600.00		35,725.00	Dr
54-Plant Wages							
	Balance Forward					42,657.30	Dr
	General	10/09	Payroll	4,902.00		47,559.30	Dr
	General	10/23	Payroll	5,223.90		52,783.20	Dr
56-Payroll Taxes							
	Balance Forward					14,013.23	Dr
	General	10/09	Pay. Tax	1,231.14		15,244.37	Dr
	General	10/23	Pay. Tax	1,241.25		16,485.62	Dr

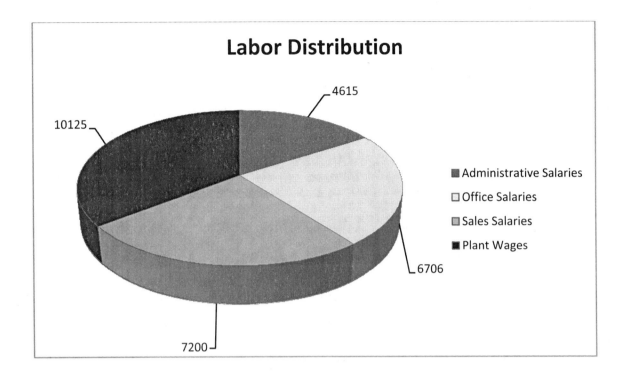

Student Audit Test: October 23 Payroll

Payroll Report
1. $1,517.90
2. $55.80
3. $11,150.25
4. $28,647.44
5. $165.90

Journal Entries Report
6. $444.70
7. $1,241.25

General Ledger
8. $3,552.28
9. $32.00

NOVEMBER 6 PAYROLL

Glo-Brite Paint Company
Employee List
11/06/--

Emp. No.	Employee Name/Address	Soc. Sec./ Mar. Stat.	# Pay Periods	G.L. Acct.	Salary/ Rate
100	BONNO, Anthony Victor 694 Bristol Avenue Philadelphia, PA 19135-0617	000-00-3481 Married W/H 4	26	54	17.65
110	FERGUSON, James Claude 808 Sixth Street Philadelphia, PA 19106-0995	000-00-8645 Married W/H 5	26	53	2,250.00
120	FORD, Catherine Louise 18 Dundee Avenue Philadelphia, PA 19151-1919	000-00-4567 Single W/H 2	26	52	900.00
130	MANN, Dewey Wilson 3007 Bisque Drive Philadelphia, PA 19199-0718	000-00-9352 Married W/H 0	26	53	1,350.00
140	O'NEILL, Joseph Tyler 2100 Broad Street Philadelphia, PA 19121-7189	000-00-1534 Married W/H 3	26	51	2,307.69
150	RUSSELL, Virginia Aloise 8004 Dowling Road Philadelphia, PA 19135-9001	000-00-6337 Single W/H 2	26	52	690.00
160	RYAN, Norman Allen 7300 Harrison Street Philadelphia, PA 19124-6699	000-00-1233 Married W/H 4	26	54	18.00
170	SOKOWSKI, Thomas James 133 Cornwells Street Philadelphia, PA 19171-5718	000-00-8832 Single W/H 2	26	54	2,050.00
180	STUDENT 7018 Erdrick Street Philadelphia, PA 19135-8517	000-00-5555 Single W/H 1	26	52	7.50
190	WILLIAMS, Ruth Virginia 9433 State Street Philadelphia, PA 19149-0819	000-00-6741 Single W/H 0	26	52	1,223.08

Glo-Brite Paint Company
Payroll Report
11/06/--

		Current	Quarterly	Yearly
100-BONNO, Anthony Victor	Gross Pay	1,412.00	4,341.90	15,663.85
54-Plant	FIT	52.35	167.64	977.64
Married Acct. 54	SIT	43.35	133.30	480.89
W/H 4 000-00-3481	Soc. Sec.—OASDI	87.54	269.19	971.15
Pay Periods 26	Medicare—HI	20.47	62.95	227.12
Salary	CIT	55.46	170.54	615.27
Hourly Rate 17.65	Group Ins.		16.50	161.30
Reg. Hours 80.00	Union Dues	8.00	24.00	96.00
O.T. Hours	Simple Plan			
Check Number 692	Employee SUTA	0.99	3.04	10.97
Check Date 11/06/--	Net Pay	1,143.84	3,494.74	12,123.51
110-FERGUSON, James Claude	Gross Pay	2,250.00	6,750.00	29,875.00
53-Sales	FIT	148.56	445.68	2,736.68
Married Acct. 53	SIT	69.08	207.24	917.18
W/H 5 000-00-8645	Soc. Sec.—OASDI	139.50	418.50	1,852.25
Pay Periods 26	Medicare—HI	32.63	97.89	433.20
Salary 2,250.00	CIT	88.38	265.14	1,173.49
Hourly Rate	Group Ins.		26.40	158.70
Reg. Hours	Union Dues			
O.T. Hours	Simple Plan			
Check Number 693	Employee SUTA	1.58	4.74	20.93
Check Date 11/06/--	Net Pay	1,770.27	5,284.41	22,582.57
120-FORD, Catherine Louise	Gross Pay	900.00	2,700.00	9,000.00
52-Office	FIT	62.45	187.35	826.35
Single Acct. 52	SIT	27.63	82.89	276.30
W/H 2 000-00-4567	Soc. Sec.—OASDI	55.80	167.40	558.00
Pay Periods 26	Medicare—HI	13.05	39.15	130.50
Salary 900.00	CIT	35.35	106.05	353.51
Hourly Rate	Group Ins.		10.50	48.30
Reg. Hours	Union Dues			
O.T. Hours	Simple Plan			
Check Number 694	Employee SUTA	0.63	1.89	6.30
Check Date 11/06/--	Net Pay	705.09	2,104.77	6,800.74
130-MANN, Dewey Wilson	Gross Pay	1,350.00	4,050.00	9,450.00
53-Sales	FIT	120.29	212.59	544.59
Married Acct. 53	SIT	41.45	124.35	290.13
W/H 0 000-00-9352	Soc. Sec.—OASDI	83.70	251.10	585.90
Pay Periods 26	Medicare—HI	19.58	58.74	137.04
Salary 1,350.00	CIT	53.03	159.09	371.20
Hourly Rate	Group Ins.		15.90	47.40
Reg. Hours	Union Dues			
O.T. Hours	Simple Plan			
Check Number 695	Employee SUTA	0.95	2.85	6.63
Check Date 11/06/--	Net Pay	1,031.00	3,225.38	7,467.11

		Current	Quarterly	Yearly
140-O'NEILL, Joseph Tyler	Gross Pay	2,307.69	6,923.07	49,615.34
51-Administrative	FIT	199.90	599.70	6,715.70
Married Acct. 51	SIT	70.85	212.55	1,523.20
W/H 3 000-00-1534	Soc. Sec.—OASDI	143.08	429.24	3,076.16
Pay Periods 26	Medicare—HI	33.46	100.38	719.42
Salary 2,307.69	CIT	90.65	271.95	1,948.90
Hourly Rate	Group Ins.		27.00	229.50
Reg. Hours	Union Dues			
O.T. Hours	Simple Plan			
Check Number 696	Employee SUTA	1.62	4.86	34.74
Check Date 11/06/--	Net Pay	1,768.13	5,277.39	35,367.72
150-RUSSELL, Virginia Aloise	Gross Pay	672.94	2,052.94	8,292.94
52-Office	FIT	30.37	134.97	776.97
Single Acct. 52	SIT	20.66	63.02	254.58
W/H 2 000-00-6337	Soc. Sec.—OASDI	41.72	127.28	514.16
Pay Periods 26	Medicare—HI	9.76	29.78	120.26
Salary 690.00	CIT	26.43	80.63	325.74
Hourly Rate	Group Ins.		8.10	39.60
Reg. Hours	Union Dues			
O.T. Hours	Simple Plan			
Check Number 697	Employee SUTA	0.47	1.43	5.80
Check Date 11/06/--	Net Pay	543.53	1,607.73	6,255.83
160-RYAN, Norman Allen	Gross Pay	1,440.00	4,536.00	19,221.30
54-Plant	FIT	55.15	191.10	1,261.10
Married Acct. 54	SIT	44.21	139.26	590.10
W/H 4 000-00-1233	Soc. Sec.—OASDI	89.28	281.23	1,191.72
Pay Periods 26	Medicare—HI	20.88	65.77	278.71
Salary	CIT	56.56	178.17	755.01
Hourly Rate 18.00	Group Ins.		16.80	180.50
Reg. Hours 80.00	Union Dues	8.00	24.00	96.00
O.T. Hours	Simple Plan			
Check Number 698	Employee SUTA	1.01	3.18	13.46
Check Date 11/06/--	Net Pay	1,164.91	3,636.49	14,854.70
170-SOKOWSKI, Thomas James	Gross Pay	2,050.00	6,150.00	22,800.00
54-Plant	FIT	263.61	628.81	2,630.81
Single Acct. 54	SIT	62.94	188.82	699.98
W/H 2 000-00-8832	Soc. Sec.—OASDI	127.10	381.30	1,413.60
Pay Periods 26	Medicare—HI	29.73	89.19	330.62
Salary 2,050.00	CIT	80.52	241.56	895.57
Hourly Rate	Group Ins.		24.00	118.50
Reg. Hours	Union Dues			
O.T. Hours	Simple Plan			
Check Number 699	Employee SUTA	1.44	4.32	15.98
Check Date 11/06/--	Net Pay	1,484.66	4,592.00	16,694.94
180-STUDENT	Gross Pay	540.00	1,620.00	7,170.00
52-Office	FIT	31.31	93.93	502.93
Single Acct. 52	SIT	16.58	49.74	220.12
W/H 1 000-00-5555	Soc. Sec.—OASDI	33.48	100.44	444.54
Pay Periods 26	Medicare—HI	7.83	23.49	103.97
Salary	CIT	21.21	63.63	281.63
Hourly Rate 7.50	Group Ins.		6.30	38.70
Reg. Hours 72.00	Union Dues			
O.T. Hours	Simple Plan			
Check Number 700	Employee SUTA	0.38	1.14	5.03
Check Date 11/06/--	Net Pay	429.21	1,281.33	5,573.08

		Current	Quarterly	Yearly
190-WILLIAMS, Ruth Virgin	Gross Pay	1,207.85	3,654.01	13,914.01
52-Office	FIT	151.32	458.54	2,064.54
Single Acct. 52	SIT	37.08	112.18	427.16
W/H 0 000-00-6741	Soc. Sec.—OASDI	74.89	226.55	862.67
Pay Periods 26	Medicare—HI	17.51	52.97	201.74
Salary 1,223.08	CIT	47.44	143.52	546.53
Hourly Rate	Group Ins.		14.40	73.80
Reg. Hours	Union Dues			
O.T. Hours	Simple Plan			
Check Number 701	Employee SUTA	0.85	2.57	9.75
Check Date 11/06/--	Net Pay	878.76	2,643.28	9,727.82
Payroll Summary	Gross Pay	14,130.48	42,777.92	185,002.44
	FIT	1,115.31	3,120.31	19,037.31
	SIT	433.83	1,313.35	5,679.64
	Soc. Sec.—OASDI	876.09	2,652.23	11,470.15
	Medicare—HI	204.90	620.31	2,682.58
	CIT	555.03	1,680.28	7,266.85
	Group Ins.		165.90	1,096.30
	Union Dues	16.00	48.00	192.00
	Simple Plan			
	Employee SUTA	9.92	30.02	129.59
	Net Pay	10,919.40	33,147.52	137,448.02

Glo-Brite Paint Company
General Journal
11/06/--

Date	Refer.	Acct.	Title	Debit	Credit
11/04	General	25	Employees SIT Payable	444.70	
11/04	General	11	Cash		444.70
11/06	General	28	Union Dues Payable	32.00	
11/06	General	11	Cash		32.00
11/06	Payroll	54	Plant Wages	4,902.00	
11/06	Payroll	53	Sales Salaries	3,600.00	
11/06	Payroll	52	Office Salaries	3,320.79	
11/06	Payroll	51	Administrative Salaries	2,307.69	
11/06	Payroll	24	Employees FIT Payable		1,115.31
11/06	Payroll	25	Employees SIT Payable		433.83
11/06	Payroll	20.1	FICA Taxes Payable—OASDI		876.09
11/06	Payroll	20.2	FICA Taxes Payable—HI		204.90
11/06	Payroll	26	Employees CIT Payable		555.03
11/06	Payroll	28	Union Dues Payable		16.00
11/06	Payroll	25.1	Employees SUTA Payable		9.92
11/06	Payroll	12	Payroll Cash		10,919.40
11/06	Pay. Tax	56	Payroll Taxes	1,157.25	
11/06	Pay. Tax	20.1	FICA Taxes Payable—OASDI		876.09
11/06	Pay. Tax	20.2	FICA Taxes Payable—HI		204.89
11/06	Pay. Tax	22	SUTA Taxes Payable		74.05
11/06	Pay. Tax	21	FUTA Taxes Payable		2.22
11/06	General	12	Payroll Cash	10,919.40	
11/06	General	11	Cash		10,919.40
	Totals			26,683.83	26,683.83

Glo-Brite Paint Company
General Ledger
11/06/--

Account	Journal	Date	Refer.	Debit	Credit	Balance	
11-Cash							
	Balance Forward					199,846.33	Dr
	General	10/09	General		11,077.87	188,768.46	Dr
	General	10/20	General		434.82	188,333.64	Dr
	General	10/23	General		11,150.25	177,183.39	Dr
	General	11/04	General		444.70	176,738.69	Dr
	General	11/06	General		32.00	176,706.69	Dr
	General	11/06	General		10,919.40	165,787.29	Dr

Account Journal	Date	Refer.	Debit	Credit	Balance	
12-Payroll Cash						
General	10/09	Payroll		11,077.87	11,077.87	Cr
General	10/09	General	11,077.87		.00	
General	10/23	Payroll		11,150.25	11,150.25	Cr
General	10/23	General	11,150.25		.00	
General	11/06	Payroll		10,919.40	10,919.40	Cr
General	11/06	General	10,919.40		.00	
20.1-FICA Taxes Payable—OASDI						
General	10/09	Payroll		878.09	878.09	Cr
General	10/09	Pay. Tax		878.09	1,756.18	Cr
General	10/23	Payroll		898.05	2,654.23	Cr
General	10/23	Pay. Tax		898.05	3,552.28	Cr
General	11/06	Payroll		876.09	4,428.37	Cr
General	11/06	Pay. Tax		876.09	5,304.46	Cr
20.2-FICA Taxes Payable—HI						
General	10/09	Payroll		205.37	205.37	Cr
General	10/09	Pay. Tax		205.36	410.73	Cr
General	10/23	Payroll		210.04	620.77	Cr
General	10/23	Pay. Tax		210.03	830.80	Cr
General	11/06	Payroll		204.90	1,035.70	Cr
General	11/06	Pay. Tax		204.89	1,240.59	Cr
21-FUTA Taxes Payable						
Balance Forward					392.94	Cr
General	10/09	Pay. Tax		19.68	412.62	Cr
General	10/23	Pay. Tax		5.16	417.78	Cr
General	11/06	Pay. Tax		2.22	420.00	Cr
22-SUTA Taxes Payable						
General	10/09	Pay. Tax		128.01	128.01	Cr
General	10/23	Pay. Tax		128.01	256.02	Cr
General	11/06	Pay. Tax		74.05	330.07	Cr
24-Employees FIT Payable						
General	10/09	Payroll		984.38	984.38	Cr
General	10/23	Payroll		1,020.62	2,005.00	Cr
General	11/06	Payroll		1,115.31	3,120.31	Cr
25-Employees SIT Payable						
General	10/09	Payroll		434.82	434.82	Cr
General	10/20	General	434.82		.00	
General	10/23	Payroll		444.70	444.70	Cr
General	11/04	General	444.70		.00	
General	11/06	Payroll		433.83	433.83	Cr

Account	Journal	Date	Refer.	Debit	Credit	Balance	
25.1-Employees SUTA Payable							
	General	10/09	Payroll		9.94	9.94	Cr
	General	10/23	Payroll		10.16	20.10	Cr
	General	11/06	Payroll		9.92	30.02	Cr
26-Employees CIT Payable							
	General	10/09	Payroll		556.30	556.30	Cr
	General	10/23	Payroll		568.95	1,125.25	Cr
	General	11/06	Payroll		555.03	1,680.28	Cr
27-Grp. Ins. Prem. Collected							
	General	10/23	Payroll		165.90	165.90	Cr
28-Union Dues Payable							
	General	10/09	Payroll		16.00	16.00	Cr
	General	10/23	Payroll		16.00	32.00	Cr
	General	11/06	General	32.00		.00	
	General	11/06	Payroll		16.00	16.00	Cr
29-Simple Contrib. Payable							
	*** No Activity **					.00	
51-Administrative Salaries							
	Balance Forward					42,692.27	Dr
	General	10/09	Payroll	2,307.69		44,999.96	Dr
	General	10/23	Payroll	2,307.69		47,307.65	Dr
	General	11/06	Payroll	2,307.69		49,615.34	Dr
52-Office Salaries							
	Balance Forward					28,350.00	Dr
	General	10/09	Payroll	3,353.08		31,703.08	Dr
	General	10/23	Payroll	3,353.08		35,056.16	Dr
	General	11/06	Payroll	3,320.79		38,376.95	Dr
53-Sales Salaries							
	Balance Forward					28,525.00	Dr
	General	10/09	Payroll	3,600.00		32,125.00	Dr
	General	10/23	Payroll	3,600.00		35,725.00	Dr
	General	11/06	Payroll	3,600.00		39,325.00	Dr
54-Plant Wages							
	Balance Forward					42,657.30	Dr
	General	10/09	Payroll	4,902.00		47,559.30	Dr
	General	10/23	Payroll	5,223.90		52,783.20	Dr
	General	11/06	Payroll	4,902.00		57,685.20	Dr

Account	Journal	Date	Refer.	Debit	Credit	Balance	
56-Payroll Taxes							
	Balance Forward					14,013.23	Dr
	General	10/09	Pay. Tax	1,231.14		15,244.37	Dr
	General	10/23	Pay. Tax	1,241.25		16,485.62	Dr
	General	11/06	Pay. Tax	1,157.25		17,642.87	Dr

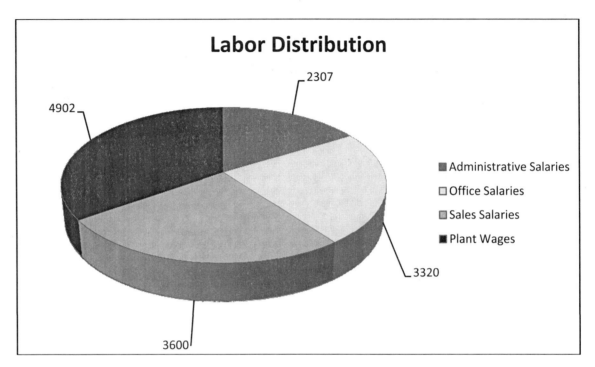

Student Audit Test: November 06 Payroll

Payroll Report
1. $199.90
2. $14,130.48
3. $555.03
4. $10,919.40

Journal Entries Report
5. $876.09
6. $204.90
7. $1,157.25

General Ledger
8. $165,787.29
9. $39,325.00

NOVEMBER 13 PAYROLL

Glo-Brite Paint Company
Payroll Report
11/13/--

		Current	Quarterly	Yearly
190-WILLIAMS, Ruth Virginia	Gross Pay	2,079.32	5,733.33	15,993.33
52-Office	FIT	342.09	800.63	2,406.63
Single Acct. 52	SIT	63.84	176.02	491.00
W/H 0 000-00-6741	Soc. Sec.—OASDI	128.92	355.47	991.59
Pay Periods 26	Medicare—HI	30.15	83.12	231.89
Salary 1,223.08	CIT	81.68	225.20	628.21
Hourly Rate	Group Ins.	14.40	28.80	88.20
Reg. Hours	Union Dues			
O.T. Hours	Simple Plan			
Check Number 702	Employee SUTA	1.46	4.03	11.21
Check Date 11/13/--	Net Pay	1,416.78	4,060.06	11,144.60
Payroll Summary	Gross Pay	2,079.32	44,857.24	187,081.76
	FIT	342.09	3,462.40	19,379.40
	SIT	63.84	1,377.19	5,743.48
	Soc. Sec.—OASDI	128.92	2,781.15	11,599.07
	Medicare—HI	30.15	650.46	2,712.73
	CIT	81.68	1,761.96	7,348.53
	Group Ins.	14.40	180.30	1,110.70
	Union Dues		48.00	192.00
	Simple Plan			
	Employee SUTA	1.46	31.48	131.05
	Net Pay	1,416.78	34,564.30	138,864.80

Glo-Brite Paint Company
General Journal
11/13/--

Date	Refer.	Acct.	Title	Debit	Credit
11/13	Payroll	52	Office Salaries	2,079.32	
11/13	Payroll	24	Employees FIT Payable		342.09
11/13	Payroll	25	Employees SIT Payable		63.84
11/13	Payroll	20.1	FICA Taxes Payable—OASDI		128.92
11/13	Payroll	20.2	FICA Taxes Payable—HI		30.15
11/13	Payroll	26	Employees CIT Payable		81.68
11/13	Payroll	27	Grp. Ins. Prem. Collected		14.40
11/13	Payroll	25.1	Employees SUTA Payable		1.46
11/13	Payroll	12	Payroll Cash		1,416.78
11/13	Pay. Tax	56	Payroll Taxes	159.07	
11/13	Pay. Tax	20.1	FICA Taxes Payable—OASDI		128.92
11/13	Pay. Tax	20.2	FICA Taxes Payable—HI		30.15
11/13	General	12	Payroll Cash	1,416.78	
11/13	General	11	Cash		1,416.78
		Totals		3,655.17	3,655.17

Glo-Brite Paint Company
General Ledger
11/13/--

Account	Journal	Date	Refer.	Debit	Credit	Balance	
11-Cash							
	Balance Forward					199,846.33	Dr
	General	10/09	General		11,077.87	188,768.46	Dr
	General	10/20	General		434.82	188,333.64	Dr
	General	10/23	General		11,150.25	177,183.39	Dr
	General	11/04	General		444.70	176,738.69	Dr
	General	11/06	General		32.00	176,706.69	Dr
	General	11/06	General		10,919.40	165,787.29	Dr
	General	11/13	General		1,416.78	164,370.51	Dr
12-Payroll Cash							
	General	10/09	Payroll		11,077.87	11,077.87	Cr
	General	10/09	General	11,077.87		.00	
	General	10/23	Payroll		11,150.25	11,150.25	Cr
	General	10/23	General	11,150.25		.00	
	General	11/06	Payroll		10,919.40	10,919.40	Cr
	General	11/06	General	10,919.40		.00	
	General	11/13	Payroll		1,416.78	1,416.78	Cr
	General	11/13	General	1,416.78		.00	

Account	Journal	Date	Refer.	Debit	Credit	Balance	
20.1-FICA Taxes Payable—OASDI							
	General	10/09	Payroll		878.09	878.09	Cr
	General	10/09	Pay. Tax		878.09	1,756.18	Cr
	General	10/23	Payroll		898.05	2,654.23	Cr
	General	10/23	Pay. Tax		898.05	3,552.28	Cr
	General	11/06	Payroll		876.09	4,428.37	Cr
	General	11/06	Pay. Tax		876.09	5,304.46	Cr
	General	11/13	Payroll		128.92	5,433.38	Cr
	General	11/13	Pay. Tax		128.92	5,562.30	Cr
20.2-FICA Taxes Payable—HI							
	General	10/09	Payroll		205.37	205.37	Cr
	General	10/09	Pay. Tax		205.36	410.73	Cr
	General	10/23	Payroll		210.04	620.77	Cr
	General	10/23	Pay. Tax		210.03	830.80	Cr
	General	11/06	Payroll		204.90	1,035.70	Cr
	General	11/06	Pay. Tax		204.89	1,240.59	Cr
	General	11/13	Payroll		30.15	1,270.74	Cr
	General	11/13	Pay. Tax		30.15	1,300.89	Cr
21-FUTA Taxes Payable							
	Balance Forward					392.94	Cr
	General	10/09	Pay. Tax		19.68	412.62	Cr
	General	10/23	Pay. Tax		5.16	417.78	Cr
	General	11/06	Pay. Tax		2.22	420.00	Cr
22-SUTA Taxes Payable							
	General	10/09	Pay. Tax		128.01	128.01	Cr
	General	10/23	Pay. Tax		128.01	256.02	Cr
	General	11/06	Pay. Tax		74.05	330.07	Cr
24-Employees FIT Payable							
	General	10/09	Payroll		984.38	984.38	Cr
	General	10/23	Payroll		1,020.62	2,005.00	Cr
	General	11/06	Payroll		1,115.31	3,120.31	Cr
	General	11/13	Payroll		342.09	3,462.40	Cr
25-Employees SIT Payable							
	General	10/09	Payroll		434.82	434.82	Cr
	General	10/20	General	434.82		.00	
	General	10/23	Payroll		444.70	444.70	Cr
	General	11/04	General	444.70		.00	
	General	11/06	Payroll		433.83	433.83	Cr
	General	11/13	Payroll		63.84	497.67	Cr

Account	Journal	Date	Refer.	Debit	Credit	Balance	
25.1-Employees SUTA Payable							
	General	10/09	Payroll		9.94	9.94	Cr
	General	10/23	Payroll		10.16	20.10	Cr
	General	11/06	Payroll		9.92	30.02	Cr
	General	11/13	Payroll		1.46	31.48	Cr
26-Employees CIT Payable							
	General	10/09	Payroll		556.30	556.30	Cr
	General	10/23	Payroll		568.95	1,125.25	Cr
	General	11/06	Payroll		555.03	1,680.28	Cr
	General	11/13	Payroll		81.68	1,761.96	Cr
27-Grp. Ins. Prem. Collected							
	General	10/23	Payroll		165.90	165.90	Cr
	General	11/13	Payroll		14.40	180.30	Cr
28-Union Dues Payable							
	General	10/09	Payroll		16.00	16.00	Cr
	General	10/23	Payroll		16.00	32.00	Cr
	General	11/06	General	32.00		.00	
	General	11/06	Payroll		16.00	16.00	Cr
29-Simple Contrib. Payable							
*** No Activity **						.00	
51-Administrative Salaries							
	Balance Forward					42,692.27	Dr
	General	10/09	Payroll	2,307.69		44,999.96	Dr
	General	10/23	Payroll	2,307.69		47,307.65	Dr
	General	11/06	Payroll	2,307.69		49,615.34	Dr
52-Office Salaries							
	Balance Forward					28,350.00	Dr
	General	10/09	Payroll	3,353.08		31,703.08	Dr
	General	10/23	Payroll	3,353.08		35,056.16	Dr
	General	11/06	Payroll	3,320.79		38,376.95	Dr
	General	11/13	Payroll	2,079.32		40,456.27	Dr
53-Sales Salaries							
	Balance Forward					28,525.00	Dr
	General	10/09	Payroll	3,600.00		32,125.00	Dr
	General	10/23	Payroll	3,600.00		35,725.00	Dr
	General	11/06	Payroll	3,600.00		39,325.00	Dr

Account Journal	Date	Refer.	Debit	Credit	Balance
54-Plant Wages					
Balance Forward					42,657.30 Dr
General	10/09	Payroll	4,902.00		47,559.30 Dr
General	10/23	Payroll	5,223.90		52,783.20 Dr
General	11/06	Payroll	4,902.00		57,685.20 Dr
56-Payroll Taxes					
Balance Forward					14,013.23 Dr
General	10/09	Pay. Tax	1,231.14		15,244.37 Dr
General	10/23	Pay. Tax	1,241.25		16,485.62 Dr
General	11/06	Pay. Tax	1,157.25		17,642.87 Dr
General	11/13	Pay. Tax	159.07		17,801.94 Dr

Student Audit Test: November 13 Payroll

Payroll Report
1. $2,406.63
2. $1,416.78
3. 52-Office

Journal Entries Report
4. $14.40

General Ledger
5. $17,801.94

NOVEMBER 20 PAYROLL

Glo-Brite Paint Company
Employee List
11/20/--

Emp. No.	Employee Name/Address	Soc. Sec./ Mar. Stat.	# Pay Periods	G.L. Acct.	Salary/ Rate
100	BONNO, Anthony Victor 694 Bristol Avenue Philadelphia, PA 19135-0617	000-00-3481 Married W/H 4	26	54	17.65
110	FERGUSON, James Claude 808 Sixth Street Philadelphia, PA 19106-0995	000-00-8645 Married W/H 5	26	53	2,250.00
120	FORD, Catherine Louise 18 Dundee Avenue Philadelphia, PA 19151-1919	000-00-4567 Single W/H 2	26	52	900.00
130	MANN, Dewey Wilson 3007 Bisque Drive Philadelphia, PA 19199-0718	000-00-9352 Married W/H 0	26	53	1,350.00
140	O'NEILL, Joseph Tyler 2100 Broad Street Philadelphia, PA 19121-7189	000-00-1534 Married W/H 3	26	51	2,307.69
150	RUSSELL, Virginia Aloise 8004 Dowling Road Philadelphia, PA 19135-9001	000-00-6337 Single W/H 2	26	52	690.00
160	RYAN, Norman Allen 7300 Harrison Street Philadelphia, PA 19124-6699	000-00-1233 Married W/H 4	26	54	18.00
170	SOKOWSKI, Thomas James 133 Cornwells Street Philadelphia, PA 19171-5718	000-00-8832 Single W/H 2	26	54	2,050.00
180	STUDENT 7018 Erdrick Street Philadelphia, PA 19135-8517	000-00-5555 Single W/H 1	26	52	7.50
190	WILLIAMS, Ruth Virginia 9433 State Street Philadelphia, PA 19149-0819	000-00-6741 Single W/H 0	26	52	1,223.08

Emp. No.	Employee Name/Address	Soc. Sec./ Mar. Stat.	# Pay Periods	G.L. Acct.	Salary/ Rate
200	WOODS, Beth Anne 8102 Franklin Court Philadelphia, PA 19105-0915	000-00-1587 Single W/H 1	26	52	1,200.00

Glo-Brite Paint Company
Payroll Report
11/20/--

		Current	Quarterly	Yearly
100-BONNO, Anthony Victor	Gross Pay	1,129.60	5,471.50	16,793.45
54-Plant	FIT	24.11	191.75	1,001.75
Married Acct. 54	SIT	34.68	167.98	515.57
W/H 4 000-00-3481	Soc. Sec.—OASDI	70.04	339.23	1,041.19
Pay Periods 26	Medicare—HI	16.38	79.33	243.50
Salary	CIT	44.37	214.91	659.64
Hourly Rate 17.65	Group Ins.	16.50	33.00	177.80
Reg. Hours 64.00	Union Dues	8.00	32.00	104.00
O.T. Hours	Simple Plan			
Check Number 703	Employee SUTA	0.79	3.83	11.76
Check Date 11/20/--	Net Pay	914.73	4,409.47	13,038.24
110-FERGUSON, James Claude	Gross Pay	2,250.00	9,000.00	32,125.00
53-Sales	FIT	73.56	519.24	2,810.24
Married Acct. 53	SIT	69.08	276.32	986.26
W/H 5 000-00-8645	Soc. Sec.—OASDI	139.50	558.00	1,991.75
Pay Periods 26	Medicare—HI	32.63	130.52	465.83
Salary 2,250.00	CIT	88.38	353.52	1,261.87
Hourly Rate	Group Ins.	26.40	52.80	185.10
Reg. Hours	Union Dues			
O.T. Hours	Simple Plan	500.00	500.00	500.00
Check Number 704	Employee SUTA	1.58	6.32	22.51
Check Date 11/20/--	Net Pay	1,318.87	6,603.28	23,901.44
120-FORD, Catherine Louise	Gross Pay	900.00	3,600.00	9,900.00
52-Office	FIT	62.45	249.80	888.80
Single Acct. 52	SIT	27.63	110.52	303.93
W/H 2 000-00-4567	Soc. Sec.—OASDI	55.80	223.20	613.80
Pay Periods 26	Medicare—HI	13.05	52.20	143.55
Salary 900.00	CIT	35.35	141.40	388.86
Hourly Rate	Group Ins.	10.50	21.00	58.80
Reg. Hours	Union Dues			
O.T. Hours	Simple Plan			
Check Number 705	Employee SUTA	0.63	2.52	6.93
Check Date 11/20/--	Net Pay	694.59	2,799.36	7,495.33

		Current	Quarterly	Yearly
130-MANN, Dewey Wilson	Gross Pay	1,350.00	5,400.00	10,800.00
53-Sales	FIT	82.79	295.38	627.38
Married Acct. 53	SIT	41.45	165.80	331.58
W/H 0 000-00-9352	Soc. Sec.—OASDI	83.70	334.80	669.60
Pay Periods 26	Medicare—HI	19.58	78.32	156.62
Salary 1,350.00	CIT	53.03	212.12	424.23
Hourly Rate	Group Ins.	15.90	31.80	63.30
Reg. Hours	Union Dues			
O.T. Hours	Simple Plan	250.00	250.00	250.00
Check Number 706	Employee SUTA	0.95	3.80	7.58
Check Date 11/20/--	Net Pay	802.60	4,027.98	8,269.71
140-O'NEILL, Joseph Tyler	Gross Pay	2,307.69	9,230.76	51,923.03
51-Administrative	FIT	94.90	694.60	6,810.60
Married Acct. 51	SIT	70.85	283.40	1,594.05
W/H 3 000-00-1534	Soc. Sec.—OASDI	143.08	572.32	3,219.24
Pay Periods 26	Medicare—HI	33.46	133.84	752.88
Salary 2,307.69	CIT	90.65	362.60	2,039.55
Hourly Rate	Group Ins.	27.00	54.00	256.50
Reg. Hours	Union Dues			
O.T. Hours	Simple Plan	700.00	700.00	700.00
Check Number 707	Employee SUTA	1.62	6.48	36.36
Check Date 11/20/--	Net Pay	1,146.13	6,423.52	36,513.85
150-RUSSELL, Virginia Aloise	Gross Pay	672.94	2,725.88	8,965.88
52-Office	FIT	30.37	165.34	807.34
Single Acct. 52	SIT	20.66	83.68	275.24
W/H 2 000-00-6337	Soc. Sec.—OASDI	41.72	169.00	555.88
Pay Periods 26	Medicare—HI	9.76	39.54	130.02
Salary 690.00	CIT	26.43	107.06	352.17
Hourly Rate	Group Ins.	8.10	16.20	47.70
Reg. Hours	Union Dues			
O.T. Hours	Simple Plan			
Check Number 708	Employee SUTA	0.47	1.90	6.27
Check Date 11/20/--	Net Pay	535.43	2,143.16	6,791.26
160-RYAN, Norman Allen	Gross Pay	1,440.00	5,976.00	20,661.30
54-Plant	FIT	35.15	226.25	1,296.25
Married Acct. 54	SIT	44.21	183.47	634.31
W/H 4 000-00-1233	Soc. Sec.—OASDI	89.28	370.51	1,281.00
Pay Periods 26	Medicare—HI	20.88	86.65	299.59
Salary	CIT	56.56	234.73	811.57
Hourly Rate 18.00	Group Ins.	16.80	33.60	197.30
Reg. Hours 80.00	Union Dues	8.00	32.00	104.00
O.T. Hours	Simple Plan	200.00	200.00	200.00
Check Number 709	Employee SUTA	1.01	4.19	14.47
Check Date 11/20/--	Net Pay	968.11	4,604.60	15,822.81
170-SOKOWSKI, Thomas James	Gross Pay	2,050.00	8,200.00	24,850.00
54-Plant	FIT	263.61	892.42	2,894.42
Single Acct. 54	SIT	62.94	251.76	762.92
W/H 2 000-00-8832	Soc. Sec.—OASDI	127.10	508.40	1,540.70
Pay Periods 26	Medicare—HI	29.73	118.92	360.35
Salary 2,050.00	CIT	80.52	322.08	976.09
Hourly Rate	Group Ins.	24.00	48.00	142.50
Reg. Hours	Union Dues			
O.T. Hours	Simple Plan			
Check Number 710	Employee SUTA	1.44	5.76	17.42
Check Date 11/20/--	Net Pay	1,460.66	6,052.66	18,155.60

		Current	Quarterly	Yearly
180-STUDENT	Gross Pay	540.00	2,160.00	7,710.00
52-Office	FIT	31.31	125.24	534.24
Single Acct. 52	SIT	16.58	66.32	236.70
W/H 1 000-00-5555	Soc. Sec.—OASDI	33.48	133.92	478.02
Pay Periods 26	Medicare—HI	7.83	31.32	111.80
Salary	CIT	21.21	84.84	302.84
Hourly Rate 7.50	Group Ins.	6.30	12.60	45.00
Reg. Hours 72.00	Union Dues			
O.T. Hours	Simple Plan			
Check Number 711	Employee SUTA	0.38	1.52	5.41
Check Date 11/20/--	Net Pay	422.91	1,704.24	5,995.99
190-WILLIAMS, Ruth Virginia	Gross Pay		5,733.33	15,993.33
52-Office	FIT		800.63	2,406.63
Single Acct. 52	SIT		176.02	491.00
W/H 0 000-00-6741	Soc. Sec.—OASDI		355.47	991.59
Pay Periods 26	Medicare—HI		83.12	231.89
Salary 1,223.08	CIT		225.20	628.21
Hourly Rate	Group Ins.		28.80	88.20
Reg. Hours	Union Dues			
O.T. Hours	Simple Plan			
Check Number	Employee SUTA		4.03	11.21
Check Date	Net Pay		4,060.06	11,144.60
200-WOODS, Beth Anne	Gross Pay			
52-Office	FIT			
Single Acct. 52	SIT			
W/H 1 000-00-1587	Soc. Sec.—OASDI			
Pay Periods 26	Medicare—HI			
Salary 1,200.00	CIT			
Hourly Rate	Group Ins.			
Reg. Hours	Union Dues			
O.T. Hours	Simple Plan			
Check Number	Employee SUTA			
Check Date	Net Pay			
Payroll Summary	Gross Pay	12,640.23	57,497.47	199,721.99
	FIT	698.25	4,160.65	20,077.65
	SIT	388.08	1,765.27	6,131.56
	Soc. Sec.—OASDI	783.70	3,564.85	12,382.77
	Medicare—HI	183.30	833.76	2,896.03
	CIT	496.50	2,258.46	7,845.03
	Group Ins.	151.50	331.80	1,262.20
	Union Dues	16.00	64.00	208.00
	Simple Plan	1,650.00	1,650.00	1,650.00
	Employee SUTA	8.87	40.35	139.92
	Net Pay	8,264.03	42,828.33	147,128.83

Glo-Brite Paint Company
General Journal
11/20/--

Date	Refer.	Acct.	Title	Debit	Credit
11/16	General	20.1	FICA Taxes Payable—OASDI	3,552.28	
11/16	General	20.2	FICA Taxes Payable—HI	830.80	
11/16	General	24	Employees FIT Payable	2,005.00	
11/16	General	11	Cash		6,388.08
11/16	General	26	Employees CIT Payable	1,125.25	
11/16	General	11	Cash		1,125.25
11/18	General	25	Employees SIT Payable	497.67	
11/18	General	11	Cash		497.67
11/20	Payroll	54	Plant Wages	4,619.60	
11/20	Payroll	53	Sales Salaries	3,600.00	
11/20	Payroll	52	Office Salaries	2,112.94	
11/20	Payroll	51	Administrative Salaries	2,307.69	
11/20	Payroll	24	Employees FIT Payable		698.25
11/20	Payroll	25	Employees SIT Payable		388.08
11/20	Payroll	20.1	FICA Taxes Payable—OASDI		783.70
11/20	Payroll	20.2	FICA Taxes Payable—HI		183.30
11/20	Payroll	26	Employees CIT Payable		496.50
11/20	Payroll	27	Grp. Ins. Prem. Collected		151.50
11/20	Payroll	28	Union Dues Payable		16.00
11/20	Payroll	29	Simple Contrib. Payable		1,650.00
11/20	Payroll	25.1	Employees SUTA Payable		8.87
11/20	Payroll	12	Payroll Cash		8,264.03
11/20	Pay. Tax	56	Payroll Taxes	994.45	
11/20	Pay. Tax	20.1	FICA Taxes Payable—OASDI		783.69
11/20	Pay. Tax	20.2	FICA Taxes Payable—HI		183.28
11/20	Pay. Tax	22	SUTA Taxes Payable		27.48
11/20	General	12	Payroll Cash	8,264.03	
11/20	General	11	Cash		8,264.03
		Totals		29,909.71	29,909.71

Glo-Brite Paint Company
General Ledger
11/20/--

Account	Journal	Date	Refer.	Debit	Credit	Balance	
11-Cash							
	Balance Forward					199,846.33	Dr
	General	10/09	General		11,077.87	188,768.46	Dr
	General	10/20	General		434.82	188,333.64	Dr
	General	10/23	General		11,150.25	177,183.39	Dr
	General	11/04	General		444.70	176,738.69	Dr
	General	11/06	General		32.00	176,706.69	Dr
	General	11/06	General		10,919.40	165,787.29	Dr
	General	11/13	General		1,416.78	164,370.51	Dr
	General	11/16	General		6,388.08	157,982.43	Dr
	General	11/16	General		1,125.25	156,857.18	Dr
	General	11/18	General		497.67	156,359.51	Dr
	General	11/20	General		8,264.03	148,095.48	Dr
12-Payroll Cash							
	General	10/09	Payroll		11,077.87	11,077.87	Cr
	General	10/09	General	11,077.87		.00	
	General	10/23	Payroll		11,150.25	11,150.25	Cr
	General	10/23	General	11,150.25		.00	
	General	11/06	Payroll		10,919.40	10,919.40	Cr
	General	11/06	General	10,919.40		.00	
	General	11/13	Payroll		1,416.78	1,416.78	Cr
	General	11/13	General	1,416.78		.00	
	General	11/20	Payroll		8,264.03	8,264.03	Cr
	General	11/20	General	8,264.03		.00	
20.1-FICA Taxes Payable—OASDI							
	General	10/09	Payroll		878.09	878.09	Cr
	General	10/09	Pay. Tax		878.09	1,756.18	Cr
	General	10/23	Payroll		898.05	2,654.23	Cr
	General	10/23	Pay. Tax		898.05	3,552.28	Cr
	General	11/06	Payroll		876.09	4,428.37	Cr
	General	11/06	Pay. Tax		876.09	5,304.46	Cr
	General	11/13	Payroll		128.92	5,433.38	Cr
	General	11/13	Pay. Tax		128.92	5,562.30	Cr
	General	11/16	General	3,552.28		2,010.02	Cr
	General	11/20	Payroll		783.70	2,793.72	Cr
	General	11/20	Pay. Tax		783.69	3,577.41	Cr

Account	Journal	Date	Refer.	Debit	Credit	Balance	
20.2-FICA Taxes Payable—HI							
	General	10/09	Payroll		205.37	205.37	Cr
	General	10/09	Pay. Tax		205.36	410.73	Cr
	General	10/23	Payroll		210.04	620.77	Cr
	General	10/23	Pay. Tax		210.03	830.80	Cr
	General	11/06	Payroll		204.90	1,035.70	Cr
	General	11/06	Pay. Tax		204.89	1,240.59	Cr
	General	11/13	Payroll		30.15	1,270.74	Cr
	General	11/13	Pay. Tax		30.15	1,300.89	Cr
	General	11/16	General	830.80		470.09	Cr
	General	11/20	Payroll		183.30	653.39	Cr
	General	11/20	Pay. Tax		183.28	836.67	Cr
21-FUTA Taxes Payable							
	Balance Forward					392.94	Cr
	General	10/09	Pay. Tax		19.68	412.62	Cr
	General	10/23	Pay. Tax		5.16	417.78	Cr
	General	11/06	Pay. Tax		2.22	420.00	Cr
22-SUTA Taxes Payable							
	General	10/09	Pay. Tax		128.01	128.01	Cr
	General	10/23	Pay. Tax		128.01	256.02	Cr
	General	11/06	Pay. Tax		74.05	330.07	Cr
	General	11/20	Pay. Tax		27.48	357.55	Cr
24-Employees FIT Payable							
	General	10/09	Payroll		984.38	984.38	Cr
	General	10/23	Payroll		1,020.62	2,005.00	Cr
	General	11/06	Payroll		1,115.31	3,120.31	Cr
	General	11/13	Payroll		342.09	3,462.40	Cr
	General	11/16	General	2,005.00		1,457.40	Cr
	General	11/20	Payroll		698.25	2,155.65	Cr
25-Employees SIT Payable							
	General	10/09	Payroll		434.82	434.82	Cr
	General	10/20	General	434.82		.00	
	General	10/23	Payroll		444.70	444.70	Cr
	General	11/04	General	444.70		.00	
	General	11/06	Payroll		433.83	433.83	Cr
	General	11/13	Payroll		63.84	497.67	Cr
	General	11/18	General	497.67		.00	Cr
	General	11/20	Payroll		388.08	388.08	Cr

Account Journal	Date	Refer.	Debit	Credit	Balance	
25.1-Employees SUTA Payable						
General	10/09	Payroll		9.94	9.94	Cr
General	10/23	Payroll		10.16	20.10	Cr
General	11/06	Payroll		9.92	30.02	Cr
General	11/13	Payroll		1.46	31.48	Cr
General	11/20	Payroll		8.87	40.35	Cr
26-Employees CIT Payable						
General	10/09	Payroll		556.30	556.30	Cr
General	10/23	Payroll		568.95	1,125.25	Cr
General	11/06	Payroll		555.03	1,680.28	Cr
General	11/13	Payroll		81.68	1,761.96	Cr
General	11/16	General	1,125.25		636.71	Cr
General	11/20	Payroll		496.50	1,133.21	Cr
27-Grp. Ins. Prem. Collected						
General	10/23	Payroll		165.90	165.90	Cr
General	11/13	Payroll		14.40	180.30	Cr
General	11/20	Payroll		151.50	331.80	Cr
28-Union Dues Payable						
General	10/09	Payroll		16.00	16.00	Cr
General	10/23	Payroll		16.00	32.00	Cr
General	11/06	General	32.00		.00	
General	11/06	Payroll		16.00	16.00	Cr
General	11/20	Payroll		16.00	32.00	Cr
29-Simple Contrib. Payable						
General	11/20	Payroll		1,650.00	1,650.00	Cr
51-Administrative Salaries						
Balance Forward					42,692.27	Dr
General	10/09	Payroll	2,307.69		44,999.96	Dr
General	10/23	Payroll	2,307.69		47,307.65	Dr
General	11/06	Payroll	2,307.69		49,615.34	Dr
General	11/20	Payroll	2,307.69		51,923.03	Dr
52-Office Salaries						
Balance Forward					28,350.00	Dr
General	10/09	Payroll	3,353.08		31,703.08	Dr
General	10/23	Payroll	3,353.08		35,056.16	Dr
General	11/06	Payroll	3,320.79		38,376.95	Dr
General	11/13	Payroll	2,079.32		40,456.27	Dr
General	11/20	Payroll	2,112.94		42,569.21	Dr

Account	Journal	Date	Refer.	Debit	Credit	Balance	
53-Sales Salaries							
	Balance Forward					28,525.00	Dr
	General	10/09	Payroll	3,600.00		32,125.00	Dr
	General	10/23	Payroll	3,600.00		35,725.00	Dr
	General	11/06	Payroll	3,600.00		39,325.00	Dr
	General	11/20	Payroll	3,600.00		42,925.00	Dr
54-Plant Wages							
	Balance Forward					42,657.30	Dr
	General	10/09	Payroll	4,902.00		47,559.30	Dr
	General	10/23	Payroll	5,223.90		52,783.20	Dr
	General	11/06	Payroll	4,902.00		57,685.20	Dr
	General	11/20	Payroll	4,619.60		62,304.80	Dr
56-Payroll Taxes							
	Balance Forward					14,013.23	Dr
	General	10/09	Pay. Tax	1,231.14		15,244.37	Dr
	General	10/23	Pay. Tax	1,241.25		16,485.62	Dr
	General	11/06	Pay. Tax	1,157.25		17,642.87	Dr
	General	11/13	Pay. Tax	159.07		17,801.94	Dr
	General	11/20	Pay. Tax	994.45		18,796.39	Dr

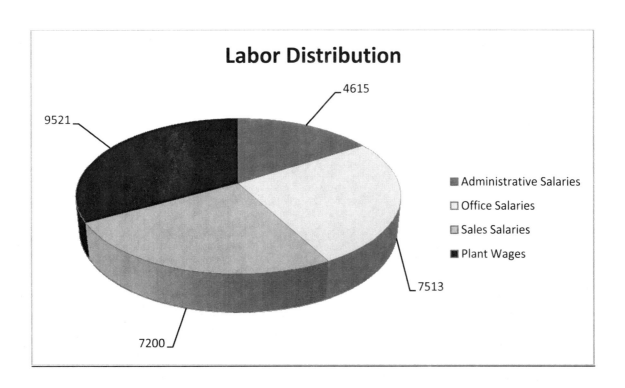

Labor Distribution

- Administrative Salaries
- Office Salaries
- Sales Salaries
- Plant Wages

Student Audit Test: November 20 Payroll

Payroll Report
1. $82.79
2. $8,264.03
3. $12,640.23

Journal Entries Report
4. $8,264.03
5. $994.45
6. $4,619.60

General Ledger
7. $388.08
8. $42,569.21
9. $1,650.00

DECEMBER 4 PAYROLL

Shortened Payroll Project starts here (continuance of the Complete Payroll Project)

Glo-Brite Paint Company
Employee List
12/04/--

Emp. No.	Employee Name/Address	Soc. Sec./ Mar. Stat.	# Pay Periods	G.L. Acct.	Salary/ Rate
100	BONNO, Anthony Victor 694 Bristol Avenue Philadelphia, PA 19135-0617	000-00-3481 Married W/H 4	26	54	17.65
110	FERGUSON, James Claude 808 Sixth Street Philadelphia, PA 19106-0995	000-00-8645 Married W/H 5	26	53	2,250.00
120	FORD, Catherine Louise 18 Dundee Avenue Philadelphia, PA 19151-1919	000-00-4567 Single W/H 2	26	52	960.00
130	MANN, Dewey Wilson 3007 Bisque Drive Philadelphia, PA 19199-0718	000-00-9352 Married W/H 0	26	53	1,350.00
140	O'NEILL, Joseph Tyler 2100 Broad Street Philadelphia, PA 19121-7189	000-00-1534 Married W/H 3	26	51	2,307.69
150	RUSSELL, Virginia Aloise 8004 Dowling Road Philadelphia, PA 19135-9001	000-00-6337 Single W/H 2	26	52	750.00
160	RYAN, Norman Allen 7300 Harrison Street Philadelphia, PA 19124-6699	000-00-1233 Married W/H 4	26	54	18.00
170	SOKOWSKI, Thomas James 133 Cornwells Street Philadelphia, PA 19171-5718	000-00-8832 Single W/H 2	26	54	2,050.00
180	STUDENT 7018 Erdrick Street Philadelphia, PA 19135-8517	000-00-5555 Single W/H 1	26	52	7.50

Emp. No.	Employee Name/Address	Soc. Sec./ Mar. Stat.	# Pay Periods	G.L. Acct.	Salary/ Rate
190	WILLIAMS, Ruth Virginia 9433 State Street Philadelphia, PA 19149-0819	000-00-6741 Single W/H 0	26	52	1,223.08
200	WOODS, Beth Anne 8102 Franklin Court Philadelphia, PA 19105-0915	000-00-1587 Single W/H 1	26	52	1,200.00
210	YOUNG, Paul Winston 7936 Holmes Drive Philadelphia, PA 19107-6107	000-00-6057 Single W/H 1	26	53	807.70

Glo-Brite Paint Company
Payroll Report
12/04/--

		Current	Quarterly	Yearly
100-BONNO, Anthony Victor	Gross Pay	1,694.40	7,165.90	18,487.85
54-Plant	FIT	86.56	278.31	1,088.31
Married Acct. 54	SIT	52.02	220.00	567.59
W/H 4 000-00-3481	Soc. Sec.—OASDI	105.05	444.28	1,146.24
Pay Periods 26	Medicare—HI	24.57	103.90	268.07
Salary	CIT	66.56	281.47	726.20
Hourly Rate 17.65	Group Ins.		33.00	177.80
Reg. Hours 80.00	Union Dues	8.00	40.00	112.00
O.T. Hours 8.00	Simple Plan			
Check Number 712	Employee SUTA	1.19	5.02	12.95
Check Date 12/04/--	Net Pay	1,350.45	5,759.92	14,388.69
110-FERGUSON, James Claude	Gross Pay	2,250.00	11,250.00	34,375.00
53-Sales	FIT	73.56	592.80	2,883.80
Married Acct. 53	SIT	69.08	345.40	1,055.34
W/H 5 000-00-8645	Soc. Sec.—OASDI	139.50	697.50	2,131.25
Pay Periods 26	Medicare—HI	32.63	163.15	498.46
Salary 2,250.00	CIT	88.38	441.90	1,350.25
Hourly Rate	Group Ins.		52.80	185.10
Reg. Hours	Union Dues			
O.T. Hours	Simple Plan	500.00	1,000.00	1,000.00
Check Number 713	Employee SUTA	1.58	7.90	24.09
Check Date 12/04/--	Net Pay	1,345.27	7,948.55	25,246.71

		Current	Quarterly	Yearly
120-FORD, Catherine Louise	Gross Pay	960.00	4,560.00	10,860.00
52-Office	FIT	71.45	321.25	960.25
Single Acct. 52	SIT	29.47	139.99	333.40
W/H 2 000-00-4567	Soc. Sec.—OASDI	59.52	282.72	673.32
Pay Periods 26	Medicare—HI	13.92	66.12	157.47
Salary 960.00	CIT	37.71	179.11	426.57
Hourly Rate	Group Ins.		21.00	58.80
Reg. Hours	Union Dues			
O.T. Hours	Simple Plan			
Check Number 714	Employee SUTA	0.67	3.19	7.60
Check Date 12/04/--	Net Pay	747.26	3,546.62	8,242.59
130-MANN, Dewey Wilson	Gross Pay	1,350.00	6,750.00	12,150.00
53-Sales	FIT	82.79	378.17	710.17
Married Acct. 53	SIT	41.45	207.25	373.03
W/H 0 000-00-9352	Soc. Sec.—OASDI	83.70	418.50	753.30
Pay Periods 26	Medicare—HI	19.58	97.90	176.20
Salary 1,350.00	CIT	53.03	265.15	477.26
Hourly Rate	Group Ins.		31.80	63.30
Reg. Hours	Union Dues			
O.T. Hours	Simple Plan	250.00	500.00	500.00
Check Number 715	Employee SUTA	0.95	4.75	8.53
Check Date 12/04/--	Net Pay	818.50	4,846.48	9,088.21
140-O'NEILL, Joseph Tyler	Gross Pay	2,307.69	11,538.45	54,230.72
51-Administrative	FIT	94.90	789.50	6,905.50
Married Acct. 51	SIT	70.85	354.25	1,664.90
W/H 3 000-00-1534	Soc. Sec.—OASDI	143.08	715.40	3,362.32
Pay Periods 26	Medicare—HI	33.46	167.30	786.34
Salary 2,307.69	CIT	90.65	453.25	2,130.20
Hourly Rate	Group Ins.		54.00	256.50
Reg. Hours	Union Dues			
O.T. Hours	Simple Plan	700.00	1,400.00	1,400.00
Check Number 716	Employee SUTA	1.62	8.10	37.98
Check Date 12/04/--	Net Pay	1,173.13	7,596.65	37,686.98
150-RUSSELL, Virginia Aloise	Gross Pay	750.00	3,475.88	9,715.88
52-Office	FIT	39.95	205.29	847.29
Single Acct. 52	SIT	23.03	106.71	298.27
W/H 2 000-00-6337	Soc. Sec.—OASDI	46.50	215.50	602.38
Pay Periods 26	Medicare—HI	10.88	50.42	140.90
Salary 750.00	CIT	29.46	136.52	381.63
Hourly Rate	Group Ins.		16.20	47.70
Reg. Hours	Union Dues			
O.T. Hours	Simple Plan			
Check Number 717	Employee SUTA	0.53	2.43	6.80
Check Date 12/04/--	Net Pay	599.65	2,742.81	7,390.91
160-RYAN, Norman Allen	Gross Pay	1,449.00	7,425.00	22,110.30
54-Plant	FIT	36.05	262.30	1,332.30
Married Acct. 54	SIT	44.48	227.95	678.79
W/H 4 000-00-1233	Soc. Sec.—OASDI	89.84	460.35	1,370.84
Pay Periods 26	Medicare—HI	21.01	107.66	320.60
Salary	CIT	56.92	291.65	868.49
Hourly Rate 18.00	Group Ins.		33.60	197.30
Reg. Hours 76.00	Union Dues	8.00	40.00	112.00
O.T. Hours 3.00	Simple Plan	200.00	400.00	400.00
Check Number 718	Employee SUTA	1.01	5.20	15.48
Check Date 12/04/--	Net Pay	991.69	5,596.29	16,814.50

		Current	Quarterly	Yearly
170-SOKOWSKI, Thomas James	Gross Pay	2,050.00	10,250.00	26,900.00
54-Plant	FIT	263.61	1,156.03	3,158.03
Single Acct. 54	SIT	62.94	314.70	825.86
W/H 2 000-00-8832	Soc. Sec.—OASDI	127.10	635.50	1,667.80
Pay Periods 26	Medicare—HI	29.73	148.65	390.08
Salary 2,050.00	CIT	80.52	402.60	1,056.61
Hourly Rate	Group Ins.		48.00	142.50
Reg. Hours	Union Dues			
O.T. Hours	Simple Plan			
Check Number 719	Employee SUTA	1.44	7.20	18.86
Check Date 12/04/--	Net Pay	1,484.66	7,537.32	19,640.26
180-STUDENT	Gross Pay	540.00	2,700.00	8,250.00
52-Office	FIT	31.31	156.55	565.55
Single Acct. 52	SIT	16.58	82.90	253.28
W/H 1 000-00-5555	Soc. Sec.—OASDI	33.48	167.40	511.50
Pay Periods 26	Medicare—HI	7.83	39.15	119.63
Salary	CIT	21.21	106.05	324.05
Hourly Rate 7.50	Group Ins.		12.60	45.00
Reg. Hours 72.00	Union Dues			
O.T. Hours	Simple Plan			
Check Number 720	Employee SUTA	0.38	1.90	5.79
Check Date 12/04/--	Net Pay	429.21	2,133.45	6,425.20
190-WILLIAMS, Ruth Virginia	Gross Pay		5,733.33	15,993.33
52-Office	FIT		800.63	2,406.63
Single Acct. 52	SIT		176.02	491.00
W/H 0 000-00-6741	Soc. Sec.—OASDI		355.47	991.59
Pay Periods 26	Medicare—HI		83.12	231.89
Salary 1,223.08	CIT		225.20	628.21
Hourly Rate	Group Ins.		28.80	88.20
Reg. Hours	Union Dues			
O.T. Hours	Simple Plan			
Check Number	Employee SUTA		4.03	11.21
Check Date	Net Pay		4,060.06	11,144.60
200-WOODS, Beth Anne	Gross Pay	1,080.00	1,080.00	1,080.00
52-Office	FIT	110.80	110.80	110.80
Single Acct. 52	SIT	33.16	33.16	33.16
W/H 1 000-00-1587	Soc. Sec.—OASDI	66.96	66.96	66.96
Pay Periods 26	Medicare—HI	15.66	15.66	15.66
Salary 1,200.00	CIT	42.42	42.42	42.42
Hourly Rate	Group Ins.			
Reg. Hours	Union Dues			
O.T. Hours	Simple Plan			
Check Number 721	Employee SUTA	0.76	0.76	0.76
Check Date 12/04/--	Net Pay	810.24	810.24	810.24
210-YOUNG, Paul Winston	Gross Pay			
53-Sales	FIT			
Single Acct. 53	SIT			
W/H 1 000-00-6057	Soc. Sec.—OASDI			
Pay Periods 26	Medicare—HI			
Salary 807.70	CIT			
Hourly Rate	Group Ins.			
Reg. Hours	Union Dues			
O.T. Hours	Simple Plan			
Check Number	Employee SUTA			
Check Date	Net Pay			

		Current	Quarterly	Yearly
Payroll Summary	Gross Pay	14,431.09	71,928.56	214,153.08
	FIT	890.98	5,051.63	20,968.63
	SIT	443.06	2,208.33	6,574.62
	Soc. Sec.—OASDI	894.73	4,459.58	13,277.50
	Medicare—HI	209.27	1,043.03	3,105.30
	CIT	566.86	2,825.32	8,411.89
	Group Ins.		331.80	1,262.20
	Union Dues	16.00	80.00	224.00
	Simple Plan	1,650.00	3,300.00	3,300.00
	Employee SUTA	10.13	50.48	150.05
	Net Pay	9,750.06	52,578.39	156,878.89

Glo-Brite Paint Company
General Journal
12/04/--

Date	Refer.	Acct.	Title	Debit	Credit
12/03	General	25	Employees SIT Payable	388.08	
12/03	General	11	Cash		388.08
12/04	Payroll	54	Plant Wages	5,193.40	
12/04	Payroll	53	Sales Salaries	3,600.00	
12/04	Payroll	52	Office Salaries	3,330.00	
12/04	Payroll	51	Administrative Salaries	2,307.69	
12/04	Payroll	24	Employees FIT Payable		890.98
12/04	Payroll	25	Employees SIT Payable		443.06
12/04	Payroll	20.1	FICA Taxes Payable—OASDI		894.73
12/04	Payroll	20.2	FICA Taxes Payable—HI		209.27
12/04	Payroll	26	Employees CIT Payable		566.86
12/04	Payroll	28	Union Dues Payable		16.00
12/04	Payroll	29	Simple Contrib. Payable		1,650.00
12/04	Payroll	25.1	Employees SUTA Payable		10.13
12/04	Payroll	12	Payroll Cash		9,750.06
12/04	Pay. Tax	56	Payroll Taxes	1,170.05	
12/04	Pay. Tax	20.1	FICA Taxes Payable—OASDI		894.73
12/04	Pay. Tax	20.2	FICA Taxes Payable—HI		209.25
12/04	Pay. Tax	22	SUTA Taxes Payable		59.59
12/04	Pay. Tax	21	FUTA Taxes Payable		6.48
12/04	General	12	Payroll Cash	9,750.06	
12/04	General	11	Cash		9,750.06
	Totals			25,739.28	25,739.28

Glo-Brite Paint Company
General Ledger
12/04/--

Account	Journal	Date	Refer.	Debit	Credit	Balance	
11-Cash							
	Balance Forward					199,846.33	Dr
	General	10/09	General		11,077.87	188,768.46	Dr
	General	10/20	General		434.82	188,333.64	Dr
	General	10/23	General		11,150.25	177,183.39	Dr
	General	11/04	General		444.70	176,738.69	Dr
	General	11/06	General		32.00	176,706.69	Dr
	General	11/06	General		10,919.40	165,787.29	Dr
	General	11/13	General		1,416.78	164,370.51	Dr
	General	11/16	General		6,388.08	157,982.43	Dr
	General	11/16	General		1,125.25	156,857.18	Dr
	General	11/18	General		497.67	156,359.51	Dr
	General	11/20	General		8,264.03	148,095.48	Dr
	General	12/03	General		388.08	147,707.40	Dr
	General	12/04	General		9,750.06	137,957.34	Dr
12-Payroll Cash							
	General	10/09	Payroll		11,077.87	11,077.87	Cr
	General	10/09	General	11,077.87		.00	
	General	10/23	Payrol		11,150.25	11,150.25	Cr
	General	10/23	General	11,150.25		.00	
	General	11/06	Payroll		10,919.40	10,919.40	Cr
	General	11/06	General	10,919.40		.00	
	General	11/13	Payroll		1,416.78	1,416.78	Cr
	General	11/13	General	1,416.78		.00	
	General	11/20	Payroll		8,264.03	8,264.03	Cr
	General	11/20	General	8,264.03		.00	
	General	12/04	Payroll		9,750.06	9,750.06	Cr
	General	12/04	General	9,750.06		.00	

Account	Journal	Date	Refer.	Debit	Credit	Balance	
20.1-FICA Taxes Payable—OASDI							
	General	10/09	Payroll		878.09	878.09	Cr
	General	10/09	Pay. Tax		878.09	1,756.18	Cr
	General	10/23	Payroll		898.05	2,654.23	Cr
	General	10/23	Pay. Tax		898.05	3,552.28	Cr
	General	11/06	Payroll		876.09	4,428.37	Cr
	General	11/06	Pay. Tax		876.09	5,304.46	Cr
	General	11/13	Payroll		128.92	5,433.38	Cr
	General	11/13	Pay. Tax		128.92	5,562.30	Cr
	General	11/16	General	3,552.28		2,010.02	Cr
	General	11/20	Payroll		783.70	2,793.72	Cr
	General	11/20	Pay. Tax		783.69	3,577.41	Cr
	General	12/04	Payroll		894.73	4,472.14	Cr
	General	12/04	Pay. Tax		894.73	5,366.87	Cr
20.2-FICA Taxes Payable—HI							
	General	10/09	Payroll		205.37	205.37	Cr
	General	10/09	Pay. Tax		205.36	410.73	Cr
	General	10/23	Payroll		210.04	620.77	Cr
	General	10/23	Pay. Tax		210.03	830.80	Cr
	General	11/06	Payroll		204.90	1,035.70	Cr
	General	11/06	Pay. Tax		204.89	1,240.59	Cr
	General	11/13	Payroll		30.15	1,270.74	Cr
	General	11/13	Pay. Tax		30.15	1,300.89	Cr
	General	11/16	General	830.80		470.09	Cr
	General	11/20	Payroll		183.30	653.39	Cr
	General	11/20	Pay. Tax		183.28	836.67	Cr
	General	12/04	Payroll		209.27	1,045.94	Cr
	General	12/04	Pay. Tax		209.25	1,255.19	Cr
21-FUTA Taxes Payable							
	Balance Forward					392.94	Cr
	General	10/09	Pay. Tax		19.68	412.62	Cr
	General	10/23	Pay. Tax		5.16	417.78	Cr
	General	11/06	Pay. Tax		2.22	420.00	Cr
	General	12/04	Pay. Tax		6.48	426.48	Cr
22-SUTA Taxes Payable							
	General	10/09	Pay. Tax		128.01	128.01	Cr
	General	10/23	Pay. Tax		128.01	256.02	Cr
	General	11/06	Pay. Tax		74.05	330.07	Cr
	General	11/20	Pay. Tax		27.48	357.55	Cr
	General	12/04	Pay. Tax		59.59	417.14	Cr

Account Journal	Date	Refer.	Debit	Credit	Balance	
24-Employees FIT Payable						
General	10/09	Payroll		984.38	984.38	Cr
General	10/23	Payroll		1,020.62	2,005.00	Cr
General	11/06	Payroll		1,115.31	3,120.31	Cr
General	11/13	Payroll		342.09	3,462.40	Cr
General	11/16	General	2,005.00		1,457.40	Cr
General	11/20	Payroll		698.25	2,155.65	Cr
General	12/04	Payroll		890.98	3,046.63	Cr
25-Employees SIT Payable						
General	10/09	Payroll		434.82	434.82	Cr
General	10/20	General	434.82		.00	
General	10/23	Payroll		444.70	444.70	Cr
General	11/04	General	444.70		.00	
General	11/06	Payroll		433.83	433.83	Cr
General	11/13	Payroll		63.84	497.67	Cr
General	11/18	General	497.67		.00	
General	11/20	Payroll		388.08	388.08	Cr
General	12/03	General	388.08		.00	
General	12/04	Payroll		443.06	443.06	Cr
25.1-Employees SUTA Payable						
General	10/09	Payroll		9.94	9.94	Cr
General	10/23	Payroll		10.16	20.10	Cr
General	11/06	Payroll		9.92	30.02	Cr
General	11/13	Payroll		1.46	31.48	Cr
General	11/20	Payroll		8.87	40.35	Cr
General	12/04	Payroll		10.13	50.48	Cr
26-Employees CIT Payable						
General	10/09	Payroll		556.30	556.30	Cr
General	10/23	Payroll		568.95	1,125.25	Cr
General	11/06	Payroll		555.03	1,680.28	Cr
General	11/13	Payroll		81.68	1,761.96	Cr
General	11/16	General	1,125.25		636.71	Cr
General	11/20	Payroll		496.50	1,133.21	Cr
General	12/04	Payroll		566.86	1,700.07	Cr
27-Grp. Ins. Prem. Collected						
General	10/23	Payroll		165.90	165.90	Cr
General	11/13	Payroll		14.40	180.30	Cr
General	11/20	Payroll		151.50	331.80	Cr

Account	Journal	Date	Refer.	Debit	Credit	Balance	
28-Union Dues Payable							
	General	10/09	Payroll		16.00	16.00	Cr
	General	10/23	Payroll		16.00	32.00	Cr
	General	11/06	General	32.00		.00	
	General	11/06	Payroll		16.00	16.00	Cr
	General	11/20	Payroll		16.00	32.00	Cr
	General	12/04	Payroll		16.00	48.00	Cr
29-Simple Contrib. Payable							
	General	11/20	Payroll		1,650.00	1,650.00	Cr
	General	12/04	Payroll		1,650.00	3,300.00	Cr
51-Administrative Salaries							
	Balance Forward					42,692.27	Dr
	General	10/09	Payroll	2,307.69		44,999.96	Dr
	General	10/23	Payroll	2,307.69		47,307.65	Dr
	General	11/06	Payroll	2,307.69		49,615.34	Dr
	General	11/20	Payroll	2,307.69		51,923.03	Dr
	General	12/04	Payroll	2,307.69		54,230.72	Dr
52-Office Salaries							
	Balance Forward					28,350.00	Dr
	General	10/09	Payroll	3,353.08		31,703.08	Dr
	General	10/23	Payroll	3,353.08		35,056.16	Dr
	General	11/06	Payroll	3,320.79		38,376.95	Dr
	General	11/13	Payroll	2,079.32		40,456.27	Dr
	General	11/20	Payroll	2,112.94		42,569.21	Dr
	General	12/04	Payroll	3,330.00		45,899.21	Dr
53-Sales Salaries							
	Balance Forward					28,525.00	Dr
	General	10/09	Payroll	3,600.00		32,125.00	Dr
	General	10/23	Payroll	3,600.00		35,725.00	Dr
	General	11/06	Payroll	3,600.00		39,325.00	Dr
	General	11/20	Payroll	3,600.00		42,925.00	Dr
	General	12/04	Payroll	3,600.00		46,525.00	Dr
54-Plant Wages							
	Balance Forward					42,657.30	Dr
	General	10/09	Payroll	4,902.00		47,559.30	Dr
	General	10/23	Payroll	5,223.90		52,783.20	Dr
	General	11/06	Payroll	4,902.00		57,685.20	Dr
	General	11/20	Payroll	4,619.60		62,304.80	Dr
	General	12/04	Payroll	5,193.40		67,498.20	Dr

Account Journal	Date	Refer.	Debit	Credit	Balance
56-Payroll Taxes					
Balance Forward					14,013.23 Dr
General	10/09	Pay. Tax	1,231.14		15,244.37 Dr
General	10/23	Pay. Tax	1,241.25		16,485.62 Dr
General	11/06	Pay. Tax	1,157.25		17,642.87 Dr
General	11/13	Pay. Tax	159.07		17,801.94 Dr
General	11/20	Pay. Tax	994.45		18,796.39 Dr
General	12/04	Pay. Tax	1,170.05		19,966.44 Dr

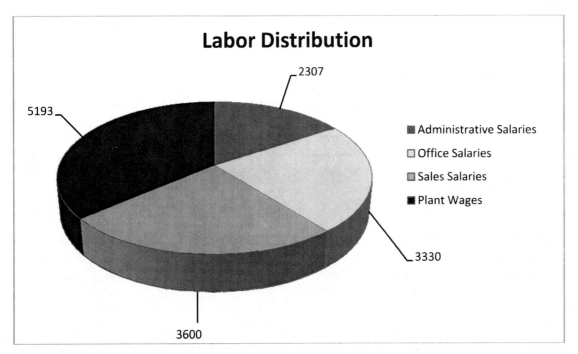

Labor Distribution

- Administrative Salaries
- Office Salaries
- Sales Salaries
- Plant Wages

2307
5193
3330
3600

Student Audit Test: December 4 Payroll

Payroll Report
1. $2,307.69
2. $89.84
3. $9,750.06
4. $566.86

Journal Entries Report
5. $2,307.69
6. $443.06
7. $1,170.05

General Ledger
8. $417.14
9. $46,525.00

DECEMBER 14 PAYROLL

Glo-Brite Paint Company
Employee List
12/14/--

Emp. No.	Employee Name/Address	Soc. Sec./ Mar. Stat.	# Pay Periods	G.L. Acct.	Salary/ Rate
100	BONNO, Anthony Victor 694 Bristol Avenue Philadelphia, PA 19135-0617	000-00-3481 Married W/H 5	26	54	17.65
110	FERGUSON, James Claude 808 Sixth Street Philadelphia, PA 19106-0995	000-00-8645 Married W/H 5	26	53	2,250.00
120	FORD, Catherine Louise 18 Dundee Avenue Philadelphia, PA 19151-1919	000-00-4567 Single W/H 2	26	52	960.00
130	MANN, Dewey Wilson 3007 Bisque Drive Philadelphia, PA 19199-0718	000-00-9352 Married W/H 0	26	53	1,350.00
140	O'NEILL, Joseph Tyler 2100 Broad Street Philadelphia, PA 19121-7189	000-00-1534 Married W/H 3	26	51	2,307.69
150	RUSSELL, Virginia Aloise 8004 Dowling Road Philadelphia, PA 19135-9001	000-00-6337 Single W/H 2	26	52	750.00
160	RYAN, Norman Allen 7300 Harrison Street Philadelphia, PA 19124-6699	000-00-1233 Married W/H 4	26	54	18.00
170	SOKOWSKI, Thomas James 133 Cornwells Street Philadelphia, PA 19171-5718	000-00-8832 Single W/H 2	26	54	2,050.00
180	STUDENT 7018 Erdrick Street Philadelphia, PA 19135-8517	000-00-5555 Single W/H 1	26	52	7.50

Emp. No.	Employee Name/Address	Soc. Sec./ Mar. Stat.	# Pay Periods	G.L. Acct.	Salary/ Rate
190	WILLIAMS, Ruth Virginia 9433 State Street Philadelphia, PA 19149-0819	000-00-6741 Single W/H 0	26	52	1,223.08
200	WOODS, Beth Anne 8102 Franklin Court Philadelphia, PA 19105-0915	000-00-1587 Single W/H 1	26	52	1,200.00
210	YOUNG, Paul Winston 7936 Holmes Drive Philadelphia, PA 19107-6107	000-00-6057 Single W/H 1	26	53	807.70

Glo-Brite Paint Company
Payroll Report
12/14/--

		Current	Quarterly	Yearly
150-RUSSELL, Virginia Aloise	Gross Pay	1,425.16	4,901.04	11,141.04
52-Office	FIT		205.29	847.29
Single Acct. 52	SIT		106.71	298.27
W/H 2 000-00-6337	Soc. Sec.—OASDI	88.36	303.86	690.74
Pay Periods 26	Medicare—HI	20.66	71.08	161.56
Salary 750.00	CIT		136.52	381.63
Hourly Rate	Group Ins.	8.70	24.90	56.40
Reg. Hours	Union Dues			
O.T. Hours	Simple Plan			
Check Number 722	Employee SUTA	1.00	3.43	7.80
Check Date 12/14/--	Net Pay	1,306.44	4,049.25	8,697.35
Payroll Summary	Gross Pay	1,425.16	73,353.72	215,578.24
	FIT		5,051.63	20,968.63
	SIT		2,208.33	6,574.62
	Soc. Sec.—OASDI	88.36	4,547.94	13,365.86
	Medicare—HI	20.66	1,063.69	3,125.96
	CIT		2,825.32	8,411.89
	Group Ins.	8.70	340.50	1,270.90
	Union Dues		80.00	224.00
	Simple Plan		3,300.00	3,300.00
	Employee SUTA	1.00	51.48	151.05
	Net Pay	1,306.44	53,884.83	158,185.33

Glo-Brite Paint Company
General Journal
12/14/--

Date	Refer.	Acct.	Title	Debit	Credit
12/09	General	28	Union Dues Payable	32.00	
12/09	General	11	Cash		32.00
12/14	Payroll	52	Office Salaries	1,425.16	
12/14	Payroll	20.1	FICA Taxes Payable—OASDI		88.36
12/14	Payroll	20.2	FICA Taxes Payable—HI		20.66
12/14	Payroll	27	Grp. Ins. Prem. Collected		8.70
12/14	Payroll	25.1	Employees SUTA Payable		1.00
12/14	Payroll	12	Payroll Cash		1,306.44
12/14	Pay. Tax	56	Payroll Taxes	109.02	
12/14	Pay. Tax	20.1	FICA Taxes Payable—OASDI		88.36
12/14	Pay. Tax	20.2	FICA Taxes Payable—HI		20.66
12/14	General	12	Payroll Cash	1,306.44	
12/14	General	11	Cash		1,306.44
		Totals		2,872.62	2,872.62

Glo-Brite Paint Company
General Ledger
12/14/--

Account	Journal	Date	Refer.	Debit	Credit	Balance	
11-Cash							
	Balance Forward					199,846.33	Dr
	General	10/09	General		11,077.87	188,768.46	Dr
	General	10/20	General		434.82	188,333.64	Dr
	General	10/23	General		11,150.25	177,183.39	Dr
	General	11/04	General		444.70	176,738.69	Dr
	General	11/06	General		32.00	176,706.69	Dr
	General	11/06	General		10,919.40	165,787.29	Dr
	General	11/13	General		1,416.78	164,370.51	Dr
	General	11/16	General		6,388.08	157,982.43	Dr
	General	11/16	General		1,125.25	156,857.18	Dr
	General	11/18	General		497.67	156,359.51	Dr
	General	11/20	General		8,264.03	148,095.48	Dr
	General	12/03	General		388.08	147,707.40	Dr
	General	12/04	General		9,750.06	137,957.34	Dr
	General	12/09	General		32.00	137,925.34	Dr
	General	12/14	General		1,306.44	136,618.90	Dr

Account	Journal	Date	Refer.	Debit	Credit	Balance	
12-Payroll Cash							
	General	10/09	Payroll		11,077.87	11,077.87	Cr
	General	10/09	General	11,077.87		.00	
	General	10/23	Payroll		11,150.25	11,150.25	Cr
	General	10/23	General	11,150.25		.00	
	General	11/06	Payroll		10,919.40	10,919.40	Cr
	General	11/06	General	10,919.40		.00	
	General	11/13	Payroll		1,416.78	1,416.78	Cr
	General	11/13	General	1,416.78		.00	
	General	11/20	Payroll		8,264.03	8,264.03	Cr
	General	11/20	General	8,264.03		.00	
	General	12/04	Payroll		9,750.06	9,750.06	Cr
	General	12/04	General	9,750.06		.00	
	General	12/14	Payroll		1,306.44	1,306.44	Cr
	General	12/14	General	1,306.44		.00	
20.1-FICA Taxes Payable—OASDI							
	General	10/09	Payroll		878.09	878.09	Cr
	General	10/09	Pay. Tax		878.09	1,756.18	Cr
	General	10/23	Payroll		898.05	2,654.23	Cr
	General	10/23	Pay. Tax		898.05	3,552.28	Cr
	General	11/06	Payroll		876.09	4,428.37	Cr
	General	11/06	Pay. Tax		876.09	5,304.46	Cr
	General	11/13	Payroll		128.92	5,433.38	Cr
	General	11/13	Pay. Tax		128.92	5,562.30	Cr
	General	11/16	General	3,552.28		2,010.02	Cr
	General	11/20	Payroll		783.70	2,793.72	Cr
	General	11/20	Pay. Tax		783.69	3,577.41	Cr
	General	12/04	Payroll		894.73	4,472.14	Cr
	General	12/04	Pay. Tax		894.73	5,366.87	Cr
	General	12/14	Payroll		88.36	5,455.23	Cr
	General	12/14	Pay. Tax		88.36	5,543.59	Cr

Account	Journal	Date	Refer.	Debit	Credit	Balance	
20.2-FICA Taxes Payable—HI							
	General	10/09	Payroll		205.37	205.37	Cr
	General	10/09	Pay. Tax		205.36	410.73	Cr
	General	10/23	Payroll		210.04	620.77	Cr
	General	10/23	Pay. Tax		210.03	830.80	Cr
	General	11/06	Payroll		204.90	1,035.70	Cr
	General	11/06	Pay. Tax		204.89	1,240.59	Cr
	General	11/13	Payroll		30.15	1,270.74	Cr
	General	11/13	Pay. Tax		30.15	1,300.89	Cr
	General	11/16	General	830.80		470.09	Cr
	General	11/20	Payroll		183.30	653.39	Cr
	General	11/20	Pay. Tax		183.28	836.67	Cr
	General	12/04	Payroll		209.27	1,045.94	Cr
	General	12/04	Pay. Tax		209.25	1,255.19	Cr
	General	12/14	Payroll		20.66	1,275.85	Cr
	General	12/14	Pay. Tax		20.66	1,296.51	Cr
21-FUTA Taxes Payable							
	Balance Forward					392.94	Cr
	General	10/09	Pay. Tax		19.68	412.62	Cr
	General	10/23	Pay. Tax		5.16	417.78	Cr
	General	11/06	Pay. Tax		2.22	420.00	Cr
	General	12/04	Pay. Tax		6.48	426.48	Cr
22-SUTA Taxes Payable							
	General	10/09	Pay. Tax		128.01	128.01	Cr
	General	10/23	Pay. Tax		128.01	256.02	Cr
	General	11/06	Pay. Tax		74.05	330.07	Cr
	General	11/20	Pay. Tax		27.48	357.55	Cr
	General	12/04	Pay. Tax		59.59	417.14	Cr
24-Employees FIT Payable							
	General	10/09	Payroll		984.38	984.38	Cr
	General	10/23	Payroll		1,020.62	2,005.00	Cr
	General	11/06	Payroll		1,115.31	3,120.31	Cr
	General	11/13	Payroll		342.09	3,462.40	Cr
	General	11/16	General	2,005.00		1,457.40	Cr
	General	11/20	Payroll		698.25	2,155.65	Cr
	General	12/04	Payroll		890.98	3,046.63	Cr

Account Journal	Date	Refer.	Debit	Credit	Balance	
25-Employees SIT Payable						
General	10/09	Payroll		434.82	434.82	Cr
General	10/20	General	434.82		.00	
General	10/23	Payroll		444.70	444.70	Cr
General	11/04	General	444.70		.00	
General	11/06	Payroll		433.83	433.83	Cr
General	11/13	Payroll		63.84	497.67	Cr
General	11/18	General	497.67		.00	
General	11/20	Payroll		388.08	388.08	Cr
General	12/03	General	388.08		.00	
General	12/04	Payroll		443.06	443.06	Cr
25.1-Employees SUTA Payable						
General	10/09	Payroll		9.94	9.94	Cr
General	10/23	Payroll		10.16	20.10	Cr
General	11/06	Payroll		9.92	30.02	Cr
General	11/13	Payroll		1.46	31.48	Cr
General	11/20	Payroll		8.87	40.35	Cr
General	12/04	Payroll		10.13	50.48	Cr
General	12/14	Payroll		1.00	51.48	Cr
26-Employees CIT Payable						
General	10/09	Payroll		556.30	556.30	Cr
General	10/23	Payroll		568.95	1,125.25	Cr
General	11/06	Payroll		555.03	1,680.28	Cr
General	11/13	Payroll		81.68	1,761.96	Cr
General	11/16	General	1,125.25		636.71	Cr
General	11/20	Payroll		496.50	1,133.21	Cr
General	12/04	Payroll		566.86	1,700.07	Cr
27-Grp. Ins. Prem. Collected						
General	10/23	Payroll		165.90	165.90	Cr
General	11/13	Payroll		14.40	180.30	Cr
General	11/20	Payroll		151.50	331.80	Cr
General	12/14	Payroll		8.70	340.50	Cr
28-Union Dues Payable						
General	10/09	Payroll		16.00	16.00	Cr
General	10/23	Payroll		16.00	32.00	Cr
General	11/06	General	32.00		.00	
General	11/06	Payroll		16.00	16.00	Cr
General	11/20	Payroll		16.00	32.00	Cr
General	12/04	Payroll		16.00	48.00	Cr
General	12/09	General	32.00		16.00	Cr

Account	Journal	Date	Refer.	Debit	Credit	Balance	
29-Simple Contrib. Payable							
	General	11/20	Payroll		1,650.00	1,650.00	Cr
	General	12/04	Payroll		1,650.00	3,300.00	Cr
51-Administrative Salaries							
	Balance Forward					42,692.27	Dr
	General	10/09	Payroll	2,307.69		44,999.96	Dr
	General	10/23	Payroll	2,307.69		47,307.65	Dr
	General	11/06	Payroll	2,307.69		49,615.34	Dr
	General	11/20	Payroll	2,307.69		51,923.03	Dr
	General	12/04	Payroll	2,307.69		54,230.72	Dr
52-Office Salaries							
	Balance Forward					28,350.00	Dr
	General	10/09	Payroll	3,353.08		31,703.08	Dr
	General	10/23	Payroll	3,353.08		35,056.16	Dr
	General	11/06	Payroll	3,320.79		38,376.95	Dr
	General	11/13	Payroll	2,079.32		40,456.27	Dr
	General	11/20	Payroll	2,112.94		42,569.21	Dr
	General	12/04	Payroll	3,330.00		45,899.21	Dr
	General	12/14	Payroll	1,425.16		47,324.37	Dr
53-Sales Salaries							
	Balance Forward					28,525.00	Dr
	General	10/09	Payroll	3,600.00		32,125.00	Dr
	General	10/23	Payroll	3,600.00		35,725.00	Dr
	General	11/06	Payroll	3,600.00		39,325.00	Dr
	General	11/20	Payroll	3,600.00		42,925.00	Dr
	General	12/04	Payroll	3,600.00		46,525.00	Dr
54-Plant Wages							
	Balance Forward					42,657.30	Dr
	General	10/09	Payroll	4,902.00		47,559.30	Dr
	General	10/23	Payroll	5,223.90		52,783.20	Dr
	General	11/06	Payroll	4,902.00		57,685.20	Dr
	General	11/20	Payroll	4,619.60		62,304.80	Dr
	General	12/04	Payroll	5,193.40		67,498.20	Dr

Account	Journal	Date	Refer.	Debit	Credit	Balance	
56-Payroll Taxes							
	Balance Forward					14,013.23	Dr
	General	10/09	Pay. Tax	1,231.14		15,244.37	Dr
	General	10/23	Pay. Tax	1,241.25		16,485.62	Dr
	General	11/06	Pay. Tax	1,157.25		17,642.87	Dr
	General	11/13	Pay. Tax	159.07		17,801.94	Dr
	General	11/20	Pay. Tax	994.45		18,796.39	Dr
	General	12/04	Pay. Tax	1,170.05		19,966.44	Dr
	General	12/14	Pay. Tax	109.02		20,075.46	Dr

Student Audit Test: December 14 Payroll

Payroll Report
1. 000-00-6337
2. $1,306.44

Journal Entries Report
3. $1,425.16

General Ledger
4. $8.70
5. $47,324.37

DECEMBER 18 PAYROLL

Glo-Brite Paint Company
Employee List
12/18/--

Emp. No.	Employee Name/Address	Soc. Sec./ Mar. Stat.	# Pay Periods	G.L. Acct.	Salary/ Rate
100	BONNO, Anthony Victor 694 Bristol Avenue Philadelphia, PA 19135-0617	000-00-3481 Married W/H 5	26	54	17.65
110	FERGUSON, James Claude 808 Sixth Street Philadelphia, PA 19106-0995	000-00-8645 Married W/H 5	26	53	2,250.00
120	FORD, Catherine Louise 18 Dundee Avenue Philadelphia, PA 19151-1919	000-00-4567 Single W/H 2	26	52	960.00
130	MANN, Dewey Wilson 3007 Bisque Drive Philadelphia, PA 19199-0718	000-00-9352 Married W/H 0	26	53	1,350.00
140	O'NEILL, Joseph Tyler 2100 Broad Street Philadelphia, PA 19121-7189	000-00-1534 Married W/H 4	26	51	2,307.69
150	RUSSELL, Virginia Aloise 8004 Dowling Road Philadelphia, PA 19135-9001	000-00-6337 Single W/H 2	26	52	750.00
160	RYAN, Norman Allen 7300 Harrison Street Philadelphia, PA 19124-6699	000-00-1233 Married W/H 4	26	54	18.00
170	SOKOWSKI, Thomas James 133 Cornwells Street Philadelphia, PA 19171-5718	000-00-8832 Single W/H 2	26	54	2,050.00
180	STUDENT 7018 Erdrick Street Philadelphia, PA 19135-8517	000-00-5555 Single W/H 1	26	52	7.50
190	WILLIAMS, Ruth Virginia 9433 State Street Philadelphia, PA 19149-0819	000-00-6741 Single W/H 0	26	52	1,223.08

Emp. No.	Employee Name/Address	Soc. Sec./ Mar. Stat.	# Pay Periods	G.L. Acct.	Salary/ Rate
200	WOODS, Beth Anne 8102 Franklin Court Philadelphia, PA 19105-0915	000-00-1587 Single W/H 1	26	52	1,200.00
210	YOUNG, Paul Winston 7936 Holmes Drive Philadelphia, PA 19107-6107	000-00-6057 Single W/H 1	26	53	807.70
220	ZIMMERMAN, Richard Lewis 900 South Clark Street Philadelphia, PA 19195-6247	000-00-1502 Married W/H 1	26	52	660.00

Glo-Brite Paint Company
Payroll Report
12/18/--

		Current	Quarterly	Yearly
100-BONNO, Anthony Victor	Gross Pay	1,835.60	9,001.50	20,323.45
54-Plant	FIT	86.40	364.71	1,174.71
Married Acct. 54	SIT	56.35	276.35	623.94
W/H 5 000-00-3481	Soc. Sec.—OASDI	113.81	558.09	1,260.05
Pay Periods 26	Medicare—HI	26.62	130.52	294.69
Salary	CIT	72.10	353.57	798.30
Hourly Rate 17.65	Group Ins.	16.50	49.50	194.30
Reg. Hours 80.00	Union Dues	9.00	49.00	121.00
O.T. Hours 12.00	Simple Plan			
Check Number 723	Employee SUTA	1.28	6.30	14.23
Check Date 12/18/--	Net Pay	1,453.54	7,213.46	15,842.23
110-FERGUSON, James Claude	Gross Pay	2,250.00	13,500.00	36,625.00
53-Sales	FIT	73.56	666.36	2,957.36
Married Acct. 53	SIT	69.08	414.48	1,124.42
W/H 5 000-00-8645	Soc. Sec.—OASDI	139.50	837.00	2,270.75
Pay Periods 26	Medicare—HI	32.63	195.78	531.09
Salary 2,250.00	CIT	88.38	530.28	1,438.63
Hourly Rate	Group Ins.	26.40	79.20	211.50
Reg. Hours	Union Dues			
O.T. Hours	Simple Plan	500.00	1,500.00	1,500.00
Check Number 724	Employee SUTA	1.58	9.48	25.67
Check Date 12/18/--	Net Pay	1,318.87	9,267.42	26,565.58

		Current	Quarterly	Yearly
120-FORD, Catherine Louise	Gross Pay	960.00	5,520.00	11,820.00
52-Office	FIT	71.45	392.70	1,031.70
Single Acct. 52	SIT	29.47	169.46	362.87
W/H 2 000-00-4567	Soc. Sec.—OASDI	59.52	342.24	732.84
Pay Periods 26	Medicare—HI	13.92	80.04	171.39
Salary 960.00	CIT	37.71	216.82	464.28
Hourly Rate	Group Ins.	11.10	32.10	69.90
Reg. Hours	Union Dues			
O.T. Hours	Simple Plan			
Check Number 725	Employee SUTA	0.67	3.86	8.27
Check Date 12/18/--	Net Pay	736.16	4,282.78	8,978.75
130-MANN, Dewey Wilson	Gross Pay	1,350.00	8,100.00	13,500.00
53-Sales	FIT	82.79	460.96	792.96
Married Acct. 53	SIT	41.45	248.70	414.48
W/H 0 000-00-9352	Soc. Sec.—OASDI	83.70	502.20	837.00
Pay Periods 26	Medicare—HI	19.58	117.48	195.78
Salary 1,350.00	CIT	53.03	318.18	530.29
Hourly Rate	Group Ins.	15.90	47.70	79.20
Reg. Hours	Union Dues			
O.T. Hours	Simple Plan	250.00	750.00	750.00
Check Number 726	Employee SUTA	0.95	5.70	9.48
Check Date 12/18/--	Net Pay	802.60	5,649.08	9,890.81
140-O'NEILL, Joseph Tyler	Gross Pay	62,307.69	73,846.14	116,538.41
51-Administrative	FIT	20,724.40	21,513.90	27,629.90
Married Acct. 51	SIT	1,912.85	2,267.10	3,577.75
W/H 4 000-00-1534	Soc. Sec.—OASDI	3,687.08	4,402.48	7,049.40
Pay Periods 26	Medicare—HI	903.46	1,070.76	1,689.80
Salary 2,307.69	CIT	2,447.45	2,900.70	4,577.65
Hourly Rate	Group Ins.	27.00	81.00	283.50
Reg. Hours	Union Dues			
O.T. Hours	Simple Plan	4,000.00	5,400.00	5,400.00
Check Number 727	Employee SUTA	43.62	51.72	81.60
Check Date 12/18/--	Net Pay	28,561.83	36,158.48	66,248.81
150-RUSSELL, Virginia Aloise	Gross Pay		4,901.04	11,141.04
52-Office	FIT		205.29	847.29
Single Acct. 52	SIT		106.71	298.27
W/H 2 000-00-6337	Soc. Sec.—OASDI		303.86	690.74
Pay Periods 26	Medicare—HI		71.08	161.56
Salary 750.00	CIT		136.52	381.63
Hourly Rate	Group Ins.		24.90	56.40
Reg. Hours	Union Dues			
O.T. Hours	Simple Plan			
Check Number	Employee SUTA		3.43	7.80
Check Date	Net Pay		4,049.25	8,697.35
160-RYAN, Norman Allen	Gross Pay	1,629.00	9,054.00	23,739.30
54-Plant	FIT	54.05	316.35	1,386.35
Married Acct. 54	SIT	50.01	277.96	728.80
W/H 4 000-00-1233	Soc. Sec.—OASDI	101.00	561.35	1,471.84
Pay Periods 26	Medicare—HI	23.62	131.28	344.22
Salary	CIT	63.99	355.64	932.48
Hourly Rate 18.00	Group Ins.	16.80	50.40	214.10
Reg. Hours 80.00	Union Dues	9.00	49.00	121.00
O.T. Hours 7.00	Simple Plan	200.00	600.00	600.00
Check Number 728	Employee SUTA	1.14	6.34	16.62
Check Date 12/18/--	Net Pay	1,109.39	6,705.68	17,923.89

		Current	Quarterly	Yearly
170-SOKOWSKI, Thomas James	Gross Pay	2,050.00	12,300.00	28,950.00
54-Plant	FIT	263.61	1,419.64	3,421.64
Single Acct. 54	SIT	62.94	377.64	888.80
W/H 2 000-00-8832	Soc. Sec.—OASDI	127.10	762.60	1,794.90
Pay Periods 26	Medicare—HI	29.73	178.38	419.81
Salary 2,050.00	CIT	80.52	483.12	1,137.13
Hourly Rate	Group Ins.	24.00	72.00	166.50
Reg. Hours	Union Dues			
O.T. Hours	Simple Plan			
Check Number 729	Employee SUTA	1.44	8.64	20.30
Check Date 12/18/--	Net Pay	1,460.66	8,997.98	21,100.92
180-STUDENT	Gross Pay	532.50	3,232.50	8,782.50
52-Office	FIT	30.56	187.11	596.11
Single Acct. 52	SIT	16.35	99.25	269.63
W/H 1 000-00-5555	Soc. Sec.—OASDI	33.02	200.42	544.52
Pay Periods 26	Medicare—HI	7.72	46.87	127.35
Salary	CIT	20.92	126.97	344.97
Hourly Rate 7.50	Group Ins.	6.30	18.90	51.30
Reg. Hours 71.00	Union Dues			
O.T. Hours	Simple Plan			
Check Number 730	Employee SUTA	0.37	2.27	6.16
Check Date 12/18/--	Net Pay	417.26	2,550.71	6,842.46
190-WILLIAMS, Ruth Virginia	Gross Pay		5,733.33	15,993.33
52-Office	FIT		800.63	2,406.63
Single Acct. 52	SIT		176.02	491.00
W/H 0 000-00-6741	Soc. Sec.—OASDI		355.47	991.59
Pay Periods 26	Medicare—HI		83.12	231.89
Salary 1,223.08	CIT		225.20	628.21
Hourly Rate	Group Ins.		28.80	88.20
Reg. Hours	Union Dues			
O.T. Hours	Simple Plan			
Check Number	Employee SUTA		4.03	11.21
Check Date	Net Pay		4,060.06	11,144.60
200-WOODS, Beth Anne	Gross Pay	1,200.00	2,280.00	2,280.00
52-Office	FIT	128.80	239.60	239.60
Single Acct. 52	SIT	36.84	70.00	70.00
W/H 1 000-00-1587	Soc. Sec.—OASDI	74.40	141.36	141.36
Pay Periods 26	Medicare—HI	17.40	33.06	33.06
Salary 1,200.00	CIT	47.14	89.56	89.56
Hourly Rate	Group Ins.	14.10	14.10	14.10
Reg. Hours	Union Dues			
O.T. Hours	Simple Plan			
Check Number 731	Employee SUTA	0.84	1.60	1.60
Check Date 12/18/--	Net Pay	880.48	1,690.72	1,690.72
210-YOUNG, Paul Winston	Gross Pay	807.70	807.70	807.70
53-Sales	FIT	69.95	69.95	69.95
Single Acct. 53	SIT	24.80	24.80	24.80
W/H 1 000-00-6057	Soc. Sec.—OASDI	50.08	50.08	50.08
Pay Periods 26	Medicare—HI	11.71	11.71	11.71
Salary 807.70	CIT	31.73	31.73	31.73
Hourly Rate	Group Ins.	9.60	9.60	9.60
Reg. Hours	Union Dues			
O.T. Hours	Simple Plan			
Check Number 732	Employee SUTA	0.57	0.57	0.57
Check Date 12/18/--	Net Pay	609.26	609.26	609.26

		Current	Quarterly	Yearly
220-ZIMMERMAN, Richard Lewis	Gross Pay			
52-Office	FIT			
Married Acct. 52	SIT			
W/H 1 000-00-1502	Soc. Sec.—OASDI			
Pay Periods 26	Medicare—HI			
Salary 660.00	CIT			
Hourly Rate	Group Ins.			
Reg. Hours	Union Dues			
O.T. Hours	Simple Plan			
Check Number	Employee SUTA			
Check Date	Net Pay			
Payroll Summary	Gross Pay	74,922.49	148,276.21	290,500.73
	FIT	21,585.57	26,637.20	42,554.20
	SIT	2,300.14	4,508.47	8,874.76
	Soc. Sec.—OASDI	4,469.21	9,017.15	17,835.07
	Medicare—HI	1,086.39	2,150.08	4,212.35
	CIT	2,942.97	5,768.29	11,354.86
	Group Ins.	167.70	508.20	1,438.60
	Union Dues	18.00	98.00	242.00
	Simple Plan	4,950.00	8,250.00	8,250.00
	Employee SUTA	52.46	103.94	203.51
	Net Pay	37,350.05	91,234.88	195,535.38

Glo-Brite Paint Company
General Journal
12/18/--

Date	Refer.	Acct.	Title	Debit	Credit
12/15	General	20.1	FICA Taxes Payable—OASDI	3,577.41	
12/15	General	20.2	FICA Taxes Payable—HI	836.67	
12/15	General	24	Employees FIT Payable	2,155.65	
12/15	General	11	Cash		6,569.73
12/15	General	26	Employees CIT Payable	1,133.21	
12/15	General	11	Cash		1,133.21
12/18	General	25	Employees SIT Payable	443.06	
12/18	General	11	Cash		443.06
12/18	General	27	Grp. Ins. Prem. Collected	8.70	
12/18	General	11	Cash		8.70
12/18	Payroll	54	Plant Wages	5,514.60	
12/18	Payroll	53	Sales Salaries	4,407.70	
12/18	Payroll	52	Office Salaries	2,692.50	
12/18	Payroll	51	Administrative Salaries	62,307.69	
12/18	Payroll	24	Employees FIT Payable		21,585.57
12/18	Payroll	25	Employees SIT Payable		2,300.14
12/18	Payroll	20.1	FICA Taxes Payable—OASDI		4,469.21
12/18	Payroll	20.2	FICA Taxes Payable—HI		1,086.39
12/18	Payroll	26	Employees CIT Payable		2,942.97
12/18	Payroll	27	Grp. Ins. Prem. Collected		167.70
12/18	Payroll	28	Union Dues Payable		18.00
12/18	Payroll	29	Simple Contrib. Payable		4,950.00
12/18	Payroll	25.1	Employees SUTA Payable		52.46
12/18	Payroll	12	Payroll Cash		37,350.05
12/18	Pay. Tax	56	Payroll Taxes	5,650.69	
12/18	Pay. Tax	20.1	FICA Taxes Payable—OASDI		4,469.21
12/18	Pay. Tax	20.2	FICA Taxes Payable—HI		1,086.38
12/18	Pay. Tax	22	SUTA Taxes Payable		83.05
12/18	Pay. Tax	21	FUTA Taxes Payable		12.05
12/18	General	12	Payroll Cash	37,350.05	
12/18	General	11	Cash		37,350.05
	Totals			126,077.93	126,077.93

Glo-Brite Paint Company
General Ledger
12/18/--

Account	Journal	Date	Refer.	Debit	Credit	Balance	
11-Cash							
	Balance Forward					199,846.33	Dr
	General	10/09	General		11,077.87	188,768.46	Dr
	General	10/20	General		434.82	188,333.64	Dr
	General	10/23	General		11,150.25	177,183.39	Dr
	General	11/04	General		444.70	176,738.69	Dr
	General	11/06	General		32.00	176,706.69	Dr
	General	11/06	General		10,919.40	165,787.29	Dr
	General	11/13	General		1,416.78	164,370.51	Dr
	General	11/16	General		6,388.08	157,982.43	Dr
	General	11/16	General		1,125.25	156,857.18	Dr
	General	11/18	General		497.67	156,359.51	Dr
	General	11/20	General		8,264.03	148,095.48	Dr
	General	12/03	General		388.08	147,707.40	Dr
	General	12/04	General		9,750.06	137,957.34	Dr
	General	12/09	General		32.00	137,925.34	Dr
	General	12/14	General		1,306.44	136,618.90	Dr
	General	12/15	General		6,569.73	130,049.17	Dr
	General	12/15	General		1,133.21	128,915.96	Dr
	General	12/18	General		443.06	128,472.90	Dr
	General	12/18	General		8.70	128,464.20	Dr
	General	12/18	General		37,350.05	91,114.15	Dr
12-Payroll Cash							
	General	10/09	Payroll		11,077.87	11,077.87	Cr
	General	10/09	General	11,077.87		.00	
	General	10/23	Payroll		11,150.25	11,150.25	Cr
	General	10/23	General	11,150.25		.00	
	General	11/06	Payroll		10,919.40	10,919.40	Cr
	General	11/06	General	10,919.40		.00	
	General	11/13	Payroll		1,416.78	1,416.78	Cr
	General	11/13	General	1,416.78		.00	
	General	11/20	Payroll		8,264.03	8,264.03	Cr
	General	11/20	General	8,264.03		.00	
	General	12/04	Payroll		9,750.06	9,750.06	Cr
	General	12/04	General	9,750.06		.00	
	General	12/14	Payroll		1,306.44	1,306.44	Cr
	General	12/14	General	1,306.44		.00	
	General	12/18	Payroll		37,350.05	37,350.05	Cr
	General	12/18	General	37,350.05		.00	

Account	Journal	Date	Refer.	Debit	Credit	Balance	
20.1-FICA Taxes Payable—OASDI							
	General	10/09	Payroll		878.09	878.09	Cr
	General	10/09	Pay. Tax		878.09	1,756.18	Cr
	General	10/23	Payroll		898.05	2,654.23	Cr
	General	10/23	Pay. Tax		898.05	3,552.28	Cr
	General	11/06	Payroll		876.09	4,428.37	Cr
	General	11/06	Pay. Tax		876.09	5,304.46	Cr
	General	11/13	Payroll		128.92	5,433.38	Cr
	General	11/13	Pay. Tax		128.92	5,562.30	Cr
	General	11/16	General	3,552.28		2,010.02	Cr
	General	11/20	Payroll		783.70	2,793.72	Cr
	General	11/20	Pay. Tax		783.69	3,577.41	Cr
	General	12/04	Payroll		894.73	4,472.14	Cr
	General	12/04	Pay. Tax		894.73	5,366.87	Cr
	General	12/14	Payroll		88.36	5,455.23	Cr
	General	12/14	Pay. Tax		88.36	5,543.59	Cr
	General	12/15		3,577.41		1,966.18	Cr
	General	12/18	Payroll		4,469.21	6,435.39	Cr
	General	12/18	Pay. Tax		4,469.21	10,904.60	Cr
20.2-FICA Taxes Payable—HI							
	General	10/09	Payroll		205.37	205.37	Cr
	General	10/09	Pay. Tax		205.36	410.73	Cr
	General	10/23	Payroll		210.04	620.77	Cr
	General	10/23	Pay. Tax		210.03	830.80	Cr
	General	11/06	Payroll		204.90	1,035.70	Cr
	General	11/06	Pay. Tax		204.89	1,240.59	Cr
	General	11/13	Payroll		30.15	1,270.74	Cr
	General	11/13	Pay. Tax		30.15	1,300.89	Cr
	General	11/16	General	830.80		470.09	Cr
	General	11/20	Payroll		183.30	653.39	Cr
	General	11/20	Pay. Tax		183.28	836.67	Cr
	General	12/04	Payroll		209.27	1,045.94	Cr
	General	12/04	Pay. Tax		209.25	1,255.19	Cr
	General	12/14	Payroll		20.66	1,275.85	Cr
	General	12/14	Pay. Tax		20.66	1,296.51	Cr
	General	12/15	General	836.67		459.84	Cr
	General	12/18	Payroll		1,086.39	1,546.23	Cr
	General	12/18	Pay. Tax		1,086.38	2,632.61	Cr

Account	Journal	Date	Refer.	Debit	Credit	Balance	
21-FUTA Taxes Payable							
	Balance Forward					392.94	Cr
	General	10/09	Pay. Tax		19.68	412.62	Cr
	General	10/23	Pay. Tax		5.16	417.78	Cr
	General	11/06	Pay. Tax		2.22	420.00	Cr
	General	12/04	Pay. Tax		6.48	426.48	Cr
	General	12/18	Pay. Tax		12.05	438.53	Cr
22-SUTA Taxes Payable							
	General	10/09	Pay. Tax		128.01	128.01	Cr
	General	10/23	Pay. Tax		128.01	256.02	Cr
	General	11/06	Pay. Tax		74.05	330.07	Cr
	General	11/20	Pay. Tax		27.48	357.55	Cr
	General	12/04	Pay. Tax		59.59	417.14	Cr
	General	12/18	Pay. Tax		83.05	500.19	Cr
24-Employees FIT Payable							
	General	10/09	Payroll		984.38	984.38	Cr
	General	10/23	Payroll		1,020.62	2,005.00	Cr
	General	11/06	Payroll		1,115.31	3,120.31	Cr
	General	11/13	Payroll		342.09	3,462.40	Cr
	General	11/16	General	2,005.00		1,457.40	Cr
	General	11/20	Payroll		698.25	2,155.65	Cr
	General	12/04	Payroll		890.98	3,046.63	Cr
	General	12/15	General	2,155.65		890.98	Cr
	General	12/18	Payroll		21,585.57	22,476.55	Cr
25-Employees SIT Payable							
	General	10/09	Payroll		434.82	434.82	Cr
	General	10/20	General	434.82		.00	
	General	10/23	Payroll		444.70	444.70	Cr
	General	11/04	General	444.70		.00	
	General	11/06	Payroll		433.83	433.83	Cr
	General	11/13	Payroll		63.84	497.67	Cr
	General	11/18	General	497.67		.00	
	General	11/20	Payroll		388.08	388.08	Cr
	General	12/03	General	388.08		.00	
	General	12/04	Payroll		443.06	443.06	Cr
	General	12/18	General	443.06		.00	
	General	12/18	Payroll		2,300.14	2,300.14	Cr

Account	Journal	Date	Refer.	Debit	Credit	Balance	
25.1-Employees SUTA Payable							
	General	10/09	Payroll		9.94	9.94	Cr
	General	10/23	Payroll		10.16	20.10	Cr
	General	11/06	Payroll		9.92	30.02	Cr
	General	11/13	Payroll		1.46	31.48	Cr
	General	11/20	Payroll		8.87	40.35	Cr
	General	12/04	Payroll		10.13	50.48	Cr
	General	12/14	Payroll		1.00	51.48	Cr
	General	12/18	Payroll		52.46	103.94	Cr
26-Employees CIT Payable							
	General	10/09	Payroll		556.30	556.30	Cr
	General	10/23	Payroll		568.95	1,125.25	Cr
	General	11/06	Payroll		555.03	1,680.28	Cr
	General	11/13	Payroll		81.68	1,761.96	Cr
	General	11/16	General	1,125.25		636.71	Cr
	General	11/20	Payroll		496.50	1,133.21	Cr
	General	12/04	Payroll		566.86	1,700.07	Cr
	General	12/15	General	1,133.21		566.86	Cr
	General	12/18	Payroll		2,942.97	3,509.83	Cr
27-Grp. Ins. Prem. Collected							
	General	10/23	Payroll		165.90	165.90	Cr
	General	11/13	Payroll		14.40	180.30	Cr
	General	11/20	Payroll		151.50	331.80	Cr
	General	12/14	Payroll		8.70	340.50	Cr
	General	12/18	General	8.70		331.80	Cr
	General	12/18	Payroll		167.70	499.50	Cr
28-Union Dues Payable							
	General	10/09	Payroll		16.00	16.00	Cr
	General	10/23	Payroll		16.00	32.00	Cr
	General	11/06	General	32.00		.00	
	General	11/06	Payroll		16.00	16.00	Cr
	General	11/20	Payroll		16.00	32.00	Cr
	General	12/04	Payroll		16.00	48.00	Cr
	General	12/09	General	32.00		16.00	Cr
	General	12/18	Payroll		18.00	34.00	Cr
29-Simple Contrib. Payable							
	General	11/20	Payroll		1,650.00	1,650.00	Cr
	General	12/04	Payroll		1,650.00	3,300.00	Cr
	General	12/18	Payroll		4,950.00	8,250.00	Cr

Account	Journal	Date	Refer.	Debit	Credit	Balance	
51-Administrative Salaries							
	Balance Forward					42,692.27	Dr
	General	10/09	Payroll	2,307.69		44,999.96	Dr
	General	10/23	Payroll	2,307.69		47,307.65	Dr
	General	11/06	Payroll	2,307.69		49,615.34	Dr
	General	11/20	Payroll	2,307.69		51,923.03	Dr
	General	12/04	Payroll	2,307.69		54,230.72	Dr
	General	12/18	Payroll	62,307.69		116,538.41	Dr
52-Office Salaries							
	Balance Forward					28,350.00	Dr
	General	10/09	Payroll	3,353.08		31,703.08	Dr
	General	10/23	Payroll	3,353.08		35,056.16	Dr
	General	11/06	Payroll	3,320.79		38,376.95	Dr
	General	11/13	Payroll	2,079.32		40,456.27	Dr
	General	11/20	Payroll	2,112.94		42,569.21	Dr
	General	12/04	Payroll	3,330.00		45,899.21	Dr
	General	12/14	Payroll	1,425.16		47,324.37	Dr
	General	12/18	Payroll	2,692.50		50,016.87	Dr
53-Sales Salaries							
	Balance Forward					28,525.00	Dr
	General	10/09	Payroll	3,600.00		32,125.00	Dr
	General	10/23	Payroll	3,600.00		35,725.00	Dr
	General	11/06	Payroll	3,600.00		39,325.00	Dr
	General	11/20	Payroll	3,600.00		42,925.00	Dr
	General	12/04	Payroll	3,600.00		46,525.00	Dr
	General	12/18	Payroll	4,407.70		50,932.70	Dr
54-Plant Wages							
	Balance Forward					42,657.30	Dr
	General	10/09	Payroll	4,902.00		47,559.30	Dr
	General	10/23	Payroll	5,223.90		52,783.20	Dr
	General	11/06	Payroll	4,902.00		57,685.20	Dr
	General	11/20	Payroll	4,619.60		62,304.80	Dr
	General	12/04	Payroll	5,193.40		67,498.20	Dr
	General	12/18	Payroll	5,514.60		73,012.80	Dr

Account	Journal	Date	Refer.	Debit	Credit	Balance	
56-Payroll Taxes							
	Balance Forward					14,013.23	Dr
	General	10/09	Pay. Tax	1,231.14		15,244.37	Dr
	General	10/23	Pay. Tax	1,241.25		16,485.62	Dr
	General	11/06	Pay. Tax	1,157.25		17,642.87	Dr
	General	11/13	Pay. Tax	159.07		17,801.94	Dr
	General	11/20	Pay. Tax	994.45		18,796.39	Dr
	General	12/04	Pay. Tax	1,170.05		19,966.44	Dr
	General	12/14	Pay. Tax	109.02		20,075.46	Dr
	General	12/18	Pay. Tax	5,650.69		25,726.15	Dr

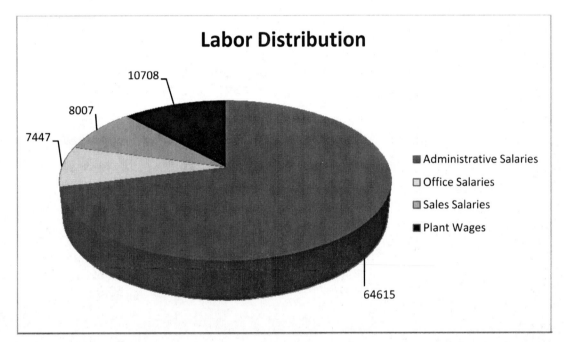

Labor Distribution

- Administrative Salaries
- Office Salaries
- Sales Salaries
- Plant Wages

10708, 8007, 7447, 64615

Student Audit Test: December 18 Payroll

Payroll Report
1. $62.94
2. $37,350.05
3. $290,500.73

Journal Entries Report
4. $62,307.69
5. $5,650.69

General Ledger
6. $91,114.15
7. $73,012.80
8. $25,726.15

OPTIONAL ACTIVITIES

STEP 7—Tax forms

See pages A–70 through A–86.

STEP 7A

Form **941 for 20--:**   **Employer's QUARTERLY Federal Tax Return**
(Rev. January 2013)   Department of the Treasury — Internal Revenue Service

OMB No. 1545-0029

Employer identification number (EIN) 0 0 – 0 0 0 0 6 6 0

Name *(not your trade name)*   Glo-Brite Paint Company

Trade name *(if any)*

Address   2215 Salvador Street
              Number   Street   Suite or room number

Philadelphia   PA   19175-0682
City   State   ZIP code

Report for this Quarter of 20--
(Check one.)

☐ **1:** January, February, March
☐ **2:** April, May, June
☐ **3:** July, August, September
☒ **4:** October, November, December

Instructions and prior year forms are available at *www.irs.gov/form941.*

Read the separate instructions before you complete Form 941. Type or print within the boxes.

Part 1:   Answer these questions for this quarter.

1	Number of employees who received wages, tips, or other compensation for the pay period including: *Mar. 12* (Quarter 1), *June 12* (Quarter 2), *Sept. 12* (Quarter 3), or *Dec. 12* (Quarter 4) **1**	10
2	Wages, tips, and other compensation **2**	138601 ▪ 05*
3	Income tax withheld from wages, tips, and other compensation **3**	26637 ▪ 20
4	If no wages, tips, and other compensation are subject to social security or Medicare tax ☐ Check and go to line 6.	

		Column 1		Column 2
5a	Taxable social security wages . .	145437 ▪ 80**	× .124 =	18034 ▪ 29
5b	Taxable social security tips . . .	▪	× .124 =	▪
5c	Taxable Medicare wages & tips . .	148276 ▪ 21	× .029 =	4300 ▪ 01
5d	Taxable wages & tips subject to Additional Medicare Tax withholding	▪	× .009 =	▪

5e	Add Column 2 from lines 5a, 5b, 5c, and 5d **5e**	22334 ▪ 30
5f	Section 3121(q) Notice and Demand—Tax due on unreported tips (see instructions) . . **5f**	▪
6	Total taxes before adjustments (add lines 3, 5e, and 5f) **6**	48971 ▪ 50
7	Current quarter's adjustment for fractions of cents **7**	▪ 07
8	Current quarter's adjustment for sick pay **8**	▪
9	Current quarter's adjustments for tips and group-term life insurance **9**	▪
10	Total taxes after adjustments. Combine lines 6 through 9 . . . . **10**	48971 ▪ 57
11	Total deposits for this quarter, including overpayment applied from a prior quarter and overpayment applied from Form 941-X or Form 944-X filed in the current quarter . . **11**	48971 ▪ 57
12a	COBRA premium assistance payments (see instructions) **12a**	▪
12b	Number of individuals provided COBRA premium assistance .	
13	Add lines 11 and 12a **13**	48971 ▪ 57
14	Balance due. If line 10 is more than line 13, enter the difference and see instructions . . **14**	▪
15	Overpayment. If line 13 is more than line 10, enter the difference [▪] Check one: ☐ Apply to next return. ☐ Send a refund.	

▶ **You MUST complete both pages of Form 941 and SIGN it.**

Next ▶

For Privacy Act and Paperwork Reduction Act Notice, see the back of the Payment Voucher.   Cat. No. 17001Z   Form **941** (Rev. 1-2013)

*Total wages paid $148,276.21 less earnings paid Russell on 12/14 ($1,425.16) less simple deductions, $8,250.00.
**Total wages paid $148,276.21 less O'Neill's nontaxable wages of $2,838.41 (in excess of $113,700).

Name (not your trade name)	Employer identification number (EIN)
Glo-Brite Paint Company	00-0000660

Part 2: Tell us about your deposit schedule and tax liability for this quarter.

If you are unsure about whether you are a monthly schedule depositor or a semiweekly schedule depositor, see Pub. 15 (Circular E), section 11.

16 Check one: ☐ Line 10 on this return is less than $2,500 or line 10 on the return for the prior quarter was less than $2,500, and you did not incur a $100,000 next-day deposit obligation during the current quarter. If line 10 for the prior quarter was less than $2,500 but line 10 on this return is $100,000 or more, you must provide a record of your federal tax liability. If you are a monthly schedule depositor, complete the deposit schedule below; if you are a semiweekly schedule depositor, attach Schedule B (Form 941). Go to Part 3.

☒ **You were a monthly schedule depositor for the entire quarter.** Enter your tax liability for each month and total liability for the quarter, then go to Part 3.

Tax liability:	Month 1	6388 . 08
	Month 2	6569 . 73
	Month 3	36013 . 76
Total liability for quarter		48971 . 57	Total must equal line 10.

☐ **You were a semiweekly schedule depositor for any part of this quarter.** Complete Schedule B (Form 941), Report of Tax Liability for Semiweekly Schedule Depositors, and attach it to Form 941.

Part 3: Tell us about your business. If a question does NOT apply to your business, leave it blank.

17 If your business has closed or you stopped paying wages . . . . ☐ Check here, and

enter the final date you paid wages [/ /] .

18 If you are a seasonal employer and you do not have to file a return for every quarter of the year . . ☐ Check here.

Part 4: May we speak with your third-party designee?

Do you want to allow an employee, a paid tax preparer, or another person to discuss this return with the IRS? See the instructions for details.

☐ Yes. Designee's name and phone number [   ] [   ]

Select a 5-digit Personal Identification Number (PIN) to use when talking to the IRS. ☐ ☐ ☐ ☐ ☐

☒ No.

Part 5: Sign here. You MUST complete both pages of Form 941 and SIGN it.

Under penalties of perjury, I declare that I have examined this return, including accompanying schedules and statements, and to the best of my knowledge and belief, it is true, correct, and complete. Declaration of preparer (other than taxpayer) is based on all information of which preparer has any knowledge.

X **Sign your name here**	*Joseph T. O'Neill*	Print your name here	Joseph T. O'Neill
		Print your title here	President
Date	02 / 01 / --	Best daytime phone	215-555-9559

Paid Preparer Use Only   Check if you are self-employed . . . ☐

Preparer's name		PTIN	
Preparer's signature		Date	/ /
Firm's name (or yours if self-employed)		EIN	
Address		Phone	
City		State		ZIP code	

Page **2**

Form **941** (Rev. 1-2013)

Source: Internal Revenue Service.

STEP 7B

Form **940** for 20--: **Employer's Annual Federal Unemployment (FUTA) Tax Return**

Department of the Treasury — Internal Revenue Service

OMB No. 1545-0028

Employer identification number (EIN)   0 0 – 0 0 0 0 6 6 0

Name (not your trade name)   Glo-Brite Paint Company

Trade name (if any)

Address   2215 Salvador Street
Number   Street   Suite or room number

Philadelphia   PA   19175-0682
City   State   ZIP code

Type of Return
(Check all that apply.)

☐ **a.** Amended

☐ **b.** Successor employer

☐ **c.** No payments to employees in 20--

☐ **d.** Final: Business closed or stopped paying wages

Instructions and prior-year forms are available at *www.irs.gov/form940.*

Read the separate instructions before you complete this form. Please type or print within the boxes.

Part 1:   **Tell us about your return. If any line does NOT apply, leave it blank.**

1a If you had to pay state unemployment tax in one state only, enter the state abbreviation .   **1a**   P   A

1b If you had to pay state unemployment tax in more than one state, you are a multi-state employer . . . .   **1b** ☐ Check here. Complete Schedule A (Form 940).

2 If you paid wages in a state that is subject to CREDIT REDUCTION . . . .   **2** ☐ Check here. Complete Schedule A (Form 940).

Part 2:   **Determine your FUTA tax before adjustments for 20--. If any line does NOT apply, leave it blank.**

3 Total payments to all employees . . . .   **3**   290500 ▪ 73

4 Payments exempt from FUTA tax . . . .   **4**   ▪

    Check all that apply: **4a** ☐ Fringe benefits   **4c** ☐ Retirement/Pension   **4e** ☐ Other
                     4b ☐ Group-term life insurance   **4d** ☐ Dependent care

5 Total of payments made to each employee in excess of $7,000 . . . .   **5**   217413 ▪ 03

6 Subtotal (line 4 + line 5 = line 6) . . . .   **6**   217413 ▪ 03

7 Total taxable FUTA wages (line 3 – line 6 = line 7) (see instructions) . . . . . .   **7**   73087 ▪ 70

8 FUTA tax before adjustments (line 7 × .006 = line 8) . . . .   **8**   438 ▪ 53

Part 3:   **Determine your adjustments. If any line does NOT apply, leave it blank.**

9 If ALL of the taxable FUTA wages you paid were excluded from state unemployment tax, multiply line 7 by .054 (line 7 × .054 = line 9). Go to line 12 . . . .   **9**   ▪

10 If SOME of the taxable FUTA wages you paid were excluded from state unemployment tax, OR you paid ANY state unemployment tax late (after the due date for filing Form 940), complete the worksheet in the instructions. Enter the amount from line 7 of the worksheet . .   **10**   ▪

11 If credit reduction applies, enter the total from Schedule A (Form 940) . . . . . .   **11**   ▪

Part 4:   **Determine your FUTA tax and balance due or overpayment for 20--. If any line does NOT apply, leave it blank.**

12 Total FUTA tax after adjustments (lines 8 + 9 + 10 + 11 = line 12) . . . .   **12**   438 ▪ 53

13 FUTA tax deposited for the year, including any overpayment applied from a prior year .   **13**   438 ▪ 53

14 Balance due (If line 12 is more than line 13, enter the excess on line 14.)
    • If line 14 is more than $500, you must deposit your tax.
    • If line 14 is $500 or less, you may pay with this return. (see instructions) . . . .   **14**   ▪

15 Overpayment (If line 13 is more than line 12, enter the excess on line 15 and check a box below.) . . . .   **15**   ▪

   ▶ You **MUST** complete both pages of this form and **SIGN** it.   Check one: ☐ Apply to next return. ☐ Send a refund.

Next ▶

For Privacy Act and Paperwork Reduction Act Notice, see the back of Form 940-V, Payment Voucher.   Cat. No. 11234O   Form **940** (2012)

Name *(not your trade name)*	**Employer identification number (EIN)**
Glo-Brite Paint Company	00-0000660

Part 5: Report your FUTA tax liability by quarter only if line 12 is more than $500. If not, go to Part 6.

16 Report the amount of your FUTA tax liability for each quarter; do NOT enter the amount you deposited. If you had no liability for a quarter, leave the line blank.

16a 1st quarter (January 1 – March 31) **16a**	204 ▪ 53	
16b 2nd quarter (April 1 – June 30) **16b**	105 ▪ 25	
16c 3rd quarter (July 1 – September 30) **16c**	83 ▪ 16	
16d 4th quarter (October 1 – December 31) **16d**	45 ▪ 59	
17 Total tax liability for the year (lines 16a + 16b + 16c + 16d = line 17) **17**	438 ▪ 53	**Total must equal line 12.**

Part 6: May we speak with your third-party designee?

Do you want to allow an employee, a paid tax preparer, or another person to discuss this return with the IRS? See the instructions for details.

☐ **Yes.** Designee's name and phone number

Select a 5-digit Personal Identification Number (PIN) to use when talking to IRS

☒ **No.**

Part 7: Sign here. You MUST complete both pages of this form and SIGN it.

Under penalties of perjury, I declare that I have examined this return, including accompanying schedules and statements, and to the best of my knowledge and belief, it is true, correct, and complete, and that no part of any payment made to a state unemployment fund claimed as a credit was, or is to be, deducted from the payments made to employees. Declaration of preparer (other than taxpayer) is based on all information of which preparer has any knowledge.

X Sign your name here *Joseph T. O'Neill*

Print your name here: Joseph T. O'Neill

Print your title here: President

Date: 02 / 01 / --

Best daytime phone: 215-555-9559

Paid Preparer Use Only   Check if you are self-employed . . . ☐

Preparer's name		PTIN	
Preparer's signature		Date	/ /
Firm's name (or yours if self-employed)		EIN	
Address		Phone	
City	State	ZIP code	

Source: Internal Revenue Service.

STEP 7C

PA Form UC-2 REV 1–12, Employer's Report for Unemployment Compensation

Read Instructions – Answer Each Item

		QTR./YEAR 1/20--	4/20--

W   INV. ☐   EXAMINED BY:

DUE DATE 1/31/20- -

1ST MONTH	2ND MONTH	3RD MONTH
10	10	11

1. TOTAL COVERED EMPLOYEES IN PAY PERIOD INCL. 12TH OF MONTH

Signature certifies that the information contained herein is true and correct to the best of the signer's knowledge.

Joseph T. O'Neill

10. SIGN HERE-DO NOT PRINT

TITLE President   DATE 2/1/- -   PHONE # 215-555-9559

11. FILED ☐ PAPER UC-2A ☐ INTERNET UC-2A ☐ MAGNETIC MEDIA UC-2A

12. FEDERAL IDENTIFICATION NUMBER 00-0000660

EMPLOYER'S CONTRIBUTION RATE

EMPLOYER'S CONTRIBUTION RATE ▷ .036785   EMPLOYER'S ACCT. NO. 000-0-3300   CHECK DIGIT 1

2. GROSS WAGES 148276.21
3. EMPLOYEE CONTRIBUTIONS 103.94
4. TAXABLE WAGES FOR EMPLOYER CONTRIBUTIONS 13597.70
5. EMPLOYER CONTRIBUTIONS DUE (RATE X ITEM 4) 500.19
6. TOTAL CONTRIBUTIONS DUE (ITEMS 3 + 5) 604.13
7. INTEREST DUE (SEE INSTRUCTIONS)
8. PENALTY DUE (SEE INSTRUCTIONS)
9. TOTAL REMITTANCE (ITEMS 6 + 7 + 8) $ 604.13

GLO-BRITE PAINT COMPANY
2215 SALVADOR STREET
PHILADELPHIA, PA 19175-0682

FOR DEPT. USE

MAKE CHECKS PAYABLE TO: PA UC FUND

PA Form UC-2A, Employer's Quarterly Report of Wages Paid to Each Employee

See Instructions on separate sheet. Information MUST be typewritten or printed in BLACK ink. Do NOT use commas (,) or dollar signs ($). If typed, disregard vertical bars and type a consecutive string of characters. If hand printed, print in CAPS and within the boxes as below:

SAMPLE Typed: 123456.00
SAMPLE Handwritten: 123456.00
SAMPLE Filled-in: ●

Employer name (make corrections on Form UC-2B)	Employer PA UC account no.	Check digit	Quarter and year Q / YYYY	Quarter ending date MM / DD / YYYY
GLO-BRITE PAINT COMPANY	000-0-3300	1	4/20--	12/31/20- -

1. Name and telephone number of preparer

2. Total number of pages in this report	3. Total number of employees listed in item 8 on all pages of Form UC-2A	4. Plant number (if approved)
1	12	

5. Gross wages, MUST agree with item 2 on UC-2 and the sum of item 11 on all pages of Form UC-2A

148276.21

6. Fill in this circle if you would like the Department to preprint your employee's names & SSNs on Form UC-2A next quarter ○

7. Employee's Social Security Number	8. Employee's name FI	MI	LAST	9. Gross wages paid this qtr Example: 123456.00	10. Credit Weeks
000003481	A	V	BONNO	9001.50	13
000008645	J	C	FERGUSON	13500.00	13
000004567	C	L	FORD	5520.00	13
000009352	D	W	MANN	8100.00	13
000001534	J	T	ONEILL	73846.14	13
000006337	V	A	RUSSELL	4901.04	11
000001233	N	A	RYAN	9054.00	13
000008832	T	J	SOKOWSKI	12300.00	13
000005555			STUDENT	3232.50	13
000006741	R	V	WILLIAMS	5733.33	7
000001587	B	A	WOODS	2280.00	6
000006057	P	W	YOUNG	807.70	4

List any additional employees on continuation sheets in the required format (see instructions).

11. Total gross wages for this page: ➡ 148276.21
12. Total number of employees for this page 12

UC-2A REV 9-05   13. Page 1 of 1

Source: PA Department of Labor & Industry.

STEP 7D

22222	Void ☐	a Employee's social security number 000-00-6741	For Official Use Only OMB No. 1 545-0008		
b Employer identification number (EIN) 00-0000660			1 Wages, tips, other compensation 15993.33	2 Federal income tax withheld 2406.63	
c Employer's name, address, and ZIP code			3 Social security wages 15993.33	4 Social security tax withheld 991.59	
Glo-Brite Paint Company *2215 Salvador Street* *Philadelphia, PA 19175-0682*			5 Medicare wages and tips 15993.33	6 Medicare tax withheld 231.89	
			7 Social security tips	8 Allocated tips	
d Control number			9	10 Dependent care benefits	
e Employee's first name and initial Ruth V.	Last name Williams	Suff.	11 Nonqualified plans	12a Code	See instructions for box 12
			13 Statutory employee ☐ Retirement plan ☐ Third-party sick pay ☐	12b Code	
9433 STATE STREET PHILADELPHIA, PA 19149-0819			14 Other	12c Code	
f Employee's address and ZIP code				12d Code	

15 State PA	Employer's state ID number 000-0-3300	16 State wages, tips, etc. 15993.33	17 State income tax 491.00	18 Local wages, tips, etc. 15993.33	19 Local income tax 628.21	20 Locality name PHILA.

Form **W-2** Wage and Tax Statement **20--**

Department of the Treasury—Internal Revenue Service
For Privacy Act and Paperwork Reduction Act Notice, see back of Copy D.

22222	Void ☐	a Employee's social security number 000-00-6337	For Official Use Only OMB No. 1 545-0008		
b Employer identification number (EIN) 00-0000660			1 Wages, tips, other compensation 9715.88*	2 Federal income tax withheld 847.29	
c Employer's name, address, and ZIP code			3 Social security wages 11141.04	4 Social security tax withheld 690.74	
Glo-Brite Paint Company *2215 Salvador Street* *Philadelphia, PA 19175-0682*			5 Medicare wages and tips 11141.04	6 Medicare tax withheld 161.56	
			7 Social security tips	8 Allocated tips	
d Control number			9	10 Dependent care benefits	
e Employee's first name and initial Virginia A.	Last name Russell	Suff.	11 Nonqualified plans	12a Code	See instructions for box 12
			13 Statutory employee ☐ Retirement plan ☐ Third-party sick pay ☐	12b Code	
8004 DOWLING ROAD PHILADELPHIA, PA 19135-9001			14 Other	12c Code	
f Employee's address and ZIP code				12d Code	

15 State PA	Employer's state ID number 000-0-3300	16 State wages, tips, etc. 9715.88*	17 State income tax 298.27	18 Local wages, tips, etc. 9715.88*	19 Local income tax 381.63	20 Locality name PHILA.

Form **W-2** Wage and Tax Statement **20--**

Department of the Treasury—Internal Revenue Service
For Privacy Act and Paperwork Reduction Act Notice, see back of Copy D.

Source: Internal Revenue Service.

*$11,141.04 – $1,425.16 (not considered wages for purposes of FIT, SIT, and CIT).

STEP 7D

22222	Void ☐	a Employee's social security number 000-00-3481	For Official Use Only OMB No. 1 545-0008			
b	Employer identification number (EIN) 00-0000660		**1** Wages, tips, other compensation 20323.45		**2** Federal income tax withheld 1174.71	
c	Employer's name, address, and ZIP code		**3** Social security wages 20323.45		**4** Social security tax withheld 1260.05	
	Glo-Brite Paint Company *2215 Salvador Street* *Philadelphia, PA 19175-0682*		**5** Medicare wages and tips 20323.45		**6** Medicare tax withheld 294.69	
			7 Social security tips		**8** Allocated tips	
d	Control number		**9**		**10** Dependent care benefits	
e Employee's first name and initial **Anthony V.**	Last name **Bonno**	Suff.	**11** Nonqualified plans		**12a** See instructions for box 12 Code	
			13 Statutory employee ☐ Retirement plan ☐ Third-party sick pay ☐		**12b** Code	
694 BRISTOL AVENUE PHILADELPHIA, PA 19135-0617			**14** Other UNION DUES 121.00		**12c** Code	
					12d Code	
f	Employee's address and ZIP code					

15 State PA	Employer's state ID number 000-0-3300	**16** State wages, tips, etc. 20323.45	**17** State income tax 623.93	**18** Local wages, tips, etc. 20323.45	**19** Local income tax 798.30	**20** Locality name PHILA.

Form **W-2** Wage and Tax Statement   **20--**

Department of the Treasury—Internal Revenue Service
For Privacy Act and Paperwork
Reduction Act Notice, see back of Copy D.

22222	Void ☐	a Employee's social security number 000-00-8645	For Official Use Only OMB No. 1 545-0008			
b	Employer identification number (EIN) 00-0000660		**1** Wages, tips, other compensation 35125.00*		**2** Federal income tax withheld 2957.36	
c	Employer's name, address, and ZIP code		**3** Social security wages 36625.00		**4** Social security tax withheld 2270.75	
	Glo-Brite Paint Company *2215 Salvador Street* *Philadelphia, PA 19175-0682*		**5** Medicare wages and tips 36625.00		**6** Medicare tax withheld 531.09	
			7 Social security tips		**8** Allocated tips	
d	Control number		**9**		**10** Dependent care benefits	
e Employee's first name and initial **James C.**	Last name **Ferguson**	Suff.	**11** Nonqualified plans		**12a** See instructions for box 12 Code **S** 1500.00	
			13 Statutory employee ☐ Retirement plan ☒ Third-party sick pay ☐		**12b** Code	
808 SIXTH STREET PHILADELPHIA, PA 19106-0995			**14** Other		**12c** Code	
					12d Code	
f	Employee's address and ZIP code					

15 State PA	Employer's state ID number 000-0-3300	**16** State wages, tips, etc. 36625.00	**17** State income tax 1124.42	**18** Local wages, tips, etc. 36625.00	**19** Local income tax 1438.63	**20** Locality name PHILA.

Form **W-2** Wage and Tax Statement   **20--**

Department of the Treasury—Internal Revenue Service
For Privacy Act and Paperwork
Reduction Act Notice, see back of Copy D.

Source: Internal Revenue Service.

*Less retirement contributions.

STEP 7D

22222	Void ☐	a Employee's social security number 000-00-4567	For Official Use Only OMB No. 1 545-0008		
b	Employer identification number (EIN) 00-0000660		1 Wages, tips, other compensation 11820.00	2 Federal income tax withheld 1031.70	
c	Employer's name, address, and ZIP code		3 Social security wages 11820.00	4 Social security tax withheld 732.84	
	Glo-Brite Paint Company 2215 Salvador Street Philadelphia, PA 19175-0682		5 Medicare wages and tips 11820.00	6 Medicare tax withheld 171.39	
			7 Social security tips	8 Allocated tips	
d	Control number		9	10 Dependent care benefits	
e Employee's first name and initial Catherine L.	Last name Ford	Suff.	11 Nonqualified plans	12a See instructions for box 12 Code	
			13 Statutory employee ☐ Retirement plan ☐ Third-party sick pay ☐	12b Code	
18 DUNDEE AVENUE PHILADELPHIA, PA 19151-1919			14 Other	12c Code	
				12d Code	
f	Employee's address and ZIP code				
15 State PA	Employer's state ID number 000-0-3300	16 State wages, tips, etc. 11820.00	17 State income tax 362.87	18 Local wages, tips, etc. 11820.00	19 Local income tax 464.28 20 Locality name PHILA.

Form **W-2** Wage and Tax Statement   **20--**

22222	Void ☐	a Employee's social security number 000-00-9352	For Official Use Only OMB No. 1 545-0008		
b	Employer identification number (EIN) 00-0000660		1 Wages, tips, other compensation 12750.00*	2 Federal income tax withheld 792.96	
c	Employer's name, address, and ZIP code		3 Social security wages 13500.00	4 Social security tax withheld 837.00	
	Glo-Brite Paint Company 2215 Salvador Street Philadelphia, PA 19175-0682		5 Medicare wages and tips 13500.00	6 Medicare tax withheld 195.78	
			7 Social security tips	8 Allocated tips	
d	Control number		9	10 Dependent care benefits	
e Employee's first name and initial Dewey W.	Last name Mann	Suff.	11 Nonqualified plans	12a See instructions for box 12 Code S 750.00	
			13 Statutory employee ☐ Retirement plan ☒ Third-party sick pay ☐	12b Code	
3007 BISQUE DRIVE PHILADELPHIA, PA 19199-0718			14 Other	12c Code	
				12d Code	
f	Employee's address and ZIP code				
15 State PA	Employer's state ID number 000-0-3300	16 State wages, tips, etc. 13500.00	17 State income tax 414.48	18 Local wages, tips, etc. 13500.00	19 Local income tax 530.29 20 Locality name PHILA.

Form **W-2** Wage and Tax Statement   **20--**

*Less retirement contributions.

STEP 7D

22222	Void ☐	a Employee's social security number 000-00-1534	For Official Use Only OMB No. 1 545-0008		
b	Employer identification number (EIN) 00-0000660		1 Wages, tips, other compensation 111138.41*		2 Federal income tax withheld 27629.90
c	Employer's name, address, and ZIP code		3 Social security wages 113700.00		4 Social security tax withheld 7049.40
	Glo-Brite Paint Company 2215 Salvador Street Philadelphia, PA 19175-0682		5 Medicare wages and tips 116538.41		6 Medicare tax withheld 1689.80
			7 Social security tips		8 Allocated tips
d	Control number		9		10 Dependent care benefits
e Employee's first name and initial Joseph T.	Last name O'Neill	Suff.	11 Nonqualified plans	12a See instructions for box 12 Code S 5400.00	
			13 Statutory Employee ☐ Retirement plan ☒ Third-party sick pay ☐	12b Code	
2100 BROAD STREET PHILADELPHIA, PA 19121-7189			14 Other	12c Code	
				12d Code	
f	Employee's address and ZIP code				

15 State PA	Employer's state ID number 000-0-3300	16 State wages, tips, etc. 116538.41	17 State income tax 3577.75	18 Local wages, tips, etc. 116538.41	19 Local income tax 4577.65	20 Locality name PHILA.

Form **W-2** **Wage and Tax Statement** **20--**

Department of the Treasury—Internal Revenue Service
For Privacy Act and Paperwork
Reduction Act Notice, see back of Copy D.

22222	Void ☐	a Employee's social security number 000-00-1233	For Official Use Only OMB No. 1 545-0008		
b	Employer identification number (EIN) 00-0000660		1 Wages, tips, other compensation 23139.30*		2 Federal income tax withheld 1386.35
c	Employer's name, address, and ZIP code		3 Social security wages 23739.30		4 Social security tax withheld 1471.84
	Glo-Brite Paint Company 2215 Salvador Street Philadelphia, PA 19175-0682		5 Medicare wages and tips 23739.30		6 Medicare tax withheld 344.22
			7 Social security tips		8 Allocated tips
d	Control number		9		10 Dependent care benefits
e Employee's first name and initial Norman A.	Last name Ryan	Suff.	11 Nonqualified plans	12a See instructions for box 12 Code S 600.00	
			13 Statutory employee ☐ Retirement plan ☒ Third-party sick pay ☐	12b Code	
7300 HARRISON STREET PHILADELPHIA, PA 19124-6699			14 Other UNION DUES 121.00	12c Code	
				12d Code	
f	Employee's address and ZIP code				

15 State PA	Employer's state ID number 000-0-3300	16 State wages, tips, etc. 23739.30	17 State income tax 728.80	18 Local wages, tips, etc. 23739.30	19 Local income tax 932.48	20 Locality name PHILA.

Form **W-2** **Wage and Tax Statement** **20--**

Department of the Treasury—Internal Revenue Service
For Privacy Act and Paperwork
Reduction Act Notice, see back of Copy D.

Source: Internal Revenue Service.

*Less retirement contributions.

STEP 7D

22222	Void ☐	a Employee's social security number 000-00-8832	For Official Use Only OMB No. 1 545-0008			

b Employer identification number (EIN) 00-0000660	1 Wages, tips, other compensation 28950.00	2 Federal income tax withheld 3421.64

c Employer's name, address, and ZIP code	3 Social security wages 28950.00	4 Social security tax withheld 1794.90

Glo-Brite Paint Company
2215 Salvador Street
Philadelphia, PA 19175-0682

5 Medicare wages and tips 28950.00	6 Medicare tax withheld 419.81
7 Social security tips	8 Allocated tips
d Control number	9	10 Dependent care benefits

e Employee's first name and initial Thomas J.	Last name Sokowski	Suff.	11 Nonqualified plans	12a See instructions for box 12 Code

13 Statutory employee ☐	Retirement plan ☐	Third-party sick pay ☐	12b Code

133 CORNWELLS STREET
PHILADELPHIA, PA 19171-5718

14 Other	12c Code
	12d Code

f Employee's address and ZIP code

15 State PA	Employer's state ID number 000-0-3300	16 State wages, tips, etc. 28950.00	17 State income tax 888.80	18 Local wages, tips, etc. 28950.00	19 Local income tax 1137.13	20 Locality name PHILA.

Form **W-2** Wage and Tax Statement   **20--**

Department of the Treasury—Internal Revenue Service
For Privacy Act and Paperwork Reduction Act Notice, see back of Copy D.

22222	Void ☐	a Employee's social security number 000-00-5555	For Official Use Only OMB No. 1 545-0008			

b Employer identification number (EIN) 00-0000660	1 Wages, tips, other compensation 8782.50	2 Federal income tax withheld 596.11

c Employer's name, address, and ZIP code	3 Social security wages 8782.50	4 Social security tax withheld 544.52

Glo-Brite Paint Company
2215 Salvador Street
Philadelphia, PA 19175-0682

5 Medicare wages and tips 8782.50	6 Medicare tax withheld 127.35
7 Social security tips	8 Allocated tips
d Control number	9	10 Dependent care benefits

e Employee's first name and initial STUDENT	Last name	Suff.	11 Nonqualified plans	12a See instructions for box 12 Code

13 Statutory employee ☐	Retirement plan ☐	Third-party sick pay ☐	12b Code

7018 ERDRICK ST.
PHILADELPHIA, PA 19135-8517

14 Other	12c Code
	12d Code

f Employee's address and ZIP code

15 State PA	Employer's state ID number 000-0-3300	16 State wages, tips, etc. 8782.50	17 State income tax 269.63	18 Local wages, tips, etc. 8782.50	19 Local income tax 344.97	20 Locality name PHILA.

Form **W-2** Wage and Tax Statement   **20--**

Department of the Treasury—Internal Revenue Service
For Privacy Act and Paperwork Reduction Act Notice, see back of Copy D.

Source: Internal Revenue Service.

STEP 7D

22222	Void ☐	a Employee's social security number 000-00-1587	For Official Use Only OMB No. 1 545-0008		
b Employer identification number (EIN) 00-0000660			**1** Wages, tips, other compensation 2280.00	**2** Federal income tax withheld 239.60	
c Employer's name, address, and ZIP code			**3** Social security wages 2280.00	**4** Social security tax withheld 141.36	
Glo-Brite Paint Company *2215 Salvador Street* *Philadelphia, PA 19175-0682*			**5** Medicare wages and tips 2280.00	**6** Medicare tax withheld 33.06	
			7 Social security tips	**8** Allocated tips	
d Control number			**9**	**10** Dependent care benefits	
e Employee's first name and initial Beth A.	Last name Woods	Suff.	**11** Nonqualified plans	**12a** See instructions for box 12 Code	
			13 Statutory employee ☐ Retirement plan ☐ Third-party sick pay ☐	**12b** Code	
8102 FRANKLIN COURT PHILADELPHIA, PA 19105-0915			**14** Other	**12c** Code	
				12d Code	
f Employee's address and ZIP code					

15 State PA	Employer's state ID number 000-0-3300	**16** State wages, tips, etc. 2280.00	**17** State income tax 70.00	**18** Local wages, tips, etc. 2280.00	**19** Local income tax 89.56	**20** Locality name PHILA.

Form **W-2** Wage and Tax Statement   **20--**   Department of the Treasury—Internal Revenue Service
For Privacy Act and Paperwork Reduction Act Notice, see back of Copy D.

22222	Void ☐	a Employee's social security number 000-00-6057	For Official Use Only OMB No. 1 545-0008		
b Employer identification number (EIN) 00-0000660			**1** Wages, tips, other compensation 807.70	**2** Federal income tax withheld 69.95	
c Employer's name, address, and ZIP code			**3** Social security wages 807.70	**4** Social security tax withheld 50.08	
Glo-Brite Paint Company *2215 Salvador Street* *Philadelphia, PA 19175-0682*			**5** Medicare wages and tips 807.70	**6** Medicare tax withheld 11.71	
			7 Social security tips	**8** Allocated tips	
d Control number			**9** Advance EIC payment	**10** Dependent care benefits	
e Employee's first name and initial Paul W.	Last name Young	Suff.	**11** Nonqualified plans	**12a** See instructions for box 12 Code	
			13 Statutory employee ☐ Retirement plan ☐ Third-party sick pay ☐	**12b** Code	
7936 HOLMES DRIVE PHILADELPHIA, PA 19107-6107			**14** Other	**12c** Code	
				12d Code	
f Employee's address and ZIP code					

15 State PA	Employer's state ID number 000-0-3300	**16** State wages, tips, etc. 807.70	**17** State income tax 24.80	**18** Local wages, tips, etc. 807.70	**19** Local income tax 31.73	**20** Locality name PHILA.

Form **W-2** Wage and Tax Statement   **20--**   Department of the Treasury—Internal Revenue Service
For Privacy Act and Paperwork Reduction Act Notice, see back of Copy D.

Source: Internal Revenue Service.

STEP 7E

DO NOT STAPLE

33333	a Control number	For Official Use Only ▶ OMB No. 1545-0008

b Kind of Payer (Check one)	941 [X]	Military	943	944	Kind of Employer (Check one)	None apply [X]	501c non-govt.		Third-party sick pay (Check if applicable)
	CT-1	Hshld. emp.	Medicare govt. emp.			State/local non-501c	State/local 501c	Federal govt.	

c Total number of Forms W-2	d Establishment number	1 Wages, tips, other compensation	2 Federal income tax withheld
12		280825.57*	42554.20

e Employer identification number (EIN)	3 Social security wages	4 Social security tax withheld
	287662.32**	17835.07

f Employer's name	5 Medicare wages and tips	6 Medicare tax withheld
GLO-BRITE PAINT COMPANY	290500.73	4212.35

2215 SALVADOR STREET
PHILADELPHIA, PA 19175-0682

7 Social security tips	8 Allocated tips

9	10 Dependent care benefits

11 Nonqualified plans	12a Deferred compensation
	8250.00

g Employer's address and ZIP code

h Other EIN used this year	13 For third-party sick pay use only	12b

15 State	Employer's state ID number	14 Income tax withheld by payer of third-party sick pay
PA	000-0-3300	

16 State wages, tips, etc.	17 State income tax	18 Local wages, tips, etc.	19 Local income tax
289075.57***	8874.76	289075.57	11354.86

Contact person	Telephone number	For Official Use Only
Student		

Email address	Fax number

Under penalties of perjury, I declare that I have examined this return and accompanying documents and, to the best of my knowledge and belief, they are true, correct, and complete.

Signature ▶ *Joseph T. O'Neill*   Title ▶ President   Date ▶ 2/1/--

Form **W-3** Transmittal of Wage and Tax Statements   20__   Department of the Treasury Internal Revenue Service

Source: Internal Revenue Service.

*$290,500.73 – $1,425.16 (Russell's earnings on December 14) – $8,250.00 (SIMPLE Contributions).

**$290,500.73 – $2,838.41 (O'Neill's nontaxable wages for OASDI).

***$290,500.73 – $1,425.16.

STEP 7F

pennsylvania DEPARTMENT OF REVENUE REV-1667 R AS (08-10) (I)

W-2 TRANSMITTAL

YEAR 2 0 - -
EMPLOYER ACCOUNT ID 0 0 0 0 3 0 0
ENTITY ID (EIN) 0 0 0 0 0 6 6 0
DUE DATE JANUARY 31

Part I W-2 RECONCILIATION

1a	Number of W-2 forms attached	12
1b	Number of 1099 forms with PA withholding tax	
1c	Number of W-2s reported on magnetic tape(s)	
1d	Number of W-2s reported on compact discs	
2	Total compensation subject to PA withholding tax	$ 2 8 9 0 7 5 . 5 7
3	PA INCOME TAX WITHHELD	$ 8 8 7 4 . 7 6

Part II ANNUAL RECONCILIATION

	Wages paid subject to PA withholding tax	PA tax withheld
1st Quarter	34088.70	1046.52
2nd Quarter	45535.62	1397.94
3rd Quarter	62600.20	1921.83
4th Quarter	146851.05*	4508.47
TOTAL	289075.57	8874.76

Part III FOR MEDIA REPORTING

NUMBER OF TAPES	NUMBER OF CD's

BUSINESS NAME AND ADDRESS

LEGAL NAME

TRADE NAME

ADDRESS

CITY, STATE, ZIP

DO NOT SEND PAYMENT WITH THIS FORM.

Attach adding machine tape(s) or some acceptable listing of tax withheld as reported on accompanying W-2 form(s) to substantiate reported PA withholding tax. This tape or listing applies only to paper W-2s, not media reporting.

SIGNATURE *Joseph T. O'Neill*

DATE 02/01/20--
DAYTIME TELEPHONE # (215) 555-9559
EXT.
TITLE President

Source: PA Department of Revenue.

*$148,276.21 – $1,425.16 (Russell's earnings on December 14).

STEP 7G

9595	☐ VOID	☐ CORRECTED			

PAYER'S name, street address, city or town, province or state, country, ZIP or foreign postal code, and telephone no. GLO-BRITE PAINT COMPANY 2215 SALVADOR ST PHILADELPHIA, PA 19175-0682	**1** Rents $	OMB No. 1545-0115 20-- Form **1099-MISC**	**Miscellaneous Income**
	2 Royalties $		
	3 Other income $ 1425.16	**4** Federal income tax withheld $	**Copy A** **For**
PAYER'S federal identification number	RECIPIENT'S identification number	**5** Fishing boat proceeds	**6** Medical and health care payments	**Internal Revenue Service Center**
00-0000660	00-00-6337			
		$	$	File with Form 1096.
RECIPIENT'S name The Estate of Virginia Aloise Russell	**7** Nonemployee compensation	**8** Substitute payments in lieu of dividends or interest	For Privacy Act and Paperwork Reduction Act Notice, see the
Street address (including apt. no.) 8004 Dowling Road	$	$	**20-- General Instructions for Certain**
	9 Payer made direct sales of $5,000 or more of consumer products to a buyer (recipient) for resale ▶ ☐	**10** Crop insurance proceeds $	
City or town, province or state, country, and ZIP or foreign postal code PHILADELPHIA, PA 19135-9001	**11** Foreign tax paid $	**12** Foreign country or U.S. possession	**Information Returns.**
Account number (see instructions)	2nd TIN not. ☐	**13** Excess golden parachute payments $	**14** Gross proceeds paid to an attorney $	
15a Section 409A deferrals $	**15b** Section 409A income $	**16** State tax withheld $ $	**17** State/Payer's state no.	**18** State income $ $

Form **1099-MISC**   Cat. No. 14425J   www.irs.gov/form1099misc   Department of the Treasury - Internal Revenue Service

Do Not Cut or Separate Forms on This Page — Do Not Cut or Separate Forms on This Page

Source: Internal Revenue Service.

STEP 7H

Do Not Staple   6969

Form **1096**	Annual Summary and Transmittal of	OMB No. 1545-0108
Department of the Treasury Internal Revenue Service	U.S. Information Returns	20--

FILER'S name

GLO-BRITE PAINT COMPANY

Street address (including room or suite number)

2215 SALVADOR ST

City or town, province or state, country, and ZIP or foreign postal code

PHILADELPHIA, PA 19175-0682

Name of person to contact	Telephone number
Student	(215) 555-9559
Email address	Fax number

For Official Use Only

1 Employer identification number	2 Social security number	3 Total number of forms	4 Federal income tax withheld	5 Total amount reported with this Form 1096
00-0000660		1	$ 0	$ 1425.16

6 Enter an "X" in only one box below to indicate the type of form being filed.

7 If this is your **final return**, enter an "X" here ▶ ☐

W-2G 32	1097-BTC 50	1098 81	1098-C 78	1098-E 84	1098-T 83	1099-A 80	1099-B 79	1099-C 85	1099-CAP 73	1099-DIV 91	1099-G 86	1099-H 71	1099-INT 92	1099-K 10	1099-LTC 93	1099-MISC 95	1099-OID 96
☐	☐	☐	☐	☐	☐	☐	☐	☐	☐	☐	☐	☐	☐	☐	☐	☒	☐

1099-PATR 97	1099-Q 31	1099-R 98	1099-S 75	1099-SA 94	3921 25	3922 26	5498 28	5498-ESA 72	5498-SA 27
☐	☐	☐	☐	☐	☐	☐	☐	☐	☐

Return this entire page to the Internal Revenue Service. Photocopies are not acceptable.

Under penalties of perjury, I declare that I have examined this return and accompanying documents, and, to the best of my knowledge and belief, they are true, correct, and complete.

Signature ▶ *Joseph T. O'Neill*   Title ▶ President   Date ▶ 2/1/--

Source: Internal Revenue Service.

STEP 7I

PA Employer's Quarterly Reconciliation Worksheet

Company Name	**Glo-Brite Paint Co.**
Account Number	**00003300**
ID #	**00-0000660**
Telephone #	**(215) 555-9559**
Quarter Ending Date	**12/31/--**

Record of PA Withholding Tax:

1st half of month	**434.82**	1.	Total Compensation	**146,851.05***
2nd half of month	**444.70**	2.	Total Pa. W/H/ Tax	**4,508.47**
1st half of month	**497.67**	3.	Total Deposits/Quarter	**4,508.47**
2nd half of month	**388.08**	4.	Tax Due	**—**
1st half of month	**443.06**			
2nd half of month	**2,300.14**			
TOTAL	**4,508.47**			

*$148,276.21 less exempt wages paid Russell on December 14 ($1,425.16).

STEP 7J

CITY OF PHILADELPHIA	City Account Number
ANNUAL RECONCILIATION OF	0 0 0 1 8 5 5
20-- EMPLOYER WAGE TAX	
DUE DATE: FEBRUARY 28, 20--	Federal Identification Number

5 0 1 1

Name and Address
Glo-Brite Paint Company

2215 Salvador Street
Philadelphia, PA 19175-0682

Federal Identification Number
0 0 - 0 0 0 0 6 6 0

To file online, click on "Online Services" at
www.phila.gov/revenue.

If your business terminated in 20--, enter the termination date **AND** file a CHANGE FORM.

YOU MUST USE THE CHANGE FORM TO REPORT A CHANGE OF ADDRESS.   *If this is an amended return place an "X" here:*

A. Enter the number of Philadelphia Residents for whom wage tax was remitted for the pay period including
   March 12, 20-- .... A. **1 0**

B. Enter the number of **nonresidents** (employees living outside Philadelphia city limits) for whom wage tax
   was remitted for the pay period including March 12, 20-- .... B.

C. Total number of employees **for all company locations** reported on the Employer's Federal Quarterly
   Tax Return for the first quarter of 20-- (for the pay period including March 12, 20--) .... C. **1 0**

D. Number of employees working **at company locations within Philadelphia city limits**, for the pay period
   including March 12, 20-- .... D. **1 0**

1. Gross Compensation per W-2 forms for all employees .... 1. ____ , 2 8 9 , 0 7 6 . 0 0 *

2. Non-Taxable Gross Compensation included in Line 1.
   (Paid to nonresidents working outside of Philadelphia) .... 2. ____ , ____ , ____ . 0 0

3. Gross Compensation per W-2 forms on which Philadelphia Wage Tax was
   withheld or due (Line 1 minus Line 2) .... 3. ____ , 2 8 9 , 0 7 6 . 0 0

4. Total Taxable Gross Compensation paid to **residents** of Philadelphia in 20-- .... 4. ____ , 2 8 9 , 0 7 6 . 0 0

5. Tax Due (Line 4 times .03928) .... 5. ____ , 1 1 , 3 5 5 . 0 0

6. Total Taxable Gross Compensation paid to **nonresidents** of Philadelphia in 20-- .... 6. ____ , ____ , ____ . 0 0

7. Tax Due (Line 6 times .034985) .... 7. ____ , ____ , ____ . 0 0

8. **Total Tax Due** (Line 5 plus Line 7) .... 8. ____ , 1 1 , 3 5 5 . 0 0

9. **Tax previously paid for 20--** .... 9. ____ , 1 1 , 3 5 5 . 0 0

10. **ADDITIONAL TAX DUE** If Line 8 is greater than Line 9, enter the amount here .... 10. ____ , ____ . 0 0

11. **TAX OVERPAID** If Line 9 is greater than Line 8, enter the amount here.
    See instructions for filing a Refund Petition .... 11. ____ , ____ , ____ . 0 0

Under penalties of perjury, as set forth in 18 PA C.S. §§ 4902-4903 as amended, I swear that I have reviewed this return
and accompanying statements and schedules, and to the best of my knowledge and belief, they are true and complete.

Taxpayer Signature *Joseph T. O'Neill*   Date *2/11 - -*   Phone # *(215) 555-9559*

Preparer Signature_____   Date_____   Phone #_____

2011 Wage Internet 5-28-2011 Ver 1.0

Source: Philadelphia Revenue Department.

*$290,500.73 less exempt wages paid Russell on December 14 ($1,425.16).

STEPS 8 & 9

Glo-Brite Paint Company
General Journal
02/01/--

Date	Refer.	Acct.	Title	Debit	Credit
01/06	General	25	Employees SIT Payable	2,300.14	
01/06	General	11	Cash		2,300.14
01/08	General	28	Union Dues Payable	34.00	
01/08	General	11	Cash		34.00
01/15	General	20.1	FICA Taxes Payable—OASDI	10,904.60	
01/15	General	20.2	FICA Taxes Payable—HI	2,632.61	
01/15	General	24	Employees FIT Payable	22,476.55	
01/15	General	11	Cash		36,013.76
01/15	General	26	Employees CIT Payable	3,509.83	
01/15	General	11	Cash		3,509.83
02/01	General	21	FUTA Taxes Payable	438.53	
02/01	General	11	Cash		438.53
02/01	General	22	SUTA Taxes Payable	500.19	
02/01	General	25.1	Employees SUTA Payable	103.94	
02/01	General	11	Cash		604.13
			Totals	42,900.39	42,900.39

Student Audit Test: Optional Activities

Journal Entries Report
1. $2,300.14
2. $34.00
3. $10,904.60
4. $3,509.83
5. $438.53
6. $500.19
7. $103.94

EXAMINATION QUESTIONS

To aid instructors using *Payroll Accounting*, we have provided a section of examination questions in this manual. The section contains true-false and multiple-choice questions for Chapter 1, with the addition of short problems for Chapters 2, 3, 4, 5, and 6, arranged according to the presentation of the subject matter within these chapters of the textbook.

There is a sufficient number of test questions so that you may vary your examinations from semester to semester or prepare different examinations for each section of the course you may be teaching. Each of the true-false and multiple-choice questions is preceded by a letter answer to the question and a page reference to the textbook page upon which the answer may be found.

CHAPTER 1

True-False Questions

T
1–3
1. The current minimum wage set by the Fair Labor Standards Act is $7.25 per hour.

F
1–3
2. The FLSA imposes no recordkeeping requirements on employers.

T
1–3
3. The employer is required by the FLSA to display a poster that informs employees of the provisions of the law.

F
1–3
4. All states have set their minimum wage to be the same as the federal government.

F
1–4
5. Restrictions on the employment of child labor are established by the Federal Insurance Contributions Act.

F
1–4
6. The FLSA provides health insurance for the aged and disabled (Medicare).

T
1–4
7. The tax paid to the federal government for unemployment taxes is used for paying state and federal administrative expenses of the unemployment program.

T
1–4
8. The Self-Employment Contributions Act imposes a tax on the net earnings from self-employment derived by an individual from any trade or business.

F
1–4
9. Each state imposes an income tax on employees that is 2 percent of gross wages.

F
1–4
10. Only six states do not impose a state unemployment tax on employers in their state.

T   **11.** One of the provisions of coverage of the Civil Rights Act is that the
1–6   employer must have 15 or more workers.

F   **12.** Title VII of the Civil Rights Act protects all employees from arbitrary
1–6   dismissal.

T   **13.** By the use of executive orders, the federal government has banned
1–7   discrimination in employment on government contracts.

T   **14.** Employers not subject to Title VII coverage may come within the scope
1–7   of the Civil Rights Act by reason of a contract or subcontract involving
             federal funds.

T   **15.** Under the Civil Rights Act of 1964, the U.S. government is classified
1–6   as an exempt employer.

T   **16.** An exception to the protection that the Age Discrimination in Employ-
1–7   ment Act provides for all workers over 40 involves executives who are
             65 or older and who have held high policy-making positions during the
             two-year period prior to retirement.

T   **17.** Under the Federal Personal Responsibility and Work Opportunity Rec-
1–7   onciliation Act, every employer is required to report the name, address,
             and social security number of each new employee to the appropriate
             state agency.

T   **18.** Form I-9 must be completed by each new hire.
1–8

F   **19.** Employers are now required to photocopy new employees' Form I-9
1–8   documents.

T   **20.** In order for the Walsh-Healey Public Contracts Act to protect laborers
1–8   for contractors who furnish materials to any agency of the United
             States, the contract amount must be at least $10,000.

F   **21.** Under FMLA, the time off must be used in one uninterrupted period of
1–9   time.

T   **22.** Under the Family and Medical Leave Act, an employer can substitute
1–9   an employee's earned paid leave for any part of the 12-week family
             leave.

F   **23.** FUTA was designed to ensure that workers who are covered by pen-
1–10   sion plans receive benefits from those plans.

T   **24.** Under ERISA, vesting conveys to employees the right to share in a
1–10   retirement fund in the event they are terminated before the normal
             retirement age.

T 1–10	**25.**	Under ERISA, if there is a pension plan, every employee is eligible after reaching age 21 or completing one year of service, whichever is later.
T 1–10	**26.**	ERISA provides for full vesting of the employer's contributions in three years or gradually over six.
F 1–11	**27.**	The total cost of workers' compensation insurance is borne by the employees.
T 1–11	**28.**	Workers' compensation insurance premiums for employers vary according to the different degrees of danger in various classes of jobs and employers' accident experience rate.
F 1–11	**29.**	Workers' compensation benefits are paid directly to the employer.
F 1–12	**30.**	Only one state has passed a law to provide disability benefits to employees absent from their jobs due to illness, accident, or disease not arising out of their employment.
F 1–13	**31.**	The *requisition for personnel form* is sent to the Payroll Department so that the new employee can be properly added to the payroll.
F 1–14	**32.**	Employment application forms are usually discarded when the applicant is hired.
T 1–14	**33.**	Questions pertaining to religion, gender, national origin, or age are allowed on application forms when these are bona fide occupational qualifications for a job.
F 1–14	**34.**	Most firms are now using a standard *reference inquiry form*, supplied by the IRS.
T 1–17	**35.**	If an investigative consumer report is being checked, the job applicant must be notified in writing by the employer that such a report is being sought.
F 1–19	**36.**	There are no states that allow employees to access their personnel files.
F 1–19	**37.**	The *payroll register* is a separate payroll record that is kept on each employee.
T 1–19	**38.**	A *payroll register* lists all employees who have earned remuneration, the amount of remuneration, the deductions, and the net amount paid for each pay period.
F 1–20	**39.**	The amounts needed for the payroll entries in the journal come from the *employee's earnings record*.
F 1–21	**40.**	The trend toward outsourcing of payroll operations has weakened in recent years.

Multiple-Choice Questions

c
1–3

1. Which of the following is *not* a provision of the Fair Labor Standards Act (FLSA)?
   a. Restricts the employment of child labor
   b. Sets up minimum wage
   c. Forbids discrimination in hiring
   d. Mandates equal pay for equal work, regardless of sex
   e. All are provisions of the FLSA.

a
1–4

2. Which of the following is *not* part of the social security program?
   a. Federal Income Tax Law
   b. Federal Old-Age and Survivors' Trust Fund
   c. Medicare
   d. Self-Employment Contributions Act
   e. All are part of the social security program.

b
1–4

3. Which of the following acts levies a tax on employers and employees that is credited to the Federal Old-Age and Survivors' Trust Fund and the Federal Disability Insurance Trust Fund?
   a. Federal Income Tax Act
   b. Federal Insurance Contributions Act
   c. Fair Labor Standards Act
   d. Federal Unemployment Tax Act
   e. Employee Retirement Income Security Act

e
1–7

4. The Age Discrimination in Employment Act provides protection to virtually all workers over the age of:
   a. 18.
   b. 65.
   c. 21.
   d. 55.
   e. 40.

b
1–8

5. Form I-9, which is completed by each employee, deals with:
   a. contributions to individual retirement accounts.
   b. verification of employment eligibility.
   c. eligibility for unemployment benefits.
   d. eligibility for Medicare benefits.
   e. none of the above.

e
1–8

6. Which of the following acts deals with the minimum wage paid to laborers for contractors on federal government construction contracts?
   a. Walsh-Healey Public Contracts Act
   b. Fair Labor Standards Act
   c. McNamara-O'Hara Service Contract Act
   d. Occupational Safety and Health Act
   e. None of the above

c
1–10

7. ERISA provides for full vesting of the employer's contribution to an employee's pension fund in three years or gradually over:
   a. ten years.
   b. five years.
   c. six years.
   d. seven years.
   e. No gradual vesting is allowed.

c
1–14

8. Prehire questions pertaining to religion, gender, national origin, or age are allowed if:
   a. all employees are asked the same questions.
   b. only foreign-born applicants are asked these questions.
   c. these factors are bona fide occupational qualifications for the job.
   d. they are not in written form.
   e. the applicant is married.

d
1–17

9. Which of the following forms is used to notify the Payroll Department to add a new employee to the payroll?
   a. Employee's earnings record
   b. Change in payroll rate form
   c. Reference inquiry form
   d. Hiring notice
   e. None of the above

b
1–19

10. Which of the following records lists all employees who earn remuneration, the amount of remuneration, the deductions, and the net amount paid for each payroll period?
   a. Employee history record
   b. Payroll register
   c. Change in payroll rate form
   d. Reference inquiry form
   e. None of the above

CHAPTER 2

True-False Questions

F 2–2   **1.** Under the FLSA enterprise coverage test, hospitals and nursing homes are only covered if their annual charges for services are at least $500,000.

T 2–2   **2.** Institutions of higher education are extended coverage under FLSA without regard to their annual sales volume.

F 2–2   **3.** If a business does not meet the enterprise coverage test, none of its workers qualify for individual employee coverage.

F 2–3   **4.** Domestics are excluded from coverage under the FLSA individual employee coverage.

F 2–4   **5.** Under the FLSA, severance pay is excluded from the definition of wages.

F 2–4   **6.** The term *wage* refers to remuneration paid only on an hourly basis.

T 2–4   **7.** Employees paid biweekly receive their remuneration every two weeks.

F 2–4   **8.** In May 2013, workers who receive the minimum hourly wage are paid $6.10 an hour.

F 2–5   **9.** A retail shop may employ a full-time student at $5.00 per hour.

T 2–5   **10.** A college may employ its own full-time students at 85 percent of the minimum wage.

F 2–5   **11.** All major cities have enacted ordinances establishing a so-called "living wage" at $8.25 per hour.

F 2–6   **12.** The FLSA defines a tipped employee as one who regularly receives tips of more than $20 a month.

T 2–6   **13.** An employer can credit up to $5.12 of a tipped employee's minimum wage as coming from the tips received by that employee.

T 2–7   **14.** The FLSA requires that workers receive overtime pay for all hours worked in excess of 40 in a workweek.

F 2–7   **15.** The FLSA requires that workers receive overtime pay of twice the employees' regular hourly rate for hours worked on Sunday.

T 2–8   **16.** Employees who are receiving remedial education may work up to 10 hours overtime each week without receiving overtime pay.

T 2–8	**17.**	Public safety employees of a state can be granted compensatory time off in lieu of overtime compensation.
F 2–8	**18.**	No employer can grant compensatory time off to employees in place of overtime pay.
F 2–9	**19.**	Exempt professional employees are exempt from all provisions of the FLSA—minimum wages, overtime pay, and equal pay.
T 2–9	**20.**	Employees paid by the hour without a guarantee of a weekly minimum salary do not qualify for the salary test for white-collar workers.
T 2–9	**21.**	One of the tests to be met for the white-collar exemption for an executive is to be paid a salary of at least $455 per week.
F 2–11	**22.**	The Equal Pay Act stipulates that there cannot be any wage differentials between the sexes.
F 2–11	**23.**	Under no conditions may children under age 16 be employed in food service establishments.
F 2–11	**24.**	The FLSA sets no limits upon the number of hours that a 15-year-old person may work so long as the overtime pay provisions are met.
F 2–12	**25.**	The FLSA requires that employees be given the day off on all Monday holidays or be paid time and one-half for those Mondays.
F 2–13	**26.**	When employees spend time changing clothes on the employer's premises, this time must be counted as part of their principal activities for which they are always fully compensated.
T 2–14	**27.**	Provided employees can use the on-call time for their own purposes, this time is not compensable.
F 2–14	**28.**	The FLSA requires that employees be given at least two 15-minute rest periods each workday.
T 2–14	**29.**	Bona fide meal periods when the employee is completely relieved from duty are not considered working time.
F 2–14	**30.**	"Engaged to wait" and "waiting to be engaged" are both considered work time.
F 2–15	**31.**	The courts have ruled that preliminary and postliminary activities, even if indispensable to the main activities of an employee, do not constitute work time.
T 2–16	**32.**	Employers may adopt the practice of recording an employee's starting and stopping time to the nearest quarter of an hour.
F 2–16	**33.**	The FLSA contains detailed specifications of the methods that employers must follow in keeping time records.
T 2–17	**34.**	Under the continental system of recording time, 9:00 A.M. is recorded as 900 while 9:00 P.M. is recorded as 2100.

F 2–22 **35.** In converting semimonthly wage rates to hourly rates, divide the semi-monthly rate by 4 to arrive at the weekly rate, then divide this rate by the standard number of hours.

T 2–25 **36.** Under the piece-rate system, workers are paid according to their output.

F 2–27 **37.** Although commissions are considered payments for hours worked, in all cases they are excluded when determining the regular hourly rate.

T 2–27 **38.** To calculate the overtime pay rate for a commissioned worker, divide the total commission by the hours worked, and then take one-half of the resulting rate of pay.

T 2–27 **39.** Nondiscretionary bonuses are part of the determination of regular rate of pay.

T 2–28 **40.** Payments made to a bona fide profit-sharing plan that meets the standards set by the secretary of labor's regulations are not deemed wages in determining the regular rate of pay.

Multiple-Choice Questions

d 2–2 **1.** Under *enterprise coverage*, all employees of a business are covered by the FLSA if the organization is:
a. a nursing home.
b. a public agency.
c. a hospital.
d. all of the above.
e. none of the above.

d 2–2, 2–3 **2.** Under *individual employee coverage*, the worker is covered by the FLSA if:
a. the worker produces goods for interstate commerce.
b. the worker is a housekeeper in a private home for 16 hours a week.
c. the domestic receives cash wages of at least $1,800 from the employer in the calendar year.
d. all of the above.
e. none of the above.

a 2–4 **3.** Under the FLSA, regular rate of pay does not include:
a. vacation pay.
b. severance pay.
c. overtime pay.
d. earned bonuses.
e. All of the above are considered wages.

e
2–4

4. In August 2014, the minimum hourly wage was:
   a. $3.35.
   b. $7.15.
   c. $5.85.
   d. $5.15.
   e. none of the above.

e
2–6

5. The tips received by a tipped employee are less than $5.12 of the minimum hourly tip credit rate. The maximum permissible tip credit is:
   a. $30 a month.
   b. $5.12 an hour.
   c. 45% of the employee's minimum wage.
   d. 50% of the employee's minimum wage.
   e. the amount of tips actually received by the employee.

c
2–7

6. Under the FLSA, overtime pay is required for:
   a. any hours worked in excess of 8 in one day.
   b. all work on Sunday.
   c. all hours worked in excess of 40 in a workweek.
   d. all hours worked on Christmas.
   e. all of the above.

e
2–9

7. Workers exempt from all of the FLSA requirements include:
   a. employees paid by the hour.
   b. clerk-typists earning less than $200 a week.
   c. taxicab drivers.
   d. motion picture theater employees.
   e. none of the above.

c
2–11

8. Under the Equal Pay Act:
   a. employers must pay a married male a higher wage rate than a single female if both are performing equal work.
   b. white-collar workers are exempt from its requirements.
   c. wage differentials based on a seniority system are allowed.
   d. if there is an unlawful pay differential, employers may reduce the higher rate to equal the lower rate.
   e. none of the above.

a
2–12

9. If an employer is unable to obtain a certificate of age or a work permit for a minor employee, the employer may rely upon what document as evidence of age?
   a. Baptism record
   b. Mother's statement as to date of birth
   c. High school enrollment form showing date of birth
   d. Minor employee's statement as to date of birth
   e. None of the above

e **10.** Which of the following is *not* required by the FLSA?
2–12, 2–13
    a. Extra pay for work on holidays
    b. Two weeks' vacation pay after one year of service
    c. Restriction on hours worked by a 17-year-old worker
    d. All of the above are required.
    e. None of the above is required.

d **11.** Those tasks that employees must perform and which include any work of
2–13 consequence performed for the employer are known as:
    a. preliminary activities.
    b. postliminary activities.
    c. work activities.
    d. principal activities.
    e. none of the above.

d **12.** Rest periods and coffee breaks may be required by all of the following
2–14 *except*:
    a. a union contract.
    b. a state legislation.
    c. a municipal legislation.
    d. the FLSA.
    e. none of the above.

b **13.** Training sessions are counted as working time when the following condi-
2–15 tion is met:
    a. the employee's attendance is voluntary.
    b. the employer requires the employee's attendance.
    c. the training sessions are for the primary benefit of the employee.
    d. the session takes place outside the regular working hours.
    e. the session is not directly related to the employee's work.

d **14.** The Wage and Hour Division allows the practice of recording an em-
2–16 ployee's starting and stopping time to:
    a. the nearest five minutes.
    b. the nearest tenth of an hour.
    c. the nearest quarter of an hour.
    d. all of the above.
    e. none of the above.

c **15.** The FLSA requires:
2–16
    a. that employers use time cards to record the employees' time worked.
    b. that employers use the continental time system to record all time worked by employees.
    c. that employers keep records that show the hours each employee worked each workday and each workweek.
    d. that employees sign each clock card.
    e. none of the above.

c
2–17

16. Under the continental system of recording time, 9:20 P.M. is recorded as:
   a.   P2120.
   b.   9:20P.
   c.   2120.
   d.   2220.
   e.   none of the above.

e
2–20

17. If an employee works two jobs at two different wage rates for the same employer during the same pay week, any overtime pay must be calculated by using an overtime hourly rate of:
   a.   one and one-half the higher of the two wage rates.
   b.   one and one-half the lowest of the two wage rates.
   c.   one-half of the higher of the two wage rates.
   d.   one-half of the two rates combined.
   e.   none of the above.

e
2–23

18. Employers may pay nonexempt employees who work fluctuating schedules a fixed salary. In these cases, the extra pay is:
   a.   calculated at a time and one-half rate.
   b.   calculated at a double time rate.
   c.   calculated at the regular rate of pay.
   d.   unpaid.
   e.   none of the above.

a
2–25

19. To determine a pieceworker's *regular hourly rate* for one week:
   a.   divide the total weekly earnings from piece rates and all other sources by the hours worked in the week.
   b.   divide the total weekly earnings from piece rates by the number of pieces produced.
   c.   divide the total weekly earnings from piece rates, less earnings from other sources, by the hours worked in a week.
   d.   add the total weekly earnings from piece rates and all other sources and divide by the total number of pieces produced.
   e.   do none of the above.

b
2–26

20. A stated percentage of revenue paid an employee who transacts a piece of business or performs a service is called:
   a.   a piece rate.
   b.   a commission.
   c.   a regular hourly rate.
   d.   a remunerative salary.
   e.   none of the above.

Problem-Solving

NOTE: In all problems, *unless instructed otherwise*, compute the hourly and overtime rates as follows:

1. Carry the hourly rate and the overtime rate to 3 decimal places and then round off to 2 decimal places (round the hourly rate to 2 decimal places before multiplying by one and one-half to determine the overtime rate).
2. If the third decimal place is 5 or more, round to the next higher cent.
3. If the third decimal place is less than 5, drop the third decimal place.

Also, use the minimum hourly wage of $7.25 in solving these problems and all that follow.

1. Abel works a 37½-hour week at $7.75 an hour. Overtime hours are paid at 1½ times the regular rate.

   (a)   Abel's regular weekly earnings are (37½ × $7.75) $290.63
   (b)   Abel's overtime rate is ($7.75 × 1.5) .... $ 11.63
   (c)   Abel works 6 hours overtime during one week.
         Abel's weekly gross earnings are [$290.63 + (6 × $11.63)] $360.41

2. Jack Kentson works a 40-hour week with overtime paid at 1½ times his regular rate of pay of $14.88. This week he worked 42 hours, which resulted in a gross pay of [(40 × $14.88) + (2 × $14.88 × 1.5)] $639.84

3. Carolyn Clark, a full-time student at Atlanta State University, works at the Barclay Dress Shop. In order not to violate the FLSA, the least salary that Barclay could pay Clark for her 28-hour workweek is (28 × $6.17) $172.76

4. Bakker is paid an hourly rate of $7.65. For 130 minutes spent on a certain job, Bakker is paid ($7.65 × 130/60) .... $ 16.58

5. Annette Henri is paid an hourly wage of $8.90 for a 32-hour workweek of 4 days, 8 hours daily. For any work on the fifth day and on Saturdays, she is paid one and one-half times her regular hourly rate. During a certain week, in addition to her regular 32 hours, Henri worked 6 hours on the fifth day and 5 hours on Saturday. For this workweek, Henri's total earnings are [(32 × $8.90) + (11 × $8.90 × 1.5)]............................. $431.65

6. Jose Cruz earns $2,275 each month and works 37½ hours each week. His employer pays him overtime (for hours beyond 37½) and uses the overtime premium approach. Cruz's overtime premium hourly rate is ($2,275 × 12 = $27,300 ÷ 52 = $525 ÷ 37½ = $14.00 × ½)................... $ 7.00

7. Every two weeks, Linda Corson is paid $650. Corson works a 32-hour week. For overtime, she receives extra pay at the regular hourly rate up to 40 hours. For any hours beyond 40 during the workweek, she receives time and one-half. During one biweekly pay period, she worked 17 hours overtime. Only 3 hours of the overtime were beyond 40 hours in any one week. Corson's gross earnings for the biweekly pay period are {$650 ÷ 64 = $10.16; [$650 + (14 × $10.16) + (3 × $10.16 × 1.5)]} $837.96

8. Carla Maloney is a waitress who regularly receives $80 each week in tips and works 40 hours each week. The minimum gross weekly pay, excluding tips, that the restaurant could pay Maloney without violating the FLSA is [(40 × $7.25) – $80].. $210.00

9. Elder is paid a monthly salary of $2,250. Overtime is paid for hours beyond 40 in each workweek. One week, Elder works 7 hours overtime. Elder's gross pay for the week is {(12 × $2,250) ÷ 52 = $519.23 ÷ 40 = $12.98; [$519.23 + (7 × $12.98 × 1.5)]}... $655.52

10. Kevin Kurtz is a newly hired exempt employee who earns an annual salary of $67,600. Since he started work on Thursday (5-day week ends on Friday), his pay for the first week of work would be [($67,600 ÷ 52) × 2/5] $520.00

11. Fall is paid a biweekly salary of $637.50. Overtime is paid for hours beyond 40 in each workweek. One week, Fall works 3 hours overtime. Fall's pay for this biweekly pay period is ($637.50 ÷ 80 = $7.97 × 1.5 = $11.96 × 3 = $35.88 + $637.50) $673.38

12. Gates is paid a semimonthly salary of $800.00. Overtime is paid for hours beyond 40 in each workweek. One week, Gates works 6¾ hours overtime. Gates' pay for this semimonthly pay period is (24 × $800 = $19,200 ÷ 52 = $369.23 ÷ 40 = $9.23 × 1.5 = $13.85 × 6¾ = $93.49 + $800) $893.49

13. Stacy Forvour is a salaried employee who works fluctuating workweeks. She is paid $680 per workweek. This week, she worked 46 hours. Forvour's total gross pay if her employer uses the special half-rate (based on total hours worked) for overtime pay is ($680 ÷ 46 = $14.78 × ½ = $7.39 × 6 = $44.34 + $680) $724.34

14. Casey Klemons' agreement (BELO plan) with his employer provides for a pay rate of $16.50 per hour with a maximum of 50 hours. How much would Klemons be paid for a week in which he worked 46 hours? [50 × $16.50 = $825; (10 × 0.5 × $16.50 = $82.50 + $825)]...................... $907.50

15. Hall receives 18½ cents for every unit produced. Hall produces 575 units in an 8-hour workday. Hall's daily wages are (575 × $0.185) $106.38

16. Ides receives 16 cents for every unit produced. Ides produces 2,976 pieces in a 43-hour workweek. For overtime, Ides is paid a sum equal to one-half the regular hourly pay rate multiplied by the number of overtime hours. Ides' total piecework and overtime earnings are ($2,976 \times \$0.16 = \$476.16 \div 43 = \$11.07 \times 0.5 = \$5.54 \times 3 = \$16.62 + \$476.16$).......... $492.78

17. Gorman is paid $10.50 per hour for a 35-hour workweek. This past week, he worked an extra 10 hours on a job at a pay rate of $13.00 per hour. If he is only paid overtime for hours over 40 and the employer uses the average rate method, his total earnings for the 45 hours of work was [($35 \times \$10.50$) + ($10 \times \$13.00$) = $497.50 \div 45 = \$11.06 \times 0.5$ = (5.53×5) + $497.50] $525.15

18. Kenneth Anderson works two separate jobs for Mesa Company. During the week, Job A consisted of 38 hours at $20 per hour; Job B involved 15 hours at $14 per hour. If Mesa uses the average rate basis for calculating overtime, Anderson's pay for that week is [($38 \times \$20$) + ($15 \times \$14$) = $970 \div 53 = \$18.30 \times 0.5 = \$9.15 \times 13 = \$118.95 + \$970]................... $1,088.95

19. Kerr receives an annual $25,700 base salary for working the territory in Arizona. A quota of $900,000 in sales has been set for that state. Kerr receives an 8% commission on all sales in excess of $900,000. This year, the sales are $965,000. The total earnings due Kerr this year are ($965,000 − $900,000 = $65,000 \times 0.08 = \$5,200 + \$25,700$)....... $30,900.00

20. Kelli England earns $12.30 per hour and has earned a production bonus this week of $37.10. If England worked 44 hours this week, her gross pay is ($44 \times \$12.30 = \$541.20 + \$37.10 = \$578.30 \div 44$ = $13.14 \times 0.5 = \$6.57 \times 4 = \$26.28 + \$578.30$) $604.58

CHAPTER 3

True-False Questions

F 3–2	1.	The Federal Insurance Contributions Act levies a tax upon the gross earnings of self-employed persons.
T 3–2	2.	FICA includes partnerships in its definition of *employer*.
F 3–2	3.	In its definition of *employee*, FICA clearly distinguishes between classes or grades of employees.
F 3–3	4.	The highest paid executives of a firm are excluded from coverage under the Federal Insurance Contributions Act (FICA).
T 3–3	5.	A worker hired by the federal government in 2014 is covered under FICA.
T 3–3	6.	Employees of a state government hired before January 1, 1986, and covered by a public retirement plan, are exempt from FICA coverage.
T 3–4	7.	Peter, age 17 and employed by his family-owned corporation, is covered under FICA.
T 3–5	8.	Employers do not pay payroll taxes on payments made to independent contractors.
T 3–6	9.	Dismissal pay is considered taxable wages under FICA.
F 3–7	10.	Under FICA only, cash tips of more than $100 in a month are defined as taxable wages.
T 3–7	11.	Employees may use Form 4070 to report the amount of their tips to their employers.
F 3–8	12.	FICA does not consider the first six months of sick pay as taxable wages.
F 3–7	13.	In computing their own FICA taxes, employers may exclude the total amount of tips reported to them by their tipped employees.
T 3–8	14.	FICA defines *wages* as including the cash value of meals provided for the convenience of the employees.
T 3–8	15.	Payments made to a worker's spouse for hospital expenses in connection with an accident disability are not considered wages under FICA.
T 3–8	16.	Employer payments made directly to employees in lieu of health insurance coverage are taxable wages.

F   **17.**   Exempt *educational assistance* includes payments for tools that
3–9   employees keep after they complete a course of instruction.

T   **18.**   Each year, the FICA (OASDI portion) taxable wage base is automatically
3–10   adjusted whenever a cost of living raise in social security benefits
                    becomes available.

T   **19.**   The FICA tax rates and taxable wage bases are *exactly the same* for
3–9   employees and employers.

T   **20.**   Employees are liable for their FICA taxes only until the taxes have been
3–10   collected from their pay by their employer.

F   **21.**   OASDI taxes are levied when the wages are *earned by*, rather than when
3–10   *paid to*, employees.

T   **22.**   If an employee, who works two or more separate jobs, pays OASDI taxes
3–11   on wages in excess of the taxable wage base, the employee is entitled to
                    a refund of the overpayment.

F   **23.**   Under SECA, *all* of an individual's self-employment income is counted in
3–12   determining the OASDI tax.

T   **24.**   Self-employed persons include their self-employment taxes in their
3–13   quarterly payment of estimated federal income taxes.

T   **25.**   All employers of one or more persons must file an application for an
3–14   identification number.

F   **26.**   The Social Security Act does not require self-employed persons to have
3–14   an account number.

F   **27.**   The Social Security Act requires workers to obtain a new account
3–14   number each time they change jobs.

F   **28.**   Nonagricultural employers who withhold income taxes and are liable for
3–16   social security taxes must file a monthly tax and information return.

T   **29.**   The requirements for depositing FICA taxes and income taxes withheld
3–16   from nonagricultural employees' wages vary according to the amount of
                    such taxes reported during a "lookback period."

F   **30.**   State and local government employers must make their tax deposits
3–16   according to a different schedule than private employers.

F   **31.**   A monthly depositor is one who reported employment taxes of $50,000 or
3–18   more for the four quarters in the lookback period.

T   **32.**   Monthly depositors are required to deposit their taxes by the 15th day of
3–18   the following month.

T
3–18

33. The employees of a semiweekly depositor are paid every Tuesday. The accumulated payroll taxes must be deposited on or before the following Friday.

F
3–18

34. An employer's social security and withheld income taxes for the quarter are less than $2,500. The employer must deposit the taxes at its bank at the time of filing the fourth quarter Form 941.

T
3–18

35. If the accumulated employment taxes during a quarter are less than $2,500, no deposits are required.

F
3–19

36. Under the safe harbor rule, when employers deposit their tax liabilities, they may have a shortfall of no more than $200 without incurring any penalty.

F
3–20

37. Noncash items given to household employees by their employers are subject to FICA tax.

T
3–20

38. Businesses with $2,500 or less in quarterly tax liabilities can pay the taxes when they file Form 941.

T
3–21

39. Form 941 is used by employers to make their quarterly return of FICA taxes and withheld income taxes.

T
3–24

40. On Form 941, the employer does not show the date of each tax deposit during the quarter.

F
3–26

41. Form 941 is due on or before the 15th day of the month following the close of the calendar quarter for which the return is made.

T
3–27

42. Employers file Form 941 with the IRS center of the region in which the employer's principal place of business is located.

F
3–27

43. Form 944 (annual form) can be used by all new employers instead of Form 941.

T
3–28

44. Employers who fail to file employment tax returns are subject to both civil and criminal penalties.

T
3–28

45. If an employer fails to file an employment tax return on the due date, a penalty based on a certain percentage of the amount of tax required to be reported may be added to the tax.

Multiple-Choice Questions

e
3–2

1. The taxes imposed under the Social Security Act consist of:
   a. two taxes on employers.
   b. two taxes on employees.
   c. OASDI and HI taxes.
   d. taxes on the net earnings of the self-employed.
   e. all of the above.

b
3–2

2. FICA defines all of the following as employees *except*:
   a. vice presidents.
   b. partners.
   c. superintendents.
   d. full-time life insurance salespersons.
   e. payroll managers.

d
3–3

3. FICA excludes from coverage all of the following kinds of employment *except*:
   a. domestic service performed in a college sorority by a student.
   b. service performed by a 16-year-old child in the employ of the mother.
   c. babysitting service performed by a 35-year-old person who receives $40 in cash during the calendar quarter.
   d. federal government secretaries hired in 1990.
   e. services performed by a railroad worker for an employer covered by the Railroad Retirement Tax Act.

c
3–7

4. FICA defines all of the following as wages *except*:
   a. year-end bonuses.
   b. standby payments.
   c. total cash tips of $15 received by a tipped employee in May.
   d. employees' social security taxes paid for by the employer.
   e. first six months of sick pay.

a
3–8

5. Each of the following items is accurately defined under FICA as taxable wages *except*:
   a. value of meals furnished employees for the employer's convenience.
   b. value of meals furnished employees for the employees' convenience.
   c. commissions.
   d. dismissal pay.
   e. $500 award for productivity improvement suggestion.

b
3–8

6. Which of the following payments are not taxable for FICA?
   a. Back-pay awards.
   b. Wage supplements to cover difference between employees' salaries and their military pay.
   c. Dismissal pay.
   d. Difference between employees' regular wages and the amount received for jury duty.
   e. Retroactive wage increase.

b
3–9

7. The OASDI taxable wage base is correctly defined as:
    a. all amounts earned by an employee during a calendar year.
    b. the maximum amount of wages during a calendar year that is subject to the OASDI tax.
    c. all amounts paid an employee during a calendar year.
    d. all amounts either earned by, or paid to, an employee during a calendar year.
    e. none of the above.

c
3–10

8. Which of the following statements does *not* describe an employee's FICA taxes and withholdings?
    a. The employee's taxes are collected by the employer and paid to the IRS along with the employer's taxes.
    b. The employee's taxes are deducted from the employee's wages at the time of payment.
    c. The employee's liability for the FICA taxes continues even after the employer has withheld them.
    d. The amount of tax to be withheld is computed by multiplying the employee's taxable wages by the current tax rate.
    e. The employee is entitled to a refund for overpayment of FICA taxes resulting from having worked for more than one employer.

e
3–12

9. The FICA tax rates for the self-employed are:
    a. 6.2% (OASDI) and 1.45% (HI).
    b. 12.4% (OASDI) and 1.45% (HI).
    c. 6.2% (OASDI) and 2.9% (HI).
    d. 10.0% (OASDI) and 1.0% (HI).
    e. none of the above.

c
3–18

10. Which of the following deposit requirements pertains to a monthly depositor who has accumulated employment taxes of $2,900 at the end of October?
    a. No deposit is required.
    b. The undeposited taxes should be carried over to the end of November.
    c. The taxes must be deposited on or before November 15.
    d. The taxes must be deposited on or before the next banking day.
    e. None of the above.

d
3–18

11. Which of the following deposit requirements pertains to a *semiweekly* depositor who has accumulated employment taxes of $17,500 on payday, Saturday, May 17?
    a. No deposit is required until May 19, the next banking day.
    b. The undeposited taxes should be carried over to the next payday on May 24.
    c. The taxes must be deposited on or before Tuesday, May 20.
    d. The taxes must be deposited on or before Friday, May 23.
    e. None of the above.

a   **12.** To be designated a semiweekly depositor, how much in employment
3–18   taxes would an employer have reported for the four quarters in the
                lookback period?
                a.   More than $50,000.
                b.   More than $100,000.
                c.   Less than $50,000.
                d.   More than $2,500.
                e.   None of the above.

b   **13.** Which of the following deposit requirements pertains to a nonagricultural
3–18   employer who has employer FICA taxes and withheld employee FICA
                taxes and income taxes of $125,000 at the end of payday on Friday,
                August 15?
                a.   No deposit is required until Tuesday, August 19.
                b.   The taxes must be deposited by the close of the next banking day.
                c.   The taxes must be deposited on or before August 31.
                d.   The undeposited taxes should be carried over to the end of
                     September.
                e.   None of the above.

d   **14.** Ashe, an employer, has made timely deposits of FICA taxes and withheld
3–26   income taxes during the first quarter of 2014. The latest date on which
                she may file Form 941 is:
                a.   April 10.
                b.   April 30.
                c.   May 1.
                d.   May 12.
                e.   May 15.

a   **15.** Barr fails to make a timely deposit of FICA taxes and withheld income
3–30   taxes until five days after the due date. The penalty facing Barr is:
                a.   2% of the undeposited taxes.
                b.   5% of the undeposited taxes.
                c.   10% of the undeposited taxes.
                d.   25% of the undeposited taxes.
                e.   none of the above.

Problem-Solving

NOTE: In all the following problems, use these tax rates and taxable wage: OASDI — (Employees' and Employers' 6.2%, Self-Employed 12.4%) on first $113,700; HI — (Employees' and Employers' 1.45%, Self-Employed 2.9%) on all taxable wages.

1.   Crow earned $585.15 during the week ended March 1, 20--. Prior to payday, Crow had cumulative gross earnings of $4,733.20.

   (a) The amount of OASDI taxes to withhold from Crow's pay is ($585.15 × 6.2%) $36.28

   (b) The amount of HI taxes to withhold from Crow's pay is ($585.15 × 1.45%) $8.48

2.   Dee is paid $1,345 on November 8, 20--. Dee had cumulative gross earnings, including overtime pay, of $112,400 prior to this pay.

   (a) The amount of OASDI taxes to withhold from Dee's pay is ($1,300 × 6.2%) $80.60

   (b) The amount of HI taxes to withhold from Dee's pay is ($1,345 × 1.45%) $19.50

3.   Beginning with the first pay of the year, Carson will make $2,700 each week. In which numbered pay of the year will Carson hit the OASDI taxable limit? ($113,700 ÷ $2,700)...   43rd pay

4.   On the last weekly pay of the first quarter, Lorenz is paid her current pay of $90 per day for four days worked and one day sick pay (total— $450). She is also paid her first-quarter commission of $1,200 in this pay. How much will be deducted for:

   (a) OASDI tax ($1,650 × 6.2%)... $102.30

   (b) HI tax ($1,650 × 1.45%) $23.93

5.   Eager, a tipped employee, reported to his employer that he had received $320 in tips during March. On the next payday, April 4, he was paid his regular salary of $250.

   (a) The amount of OASDI taxes to withhold from Eager's pay is ($570 × 6.2%) $35.34

   (b) The amount of HI taxes to withhold from Eager's pay is ($570 × 1.45%) $8.27

6. Fess receives wages totaling $74,500 and has net earnings from self-employment amounting to $51,300. In determining her taxable self-employment income for the OASDI tax, how much of her net self-employment earnings must Fess count? ($113,700 – $74,500) ... $39,200

7. During 20--, Garr was paid a weekly salary of $2,250. The amount of FICA to be withheld from the following payments is:

	OASDI	HI
(a) For the 50th week ($2,250 × 6.2%), ($2,250 × 1.45%).	$139.50	$32.63
(b) For the 51st week {[$113,700 – ($2,250 × 50)] × 6.2%}	74.40	32.63
(c) For the 52nd week	0.00	32.63

8. On August 1, Huff (part-time waitress) reported on Form 4070 the cash tips of $158.50 that she received in July. During August, Huff was paid wages of $550 by her employer.

   Determine:

   (a) The amount of social security taxes that the employer should withhold from Huff's wages during August:
   OASDI ($708.50 × 6.2%) ... $43.93   HI ($708.50 × 1.45%) $10.27

   (b) The amount of the employer's social security taxes on Huff's wages and tips during August:
   OASDI .... $43.93   HI $10.27

9. In this pay, Moss Company deducted OASDI taxes of $3,574.24 and HI taxes of $1,233.95 from the $85,100.90 of taxable wages paid. What is Moss Company's portion of the social security taxes for:

   (a) OASDI ($85,100.90 × 6.2%) $5,276.26

   (b) HI ($85,100.90 × 1.45%) $1,233.96

10. Jax Company's (a monthly depositor) tax liability (amount withheld from employees' wages for federal income tax and FICA tax plus the company's portion of the FICA tax) for July was $1,210. No deposit was made by the company until August 24.

    Determine:

    (a) The date by which the deposit should have been made .... August 15

    (b) The penalty for failure to make timely deposit ($1,210 × 5%) $60.50

    (c) The penalty for failure to fully pay tax when due ($1,210 × 0.5%) .. $6.05

    (d) The interest on taxes due and unpaid (assume a 3% interest rate), ($1,210 × 3% × 9/365) $0.90

11. Ralston is the sole proprietor of Cut & Curl. During the year, his
net earnings were $79,700. What are his self-employment taxes
(OASDI and HI) on these earnings? [$79,700 × (12.4% + 2.9%)]....... $12,194.10

12. Lidge Company of Texas (TX) pays its employees monthly. The following
payroll information is for the second quarter of the year.

		WITHHOLDINGS			EMPLOYER'S	
	Wages	OASDI	HI	FIT	OASDI	HI
April	$ 86,100	$ 5,338.20	$1,248.46	$ 9,650	$ 5,338.20	$1,248.45
May	92,500	5,735.00	1,341.26	10,005	5,735.00	1,341.25
June	73,400	4,550.80	1,064.30	8,995	4,550.80	1,064.30
Totals	$252,000	$15,624.00	$3,654.02	$28,650	$15,624.00	$3,654.00

The number of employees on March 12 was 11.

Complete the following portion of Form 941.

Part 1:	Answer these questions for this quarter.		
1	Number of employees who received wages, tips, or other compensation for the pay period including: *Mar. 12* (Quarter 1), *June 12* (Quarter 2), *Sept. 12* (Quarter 3), or *Dec. 12* (Quarter 4)	1	11
2	Wages, tips, and other compensation	2	252000 • 00
3	Income tax withheld from wages, tips, and other compensation	3	28650 • 00
4	If no wages, tips, and other compensation are subject to social security or Medicare tax	☐ Check and go to line 6.	

		Column 1		Column 2
5a	Taxable social security wages . .	252000 • 00	× .124 =	31248 • 00
5b	Taxable social security tips	•	× .124 =	•
5c	Taxable Medicare wages & tips. .	252000 • 00	× .029 =	7308 • 00
5d	Taxable wages & tips subject to Additional Medicare Tax withholding	•	× .009 =	•
5e	Add Column 2 from lines 5a, 5b, 5c, and 5d	5e		38556 • 00
5f	Section 3121(q) Notice and Demand—Tax due on unreported tips (see instructions) . .	5f		•

Source: Internal Revenue Service.

13. Complete the following portion of Form 941 from the information presented in Problem 12.

6	Total taxes before adjustments (add lines 3, 5e, and 5f)	6	67206 ▪	00
7	Current quarter's adjustment for fractions of cents	7	▪	02
8	Current quarter's adjustment for sick pay	8	▪	
9	Current quarter's adjustments for tips and group-term life insurance	9	▪	
10	Total taxes after adjustments. Combine lines 6 through 9	10	67206 ▪	02
11	Total deposits for this quarter, including overpayment applied from a prior quarter and overpayment applied from Form 941-X or Form 944-X filed in the current quarter . . .	11	67206 ▪	02
12a	COBRA premium assistance payments (see instructions)	12a	▪	
12b	Number of individuals provided COBRA premium assistance . .			
13	Add lines 11 and 12a	13	67206 ▪	02
14	Balance due. If line 10 is more than line 13, enter the difference and see instructions . . .	14	▪	
15	Overpayment. If line 13 is more than line 10, enter the difference [ ] ▪ Check one: ☐ Apply to next return. ☐ Send a refund.			

▶ **You MUST complete both pages of Form 941 and SIGN it.**   Next ▶

For Privacy Act and Paperwork Reduction Act Notice, see the back of the Payment Voucher.   Cat. No. 17001Z   Form **941** (Rev. 1-2013)

Source: Internal Revenue Service.

14. From the information presented in Problem 12, complete Part 2 of Form 941.

Part 2:	**Tell us about your deposit schedule and tax liability for this quarter.**

If you are unsure about whether you are a monthly schedule depositor or a semiweekly schedule depositor, see Pub. 15 (Circular E), section 11.

16 Check one: ☐   Line 10 on this return is less than $2,500 or line 10 on the return for the prior quarter was less than $2,500, and you did not incur a $100,000 next-day deposit obligation during the current quarter. If line 10 for the prior quarter was less than $2,500 but line 10 on this return is $100,000 or more, you must provide a record of your federal tax liability. If you are a monthly schedule depositor, complete the deposit schedule below; if you are a semiweekly schedule depositor, attach Schedule B (Form 941). Go to Part 3.

☒   **You were a monthly schedule depositor for the entire quarter.** Enter your tax liability for each month and total liability for the quarter, then go to Part 3.

Tax liability:	Month 1	22823 ▪ 31
	Month 2	24157 ▪ 51
	Month 3	20225 ▪ 20
Total liability for quarter		67206 ▪ 02 Total must equal line 10.

☐   **You were a semiweekly schedule depositor for any part of this quarter.** Complete Schedule B (Form 941), Report of Tax Liability for Semiweekly Schedule Depositors, and attach it to Form 941.

Source: Internal Revenue Service.

15. What are the payment due dates of each of the monthly liabilities assuming all the deposits were made on time, and the due date of the filing of Form 941? .... May 15
June 16
July 15
August 11

CHAPTER 4

True-False Questions

T 4–2	**1.**	Before any federal income taxes may be withheld, there must be, or must have been, an employer-employee relationship.
F 4–2	**2.**	Since not-for-profit corporations are exempt from federal income taxes, they are not defined as employers under the federal income tax withholding law.
T 4–2	**3.**	Under the federal income tax withholding law, a definition of *employee* excludes partners.
F 4–2	**4.**	The amount of federal income taxes to be withheld is determined after subtracting from the employee's gross wages any local and state taxes.
T 4–3	**5.**	Under the federal income tax withholding law, income taxes are not withheld from the value of meals that employers furnish workers on the employers' premises for the employers' convenience.
F 4–4	**6.**	Noncash fringe benefits that are provided employees are treated as nontaxable income and thus are excluded from federal income tax withholding.
F 4–4	**7.**	All taxable noncash fringe benefits received during the year can only be added to the employees' taxable pay on the last payday of the year.
T 4–5	**8.**	Cash tips of $20 or more received by a tipped employee in a calendar month are treated as remuneration subject to federal income tax withholding.
T 4–5	**9.**	A waiter receives cash tips amounting to $120 in July. The waiter must report the amount of the cash tips to the employer by August 12 (August 10 is a Sunday).
T 4–5	**10.**	The withholding of federal income and FICA taxes from a tipped employee is made from the employee's wages that are under the employer's control.
F 4–5	**11.**	An employer must withhold federal income taxes on both the tips reported by tipped employees and the tips that the employer allocates to the employees.
F 4–6	**12.**	There is no limit to the amount of educational assistance that is exempt from federal income tax withholdings.
T 4–6	**13.**	The payments to a cook employed by a college fraternity are excluded from federal income tax withholding.
F 4–9	**14.**	There is no limit to the amount that an employer can contribute in an employee's SIMPLE retirement account.

F 4–9	**15.**	In the case of a 401(k) plan, employees age 50 or over can shelter an extra $10,000 of their wages from federal income tax.
T 4–9	**16.**	Persons eligible for deductible IRA contributions may put aside a specified amount of their compensation without paying federal income taxes on that amount.
T 4–9	**17.**	The IRA format of the SIMPLE plan allows employees to make tax-free contributions of up to $12,000.
T 4–9	**18.**	In the IRA form of the Simple Retirement Account, employers must match the employee's contribution, dollar-for-dollar, up to 3% of the employee's compensation.
F 4–10	**19.**	Evers, who works for two employers, is entitled to three personal allowances. Evers must claim the three allowances with each of the two employers during the entire calendar year.
F 4–11	**20.**	After completion of Form W-4, an employer must copy the employee's social security card and place it in the employee's employment file.
T 4–11	**21.**	If married employees do not claim their marital status on Form W-4, the employer must withhold according to the withholding tables for single employees.
F 4–12	**22.**	The special withholding allowance may be claimed only by those employees who do not itemize deductions on their income tax returns.
F 4–12	**23.**	Gere became the father of triplets on June 20. He must file an amended Form W-4 on or before June 30.
F 4–12	**24.**	On August 6, Hunt filed an amended Form W-4 to show a decrease in the number of allowances claimed. Hunt's employer must put the new withholding allowance certificate into effect before the next weekly payday on August 8.
F 4–12	**25.**	A person holding two jobs may have additional income tax withheld by increasing the number of withholding allowances claimed.
T 4–13	**26.**	An employee submits an invalid Form W-4 to the employer and does not replace it with a valid form. The employer should withhold federal income taxes at the rate for a single person claiming no exemptions.
F 4–13	**27.**	An employer is required to submit a copy of the employee's Form W-4 to the IRS if the employee has claimed 15 or more withholding allowances.
T 4–14	**28.**	By completing Form W-4P, a person can elect to have no income tax withheld from the annuity amounts the person receives.
F 4–15	**29.**	Of the two main methods of withholding, only the wage-bracket method distinguishes unmarried persons from married persons.
F 4–15	**30.**	The standard deduction varies according to whether the wage-bracket method or the percentage method is used.
F 4–18	**31.**	When you pay supplemental wages at the same time as regular wages, the method of calculating the withholding is the same for vacation payments as for semiannual bonuses.

F   **32.**   In calculating a "gross-up" amount of a bonus payment, an employer
4–20   does not use the OASDI/HI tax rates in the formula.

T   **33.**   Employees must be given Form W-2 on or before January 31 following
4–21   the close of the calendar year.

T   **34.**   Form W-3 is filed with the Social Security Administration when
4–24   transmitting information returns on Forms W-2.

T   **35.**   If you, an employer, are filing 550 Forms W-2, you must use electronic
4–30   filing rather than paper Forms W-2.

F   **36.**   For state income tax purposes, all states treat 401(k) plan payroll
4–30   deductions as nontaxable.

Multiple-Choice Questions

a   **1.**   Under the federal income tax withholding law, which of the following is
4–2   *not* defined as an *employee*?
  a.   Partner who draws compensation for services rendered the
       partnership
  b.   General manager, age 66
  c.   Payroll clerk hired one week ago
  d.   Governor of the state of Florida
  e.   Secretary employed by a not-for-profit corporation

e   **2.**   Which of the following noncash fringe benefits does not represent
4–4   taxable income subject to federal income tax withholding?
  a.   Flight on employer-provided airline
  b.   Personal use of company car
  c.   Sick pay
  d.   Employer-paid membership to a country club
  e.   All of the above are taxable.

b   **3.**   For which of the following payments is the employer required to
4–5   withhold federal income taxes?
  a.   Advances made to sales personnel for traveling expenses
  b.   Tipped employee's monthly tips of $120
  c.   Deceased person's wages paid to the estate
  d.   Minister of Presbyterian church
  e.   All of the above

c
4–5

4. Which of the following statements correctly describes the withholding of federal income taxes and social security taxes on tips?
   a. Tips amounting to $10 or more in a calendar month must be reported by tipped employees to their employers.
   b. The withholding of federal income taxes on employees' reported tip income is made from the amount of tips reported by employees.
   c. When employees report taxable tips in connection with employment in which they also receive regular wages, the amount of tax to be withheld on the tips is computed as if the tips were a supplemental wage payment.
   d. Employers do not withhold FICA taxes on the tipped employees' reported tip income.
   e. None of the above statements is correct.

e
4–6

5. All of the following are properly defined as wages subject to the withholding of federal income taxes *except*:
   a. year-end bonus.
   b. kitchen appliances given by manufacturer in lieu of cash wages.
   c. dismissal payment.
   d. vacation pay.
   e. payments made under worker's compensation law.

e
4–7

6. Which of the following cannot be included in a cafeteria plan?
   a. Health insurance
   b. Group-term life insurance (first $50,000 of coverage)
   c. Dependent care assistance (first $5,000)
   d. Self-insured medical reimbursement plan
   e. Educational assistance

b
4–10

7. A personal allowance:
   a. amounted to $2,000 in 2014.
   b. may be claimed to exempt a portion of the employee's earnings from withholding.
   c. is indexed for inflation every calendar quarter.
   d. may be claimed at the same time with each employer for whom an employee is working during the year.
   e. for one person is a different amount for a single versus a married taxpayer.

d
4–11

8. Beech refuses to state her marital status on Form W-4 which she gave to you, the payroll manager, when she was hired. You should:

    a. tell Beech that it is OK since you know that she was recently divorced and is reluctant to talk about it.

    b. inform Beech that she will have to write the IRS and give her reasons for refusing to state her marital status.

    c. tell Beech that you will have to withhold income taxes as if she were married and had claimed one allowance.

    d. tell Beech that you will have to withhold income taxes according to the withholding table for a single employee with no allowances.

    e. advise Beech to write "It is no business of yours." in the margin of her Form W-4.

c
4–12

9. Arch gives you an amended Form W-4 dated March 13, 2014, on which he claims two additional withholding allowances. He asks you to refund the excess taxes that were deducted from January 1 to March 13 when Arch claimed only one withholding allowance. You should:

    a. repay the overwithheld taxes on Arch's next payday.

    b. tell Arch that you will spread out a refund of the overwithheld taxes equally over the next six pays.

    c. inform Arch that you are unable to repay the overwithheld taxes that were withheld before March 13 and that the adjustment will have to be made when he files his annual income tax return.

    d. tell Arch to write the IRS immediately and ask for a refund of the overwithheld taxes.

    e. inform Arch that you will appoint a committee to study his request.

a
4–13

10. To curb the practice of employees filing false Forms W-4, the IRS requires that an employer submit to the agency a copy of each Form W-4:

    a. the IRS has requested in writing.

    b. on which an employee, usually earning $180 each week at the time Form W-4 was filed, now claims to be exempt from withholding.

    c. on which an employee claims to be single but has 9 withholding allowances.

    d. on which a married employee claims no withholding allowances.

    e. on which a recently divorced employee claims 5 withholding allowances and authorizes an additional $10 to be withheld each week.

b   **11.** Which of the following forms is used to report the amount of
4–28   distributions from pension and retirement plans?
              a. Form W-2c
              b. Form 1099-R
              c. Form 1099-PEN
              d. Form W-3p
              e. Form W-4

d   **12.** An employer must file an information return under all of the following
4–28   conditions *except*:
              a. to report $1,000 of compensation paid to an individual who is not
                  an employee.
              b. to report the wages totaling $600 paid to an independent
                  contractor during the calendar year.
              c. to report dividends totaling $600 paid to an individual during the
                  calendar year.
              d. to report commissions of $500 paid to a self-employed salesman.
              e. An information return must be filed under each of the above
                  conditions.

c   **13.** Which of the following forms is used to report rents paid over $600 to
4–28   landlords?
              a. Form 1099–R
              b. Form 1099–INT
              c. Form 1099–MISC
              d. Form 1099–G
              e. Form 8027

d   **14.** A company must withhold federal income taxes from payments made
4–29   to independent contractors in which of the following cases?
              a. When there is a signed contract between the parties
              b. When the contractor is paid more than $10,000
              c. When the contractor is a corporation
              d. When the contractor has not provided a taxpayer identification
                  number and the contract is $600 or more
              e. All of the above

Problem-Solving

Note: Use the tables on the following pages to calculate the answers to the problems listed.

1. Determine the income tax to withhold from the biweekly wages of the following employees (wage-bracket):

Karen Overton (single, 0 allowances), $595 wages	$59.00
Nancy Haller (married, 4 allowances), $535 wages	0.00
Alan Glasgow (married, 1 allowance), $785 wages	32.00
Joseph Kerr (single, 4 allowances), $900 wages	23.00
Ginni Lorenz (single, 1 allowance), $460 wages	23.00

2. Edward Dorsey is a part-time employee, and during the biweekly pay period he earned $395. In addition, he is being paid a bonus of $300 along with his regular pay. If Dorsey is single and claims two withholding allowances, how much would be deducted from his pay for FIT? (There are two ways to determine his deduction—do not use table for percentage method.)

(a)	($695 in wage-bracket table)	$31.00
(b)	($395 in wage-bracket table + 25% of $300)	76.00

3. Ted Duerson, previously unemployed for the calendar year, earned $13,200 during the biweekly period from September 22 to October 3 (20th payroll period). He has made a written request for the part-year employment method of withholding. If Duerson is married and claims zero withholding allowances, how much FIT tax would be withheld from his gross pay using the part-year employment method (using the wage-bracket table)? $13,200 ÷ 20 = $660 = $35 tax × 20 pays $700

4. Carson Smart is paid $1,200 every two weeks plus a taxable lodging allowance of $100. He is a participant in the company 401(k) plan and has $150 deducted from his pay for his contribution to the plan. He is married with two allowances. How much would be deducted from his pay for federal income tax (using the wage-bracket table)? ($1,200 + $100 – $150 = $1,150 in wage-bracket table) $53.00

5. Calculate the amount to withhold from the following employees using the biweekly table of the percentage method.

Kenneth Karcher (single, 1 allowance = $150.00), $895 wages	$ 81.85[a]
Mary Kenny (married, 2 allowances = $300.00), $1,900 wages	157.80[b]
Thomas Carney (single, 0 allowances), $1,460 wages	189.10[c]

    [a]$895.00 – $150.00 = $745.00 – $428.00 = $317.00 × 0.15 = $47.55 + $34.30 = $81.85

    [b]$1,900.00 – $300.00 = $1,600.00 – $1,006.00 = $594.00 × 0.15 = $89.10 + $68.70 = $157.80

    [c]$1,460.00 – $0 = $1,460.00 – $428.00 = $1,032.00 × 0.15 = $154.80 + $34.30 = $189.10

6. Use the appropriate table to determine the amount to withhold for federal income tax from each of the following biweekly wages (biweekly withholding allowance = $150.00):

Patrick Patrone (single, 2 allowances), $925 wages .... $ 65.00[a]
Carson Leno (married, 4 allowances), $1,195 wages .... 27.00[a]
Carli Lintz (single, 0 allowances), $700 wages.. 77.00[a]
Gene Hartz (single, 1 allowance), $2,500 wages .... 409.70[b]
Mollie Parmer (married, 2 allowances), $3,600 wages............................. 432.00[c]

[a]Wage-bracket
[b]$2,500.00 − $150.00 = $2,350.00 − $1,479.00 = $871.00 × 0.25 = $217.75 + $191.95 = $409.70
[c]$3,600.00 − 2($150.00) = $3,300.00 − $3,108.00 = $192.00 × 0.25 = $48.00 + $384.00 = $432.00

SINGLE Persons—BIWEEKLY Payroll Period

(For Wages Paid through December 20--)

And the wages are—		And the number of withholding allowances claimed is—										
At least	But less than	0	1	2	3	4	5	6	7	8	9	10
		The amount of income tax to be withheld is—										
250	260	17	2	0	0	0	0	0	0	0	0	0
260	270	18	3	0	0	0	0	0	0	0	0	0
270	280	19	4	0	0	0	0	0	0	0	0	0
280	290	20	5	0	0	0	0	0	0	0	0	0
290	300	21	6	0	0	0	0	0	0	0	0	0
300	310	22	7	0	0	0	0	0	0	0	0	0
310	320	23	8	0	0	0	0	0	0	0	0	0
320	330	24	9	0	0	0	0	0	0	0	0	0
330	340	25	10	0	0	0	0	0	0	0	0	0
340	350	26	11	0	0	0	0	0	0	0	0	0
350	360	27	12	0	0	0	0	0	0	0	0	0
360	370	28	13	0	0	0	0	0	0	0	0	0
370	380	29	14	0	0	0	0	0	0	0	0	0
380	390	30	15	0	0	0	0	0	0	0	0	0
390	400	31	16	1	0	0	0	0	0	0	0	0
400	410	32	17	2	0	0	0	0	0	0	0	0
410	420	33	18	3	0	0	0	0	0	0	0	0
420	430	34	19	4	0	0	0	0	0	0	0	0
430	440	35	20	5	0	0	0	0	0	0	0	0
440	450	37	21	6	0	0	0	0	0	0	0	0
450	460	38	22	7	0	0	0	0	0	0	0	0
460	470	40	23	8	0	0	0	0	0	0	0	0
470	480	41	24	9	0	0	0	0	0	0	0	0
480	490	43	25	10	0	0	0	0	0	0	0	0
490	500	44	26	11	0	0	0	0	0	0	0	0
500	520	47	28	13	0	0	0	0	0	0	0	0
520	540	50	30	15	0	0	0	0	0	0	0	0
540	560	53	32	17	2	0	0	0	0	0	0	0
560	580	56	34	19	4	0	0	0	0	0	0	0
580	600	59	36	21	6	0	0	0	0	0	0	0
600	620	62	39	23	8	0	0	0	0	0	0	0
620	640	65	42	25	10	0	0	0	0	0	0	0
640	660	68	45	27	12	0	0	0	0	0	0	0
660	680	71	48	29	14	0	0	0	0	0	0	0
680	700	74	51	31	16	1	0	0	0	0	0	0
700	720	77	54	33	18	3	0	0	0	0	0	0
720	740	80	57	35	20	5	0	0	0	0	0	0
740	760	83	60	38	22	7	0	0	0	0	0	0
760	780	86	63	41	24	9	0	0	0	0	0	0
780	800	89	66	44	26	11	0	0	0	0	0	0
800	820	92	69	47	28	13	0	0	0	0	0	0
820	840	95	72	50	30	15	0	0	0	0	0	0
840	860	98	75	53	32	17	2	0	0	0	0	0
860	880	101	78	56	34	19	4	0	0	0	0	0
880	900	104	81	59	36	21	6	0	0	0	0	0
900	920	107	84	62	39	23	8	0	0	0	0	0
920	940	110	87	65	42	25	10	0	0	0	0	0

Source: Internal Revenue Service.

MARRIED Persons—BIWEEKLY Payroll Period

(For Wages Paid through December 20--)

And the wages are—		And the number of withholding allowances claimed is—										
At least	But less than	0	1	2	3	4	5	6	7	8	9	10
		The amount of income tax to be withheld is—										
500	520	19	4	0	0	0	0	0	0	0	0	0
520	540	21	6	0	0	0	0	0	0	0	0	0
540	560	23	8	0	0	0	0	0	0	0	0	0
560	580	25	10	0	0	0	0	0	0	0	0	0
580	600	27	12	0	0	0	0	0	0	0	0	0
600	620	29	14	0	0	0	0	0	0	0	0	0
620	640	31	16	1	0	0	0	0	0	0	0	0
640	660	33	18	3	0	0	0	0	0	0	0	0
660	680	35	20	5	0	0	0	0	0	0	0	0
680	700	37	22	7	0	0	0	0	0	0	0	0
700	720	39	24	9	0	0	0	0	0	0	0	0
720	740	41	26	11	0	0	0	0	0	0	0	0
740	760	43	28	13	0	0	0	0	0	0	0	0
760	780	45	30	15	0	0	0	0	0	0	0	0
780	800	47	32	17	2	0	0	0	0	0	0	0
800	820	49	34	19	4	0	0	0	0	0	0	0
820	840	51	36	21	6	0	0	0	0	0	0	0
840	860	53	38	23	8	0	0	0	0	0	0	0
860	880	55	40	25	10	0	0	0	0	0	0	0
880	900	57	42	27	12	0	0	0	0	0	0	0
900	920	59	44	29	14	0	0	0	0	0	0	0
920	940	61	46	31	16	1	0	0	0	0	0	0
940	960	63	48	33	18	3	0	0	0	0	0	0
960	980	65	50	35	20	5	0	0	0	0	0	0
980	1,000	67	52	37	22	7	0	0	0	0	0	0
1,000	1,020	69	54	39	24	9	0	0	0	0	0	0
1,020	1,040	72	56	41	26	11	0	0	0	0	0	0
1,040	1,060	75	58	43	28	13	0	0	0	0	0	0
1,060	1,080	78	60	45	30	15	0	0	0	0	0	0
1,080	1,100	81	62	47	32	17	2	0	0	0	0	0
1,100	1,120	84	64	49	34	19	4	0	0	0	0	0
1,120	1,140	87	66	51	36	21	6	0	0	0	0	0
1,140	1,160	90	68	53	38	23	8	0	0	0	0	0
1,160	1,180	93	71	55	40	25	10	0	0	0	0	0
1,180	1,200	96	74	57	42	27	12	0	0	0	0	0
1,200	1,220	99	77	59	44	29	14	0	0	0	0	0
1,220	1,240	102	80	61	46	31	16	1	0	0	0	0
1,240	1,260	105	83	63	48	33	18	3	0	0	0	0
1,260	1,280	108	86	65	50	35	20	5	0	0	0	0
1,280	1,300	111	89	67	52	37	22	7	0	0	0	0
1,300	1,320	114	92	69	54	39	24	9	0	0	0	0
1,320	1,340	117	95	72	56	41	26	11	0	0	0	0
1,340	1,360	120	98	75	58	43	28	13	0	0	0	0
1,360	1,380	123	101	78	60	45	30	15	0	0	0	0
1,380	1,400	126	104	81	62	47	32	17	2	0	0	0

TABLE 2—BIWEEKLY Payroll Period

(a) SINGLE person (including head of household)—

If the amount of wages (after subtracting withholding allowances) is:

Not over $85 . . . . The amount of income tax to withhold is: $0

Over—	But not over—	The amount of income tax to withhold is:	of excess over—
$85	—$428	$0.00 plus 10%	—$85
$428	—$1,479	$34.30 plus 15%	—$428
$1,479	—$3,463	$191.95 plus 25%	—$1,479
$3,463	—$7,133	$687.95 plus 28%	—$3,463
$7,133	—$15,406	$1,715.55 plus 33%	—$7,133
$15,406	—$15,469	$4,445.64 plus 35%	—$15,406
$15,469	. . . .	$4,467.69 plus 39.6%	—$15,469

(b) MARRIED person—

If the amount of wages (after subtracting withholding allowances) is:

Not over $319 . . . . The amount of income tax to withhold is: $0

Over—	But not over—	The amount of income tax to withhold is:	of excess over—
$319	—$1,006	$0.00 plus 10%	—$319
$1,006	—$3,108	$68.70 plus 15%	—$1,006
$3,108	—$5,950	$384.00 plus 25%	—$3,108
$5,950	—$8,898	$1,094.50 plus 28%	—$5,950
$8,898	—$15,640	$1,919.94 plus 33%	—$8,898
$15,640	—$17,627	$4,144.80 plus 35%	—$15,640
$17,627	. . . .	$4,840.25 plus 39.6%	—$17,627

Source: Internal Revenue Service.

CHAPTER 5

True-False Questions

F 5–2	1.	Unemployment taxes (FUTA and SUTA) do not have to be paid by an employer who has only part-time employees.
T 5–2	2.	The Social Security Act ordered every state to set up an unemployment compensation program.
F 5–3	3.	Partnerships do not have to pay unemployment taxes on the wages of their employees.
F 5–3	4.	Once a company attains the status of employer for FUTA purposes, that status continues for four calendar years.
T 5–3	5.	A traveling salesperson who solicits and transmits to the principal orders for merchandise for resale is considered an employee under FUTA.
T 5–4	6.	Services performed by a child under the age of 21 for a parent–employer are excluded from FUTA coverage.
T 5–4	7.	Services performed in the employ of a religious organization that is exempt from federal income tax are also exempt from FUTA coverage.
T 5–4	8.	Directors of corporations who only attend and participate in board of directors' meetings are not covered as employees under FUTA.
T 5–4	9.	Insurance agents paid solely on a commission basis are not considered employees under FUTA.
F 5–5	10.	If an employee works in more than one state, the employer must pay a separate SUTA tax to each of those states in which the employee earns wages.
F 5–7	11.	For FUTA purposes, the cash value of remuneration paid in any medium other than cash is not considered taxable wages.
F 5–7	12.	Advance payments for work done in the future are not taxable wages for FUTA purposes.
T 5–7	13.	FUTA and SUTA coverages extend to U.S. citizens working abroad for American employers.
F 5–7	14.	In the case of a part-time employee, the employer pays a FUTA tax on only the first $3,500 of earnings (one-half the regular limit).
T 5–7	15.	Christmas gifts, excluding noncash gifts of nominal value, are taxable wages for unemployment purposes.
F 5–8	16.	Retirement pay is taxable wages for FUTA purposes.

T
5–8

17. Educational assistance payments made to workers to improve skills required of their jobs are nontaxable for unemployment purposes.

T
5–9

18. If an employee has more than one employer during the current year, the taxable wage base applies separately to each of those employers, unless one employer has transferred the business to the second.

F
5–9

19. Every employer is entitled to a 5.4 percent credit against the gross FUTA tax of 6.0 percent.

F
5–9

20. For FUTA purposes, an employer must pay a higher FUTA tax rate on executives than on nonsupervisory personnel.

T
5–9

21. In order to obtain the maximum credit allowed against the federal unemployment tax, the employer must have paid its SUTA contributions by the due date of Form 940.

F
5–11

22. Even if a state repays its Title XII advances, all employers in that state are subject to a credit reduction in the year of the advance.

T
5–11

23. If an employer is subject to a credit reduction because of Title XII advances, the penalty for the entire year will be paid only with the deposit for the last quarter of the year.

F
5–12

24. There is a uniform rate of unemployment benefits payable by all states.

F
5–14

25. If an employer pays unemployment taxes to two states, it will have the same SUTA tax rate in both states.

F
5–14

26. Currently, none of the states imposes an unemployment tax on employees.

T
5–16

27. In some states, employers may obtain reduced unemployment compensation rates by making voluntary contributions to the state fund.

F
5–17

28. "Dumping" is legal in all but a few states.

F
5–21

29. On Form 940, even if the total FUTA tax is more than $500, there is no listing of quarterly federal unemployment tax liabilities.

F
5–22

30. Form 940 must be mailed to the IRS by January 15.

T
5–22

31. The mailing of Form 940 is considered timely if it is postmarked on or before the due date.

T
5–22

32. If an employer's quarterly tax liability is $525, it must be paid on or before the last day of the month following the end of the quarter.

F
5–22

33. FUTA tax deposits cannot be paid electronically.

F
5–24

34. Unlike Form 941, there is no penalty for the late filing of Form 940.

T   **35.**   In most states, the contribution reports and the wage information reports
5–25   are filed quarterly.

Multiple-Choice Questions

c   **1.**   A federal unemployment tax is levied on:
5–2   a.   employees only.
                 b.   both employers and employees.
                 c.   employers only.
                 d.   government employers only.
                 e.   no one.

e   **2.**   For FUTA purposes, an employer can be any one of the following *except*:
5–3   a.   an individual.
                 b.   a partnership.
                 c.   a trust.
                 d.   a corporation.
                 e.   All of the above can be employers.

d   **3.**   Included under the definition of employees for FUTA purposes are:
5–4   a.   independent contractors.
                 b.   insurance agents paid solely on commission.
                 c.   student nurses.
                 d.   officers of a corporation.
                 e.   members of partnerships.

c   **4.**   Which of the following is *not* a factor considered in determining coverage
5–5   of interstate employees?
                 a.   Location of base of operations
                 b.   Place where work is localized
                 c.   Location of company's payroll department
                 d.   Location of employee's residence
                 e.   Location of place from which operations are controlled

d   **5.**   An aspect of the interstate reciprocal arrangement concerns:
5–7   a.   the status of Americans working overseas.
                 b.   the taxability of dismissal payments.
                 c.   the determination of an employer's experience rating.
                 d.   the transfer of an employee from one state to another during the
                      year.
                 e.   none of the above.

a

5–7

6. Which of the following payments are taxable payments for federal unemployment tax?
   a.   Christmas gifts, excluding noncash gifts of nominal value
   b.   Caddy fees
   c.   Courtesy discounts to employees and their families
   d.   Workers' compensation payments
   e.   Value of meals and lodging furnished employees for the convenience of the employer

a

5–8

7. Which of the following types of payments are *not* taxable wages for federal unemployment tax?
   a.   Retirement pay
   b.   Cash prizes and awards for doing outstanding work
   c.   Dismissal pay
   d.   Bonuses as remuneration for services
   e.   Payment under a guaranteed annual wage plan

b

5–9

8. If the employer is tardy in paying the state contributions, the credit against the federal tax is limited to what percent of the late payments that would have been allowed as a credit if the contributions had been paid on time?
   a.   6.2%
   b.   90%
   c.   5.13%
   d.   20%
   e.   0%

d

5–10

9. Which of the following provides for a reduction in the employer's state unemployment tax rate based on the employer's experience with the risk of unemployment?
   a.   Voluntary contribution
   b.   Title XII advances
   c.   Pooled-fund laws
   d.   Experience-rating plan
   e.   None of the above

d

5–11

10. In order to avoid a credit reduction for Title XII advances, a state must repay the loans by:
   a.   the end of the year of the loans.
   b.   the end of the year the credit reduction is scheduled to take effect.
   c.   the end of the third year after the year of the loans.
   d.   November 10 of the year the credit reduction is scheduled to take effect.
   e.   June 30 of the year after the loans.

b
5–16

11. Voluntary contributions to a state's unemployment department are:
   a. allowed in all states.
   b. designed to increase an employer's reserve account in order to lower the employer's contribution rate.
   c. capable of being paid at any time with no time limit.
   d. returned to the employer at the end of the following year.
   e. sent directly to the IRS.

b
5–21

12. The person who is *not* an authorized signer of Form 940 is:
   a. the individual, if a sole proprietorship.
   b. the accountant from the company's independent auditing firm.
   c. the president, if a corporation.
   d. a fiduciary, if a trust.
   e. All of the above are authorized signers.

c
5–22

13. If the employer has made timely deposits that pay the FUTA tax liability in full, the filing of Form 940 can be delayed until:
   a. December 31.
   b. February 15.
   c. February 10.
   d. February 1.
   e. March 31.

a
5–22

14. When making a payment of FUTA taxes, the employer must make the deposit by the:
   a. end of the month after the quarter.
   b. 15th of the month after the quarter.
   c. 10th of the month after the quarter.
   d. end of the following quarter.
   e. same day of the FICA and FIT deposits.

b
5–22

15. An employer must pay the quarterly FUTA tax liability if the liability is more than:
   a. $3,000.
   b. $500.
   c. $1,000.
   d. $1.
   e. $100.

Problem-Solving

NOTE: In the following problems, use the net FUTA tax rate of 0.6% on the first $7,000 of taxable wages.

1. Niemann Company has a SUTA tax rate of 7.1%. The taxable payroll for the year for FUTA and SUTA is $82,600.

    (a) The amount of FUTA tax for the year is ($82,600 × 0.006) $495.60

    (b) The amount of SUTA tax for the year is ($82,600 × 0.071) $5,864.60

2. Stys Company's payroll for the year is $1,210,930. Of this amount, $510,710 is for wages paid in excess of $7,000 to each individual employee. The SUTA tax rate for the company is 3.2% on the first $7,000 of each employee's earnings.

    (a) The amount of FUTA tax for the year is [($1,210,930 – $510,710)
        × 0.006] $4,201.32

    (b) The amount of SUTA tax for the year is [($1,210,930 – $510,710)
        × 0.032] $22,407.04

3. Michael Mirer worked for Dawson Company for six months this year and earned $11,200. The other six months, he earned $6,900 working for McBride Company (a separate company). The amount of FUTA taxes to be paid on Mirer's wages by the two companies is:

    (a) Dawson Company ($7,000 × 0.006) $42.00

    (b) McBride Company ($6,900 × 0.006) $41.40

4. John Gercke is an employee of The Woolson Company. During the first part of the year, he earned $6,800 while working in State A. For the remainder of the year, the company transferred him to State B where he earned $16,500. The Woolson Company's tax rate in State A is 4.2%, and in State B it is 3.15% on the first $7,000. Assuming that reciprocal arrangements exist between the two states, determine the SUTA tax that the company paid to:

    (a) State A ($6,800 × 0.042) $285.60

    (b) State B [($7,000 – $6,800) × 0.0315] $6.30

5. Aaron Norman earned $24,900 for the year from Marcus Company. The company is subject to a SUTA tax of 4.7% on the first $9,900 of earnings. Determine:

    (a) the employer's FUTA tax on Norman's earnings ($7,000 × 0.006) $42.00

    (b) the employer's SUTA tax on Norman's earnings ($9,900 × 0.047) $465.30

6. Ted Carman worked for Rivertide Country Club and earned $28,500 during the year. He also worked part time for Harrison Furniture Company and earned $12,400 during the year. The SUTA tax rate for Rivertide Country Club is 4.2% on the first $8,000, and the rate for Harrison Furniture Company is 5.1% on the first $8,000. Calculate the FUTA and SUTA taxes paid by the employers on Carman's earnings.

	FUTA	SUTA
(a) Rivertide Country Club	$42.00 ($7,000 × 0.006)	$336.00 ($8,000 × 0.042)
(b) Harrison Furniture Company	$42.00 ($7,000 × 0.006)	$408.00 ($8,000 × 0.051)

7. Queno Company had FUTA taxable wages of $510,900 during the year. Determine its:

(a) gross FUTA tax ($510,900 × 0.060) $30,654.00

(b) FUTA tax credits (assuming no penalties) ($510,900 × 0.054) $27,588.60

(c) net FUTA tax ($510,900 × 0.006) $3,065.40

8. Faruga Company had FUTA taxable payrolls for the four quarters of 2014 of $28,400; $19,600; $16,500; and $8,900, respectively. The company was located in a state that was subject to a FUTA credit reduction of 0.3%. What was the amount of Faruga's first required deposit of FUTA taxes? [$28,400 + $19,600 + $16,500 + $8,900 = $73,400 × 0.006 = $440.40 + ($73,400 × 0.003)] $660.60

9. Hunter Company had a FUTA taxable payroll of $192,700 for the year. Since the company is located in a state that has a 0.3% FUTA credit reduction due to unpaid loans, determine Hunter's FUTA tax liability for the year [$192,700 × (0.6% + 0.3%)] $1,734.30

10. In the first quarter of the year, Henry Gibson earned $3,000 in wages and reported $2,400 in tips to his employer. How much would the employer's FUTA tax be for the first quarter on Gibson? ($5,400 × 0.006) $32.40

11. In Part 5 of Form 940, Peterson Company reported FUTA tax liabilities as follows:

First quarter:	$397.50
Second quarter:	$209.10
Third quarter:	$274.50
Fourth quarter:	$262.20

List the amounts and the dates of each required FUTA tax payment:

amount	$606.60 ($397.50 + $209.10)	date	7/31/year 1
amount	$536.70 ($274.50 + $262.20)	date	1/31/year 2
amount	$_____	date	_____
amount	$_____	date	_____

12. Sparks Company's SUTA rate for next year is 3.25% because its reserve ratio falls into the state's 10% to less than 12% category [(contributions – benefits paid) ÷ average payroll = $414,867 ÷ $3,521,790 = 11.78%]. If the next bracket (12% to less than 14%) would give the company a lower tax rate of 3.05%, what would be the least amount of the voluntary contribution needed to qualify the company for the 3.05% SUTA tax rate? (12% × $3,521,790 = $422,614.80; $422,614.80 – $414,867.00) $7,747.80

13. Complete Part 2 of Form 940 based on the following information:

Total payroll for the year	$913,590
Payroll to employees in excess of $7,000	$421,930
Employer contributions into employees' 401(k) plans	$23,710

Part 2:	Determine your FUTA tax before adjustments for 20--. If any line does NOT apply, leave it blank.		
3	Total payments to all employees	3	913590 . 00
4	Payments exempt from FUTA tax 4	23710 . 00	
	Check all that apply: **4a** ☐ Fringe benefits **4c** ☑ Retirement/Pension **4e** ☐ Other		
	4b ☐ Group-term life insurance **4d** ☐ Dependent care		
5	Total of payments made to each employee in excess of $7,000 5	421930 . 00	
6	Subtotal (line 4 + line 5 = line 6)	6	445640 . 00
7	Total taxable FUTA wages (line 3 – line 6 = line 7) (see instructions)	7	467950 . 00
8	FUTA tax before adjustments (line 7 x .006 = line 8)	8	2807 . 70

Source: Internal Revenue Service.

14. If the employer in Problem 13 is located in Wisconsin which has a FUTA credit reduction of 0.6%, what would be the amount of the credit reduction? (0.006 × $467,950).......$2,807.70

15. Continuing with Problem 14, complete Part 5 of Form 940 given the breakdown of
FUTA taxable wages for the year to be:

1st Quarter	$237,000
2nd Quarter	$168,000
3rd Quarter	$54,000
4th Quarter	$8,950
Yearly total	$467,950

Part 5:	Report your FUTA tax liability by quarter only if line 12 is more than $500. If not, go to Part 6.

16 Report the amount of your FUTA tax liability for each quarter; do **NOT** enter the amount you deposited. If you had no liability for
a quarter, leave the line blank.

16a **1st quarter** (January 1 – March 31)	**16a**	1422 ▪ 00
16b **2nd quarter** (April 1 – June 30)	**16b**	1008 ▪ 00
16c **3rd quarter** (July 1 – September 30)	**16c**	324 ▪ 00
16d **4th quarter** (October 1 – December 31)	**16d**	2861 ▪ 40*
17 Total tax liability for the year (lines 16a + 16b + 16c + 16d = line 17) **17**		5615 ▪ 40

Total must equal line 12.

Source: Internal Revenue Service.

*($8,950 × 0.006) + ($467,950 × 0.006) = $2,861.40

CHAPTER 6

True-False Questions

F
6–2
1. An employee's marital status and number of withholding allowances never appear on the payroll register.

F
6–3
2. Companies usually provide a separate column in the payroll register to record the employer's payroll taxes.

F
6–4
3. An employer will use the payroll register to keep track of an employee's accumulated wages.

T
6–4
4. In order to prepare Forms W-2, an employer would utilize the employee's earnings record.

T
6–6
5. Once the journal entry for the payroll is complete, the information is posted to the appropriate general ledger accounts.

T
6–6
6. Deductions from gross pay in the payroll register are reflected on the credit side of the journal entry to record the payroll.

F
6–6
7. If wages are paid weekly, postings to the employee's earnings record would be done once a month.

F
6–6
8. Each payday, the total of net pays that the employer incurs is the wage expense that must be debited.

F
6–6
9. Tax withholdings from employees' pays reduce the amount of the debit to Salary Expense in the payroll entry.

F
6–6
10. The wage and salaries expense account is an operating expense account debited for total net pay each payroll period.

F
6–6
11. FIT Payable is a liability account used to record employees' withheld federal income tax and also the employer's match of that tax.

T
6–6
12. A debit to the employees FIT payable account removes the liability for the amount of federal income taxes withheld from employees' wages.

T
6–8
13. Amounts withheld from employees' wages for health insurance are credited to a liability account.

T
6–8
14. When withheld union dues are turned over to the union by the employer, a journal entry is made debiting the liability account and crediting the cash account.

F
6–9
15. Under the provisions of the Consumer Credit Protection Act, an employer can discharge an employee simply because the employee's wage is subject to garnishment for a single indebtedness.

F
6–9
16. Under the Consumer Credit Protection Act, disposable earnings are the earnings remaining after any deductions for health insurance.

T   **17.** Tips received by employees are not included as disposable earnings
6-9   subject to garnishment.

F   **18.** Service charges that are passed on to the employee by the employer
6-9   are not part of the disposable earnings subject to garnishment.

T   **19.** The total of the net amount paid to employees each payday is credited
6–11   to either the cash account or the salaries payable account.

F   **20.** Every state allows employers to make e-payment options as a
6–14   condition of employment.

F   **21.** When recording FICA taxes, different liability accounts should be set
6–15   up for the employees' and employer's portions of the tax.

F   **22.** FUTA Taxes Payable is an expense account in which are recorded the
6–16   employer's federal unemployment taxes.

T   **23.** The payroll taxes incurred by an employer are FICA, FUTA, and
6–15   SUTA.

T   **24.** The payroll taxes account is an expense account that is debited for the
6–15   FICA, FUTA, and SUTA taxes on the employer.

T   **25.** The FICA taxes on the employer represent both business expenses
6–16   and liabilities of the employer.

T   **26.** The entry to record the employer's payroll taxes usually includes
6–16   credits to the liability accounts for FICA (OASDI and HI), FUTA, and
              SUTA taxes.

F   **27.** The employer's payroll tax expenses are recorded by all employers at
6–16   the time these taxes are actually paid.

F   **28.** FICA Taxes Payable—OASDI is a liability account debited for the
6–17   employer's portion of the FICA tax.

F   **29.** Since the credit against the FUTA tax (for SUTA contributions) is made
6–16   on Form 940, the employer's payroll tax entries should include the
              FUTA tax at the gross amount (6.0%).

T   **30.** The FUTA tax part of the payroll tax entry is recorded at the net
6–16   amount (0.6%) of the taxable payroll.

F   **31.** Since FUTA tax is paid only once a quarter, the FUTA tax expense is
6–16   recorded only at the time of payment.

F   **32.** At the time that the entry is made to record the employer's payroll
6–16   taxes, the SUTA tax is recorded at the net amount (0.6%).

T   **33.** Since the FUTA tax is a social security tax, it can be charged to the
6–17   same expense account as the other payroll taxes on the employer, the
              payroll taxes account.

F
6–19

34. If employees must contribute to the state unemployment fund, this deduction should be shown in the payroll tax entry.

T
6–21

35. When the federal tax deposit is made, the employees' and employer's shares of FICA taxes are paid along with the employees' FIT taxes withheld.

T
6–21

36. In the adjusting entry to accrue wages at the end of the accounting period, there is no need to credit any tax withholding accounts.

F
6–22

37. The adjusting entry to record the accrued vacation pay at the end of an accounting period includes credits to the tax withholding liability accounts.

F
6–22

38. Since vacation time is paid when used, there is no need to accrue this time in a liability account at the end of each accounting period.

T
6–23

39. Union Dues Payable is a liability account credited with the deductions made from union members' wages for their union dues.

F
6–27

40. Posting to the general ledger for payroll entries is done only at the end of each calendar year.

Multiple-Choice Questions

d
6–3

1. Carmen Gaetano worked 46 hours during this payweek. He is paid time-and-a-half for hours over 40 and his pay rate is $17.90/hour. What was his *overtime premium* pay for this workweek?
a. $107.40
b. $161.10
c. $50.70
d. $53.70
e. $26.85

b
6–4

2. The employee's earnings record provides information for each of the following *except*:
a. completing Forms W-2.
b. completing the journal entry to record the payroll.
c. determining when the accumulated wages of an employee reach cutoff levels.
d. preparing reports required by state unemployment compensation laws.
e. preparing the payroll register.

c
6–6

3. Which of these accounts shows the total gross earnings that the employer incurs as an expense each payday?
a. Payroll Taxes
b. Federal Income Taxes Payable
c. Wages Expense
d. Salaries Payable
e. None of the above

b
6–15

4. Which of the following accounts is an expense account in which an employer records the FICA, FUTA, and SUTA taxes?
  a. Wages Expense
  b. Payroll Taxes
  c. SUTA Taxes Payable
  d. Salaries Payable
  e. None of the above

e
6–16

5. Which of the following is *not* an expense of the employer?
  a. FUTA tax
  b. FICA tax—HI
  c. FICA tax—OASDI
  d. SUTA tax
  e. Union dues withheld

a
6–21

6. The entry to deposit FICA taxes and federal income taxes withheld involves all of the following accounts *except*:
  a. Payroll Taxes.
  b. FICA Taxes Payable—OASDI.
  c. FICA Taxes Payable—HI.
  d. Employees FIT Payable.
  e. Cash.

d
6–21

7. When recording the deposit of FUTA taxes owed, the proper entry is:
  a. FUTA Tax Expense
        Cash
  b. Payroll Taxes
        Cash
  c. Payroll Taxes
        FUTA Taxes Payable
  d. FUTA Taxes Payable
        Cash
  e. FUTA Tax Expense
        FUTA Taxes Payable

a
6–22

8. The entry made at the end of the accounting period to record wages incurred but unpaid is:
   a. Wages Expense
       Wages Payable
   b. Wages Expense
       FICA Taxes Payable—OASDI
       FICA Taxes Payable—HI
       FIT Payable
       Wages Payable
   c. Wages Payable
       Cash
   d. Wages Expense
       Cash
   e. Wages Expense
       Payroll Taxes
       Wages Payroll

c
6–22

9. Which of the following items would require an adjusting entry at the end of each accounting period?
   a. Garnishment for child support payments
   b. Withholdings for a 401(k) plan
   c. Vacation pay earned by employees
   d. Union dues withheld
   e. None of the above

d
6–22

10. In recording the monthly adjusting entry for accrued wages at the end of the accounting period, the amount of the adjustment would usually be determined by:
   a. collecting the timesheets for the days accrued.
   b. using the same amount as the prior month's adjustment.
   c. using the wages of the salaried workers only.
   d. a percentage of the previous week's gross payroll.
   e. a percentage of the previous week's net payroll.

Problem-Solving

The totals from the *first* payroll of the year are shown below.

Total Earnings	FICA OASDI	FICA HI	FIT W/H	State Tax	Union Dues	Net Pay
$36,195.10	$2,244.10	$524.83	$6,515.00	$361.95	$500.00	$26,049.22

1. Journalize the entry to record the payroll.
2. Journalize the entry to record the employer's payroll taxes (assume a SUTA rate of 3.7%).
3. Journalize the entry to deposit the FICA and FIT taxes.

1. Wages Expense.. 36,195.10
          FICA Taxes Payable—OASDI 2,244.10
          FICA Taxes Payable—HI..................................   524.83
          Employees FIT Payable 6,515.00
          Employees SIT Payable 361.95
          Union Dues Payable...   500.00
          Cash 26,049.22

2. Payroll Taxes 4,325.32
          FICA Taxes Payable—OASDI 2,244.10
          FICA Taxes Payable—HI..................................   524.83
          FUTA Taxes Payable 217.17
          SUTA Taxes Payable 1,339.22

3. FICA Taxes Payable—OASDI 4,488.20
          FICA Taxes Payable—HI....................................... 1,049.66
          Employee FIT Payable... 6,515.00
          Cash 12,052.86

2014 *edition*

PAYROLL ACCOUNTING

Bieg/Toland

TEST 1

Student   **INSTRUCTOR'S COPY**

Chapter 1   Date _____

SCORING RECORD

Section	Total Points	Deductions	Score
A	60		
B	40		
Total	100		

Section A—DIRECTIONS: Each of the following statements is either true or false. Unless directed otherwise by your instructor, indicate your choice in the Answers column by writing "T" for a true answer or "F" for a false answer. (2 points for each correct answer)

		Answers	For Scoring

1. The Fair Labor Standards Act is commonly known as the Federal Wage and Hour Law. .... **T**   1.____
2. The Federal Insurance Contributions Act covers restrictions on the employment of child labor... **F**   2.____
3. The Federal Income Tax Withholding Law requires that all employment data be kept on file permanently. .... **F**   3.____
4. In cases where both federal and state regulations cover the minimum wage for the same employee, the federal rate is always used as the standard minimum wage. .... **F**   4.____
5. Those records that are required by the various payroll laws must generally be kept on file for only the current year. .... **F**   5.____
6. Unions and employment agencies are excluded from coverage under the Civil Rights Act of 1964. . **F**   6.____
7. Employers' photocopying of new employees' I-9 documents is not required under the Immigration Reform and Control Act. .... **T**   7.____
8. The Age Discrimination in Employment Act protects virtually all workers, but only to the age of 70. **F**   8.____
9. FICA taxes are levied upon employers only. .... **F**   9.____
10. Criminal background checks can be used by employers on all job applicants. .... **F**   10.____
11. Most employers are faced with two unemployment taxes—federal and state. .... **T**   11.____
12. Every state imposes state unemployment taxes on employers in their state. .... **T**   12.____
13. The Age Discrimination Act covers employers engaged in an industry affecting interstate commerce (who employ 20 or more workers), employment agencies, and labor unions. .... **T**   13.____
14. The FUTA tax paid to the federal government is used to pay benefits to the unemployed workers who qualify for the benefits. .... **F**   14.____
15. Employers receive credit against their SUTA tax for their FUTA contributions. .... **F**   15.____
16. Some states allow employers to drug test in a limited number of situations. .... **T**   16.____
17. Once vested, workers have the right to receive a pension at retirement age, even if they no longer work for that company. .... **T**   17.____
18. Under the Family and Medical Leave Act, employers can exempt the highest paid 10 percent of their workforce from its provisions. .... **T**   18.____
19. Under federal law, new-hire reporting also applies to newly hired independent contractors. .... **F**   19.____
20. Form I-9, Employment Eligibility Verification, is completed only by employees who were born outside the United States. .... **F**   20.____

SECTION A (continued)

		For Answers	Scoring

21. The deadline for an employee to complete Form I-9 is one year from the date of hire..................... **F** 21. ___

22. Under the Family and Medical Leave Act, an employer can substitute an employee's earned paid leave for any part of the 12-week family leave. .... **T** 22. ___

23. Workers' compensation insurance applies only to work-related injury, illness, or death. .... **T** 23. ___

24. Prehire questions pertaining to religion, gender, national origin, or age are allowed when these factors are bona fide occupational requirements for a job.. **T** 24. ___

25. In the event employment is denied because of the information obtained from an investigative consumer report, the employer is required to inform the individual that this was the reason for denying employment. .... **T** 25. ___

26. Employers cannot terminate an employee for providing false information on an application form once the employee begins employment... **F** 26. ___

27. The hiring notice is a written record sent to the Payroll Department so that the new employee can be added to the payroll... **T** 27. ___

28. The payroll register is used by employers in preparing Form W-2, the wage and tax statement sent to each employee at year-end. .... **F** 28. ___

29. The payroll register is used to provide the information needed to record the payroll entries made in the journal on each payday... **T** 29. ___

30. The FLSA requires all employees to be paid weekly. .... **F** 30. ___

Section B—DIRECTIONS: Complete each of the following sentences by writing in the Answers column the letter of the word or words that correctly completes each statement. (5 points for each correct answer)

		For Answers	Scoring

1. Which of the following laws establishes the minimum wage? (A) Fair Labor Standards Act, (B) Federal Personal Responsibility and Work Opportunity Reconciliation Act, (C) Federal Insurance Contributions Act, (D) Federal Unemployment Tax Act, (E) Fair Employment Laws. .... **A** 1. ___

2. Which of the following bases for discrimination in employment practices is not covered in Title VII of the Civil Rights Act of 1964 as amended? (A) Color, (B) Religion, (C) Age, (D) Sex, (E) National origin.... **C** 2. ___

3. Which of the following acts covers employee pension and welfare plans? (A) Federal Unemployment Tax Act, (B) Federal Insurance Contributions Act, (C) Age Discrimination in Employment Act, (D) Family and Medical Leave Act, (E) Employee Retirement Income Security Act. .... **E** 3. ___

4. Medicare is a two-part health insurance program that was part of an amendment to what act? (A) Federal Insurance Contributions Act, (B) Federal Income Tax Withholding Law, (C) Federal Unemployment Tax Act, (D) Affordable Care Act, (E) Fair Labor Standards Act .... **A** 4. ___

5. Which of the following statements is *not* a provision of ERISA? (A) ERISA applies to pension and welfare plans established by any employer engaged in commerce. (B) ERISA establishes minimum vesting schedules that protect the workers' benefits. (C) ERISA provides that all employees are eligible to set up their own individual retirement accounts. (D) ERISA requires each employer to establish a pension plan. (E) All of the above are provisions of ERISA... **D** 5. ___

6. Which of the following acts deals with the minimum wage paid to laborers for contractors who supply materials to any agency of the United States? (A) Davis-Bacon, (B) Walsh-Healey Public Contracts, (C) Federal Insurance Contributions, (D) McNamara-O'Hara Service Contract, (E) None of these.. **B** 6. ___

7. Which of the following forms is used to complete each employee's Form W-2, Wage and Tax Statement? (A) Payroll register, (B) Employee's paycheck, (C) Change in payroll rate form, (D) Employee's individual retirement account, (E) Employee's earnings record .... **E** 7. ___

8. Which of the following items does *not* always appear on both the payroll register and the employee's earnings record in the weekly payroll recording? (A) Gross weekly pay, (B) Net amount of the paycheck, (C) Federal income tax deducted, (D) Cumulative earnings, (E) All of the above appear on both records. .... **D** 8. ___

2014 *edition*

PAYROLL ACCOUNTING

Bieg/Toland

TEST 2

Student   **INSTRUCTOR'S COPY**

Chapter 2   Date _____

SCORING RECORD

Section	Total Points	Deductions	Score
A	40		
B	60		
Total	100		

Section A—DIRECTIONS: Each of the following statements is either true or false. Unless directed otherwise by your instructor, indicate your choice in the Answers column by writing "T" for a true answer or "F" for a false answer. (2 points for each correct answer)

		Answers	For Scoring

1. An enterprise is covered under the FLSA if there are at least two employees engaged in interstate commerce and if the enterprise has a gross annual sales volume of at least $400,000. ..... **F**   1.____

2. Under the FLSA, "mom and pop stores" are excluded from enterprise coverage. ..... **T**   2.____

3. If a small amount of tips is turned over to the employer, the tip credit can still be applied against the minimum wage. ..... **F**   3.____

4. A discretionary bonus is not included in the calculation of the regular rate of pay. ..... **T**   4.____

5. Employees who regularly work less than 20 hours a week are not covered by the minimum wage requirements. ..... **F**   5.____

6. A full-time student may be employed by a retail shop at 85 percent of the minimum wage. ..... **T**   6.____

7. An employer may only credit up to half of a tipped employee's minimum wage as coming from the tips actually received. ..... **F**   7.____

8. Partial-day absences cannot be deducted from an exempt employee's salary. ..... **T**   8.____

9. The FLSA provides for the payment of "double time" for any hours worked on holidays. ..... **F**   9.____

10. Wage differentials between sexes would be allowed if the different wage rates were based on a seniority system. ..... **T**   10.____

11. Blue-collar workers do not have to be paid for overtime if they have earned more than $90,000 for the year. ..... **F**   11.____

12. The FLSA requires employees to be paid for a rest period of 30 minutes or less. ..... **F**   12.____

13. Employers are not required to pay an employee for hours not worked because of illness. ..... **T**   13.____

14. Time spent in training sessions is never counted as working time. ..... **F**   14.____

15. The FLSA specifies that the employer must record an employee's starting and stopping time to the nearest tenth of an hour. ..... **F**   15.____

16. A worker who is regularly paid on a biweekly basis should receive 24 paychecks each year. ..... **F**   16.____

17. In order to qualify for the "white-collar" exemption as outside salespeople, the employees must be paid a minimum salary of at least $455/week. ..... **F**   17.____

18. Commissions are considered to be payments for hours worked and must be included in determining the regular hourly rate. ..... **T**   18.____

19. In calculating the overtime premium pay, the overtime hours are multiplied by one-half the regular hourly rate. ..... **T**   19.____

20. A nondiscretionary bonus is one that is either known in advance or is set up as an inducement to achieve certain goals. ..... **T**   20.____

Section B—DIRECTIONS: Solve the following problems and record the answers in the Answers column. Carry each hourly rate and each overtime rate to 3 decimal places and then round off to 2 decimal places. (6 points for each correct answer)

	Answers	For Scoring

1. Diane Duke works a standard 40-hour workweek. She is paid time and one-half for all hours over 40 in each workweek. Her regular hourly wage rate is $8.90. One week, Duke worked 49 hours. Her total gross earnings for the week are [(40 × $8.90) + (9 × $8.90 × 1.5)] .... $ __476.15__ 1.___

2. Charles Rollins earns $2,400 each month and works 35 hours each week.

   (a) His hourly rate is [($2,400 × 12) ÷ 52 ÷ 35]... $ __15.82__ 2a.___

   (3 pts.)

   (b) His overtime rate is ($15.82 × 1.5).. $ __23.73__ 2b.___

   (3 pts.)

3. Ken Gorman is paid $405.00 for a 37½-hour workweek. Overtime is paid at time and one-half for hours beyond 40 in each workweek. One week, Gorman works 48 hours. If he is paid his regular hourly rate for the first 40 hours, Gorman's gross pay is $405 ÷ 37½ = $10.80/hour; [$405 + (2.5 × $10.80) + (8 × $16.20)] .... $ __561.60__ 3.___

4. Susan Tate receives an hourly wage of $8.25 for a 40-hour week of 5 days, 8 hours daily. For Saturday work, she is paid 1½ times the regular rate. For Sunday work, she is paid 2 times the regular rate. One week, she worked 50 hours—4 hours of which were on Saturday and 6 hours on Sunday. Her total earnings for the week are [(40 × $8.25) + (4 × $12.38) + (6 × $16.50)]... $ __478.52__ 4.___

5. Ronald Dowd receives an annual base salary of $47,500 as a salesman in the Southern region, which has an annual sales quota of $450,000. For all sales over this quota, Dowd receives a commission of 4½%. For the current year, sales in the Southern region total $698,000. The amount of salary and commissions due to Dowd is [$47,500 + ($248,000 × 0.045)].. $ __58,660__ 5.___

6. Charles Geiger is a nonexempt salaried employee who works fluctuating workweeks. He is paid $760 per workweek. This week, he worked 50 hours. Determine Geiger's total gross pay if his employer uses the special half-rate (based on total hours worked) for overtime pay ($760 ÷ 50 = $15.20 × 0.5 = $7.60 × 10 = $76.00 + $760) .... $ __836.00__ 6.___

7. Ron Morris earns $11.80 per hour and worked 44 hours this week. In addition, he earned a production bonus of $35.20 for the week. His gross pay for the week is (44 × $11.80 = $519.20 + $35.20 = $554.40 ÷ 44 = $12.60 × 0.5 = $6.30 × 4 = $25.20 + $554.40)........ $ __579.60__ 7.___

8. Bob Knox is paid on a piece-rate basis. He is paid 22 cents for each unit he produces. For overtime work, he receives in addition to his piece-rate earnings a sum equal to one-half the regular hourly pay multiplied by the hours worked in excess of 40 in a week. During a particular week, Knox worked 45 hours and produced 1,890 units. His total earnings for the week are (1,890 × $0.22 = $415.80 ÷ 45 = $9.24 × 0.5 = $4.62 × 5 = $23.10 + $415.80).. $ __438.90__ 8.___

9. Carson Morris worked two separate jobs for Horwath Company during the week. Job A consisted of 36 hours at $16.00 per hour; Job B entailed 14 hours at $17.50 per hour. Determine his gross pay for that week if the employer uses the average rate basis for the overtime pay [(36 × $16.00) + (14 × $17.50) = $821 ÷ 50 = $16.42 × 0.5 = $8.21 × 10 = $82.10 + $821.00]... $ __903.10__ 9.___

10. Cecil Green is a waiter who regularly receives $90 each week in tips and works 40 hours each week. Green's employer claims the maximum weekly tip credit that is allowed in this case. The gross weekly pay, excluding tips, that the restaurant should pay Green without violating the FLSA is (40 × $7.25 = $290.00 – $90.00) .... $ __200.00__ 10.___

2014 *edition*
PAYROLL ACCOUNTING
Bieg/Toland

TEST 3

Student ___INSTRUCTOR'S COPY___

Chapter 3   Date _____

SCORING RECORD

Section	Total Points	Deductions	Score
A	40		
B	60		
Total	100		

Section A—DIRECTIONS: Each of the following statements is either true or false. Unless directed otherwise by your instructor, indicate your choice in the Answers column by writing "T" for a true answer or "F" for a false answer. (1 point for each correct answer)

		Answers	For Scoring
1.	A child working for his father's corporation is not exempt from coverage under FICA.	T	1. ____
2.	Under FICA, each partner in a partnership is defined as an employee of that organization.	F	2. ____
3.	Part-time employees pay a FICA tax at half the tax rate of full-time employees.	F	3. ____
4.	Once a person reaches the age of 65, social security taxes are not taken out of his or her paycheck.	F	4. ____
5.	Year-end bonuses paid to employees are not subject to the hospital insurance (HI) part of the FICA tax.	F	5. ____
6.	Under FICA, employers must collect the employee's FICA taxes on tips reported by each employee.	T	6. ____
7.	Employees and independent contractors pay different FICA tax rates.	T	7. ____
8.	Employer contributions for retirement plan payments for employees are defined as wages and are thus subject to FICA taxes.	F	8. ____
9.	If on any day during a deposit period an employer has accumulated $100,000 or more in undeposited employment taxes, the taxes must be deposited on the next banking day.	T	9. ____
10.	If an employee defers compensation into a 401(k) plan, the deferral (payroll deduction) is still subject to social security taxes.	T	10. ____
11.	Employers must withhold FICA taxes on payments that are made to independent contractors.	F	11. ____
12.	Self-employed persons who also work other jobs as employees do not have to pay any FICA taxes on their net self-employment earnings.	F	12. ____
13.	The requirements for depositing FICA taxes and income taxes withheld from employees' wages vary according to the amount of such taxes reported during a "lookback period."	T	13. ____
14.	A monthly depositor's employment taxes total $3,800 on Wednesday, March 31, 20--, the end of the calendar quarter. The taxes should be deposited on or before the following Tuesday (April 6).	F	14. ____
15.	On payday, Friday, a semiweekly depositor has accumulated employment taxes totaling $13,900. The taxes should be deposited on or before the following Wednesday.	T	15. ____
16.	Employers who file Form 941 electronically are given an extra 10 days from the normal due date to make their deposits.	F	16. ____
17.	Once the initial Form 941 is filed by a company, the company does not need to file Form 941 for a quarter in which there are no taxes to report.	F	17. ____
18.	Every employer has the right to choose the method (electronic or paper coupon) of depositing employment taxes.	F	18. ____
19.	If the last day for filing Form 941 falls on Saturday, the return may be filed on the next business day.	T	19. ____
20.	If tax deposits are made on time, there is no penalty for late filing of Form 941.	F	20. ____

Section B—DIRECTIONS: Complete Problems 1 and 2 by recording your answers in the spaces provided. Use the following tax rates and taxable wage bases: Employees' and Employer's OASDI—6.2% both on $113,700; HI—1.45% both on $113,700; HI—1.45% for employees and employers on the total wages paid.

1. During 2014, Amanda Hines, president of Dunne, Inc., was paid a semimonthly salary of $6,400. Determine the following amounts. (2 points for each correct answer)

	OASDI	HI
(a) The amount of FICA taxes to withhold from her 9th pay is	$ 396.80	$ 92.80
(b) The amount of FICA taxes to withhold from her 18th pay is {[$113,700 – ($6,400 × 17)] × 0.062}	$ 303.80	$ 92.80
(c) The amount of FICA taxes to withhold from her 24th pay is	$ 0.00	$ 92.80

2. Karlie Hastings is a writer (employee) for the *Santa Fe Gazette* and has an annual salary of $49,000. This year, she also realized net self-employment earnings of $75,000 from a book she wrote. What portion of her self-employment earnings is subject to the two parts of the social security tax? (5 points for each correct answer)

(a) OASDI taxable self-employment earnings ($113,700 – $49,000)	$ 64,700	(c) OASDI self-employment tax ($64,700 × 0.124)	$ 8,022.80
(b) HI taxable self-employment earnings	$ 75,000	(d) HI self-employment tax ($75,000 × 0.029)	$ 2,175.00

3. At Haddon, Inc., the office workers are employed for a 40-hour workweek and are paid on either an annual, monthly, or hourly basis. All office workers are entitled to overtime pay for all hours worked beyond 40 each workweek at 1½ times the regular hourly rates.

On the form below, calculate for each worker: (a) regular earnings, (b) overtime earnings, (c) total regular and overtime earnings, (d) FICA taxable wages, (e) FICA taxes to be withheld, and (f) net pay for the week ended December 19, 20--. Assume that there are 52 weekly payrolls in 20--. Also, determine the total for each of these six items. (1 point for each correct answer)

Weekly Payroll for Period Ending December 19, 20--

Employee	Salary	Hrs. Worked	Regular Earnings (A)	Overtime Earnings (B)	Total Reg. and O/T Earnings (C)	Cum. Taxable Wages as of Last Pay Period (12/12/--)	FICA Taxable Wages This Pay Period (D) OASDI	HI	FICA Taxes to be Withheld (E) OASDI	HI	Net Pay (F)
OFFICE: King, M.	$114,400 per yr.	40	$2,200.00	—	$2,200.00	$112,200.00	$1,500.00*	$2,200.00	$ 93.00	$31.90	$2,075.10
Manera, E.	$2,600 per mo.	40	600.00	—	600.00	$29,448.70	600.00	600.00	37.20	8.70	554.10
Tate, S.	$1,625 per mo.	48	375.00	$112.56	487.56	$18,000.00	487.56	487.56	30.23	7.07	450.26
Yee, L.	$7.25 per hr.	44½	290.00	48.96	338.96	$10,675.13	338.96	338.96	21.02	4.91	313.03
PLANT: Diaz, R.	$12.50 per hr.	48	500.00	150.00	650.00	$14,778.96	650.00	650.00	40.30	9.43	600.27
Zagst, J.	$14.50 per hr.	52	580.00	261.00	841.00	$24,703.02	841.00	841.00	52.14	12.19	776.67
Totals	...	...	$4,545.00	$572.52	$5,117.52	...	$4,417.52	$5,117.52	$273.89	$74.20	$4,769.43

Employer's FICA Taxes: OASDI $ 273.89   HI $ 74.20

*($113,700 – $112,200)

2014 edition
PAYROLL ACCOUNTING
Bieg/Toland

TEST 4

Student ___INSTRUCTOR'S COPY___

Chapter 4   Date _____

SCORING RECORD

Section	Total Points	Deductions	Score
A	20		
B	50		
C	30		
Total	100		

Section A—DIRECTIONS: Complete each of the following sentences by writing in the Answers column the letter of the word or words that correctly completes each statement. (2 points for each correct answer)

	Answers	For Scoring

1. Which of the following fringe benefits is taxable? (A) membership in a country club, (B) use of on-premise athletic facility, (C) job-placement assistance, (D) qualified employee discounts, (E) reduced tuition for education. .... **A**   1.____

2. All of the following persons are classified as *employees* under the federal income tax withholding law *with the exception of* (A) a first-line supervisor, (B) the president of a corporation, (C) a partner, (D) an elected official in the state government, (E) an officer of the federal government. .... **C**   2.____

3. If an employee files an amended W-4, the employer must make the W-4 effective no later than the (A) next payday, (B) start of the first payroll period ending on or after the 30th day from the W-4 receipt date, (C) 10th day from the W-4 receipt date, (D) first pay in the next quarter, (E) first pay in the next year. .... **B**   3.____

4. Ron Case, married with four dependents, failed to complete and file Form W-4 with his employer. The employer should (A) withhold federal income taxes as if Case were single and claimed six allowances, (B) withhold federal income taxes as if Case were married and claimed no allowances, (C) withhold federal income taxes at a rate of 25% of Case's wages, (D) refuse to pay Case until his Form W-4 is filed, (E) take none of the above actions. .... **E**   4.____

5. Employers must submit Forms W-4 to the IRS for (A) all Forms W-4, (B) those claiming more than 10 allowances, (C) all Forms W-4 claiming exemption, (D) those requested in writing by the IRS, (E) those requesting additional amounts to be withheld. .... **D**   5.____

6. The withholding on vacation wage payments is (A) a flat 15%, (B) based on the total amount of the wage payment plus the vacation pay, (C) taxed as though it were a regular payment for the periods occurring during the vacation period, (D) tax-free, (E) a flat 25%. .... **C**   6.____

7. A publisher is preparing information returns to report the royalties paid to authors (nonemployees) during the prior calendar year. The proper information return to be completed is (A) Form W-2, (B) Form W-3, (C) Form 1099-MISC, (D) Form 1099-DIV, (E) any of the above forms. .... **C**   7.____

8. Which of the following forms is not completed by the employer? (A) W-2, (B) W-3, (C) Form 941, (D) W-4, (E) Form 1099-MISC .... **D**   8.____

9. Both the percentage method and the wage-bracket method of withholding have each of the following characteristics except (A) unmarried persons are distinguished from married persons, (B) a table of allowances values is used, (C) employees are given the full benefit of the allowances they claim, (D) tables and wage-bracket charts are used to determine the amount withheld, (E) the standard deduction is taken into account. .... **B**   9.____

10. Wolf Company is giving a net bonus check of $500 to all of its employees. If each of the payments are subject to FIT (25% supplemental rate) and FICA taxes, but no state taxes, the gross amount of each bonus check would be (A) $742.39*, (B) $663.75, (C) $656.00, (D) $662.75, (E) none of these. .... **A**   10.____

$$*\left(\frac{\$500}{1-0.25-0.062-0.0145}\right)$$

ATS–7

Section B—DIRECTIONS: Complete the following payroll register for employees of Corby Company for the week ended March 7. Taxable earnings should be computed on the basis of a 40-hour week with overtime earnings being paid at time and one-half for all hours over 40 each workweek (no overtime for salaried employees).

Note: Carry each overtime hourly rate out to 3 decimal places and then round off to 2 decimal places.

All employees' wages are subject to the OASDI tax of 6.2% and the HI tax of 1.45%.

(left side)

PAYROLL REGISTER

FOR WEEK ENDING　　　March 7

EMPLOYEE'S NO.	MARITAL STATUS	NO. W/H ALLOW. CLAIMED	TIME RECORD						REGULAR EARNINGS		
			MONDAY	TUESDAY	WEDNESDAY	THURSDAY	FRIDAY	SATURDAY	NO. HOURS (REGULAR)	RATE PER HOUR	AMOUNT
41	S	2	8	7½	8	9	8	5½	40	7.25	290.00
32	M	5	8	10	10	9	8½	4	40	S	1,600.00
63	M	0	8	8	8	8	8	…	40	8.00	320.00
54	S	1	9	8	10	8	8	4	40	7.25	290.00
45	M	2	10	8	8	9	8	4½	40	7.50	300.00
16	S	0	8	9	10	9	8	4	40	7.75	310.00
7	S	1	5	6	8	8	8	4	39	7.25	282.75
28	M	3	8	8	8	8	8	…	40	7.25	290.00
49	M	0	8	9	8	8	9	6	40	7.25	290.00
10	S	1	8	8	0	9	10	5	40	S	1,450.00
			TOTALS						…	…	5,422.75

Amount of One Withholding Allowance Weekly $75.00

Percentage Method Tables for Income Tax Withholding

(For Wages Paid in 20--)

TABLE 1—WEEKLY Payroll Period

(a) SINGLE person (including head of household)—			**(b) MARRIED person**—		
If the amount of wages (after subtracting withholding allowances) is:		The amount of income tax to withhold is:	If the amount of wages (after subtracting withholding allowances) is:		The amount of income tax to withhold is:
Not over $42		$0	Not over $160		$0
Over—	But not over—	of excess over—	Over—	But not over—	of excess over—
$42	—$214 . .	$0.00 plus 10%	—$42	$160	—$503 . .	$0.00 plus 10%	—$160
$214	—$739 . .	$17.20 plus 15%	—$214	$503	—$1,554 . .	$34.30 plus 15%	—$503
$739	—$1,732 . .	$95.95 plus 25%	—$739	$1,554	—$2,975 . .	$191.95 plus 25%	—$1,554
$1,732	—$3,566 . .	$344.20 plus 28%	—$1,732	$2,975	—$4,449 . .	$547.20 plus 28%	—$2,975
$3,566	—$7,703 . .	$857.72 plus 33%	—$3,566	$4,449	—$7,820 . .	$959.92 plus 33%	—$4,449
$7,703	—$7,735 . .	$2,222.93 plus 35%	—$7,703	$7,820	—$8,813 . .	$2,072.35 plus 35%	—$7,820
$7,735		$2,234.13 plus 39.6%	—$7,735	$8,813		$2,419.90 plus 39.6%	—$8,813

SINGLE Persons—**WEEKLY** Payroll Period

(For Wages Paid through December 20--)

And the wages are–		And the number of withholding allowances claimed is—										
At least	But less than	0	1	2	3	4	5	6	7	8	9	10
		The amount of income tax to be withheld is—										
280	290	28	17	9	2	0	0	0	0	0	0	0
290	300	29	18	10	3	0	0	0	0	0	0	0
300	310	31	20	11	4	0	0	0	0	0	0	0
310	320	32	21	12	5	0	0	0	0	0	0	0
320	330	34	23	13	6	0	0	0	0	0	0	0
330	340	35	24	14	7	0	0	0	0	0	0	0
340	350	37	26	15	8	0	0	0	0	0	0	0
350	360	38	27	16	9	1	0	0	0	0	0	0
360	370	40	29	17	10	2	0	0	0	0	0	0
370	380	41	30	19	11	3	0	0	0	0	0	0
380	390	43	32	20	12	4	0	0	0	0	0	0
390	400	44	33	22	13	5	0	0	0	0	0	0
400	410	46	35	23	14	6	0	0	0	0	0	0
410	420	47	36	25	15	7	0	0	0	0	0	0
420	430	49	38	26	16	8	1	0	0	0	0	0

Source: Internal Revenue Service.

Use the partial wage-bracket tables provided to determine the amount of federal income tax to be withheld. For the salaried employees (#32 and #10), use the percentage method table.

All workers are employed in a state that imposes a 2% income tax on the gross wages earned by each worker.

(1 point for each correct answer—exclude totals row)

(right side)

_____ 20 -- _____

| OVERTIME EARNINGS | | | | | FICA TAXES | | | | | NET PAY | | |
NO. HOURS (O/T)	RATE PER HOUR	AMOUNT	TOTAL EARNINGS		OASDI	HI	FEDERAL INCOME TAX	STATE INCOME TAX	CHECK NO.		AMOUNT	EMPLOYEE'S NO.
6	10.88	65.28	$ 355.28		$ 22.03	$ 5.15	$ 16.00	$ 7.11	411		$ 304.99	41
...	...	...	1,600.00		99.20	23.20	142.60*	32.00	412		1,303.00	32
...	...	...	320.00		19.84	4.64	17.00	6.40	413		272.12	63
7	10.88	76.16	366.16		22.70	5.31	29.00	7.32	414		301.83	54
7½	11.25	84.38	384.38		23.83	5.57	8.00	7.69	415		339.29	45
8	11.63	93.04	403.04		24.99	5.84	46.00	8.06	416		318.15	16
...	...	...	282.75		17.53	4.10	17.00	5.66	417		238.46	7
...	...	...	290.00		17.98	4.21	0.00	5.80	418		262.01	28
8	10.88	87.04	377.04		23.38	5.47	22.00	7.54	419		318.65	49
...	...	...	1,450.00		89.90	21.03	254.95**	29.00	420		1,055.12	10
...	...	405.90	$5,828.65		$361.38	$84.52	$552.55	$116.58	...		$4,713.62	

* $1,600.00 – 5($75.00) = $1,225.00 – $503.00 = $722.00 × 0.15 = $108.30 + $34.30 = $142.60

** $1,450.00 – 1($75.00) = $1,375.00 – $739.00 = $636.00 × 0.25 = $159.00 + $95.95 = $254.95

MARRIED Persons—**WEEKLY** Payroll Period

(For Wages Paid through December 20--)

| And the wages are– | | And the number of withholding allowances claimed is— | | | | | | | | | | |
At least	But less than	0	1	2	3	4	5	6	7	8	9	10
		The amount of income tax to be withheld is—										
$ 0	$160	$0	$0	$0	$0	$0	$0	$0	$0	$0	$0	$0
160	165	0	0	0	0	0	0	0	0	0	0	0
165	170	1	0	0	0	0	0	0	0	0	0	0
170	175	1	0	0	0	0	0	0	0	0	0	0
175	180	2	0	0	0	0	0	0	0	0	0	0
180	185	2	0	0	0	0	0	0	0	0	0	0
185	190	3	0	0	0	0	0	0	0	0	0	0
190	195	3	0	0	0	0	0	0	0	0	0	0
195	200	4	0	0	0	0	0	0	0	0	0	0
200	210	5	0	0	0	0	0	0	0	0	0	0
210	220	6	0	0	0	0	0	0	0	0	0	0
220	230	7	0	0	0	0	0	0	0	0	0	0
230	240	8	0	0	0	0	0	0	0	0	0	0
240	250	9	1	0	0	0	0	0	0	0	0	0
250	260	10	2	0	0	0	0	0	0	0	0	0
260	270	11	3	0	0	0	0	0	0	0	0	0
270	280	12	4	0	0	0	0	0	0	0	0	0
280	290	13	5	0	0	0	0	0	0	0	0	0
290	300	14	6	0	0	0	0	0	0	0	0	0
300	310	15	7	0	0	0	0	0	0	0	0	0
310	320	16	8	1	0	0	0	0	0	0	0	0
320	330	17	9	2	0	0	0	0	0	0	0	0
330	340	18	10	3	0	0	0	0	0	0	0	0
340	350	19	11	4	0	0	0	0	0	0	0	0
350	360	20	12	5	0	0	0	0	0	0	0	0
360	370	21	13	6	0	0	0	0	0	0	0	0
370	380	22	14	7	0	0	0	0	0	0	0	0
380	390	23	15	8	0	0	0	0	0	0	0	0
390	400	24	16	9	1	0	0	0	0	0	0	0
400	410	25	17	10	2	0	0	0	0	0	0	0
410	420	26	18	11	3	0	0	0	0	0	0	0
420	430	27	19	12	4	0	0	0	0	0	0	0
430	440	28	20	13	5	0	0	0	0	0	0	0
440	450	29	21	14	6	0	0	0	0	0	0	0

Source: Internal Revenue Service.

Section C—DIRECTIONS: Each of the following statements is either true or false. Unless directed otherwise by your instructor, indicate your choice in the Answers column by writing "T" for a true answer or "F" for a false answer. (1/2 point for each correct answer)

		Answers	For Scoring
1.	A sole proprietor with two employees is exempt from the requirements of the federal income tax withholding law.	F	1.
2.	Not-for-profit corporations that are exempt from federal income taxes do not withhold federal income taxes from their employees' pay.	F	2.
3.	Cash tips of $20 or more in a month must be reported to the employer by the tipped employee by the end of the following month.	F	3.
4.	Employees who regularly receive cash tips of $20 or more in a calendar month are subject to federal income tax withholding on the tips.	T	4.
5.	Employees receiving over $1 million in supplemental wages for the year will have a 39.6% withholding rate apply to the supplemental payments in excess of $1 million.	T	5.
6.	Employees' payroll deductions into their 401(k) plans are generally made on a pretax basis and reduce the amount of gross pay that is subject to federal income tax withholding.	T	6.
7.	A worker with three employers should claim at least one withholding allowance with each employer.	F	7.
8.	The number of withholding allowances claimed by an employee is set forth on Form W-2.	F	8.
9.	Withholding allowance certificates must be retained by employers for as long as the certificates are in effect and for four years thereafter.	T	9.
10.	An employee filed a Form W-4 and claimed 22 withholding allowances. The employer should withhold 25% of the worker's gross earnings for federal income taxes until the Form W-4 is approved by the IRS.	F	10.
11.	Unmarried persons are distinguished from married persons under both the percentage method and the wage-bracket method of withholding.	T	11.
12.	Vacation pay is to be paid at the same time as a regular wage payment. In this case, the vacation pay must be combined with the regular wage payment and federal income taxes calculated on the amount of the total payment.	F	12.
13.	In the IRA form of a simple retirement account, employers can contribute as much as they want into the employee's simple retirement account, even though the employee's contribution is limited to $12,000.	F	13.
14.	The Wage and Tax Statement must be furnished to an employee on or before February 28 following the close of the calendar year.	F	14.
15.	If an employee who left the company requests a W-2 before the end of the year, it must be furnished within 30 days of the request or the final wage payment (whichever is later)	T	15.
16.	The maximum contribution that an employee (age 40) can make into a 401(k) plan that is not taxed for federal income tax withholding purposes is $25,000.	F	16.
17.	Form W-3 is filed with the Social Security Administration by employers as a transmittal of the information contained on Forms W-2.	T	17.
18.	Employers cannot send Forms W-2 to employees electronically.	F	18.
19.	To correct errors on previously filed Forms W-2, an employer must file Form W-3.	F	19.
20.	Contributions made by the employer into employees' health savings accounts are excluded from the employees' taxable income	T	20.

2014 *edition*

PAYROLL ACCOUNTING

Bieg/Toland

SCORING RECORD

Section	Total Points	Deductions	Score
A	40		
B	30		
C	30		
Total	100		

Section A—DIRECTIONS: Each of the following statements is either true or false. Unless directed otherwise by your instructor, indicate your choice in the Answers column by writing "T" for a true answer or "F" for a false answer. (2 points for each correct answer)

		Answers	For Scoring

1. The federal unemployment tax is imposed on employers, and thus, is not deducted from employees' wages .... **T**   1.____

2. Educational assistance payments to workers are considered nontaxable wages for unemployment purposes .... **T**   2.____

3. For the purpose of the FUTA tax, members of partnerships are considered employees. .... **F**   3.____

4. FUTA coverage does not include service of any nature performed outside the United States by a citizen of the United States for an American employer. .... **F**   4.____

5. The location of the employee's residence is the primary factor to be considered in determining coverage of an employee who works in more than one state .... **F**   5.____

6. A bonus paid as remuneration for services is not considered taxable wages for unemployment tax purposes even if the employee has not exceeded the taxable wage base. .... **F**   6.____

7. In the case of an employee who changes jobs during the year, only the first employer must pay FUTA tax on that employee's earnings. .... **F**   7.____

8. The maximum credit that can be applied to the FUTA tax because of SUTA contributions is 5.4%... **T**   8.____

9. If an employer pays a SUTA tax of 2.0%, the total credit that can be claimed against the FUTA tax is 2.0%. .... **F**   9.____

10. If the employer pays all of the state unemployment contributions after the filing date for Form 940, the maximum credit that can be claimed against the FUTA tax is 90% of 6.0%. .... **F**   10.____

11. Employer contributions made to employees' 401(k) plans that are included in total payments on Form 940 are also then deducted as exempt payments. .... **T**   11.____

12. The payments of FUTA taxes are included with the payments of FICA and FIT taxes and are paid as one lump sum. .... **F**   12.____

13. If an employer's FUTA tax liability for the 1st quarter is $935, no payment is required for the 1st quarter .... **F**   13.____

14. If a business has ceased operations during the year, as long as the payments of the FUTA taxes have been made, a Form 940 does not need to be completed for that year. .... **F**   14.____

15. Form 940 mailed by the due date is timely filed even if received by the IRS after the due date.. **T**   15.____

16. In certain circumstances, a FUTA tax payment can be remitted with Form 940 .... **T**   16.____

17. All of the states allow employers to make voluntary contributions into their state unemployment fund so that a lower tax contribution rate would be assigned. .... **F**   17.____

18. Employers have to pay a FUTA tax on only the first $3,500 of each part-time employee's earnings (1/2 of the full $7,000 limit). .... **F**   18.____

19. Voluntary contributions by employers into a state's unemployment fund in order to receive a reduced unemployment compensation rate are not permitted by all states. .... **T**   19.____

20. Form 940 can also be used to file an amended return .... **T**   20.____

Section B—DIRECTIONS: Determine the correct answer for each of the following problems. (5 points for each correct answer)

		Answers	For Scoring

1. Truson Company paid a 4% SUTA tax on taxable wages of $108,500. The taxable wages under FUTA were $89,400. What was the net FUTA tax of Truson Company? ($89,400 .... × 0.006)... $ **536.40**   1. _____

2. Jason Jeffries earned $10,200 while working for Brown Company. The company's SUTA tax rate is 2.9% of the first $7,000 of each employee's earnings. Compute the total unemployment taxes (SUTA and FUTA) that Brown Company should pay on Jeffries' earnings. [($7,000 × 0.006) + ($7,000 × 0.029)]... $ **245.00**   2. _____

3. Caruso Company's SUTA rate for next year is 2.9% because its reserve ratio falls in its state's 8% to less than 10% category [(contributions – benefits paid) ÷ average payroll = $93,500 ÷ $971,500 = 9.62%].
   If the next category (10% to less than 12%) would give Caruso a lower tax rate of 2.3%, what would be the amount of the voluntary contribution needed to get Caruso to that next category? [($971,500 × 10%) – $93,500] .... $ **3,650.00**   3. _____

4. Fred Stone is an employee of Henrock Company. During the first part of the year, Stone earned $4,340 while working in State Q. For the remainder of the year, the company transferred him to State S where he earned $27,000. Henrock Company's tax rate in State Q is 4.6%, and in State S, 4.0% on the first $7,000.
   If reciprocal arrangements exist between the two states, determine the SUTA tax that the company paid on Stone's earnings in State S. [($7,000 – $4,340) × 0.04] .... $ **106.40**   4. _____

5. Leinart Company had taxable wages (SUTA and FUTA) totaling $175,000. During the year, the company was late in paying its state contributions of 3.6% and is subject to the FUTA credit reduction. Determine the amount of net FUTA tax. [(5.4% – 3.6%) + (90% × 3.6%) = 5.04%; 6.0% – 5.04% = 0.96%; 0.96% × $175,000]........................... $ **1,680.00**   5. _____

6. Englesbe Company's FUTA tax liability was $289.50 FUTA tax for the 1st quarter; $129.80 for the 2nd quarter; $123.00 for the 3rd quarter; $16.00 for the 4th quarter. The company's first required payment of FUTA taxes is ($289.50 + $129.80 + $123.00) .... $ **542.30**   6. _____

Section C—DIRECTIONS: The information given below was taken from the payroll records of Clegg Company (Oregon employer) for 20--. Use the information to complete the partially illustrated Form 940 shown below. Assume that all taxes were deposited timely. (2½ points for each correct answer)

Total remuneration:
   $155,900
Included in the total remuneration is $3,000 of employer's contributions to the employees' 401(k) plans.
Remuneration in
   excess of $7,000:
   $66,670
Taxable remuneration
   by quarters:
1st quarter $43,700
2nd quarter $24,940
3rd quarter........ $14,360
4th quarter........ $ 3,230

Part 2:	Determine your FUTA tax before adjustments for 20--. If any line does NOT apply, leave it blank.		
3	Total payments to all employees	3	155900 . 00
4	Payments exempt from FUTA tax 4	3000 . 00	
	Check all that apply: 4a ☐ Fringe benefits 4c ☑ Retirement/Pension 4e ☐ Other 4b ☐ Group-term life insurance 4d ☐ Dependent care		
5	Total of payments made to each employee in excess of $7,000 5	66670 . 00	
6	Subtotal (line 4 + line 5 = line 6)	6	69670 . 00
7	Total taxable FUTA wages (line 3 – line 6 = line 7) (see instructions)	7	86230 . 00
8	FUTA tax before adjustments (line 7 x .006 = line 8)	8	517 . 38

Part 5:	Report your FUTA tax liability by quarter only if line 12 is more than $500. If not, go to Part 6.	
16	Report the amount of your FUTA tax liability for each quarter; do NOT enter the amount you deposited. If you had no liability for a quarter, leave the line blank.	
16a	1st quarter (January 1 – March 31) 16a	262 . 20
16b	2nd quarter (April 1 – June 30) 16b	149 . 64
16c	3rd quarter (July 1 – September 30) 16c	86 . 16
16d	4th quarter (October 1 – December 31) 16d	19 . 38
17	Total tax liability for the year (lines 16a + 16b + 16c + 16d = line 17) 17	517 . 38 Total must equal line 12.

Source: Internal Revenue Service.

TEST 6

Student   **INSTRUCTOR'S COPY**

Chapter 6   Date _____

SCORING RECORD

Section	Total Points	Deductions	Score
A	40		
B	60		
Total	100		

Section A—DIRECTIONS: Each of the following statements is either true or false. Unless directed otherwise by your instructor, indicate your choice in the Answers column by writing "T" for a true answer or "F" for a false answer. (2 points for each correct answer)

			Answers	For Scoring

1. In a payroll register having labor cost distribution columns, the total of each distribution column shows the amount of the gross wages or salaries for a particular department's wage expense.... **T**   1. ____

2. The information needed in preparing a journal entry to record the wages earned, deductions from wages, and net amount paid each payday is obtained from the payroll register. .... **T**   2. ____

3. In all computerized payroll systems, there is still the need to manually post from the printed payroll journal entry to the general ledger. .... **F**   3. ____

4. The payroll register is used by employers in completing Forms W-2................................. **F**   4. ____

5. The employer keeps track of each employee's accumulated wages in the employee's earnings record. .... **T**   5. ____

6. In calculating *overtime premium* earnings at one and a half times the regular hourly rate, the overtime hours are multiplied by one-half the hourly rate of pay... **T**   6. ____

7. When recording the employer's payroll taxes, a liability account entitled Employers Payroll Taxes Payable is credited for the total taxes owed (FICA, FUTA, and SUTA)........................... **F**   7. ____

8. The payment of the FUTA tax and the FICA taxes by the employer to the IRS is recorded in the same journal entry.. **F**   8. ____

9. In the case of a federal tax levy, the employee will notify the employer of the amount to take out of his or her paycheck. .... **F**   9. ____

10. FICA Taxes Payable—HI is a liability account in which is recorded the liability of the employer for the HI tax on the employer as well as for the HI tax withheld from employees' wages. .... **T**   10. ____

11. Federal tax levies are not subject to the limits imposed on garnishments under the Consumer Credit Protection Act. .... **T**   11. ____

12. Disposable earnings are the earnings remaining after withholding federal income taxes. .... **F**   12. ____

13. Direct deposit of paychecks can be forced on employees in every state..................................... **F**   13. ____

14. A garnishment cannot exceed 25 percent of an employee's gross pay. .... **F**   14. ____

SECTION A (continued)

		Answers	For Scoring

15. For the purpose of a federal tax levy, the IRS defines take-home pay as the gross pay less taxes withheld and the other payroll deductions in effect before the tax levy was received. .... **T**   15.____

16. In the case of multiple wage attachments, a garnishment for a student loan has priority over any other garnishment.. **F**   16.____

17. At the time of depositing FICA taxes and employees' federal income taxes, the account FICA Tax Expense is debited for both the employees' and the employer's portions of the FICA taxes. ... **F**   17.____

18. When union dues that have been withheld from employees' wages are turned over to the union treasurer, the account Union Dues Payable is debited.. **T**   18.____

19. The employers' OASDI portion of FICA taxes is included as part of the payroll tax entry, but the employers' HI portion of FICA taxes is not.. **F**   19.____

20. For child support garnishments, tips are considered part of an employee's disposable earnings... **T**   20.____

Section B—DIRECTIONS: Journalize each of the payroll transactions listed below. Omit the writing of the description or explanation for each journal entry, and *do not skip a line between each entry*. Then post all entries except the last one to the appropriate general ledger accounts. (8 points for each correct journal entry and ½ point for each correct account balance)

The journal page and the ledger accounts to be used in this section are supplied on the following pages. The balances listed in the general ledger accounts for Cash, FUTA Taxes Payable, SUTA Taxes Payable, Employees SIT Payable, Wages and Salaries, and Payroll Taxes are the results of all payroll transactions for the first quarter, not including the last pay of the quarter. The balances in FICA Taxes Payable—OASDI, FICA Taxes Payable—HI, and Employees FIT Payable are the amounts due from the March 15 payroll.

March 31, 20--: Paid total wages of $9,350.00. These are the wages for the last semimonthly pay of March. All of this amount is taxable under FICA (OASDI and HI). In addition, withhold $1,175 for federal income taxes and $102.03 for state income taxes. These are the only deductions made from the employees' wages.

March 31, 20--: Record the employer's payroll taxes for the last pay in March. All of the earnings are taxable under FICA (OASDI and HI), FUTA (0.6%), and SUTA (2.8%).

April 15, 20--: Made a deposit to remove the liability for the FICA taxes and the employees' federal income taxes withheld on the two March payrolls.

May 2, 20--: Made the deposit to remove the liability for FUTA taxes for the first quarter of 20--.

May 2, 20--: Filed the state unemployment contributions return for the first quarter of 20-- and paid the total amount owed for the quarter to the state unemployment compensation fund.

May 2, 20--: Filed the state income tax return for the first quarter of 20-- and paid the total amount owed for the quarter to the state income tax bureau.

December 31, 20--: In July 20--, the company changed from a semimonthly pay system to a weekly pay system. The employees were paid every Friday through the rest of 20--. Record the adjusting entry for wages accrued at the end of December ($770) but not paid until the first Friday in January. *Do not post this entry.*

December 31, 20--: The company has determined that employees have earned $19,300 in unused vacation time. Record the adjusting entry to put this expense on the books. *Do not post this entry.*

JOURNAL

PAGE 18

DATE		DESCRIPTION	POST REF.	DEBIT	CREDIT
20--					
Mar.	31	Wages and Salaries	51	9 3 5 0 00	
		FICA Taxes Payable—OASDI	20		5 7 9 70
		FICA Taxes Payable—HI	21		1 3 5 58
		Employees FIT Payable	25		1 1 7 5 00
		Employees SIT Payable	26		1 0 2 03
		Cash	11		7 3 5 7 69
	31	Payroll Taxes	52	1 0 3 3 18	
		FICA Taxes Payable—OASDI	20		5 7 9 70
		FICA Taxes Payable—HI	21		1 3 5 58
		FUTA Taxes Payable	22		5 6 10
		SUTA Taxes Payable	23		2 6 1 80
Apr.	15	FICA Taxes Payable—OASDI	20	2 2 8 7 80	
		FICA Taxes Payable—HI	21	5 3 5 06	
		Employees FIT Payable	25	2 3 0 5 00	
		Cash	11		5 1 2 7 86
May	2	FUTA Taxes Payable	22	3 1 7 22	
		Cash	11		3 1 7 22
	2	SUTA Taxes Payable	23	1 4 8 0 34	
		Cash	11		1 4 8 0 34
	2	Employees SIT Payable	26	5 8 0 74	
		Cash	11		5 8 0 74
Dec.	31	Wages and Salaries		7 7 0 00	
		Wages and Salaries Payable			7 7 0 00
	31	Vacation Benefits Expense		1 9 3 0 0 00	
		Vacation Benefits Payable			1 9 3 0 0 00

GENERAL LEDGER

ACCOUNT **CASH** ACCOUNT 11

DATE		ITEM	POST REF.	DEBIT	CREDIT	BALANCE DEBIT	BALANCE CREDIT
20--							
Mar.	31	Balance	√			4 1 9 8 4 19	
	31		J18		7 3 5 7 69	3 4 6 2 6 50	
Apr.	15		J18		5 1 2 7 86	2 9 4 9 8 64	
May	2		J18		3 1 7 22	2 9 1 8 1 42	
	2		J18		1 4 8 0 34	2 7 7 0 1 08	
	2		J18		5 8 0 74	2 7 1 2 0 34	

ACCOUNT **FICA TAXES PAYABLE—OASDI** ACCOUNT 20

DATE		ITEM	POST REF.	DEBIT	CREDIT	BALANCE DEBIT	BALANCE CREDIT
20--							
Mar.	15	Balance	√				1 1 2 8 40
	31		J18		5 7 9 70		1 7 0 8 10
	31		J18		5 7 9 70		2 2 8 7 80
Apr.	15		J18	2 2 8 7 80			—

ACCOUNT   **FICA TAXES PAYABLE—HI**   ACCOUNT   21

DATE		ITEM	POST REF.	DEBIT	CREDIT	BALANCE DEBIT	BALANCE CREDIT
20-- Mar.	15	Balance	√				2 6 3 90
	31		J18		1 3 5 58		3 9 9 48
	31		J18		1 3 5 58		5 3 5 06
Apr.	15		J18	5 3 5 06			——

ACCOUNT   **FUTA TAXES PAYABLE**   ACCOUNT   22

DATE		ITEM	POST REF.	DEBIT	CREDIT	BALANCE DEBIT	BALANCE CREDIT
20-- Mar.	15	Balance	√				2 6 1 12
	31		J18		5 6 10		3 1 7 22
May	2		J18	3 1 7 22			——

ACCOUNT   **SUTA TAXES PAYABLE**   ACCOUNT   23

DATE		ITEM	POST REF.	DEBIT	CREDIT	BALANCE DEBIT	BALANCE CREDIT
20-- Mar.	15	Balance	√				1 2 1 8 54
	31		J18		2 6 1 80		1 4 8 0 34
May	2		J18	1 4 8 0 34			——

ACCOUNT   **EMPLOYEES FIT PAYABLE**   ACCOUNT   25

DATE		ITEM	POST REF.	DEBIT	CREDIT	BALANCE DEBIT	BALANCE CREDIT
20-- Mar.	15	Balance	√				1 1 3 0 00
	31		J18		1 1 7 5 00		2 3 0 5 00
Apr.	15		J18	2 3 0 5 00			——

ACCOUNT   **EMPLOYEES SIT PAYABLE**   ACCOUNT   26

DATE		ITEM	POST REF.	DEBIT	CREDIT	BALANCE DEBIT	BALANCE CREDIT
20-- Mar.	15	Balance	√				4 7 8 71
	31		J18		1 0 2 03		5 8 0 74
May	2		J18	5 8 0 74			——

ACCOUNT   **WAGES AND SALARIES**   ACCOUNT   51

DATE		ITEM	POST REF.	DEBIT	CREDIT	BALANCE DEBIT	BALANCE CREDIT
20-- Mar.	15	Balance	√			4 3 5 1 9 20	
	31		J18	9 3 5 0 00		5 2 8 6 9 20	

ACCOUNT   **PAYROLL TAXES**   ACCOUNT   52

DATE		ITEM	POST REF.	DEBIT	CREDIT	BALANCE DEBIT	BALANCE CREDIT
20-- Mar.	15	Balance	√			4 8 0 8 88	
	31		J18	1 0 3 3 18		5 8 4 2 06	

2014 *edition*
PAYROLL ACCOUNTING
Bieg/Toland

TEST 1

Student _____

Chapter 1   Date _____

SCORING RECORD

Section	Total Points	Deductions	Score
A	60		
B	40		
Total	100		

Section A—DIRECTIONS: Each of the following statements is either true or false. Unless directed otherwise by your instructor, indicate your choice in the Answers column by writing "T" for a true answer or "F" for a false answer. (2 points for each correct answer)

	Answers	For Scoring

1. The Fair Labor Standards Act is commonly known as the Federal Wage and Hour Law. .... ____ **1.** ____

2. The Federal Insurance Contributions Act covers restrictions on the employment of child labor. .... ____ **2.** ____

3. The Federal Income Tax Withholding Law requires that all employment data be kept on file permanently. .... ____ **3.** ____

4. In cases where both federal and state regulations cover the minimum wage for the same employee, the federal rate is always used as the standard minimum wage. .... ____ **4.** ____

5. Those records that are required by the various payroll laws must generally be kept on file for only the current year. .... ____ **5.** ____

6. Unions and employment agencies are excluded from coverage under the Civil Rights Act of 1964. .... ____ **6.** ____

7. Employers' photocopying of new employees' I-9 documents is not required under the Immigration Reform and Control Act. .... ____ **7.** ____

8. The Age Discrimination in Employment Act protects virtually all workers, but only to the age of 70. .. ____ **8.** ____

9. FICA taxes are levied upon employers only. .... ____ **9.** ____

10. Criminal background checks can be used by employers on all job applicants. .... ____ **10.** ____

11. Most employers are faced with two unemployment taxes—federal and state. .... ____ **11.** ____

12. Every state imposes state unemployment taxes on employers in their state. .... ____ **12.** ____

13. The Age Discrimination Act covers employers engaged in an industry affecting interstate commerce (who employ 20 or more workers), employment agencies, and labor unions. .... ____ **13.** ____

14. The FUTA tax paid to the federal government is used to pay benefits to the unemployed workers who qualify for the benefits. .... ____ **14.** ____

15. Employers receive credit against their SUTA tax for their FUTA contributions. .... ____ **15.** ____

16. Some states allow employers to drug test in a limited number of situations. .... ____ **16.** ____

17. Once vested, workers have the right to receive a pension at retirement age, even if they no longer work for that company. .... ____ **17.** ____

18. Under the Family and Medical Leave Act, employers can exempt the highest paid 10 percent of their workforce from its provisions. .... ____ **18.** ____

19. Under federal law, new-hire reporting also applies to newly hired independent contractors. .... ____ **19.** ____

20. Form I-9, Employment Eligibility Verification, is completed only by employees who were born outside the United States. .... ____ **20.** ____

SECTION A (continued)

For
Answers Scoring

21. The deadline for an employee to complete Form I-9 is one year from the date of hire................... ____ 21. ____

22. Under the Family and Medical Leave Act, an employer can substitute an employee's earned paid leave for any part of the 12-week family leave. .... ____ 22. ____

23. Workers' compensation insurance applies only to work-related injury, illness, or death. .... ____ 23. ____

24. Prehire questions pertaining to religion, gender, national origin, or age are allowed when these factors are bona fide occupational requirements for a job.. ____ 24. ____

25. In the event employment is denied because of the information obtained from an investigative consumer report, the employer is required to inform the individual that this was the reason for denying employment. .... ____ 25. ____

26. Employers cannot terminate an employee for providing false information on an application form once the employee begins employment. .... ____ 26. ____

27. The hiring notice is a written record sent to the Payroll Department so that the new employee can be added to the payroll.. ____ 27. ____

28. The payroll register is used by employers in preparing Form W-2, the wage and tax statement sent to each employee at year-end.. ____ 28. ____

29. The payroll register is used to provide the information needed to record the payroll entries made in the journal on each payday... ____ 29. ____

30. The FLSA requires all employees to be paid weekly. .... ____ 30. ____

Section B—DIRECTIONS: Complete each of the following sentences by writing in the Answers column the letter of the word or words that correctly completes each statement. (5 points for each correct answer)

For
Answers Scoring

1. Which of the following laws establishes the minimum wage? (A) Fair Labor Standards Act, (B) Federal Personal Responsibility and Work Opportunity Reconciliation Act, (C) Federal Insurance Contributions Act, (D) Federal Unemployment Tax Act, (E) Fair Employment Laws..................... ____ 1. ____

2. Which of the following bases for discrimination in employment practices is not covered in Title VII of the Civil Rights Act of 1964 as amended? (A) Color, (B) Religion, (C) Age, (D) Sex, (E) National origin .. ____ 2. ____

3. Which of the following acts covers employee pension and welfare plans? (A) Federal Unemployment Tax Act, (B) Federal Insurance Contributions Act, (C) Age Discrimination in Employment Act, (D) Family and Medical Leave Act, (E) Employee Retirement Income Security Act. .... ____ 3. ____

4. Medicare is a two-part health insurance program that was part of an amendment to what act? (A) Federal Insurance Contributions Act, (B) Federal Income Tax Withholding Law, (C) Federal Unemployment Tax Act, (D) Affordable Care Act, (E) Fair Labor Standards Act............................ ____ 4. ____

5. Which of the following statements is *not* a provision of ERISA? (A) ERISA applies to pension and welfare plans established by any employer engaged in commerce. (B) ERISA establishes minimum vesting schedules that protect the workers' benefits. (C) ERISA provides that all employees are eligible to set up their own individual retirement accounts. (D) ERISA requires each employer to establish a pension plan. (E) All of the above are provisions of ERISA. .... ____ 5. ____

6. Which of the following acts deals with the minimum wage paid to laborers for contractors who supply materials to any agency of the United States? (A) Davis-Bacon, (B) Walsh-Healey Public Contracts, (C) Federal Insurance Contributions, (D) McNamara-O'Hara Service Contract, (E) None of these. .... ____ 6. ____

7. Which of the following forms is used to complete each employee's Form W-2, Wage and Tax Statement? (A) Payroll register, (B) Employee's paycheck, (C) Change in payroll rate form, (D) Employee's individual retirement account, (E) Employee's earnings record............................. ____ 7. ____

8. Which of the following items does *not* always appear on both the payroll register and the employee's earnings record in the weekly payroll recording? (A) Gross weekly pay, (B) Net amount of the paycheck, (C) Federal income tax deducted, (D) Cumulative earnings, (E) All of the above appear on both records.. ____ 8. ____

2014 *edition*
PAYROLL ACCOUNTING
Bieg/Toland

TEST 2

Student _____

Chapter 2   Date _____

SCORING RECORD

Section	Total Points	Deductions	Score
A	40		
B	60		
Total	100		

Section A—DIRECTIONS: Each of the following statements is either true or false. Unless directed otherwise by your instructor, indicate your choice in the Answers column by writing "T" for a true answer or "F" for a false answer. (2 points for each correct answer)

	Answers	For Scoring

1. An enterprise is covered under the FLSA if there are at least two employees engaged in interstate commerce and if the enterprise has a gross annual sales volume of at least $400,000. ...... _____ **1.** _____

2. Under the FLSA, "mom and pop stores" are excluded from enterprise coverage. ...... _____ **2.** _____

3. If a small amount of tips is turned over to the employer, the tip credit can still be applied against the minimum wage. ...... _____ **3.** _____

4. A discretionary bonus is not included in the calculation of the regular rate of pay. ...... _____ **4.** _____

5. Employees who regularly work less than 20 hours a week are not covered by the minimum wage requirements. ...... _____ **5.** _____

6. A full-time student may be employed by a retail shop at 85 percent of the minimum wage. ...... _____ **6.** _____

7. An employer may only credit up to half of a tipped employee's minimum wage as coming from the tips actually received. ...... _____ **7.** _____

8. Partial-day absences cannot be deducted from an exempt employee's salary. ...... _____ **8.** _____

9. The FLSA provides for the payment of "double time" for any hours worked on holidays. ...... _____ **9.** _____

10. Wage differentials between sexes would be allowed if the different wage rates were based on a seniority system. ...... _____ **10.** _____

11. Blue-collar workers do not have to be paid for overtime if they have earned more than $90,000 for the year. ...... _____ **11.** _____

12. The FLSA requires employees to be paid for a rest period of 30 minutes or less. ...... _____ **12.** _____

13. Employers are not required to pay an employee for hours not worked because of illness. ...... _____ **13.** _____

14. Time spent in training sessions is never counted as working time. ...... _____ **14.** _____

15. The FLSA specifies that the employer must record an employee's starting and stopping time to the nearest tenth of an hour. ...... _____ **15.** _____

16. A worker who is regularly paid on a biweekly basis should receive 24 paychecks each year. ...... _____ **16.** _____

17. In order to qualify for the "white-collar" exemption as outside salespeople, the employees must be paid a minimum salary of at least $455/week. ...... _____ **17.** _____

18. Commissions are considered to be payments for hours worked and must be included in determining the regular hourly rate. ...... _____ **18.** _____

19. In calculating the overtime premium pay, the overtime hours are multiplied by one-half the regular hourly rate. ...... _____ **19.** _____

20. A nondiscretionary bonus is one that is either known in advance or is set up as an inducement to achieve certain goals. ...... _____ **20.** _____

Section B—DIRECTIONS: Solve the following problems and record the answers in the Answers column. Carry each hourly rate and each overtime rate to 3 decimal places and then round off to 2 decimal places. (6 points for each correct answer)

	Answers	For Scoring

1. Diane Duke works a standard 40-hour workweek. She is paid time and one-half for all hours over 40 in each workweek. Her regular hourly wage rate is $8.90. One week, Duke worked 49 hours. Her total gross earnings for the week are .... $ _____   **1.** ____

2. Charles Rollins earns $2,400 each month and works 35 hours each week.

   (a) His hourly rate is .... $ _____   **2a.** ____
   (3 pts.)

   (b) His overtime rate is .... $ _____   **2b.** ____
   (3 pts.)

3. Ken Gorman is paid $405.00 for a 37½-hour workweek. Overtime is paid at time and one-half for hours beyond 40 in each workweek. One week, Gorman works 48 hours. If he is paid his regular hourly rate for the first 40 hours, Gorman's gross pay is .... $ _____   **3.** ____

4. Susan Tate receives an hourly wage of $8.25 for a 40-hour week of 5 days, 8 hours daily. For Saturday work, she is paid 1½ times the regular rate. For Sunday work, she is paid 2 times the regular rate. One week, she worked 50 hours—4 hours of which were on Saturday and 6 hours on Sunday. Her total earnings for the week are.............................. $ _____   **4.** ____

5. Ronald Dowd receives an annual base salary of $47,500 as a salesman in the Southern region, which has an annual sales quota of $450,000. For all sales over this quota, Dowd receives a commission of 4½%. For the current year, sales in the Southern region total $698,000. The amount of salary and commissions due to Dowd is.................................. $ _____   **5.** ____

6. Charles Geiger is a nonexempt salaried employee who works fluctuating workweeks. He is paid $760 per workweek. This week, he worked 50 hours. Determine Geiger's total gross pay if his employer uses the special half-rate (based on total hours worked) for over-time pay... $ _____   **6.** ____

7. Ron Morris earns $11.80 per hour and worked 44 hours this week. In addition, he earned a production bonus of $35.20 for the week. His gross pay for the week is.......................... $ _____   **7.** ____

8. Bob Knox is paid on a piece-rate basis. He is paid 22 cents for each unit he produces. For overtime work, he receives in addition to his piece-rate earnings a sum equal to one-half the regular hourly pay multiplied by the hours worked in excess of 40 in a week. During a particular week, Knox worked 45 hours and produced 1,890 units. His total earnings for the week are .... $ _____   **8.** ____

9. Carson Morris worked two separate jobs for Horwath Company during the week. Job A consisted of 36 hours at $16.00 per hour; Job B entailed 14 hours at $17.50 per hour. Determine his gross pay for that week if the employer uses the average rate basis for the overtime pay. .... $ _____   **9.** ____

10. Cecil Green is a waiter who regularly receives $90 each week in tips and works 40 hours each week. Green's employer claims the maximum weekly tip credit that is allowed in this case. The gross weekly pay, excluding tips, that the restaurant should pay Green without violating the FLSA is... $ _____   **10.** ____

2014 *edition*

PAYROLL ACCOUNTING

Bieg/Toland

TEST 3

Student _____

Chapter 3   Date _____

SCORING RECORD

Section	Total Points	Deductions	Score
A	40		
B	60		
Total	100		

Section A—DIRECTIONS: Each of the following statements is either true or false. Unless directed otherwise by your instructor, indicate your choice in the Answers column by writing "T" for a true answer or "F" for a false answer. (1 point for each correct answer)

		Answers	For Scoring

1. A child working for his father's corporation is not exempt from coverage under FICA.............. ____ **1.** ___
2. Under FICA, each partner in a partnership is defined as an employee of that organization........... ____ **2.** ___
3. Part-time employees pay a FICA tax at half the tax rate of full-time employees........................... ____ **3.** ___
4. Once a person reaches the age of 65, social security taxes are not taken out of his or her paycheck... ____ **4.** ___
5. Year-end bonuses paid to employees are not subject to the hospital insurance (HI) part of the FICA tax. .... ____ **5.** ___
6. Under FICA, employers must collect the employee's FICA taxes on tips reported by each employee. ____ **6.** ___
7. Employees and independent contractors pay different FICA tax rates..................................... ____ **7.** ___
8. Employer contributions for retirement plan payments for employees are defined as wages and are thus subject to FICA taxes. .... ____ **8.** ___
9. If on any day during a deposit period an employer has accumulated $100,000 or more in undeposited employment taxes, the taxes must be deposited on the next banking day. .... ____ **9.** ___
10. If an employee defers compensation into a 401(k) plan, the deferral (payroll deduction) is still subject to social security taxes... ____ **10.** ___
11. Employers must withhold FICA taxes on payments that are made to independent contractors. ...... ____ **11.** ___
12. Self-employed persons who also work other jobs as employees do not have to pay any FICA taxes on their net self-employment earnings... ____ **12.** ___
13. The requirements for depositing FICA taxes and income taxes withheld from employees' wages vary according to the amount of such taxes reported during a "lookback period." .... ____ **13.** ___
14. A monthly depositor's employment taxes total $3,800 on Wednesday, March 31, 20--, the end of the calendar quarter. The taxes should be deposited on or before the following Tuesday (April 6). ... ____ **14.** ___
15. On payday, Friday, a semiweekly depositor has accumulated employment taxes totaling $13,900. The taxes should be deposited on or before the following Wednesday. .... ____ **15.** ___
16. Employers who file Form 941 electronically are given an extra 10 days from the normal due date to make their deposits.. ____ **16.** ___
17. Once the initial Form 941 is filed by a company, the company does not need to file Form 941 for a quarter in which there are no taxes to report... ____ **17.** ___
18. Every employer has the right to choose the method (electronic or paper coupon) of depositing employment taxes. .... ____ **18.** ___
19. If the last day for filing Form 941 falls on Saturday, the return may be filed on the next business day. ____ **19.** ___
20. If tax deposits are made on time, there is no penalty for late filing of Form 941. .... ____ **20.** ___

AT–5

Section B—DIRECTIONS: Complete Problems 1 and 2 by recording your answers in the spaces provided. Use the following tax rates and taxable wage bases: Employees' and Employer's OASDI—6.2% both on $113,700; HI—1.45% for employees and employers on the total wages paid.

1. During 2014, Amanda Hines, president of Dunne, Inc., was paid a semimonthly salary of $6,400. Determine the following amounts. (2 points for each correct answer)

	OASDI	HI
(a) The amount of FICA taxes to withhold from her 9th pay is	$ _____	$ _____
(b) The amount of FICA taxes to withhold from her 18th pay is	$ _____	$ _____
(c) The amount of FICA taxes to withhold from her 24th pay is	$ _____	$ _____

2. Karlie Hastings is a writer (employee) for the *Santa Fe Gazette* and has an annual salary of $49,000. This year, she also realized net self-employment earnings of $75,000 from a book she wrote. What portion of her self-employment earnings is subject to the two parts of the social security tax? (5 points for each correct answer)

(a) OASDI taxable self-employment earnings .... $ _____   (c) OASDI self-employment tax .... $ _____

(b) HI taxable self-employment earnings .... $ _____   (d) HI self-employment tax .... $ _____

3. At Haddon, Inc., the office workers are employed for a 40-hour workweek and are paid on either an annual, monthly, or hourly basis. All office workers are entitled to overtime pay for all hours worked beyond 40 each workweek at 1½ times the regular hourly rates.

On the form below, calculate for each worker: (a) regular earnings, (b) overtime earnings, (c) total regular and overtime earnings, (d) FICA taxable wages, (e) FICA taxes to be withheld, and (f) net pay for the week ended December 19, 20--. Assume that there are 52 weekly payrolls in 20--. Also, determine the total for each of these six items. (1 point for each correct answer)

Weekly Payroll for Period Ending December 19, 20--

Employee	Salary	Hrs. Worked	Regular Earnings (A)	Overtime Earnings (B)	Total Reg. and O/T Earnings (C)	Cum. Taxable Wages as of Last Pay Period (12/12/--)	FICA Taxable Wages This Pay Period (D) OASDI	HI	FICA Taxes to Be Withheld (E) OASDI	HI	Net Pay (F)
OFFICE: King, M.	$114,400 per yr.	40				$112,200.00					
Manera, E.	$2,600 per mo.	40				$29,448.70					
Tate, S.	$1,625 per mo.	48				$18,000.00					
Yee, L.	$7.25 per hr.	44½				$10,675.13					
PLANT: Diaz, R.	$12.50 per hr.	48				$14,778.96					
Zagst, J.	$14.50 per hr.	52				$24,703.02					
Totals	...	...				...					

Employer's FICA Taxes: OASDI $ _____   HI $ _____

2014 *edition*

PAYROLL ACCOUNTING

Bieg/Toland

TEST 4

Student _____

Chapter 4   Date _____

SCORING RECORD

Section	Total Points	Deductions	Score
A	20		
B	50		
C	30		
Total	100		

Section A—DIRECTIONS: Complete each of the following sentences by writing in the Answers column the letter of the word or words that correctly completes each statement. (2 points for each correct answer)

Answers   For Scoring

1. Which of the following fringe benefits is taxable? (A) membership in a country club, (B) use of on-premise athletic facility, (C) job-placement assistance, (D) qualified employee discounts, (E) reduced tuition for education. .... ____ **1.** ____

2. All of the following persons are classified as *employees* under the federal income tax withholding law *with the exception of* (A) a first-line supervisor, (B) the president of a corporation, (C) a partner, (D) an elected official in the state government, (E) an officer of the federal government. .... ____ **2.** ____

3. If an employee files an amended W-4, the employer must make the W-4 effective no later than the (A) next payday, (B) start of the first payroll period ending on or after the 30th day from the W-4 receipt date, (C) 10th day from the W-4 receipt date, (D) first pay in the next quarter, (E) first pay in the next year. .... ____ **3.** ____

4. Ron Case, married with four dependents, failed to complete and file Form W-4 with his employer. The employer should (A) withhold federal income taxes as if Case were single and claimed six allowances, (B) withhold federal income taxes as if Case were married and claimed no allowances, (C) withhold federal income taxes at a rate of 25% of Case's wages, (D) refuse to pay Case until his Form W-4 is filed, (E) take none of the above actions. .... ____ **4.** ____

5. Employers must submit Forms W-4 to the IRS for (A) all Forms W-4, (B) those claiming more than 10 allowances, (C) all Forms W-4 claiming exemption, (D) those requested in writing by the IRS, (E) those requesting additional amounts to be withheld. .... ____ **5.** ____

6. The withholding on vacation wage payments is (A) a flat 15%, (B) based on the total amount of the wage payment plus the vacation pay, (C) taxed as though it were a regular payment for the periods occurring during the vacation period, (D) tax-free, (E) a flat 25%. .... ____ **6.** ____

7. A publisher is preparing information returns to report the royalties paid to authors (nonemployees) during the prior calendar year. The proper information return to be completed is (A) Form W-2, (B) Form W-3, (C) Form 1099-MISC, (D) Form 1099-DIV, (E) any of the above forms. .... ____ **7.** ____

8. Which of the following forms is not completed by the employer? (A) W-2, (B) W-3, (C) Form 941, (D) W-4, (E) Form 1099-MISC .... ____ **8.** ____

9. Both the percentage method and the wage-bracket method of withholding have each of the following characteristics except (A) unmarried persons are distinguished from married persons, (B) a table of allowances values is used, (C) employees are given the full benefit of the allowances they claim, (D) tables and wage-bracket charts are used to determine the amount withheld, (E) the standard deduction is taken into account. .... ____ **9.** ____

10. Wolf Company is giving a net bonus check of $500 to all of its employees. If each of the payments are subject to FIT (25% supplemental rate) and FICA taxes, but no state taxes, the gross amount of each bonus check would be (A) $742.39, (B) $663.75, (C) $656.00, (D) $662.75, (E) none of these.. ____ **10.** ____

AT–7

Section B—DIRECTIONS: Complete the following payroll register for employees of Corby Company for the week ended March 7. Taxable earnings should be computed on the basis of a 40-hour week with overtime earnings being paid at time and one-half for all hours over 40 each workweek (no overtime for salaried employees).

Note: Carry each overtime hourly rate out to 3 decimal places and then round off to 2 decimal places.

All employees' wages are subject to the OASDI tax of 6.2% and the HI tax of 1.45%.

(left side)

PAYROLL REGISTER

FOR WEEK ENDING — March 7

EMPLOYEE'S NO.	MARITAL STATUS	NO. W/H ALLOW. CLAIMED	MONDAY	TUESDAY	WEDNESDAY	THURSDAY	FRIDAY	SATURDAY	NO. HOURS (REGULAR)	RATE PER HOUR	AMOUNT	
			TIME RECORD						REGULAR EARNINGS			
41	S	2	8	7½	8	9	8	5½		7.25		
32	M	5	8	10	10	9	8½	4	40	S	1,600.00	
63	M	0	8	8	8	8	8	…		8.00		
54	S	1	9	8	10	8	8	4		7.25		
45	M	2	10	8	8	9	8	4½		7.50		
16	S	0	8	9	10	9	8	4		7.75		
7	S	1	5	6	8	8	8	4		7.25		
28	M	3	8	8	8	8	8	…		7.25		
49	M	0	8	9	8	8	9	6		7.25		
10	S	1	8	8	0	9	10	5	40	S	1,450.00	
			TOTALS						…	…		

Amount of One Withholding Allowance Weekly $75.00
Percentage Method Tables for Income Tax Withholding

(For Wages Paid in 20--)

TABLE 1—WEEKLY Payroll Period

(a) SINGLE person (including head of household)—

If the amount of wages (after subtracting withholding allowances) is:

Not over $42 . . . . $0

Over—	But not over—	The amount of income tax to withhold is:	of excess over—
$42	—$214 . .	$0.00 plus 10%	—$42
$214	—$739 . .	$17.20 plus 15%	—$214
$739	—$1,732 . .	$95.95 plus 25%	—$739
$1,732	—$3,566 . .	$344.20 plus 28%	—$1,732
$3,566	—$7,703 . .	$857.72 plus 33%	—$3,566
$7,703	—$7,735 . .	$2,222.93 plus 35%	—$7,703
$7,735	. . . .	$2,234.13 plus 39.6%	—$7,735

(b) MARRIED person—

If the amount of wages (after subtracting withholding allowances) is:

Not over $160 . . . . $0

Over—	But not over—	The amount of income tax to withhold is:	of excess over—
$160	—$503 . .	$0.00 plus 10%	—$160
$503	—$1,554 . .	$34.30 plus 15%	—$503
$1,554	—$2,975 . .	$191.95 plus 25%	—$1,554
$2,975	—$4,449 . .	$547.20 plus 28%	—$2,975
$4,449	—$7,820 . .	$959.92 plus 33%	—$4,449
$7,820	—$8,813 . .	$2,072.35 plus 35%	—$7,820
$8,813	. . . .	$2,419.90 plus 39.6%	—$8,813

SINGLE Persons—WEEKLY Payroll Period

(For Wages Paid through December 20--)

And the wages are—		And the number of withholding allowances claimed is—										
At least	But less than	0	1	2	3	4	5	6	7	8	9	10
		The amount of income tax to be withheld is—										
280	290	28	17	9	2	0	0	0	0	0	0	0
290	300	29	18	10	3	0	0	0	0	0	0	0
300	310	31	20	11	4	0	0	0	0	0	0	0
310	320	32	21	12	5	0	0	0	0	0	0	0
320	330	34	23	13	6	0	0	0	0	0	0	0
330	340	35	24	14	7	0	0	0	0	0	0	0
340	350	37	26	15	8	0	0	0	0	0	0	0
350	360	38	27	16	9	1	0	0	0	0	0	0
360	370	40	29	17	10	2	0	0	0	0	0	0
370	380	41	30	19	11	3	0	0	0	0	0	0
380	390	43	32	20	12	4	0	0	0	0	0	0
390	400	44	33	22	13	5	0	0	0	0	0	0
400	410	46	35	23	14	6	0	0	0	0	0	0
410	420	47	36	25	15	7	0	0	0	0	0	0
420	430	49	38	26	16	8	1	0	0	0	0	0

Source: Internal Revenue Service.

Use the partial wage-bracket tables provided to determine the amount of federal income tax to be withheld. For the salaried employees (#32 and #10), use the percentage method table.

All workers are employed in a state that imposes a 2% income tax on the gross wages earned by each worker.

(right side)

(1 point for each correct answer—exclude totals row)

20 --

NO. HOURS (O/T)	RATE PER HOUR	OVERTIME EARNINGS AMOUNT	TOTAL EARNINGS	OASDI	HI	FEDERAL INCOME TAX	STATE INCOME TAX	CHECK NO.	NET PAY AMOUNT	EMPLOYEE'S NO.
								411		41
								412		32
								413		63
								414		54
								415		45
								416		16
								417		7
								418		28
								419		49
								420		10
								...		

MARRIED Persons—WEEKLY Payroll Period

(For Wages Paid through December 20--)

And the wages are— At least	But less than	0	1	2	3	4	5	6	7	8	9	10
		The amount of income tax to be withheld is—										
$ 0	$160	$0	$0	$0	$0	$0	$0	$0	$0	$0	$0	$0
160	165	0	0	0	0	0	0	0	0	0	0	0
165	170	1	0	0	0	0	0	0	0	0	0	0
170	175	1	0	0	0	0	0	0	0	0	0	0
175	180	2	0	0	0	0	0	0	0	0	0	0
180	185	2	0	0	0	0	0	0	0	0	0	0
185	190	3	0	0	0	0	0	0	0	0	0	0
190	195	3	0	0	0	0	0	0	0	0	0	0
195	200	4	0	0	0	0	0	0	0	0	0	0
200	210	5	0	0	0	0	0	0	0	0	0	0
210	220	6	0	0	0	0	0	0	0	0	0	0
220	230	7	0	0	0	0	0	0	0	0	0	0
230	240	8	0	0	0	0	0	0	0	0	0	0
240	250	9	1	0	0	0	0	0	0	0	0	0
250	260	10	2	0	0	0	0	0	0	0	0	0
260	270	11	3	0	0	0	0	0	0	0	0	0
270	280	12	4	0	0	0	0	0	0	0	0	0
280	290	13	5	0	0	0	0	0	0	0	0	0
290	300	14	6	0	0	0	0	0	0	0	0	0
300	310	15	7	0	0	0	0	0	0	0	0	0
310	320	16	8	1	0	0	0	0	0	0	0	0
320	330	17	9	2	0	0	0	0	0	0	0	0
330	340	18	10	3	0	0	0	0	0	0	0	0
340	350	19	11	4	0	0	0	0	0	0	0	0
350	360	20	12	5	0	0	0	0	0	0	0	0
360	370	21	13	6	0	0	0	0	0	0	0	0
370	380	22	14	7	0	0	0	0	0	0	0	0
380	390	23	15	8	0	0	0	0	0	0	0	0
390	400	24	16	9	1	0	0	0	0	0	0	0
400	410	25	17	10	2	0	0	0	0	0	0	0
410	420	26	18	11	3	0	0	0	0	0	0	0
420	430	27	19	12	4	0	0	0	0	0	0	0
430	440	28	20	13	5	0	0	0	0	0	0	0
440	450	29	21	14	6	0	0	0	0	0	0	0

Source: Internal Revenue Service.

Section C—DIRECTIONS: Each of the following statements is either true or false. Unless directed otherwise by your instructor, indicate your choice in the Answers column by writing "T" for a true answer or "F" for a false answer. (1/2 point for each correct answer)

	Answers	For Scoring

1. A sole proprietor with two employees is exempt from the requirements of the federal income tax withholding law.. ___ 1.___

2. Not-for-profit corporations that are exempt from federal income taxes do not withhold federal income taxes from their employees' pay... ___ 2.___

3. Cash tips of $20 or more in a month must be reported to the employer by the tipped employee by the end of the following month. .... ___ 3.___

4. Employees who regularly receive cash tips of $20 or more in a calendar month are subject to federal income tax withholding on the tips. .... ___ 4.___

5. Employees receiving over $1 million in supplemental wages for the year will have a 39.6% withholding rate apply to the supplemental payments in excess of $1 million. .... ___ 5.___

6. Employees' payroll deductions into their 401(k) plans are generally made on a pretax basis and reduce the amount of gross pay that is subject to federal income tax withholding. .... ___ 6.___

7. A worker with three employers should claim at least one withholding allowance with each employer. ___ 7.___

8. The number of withholding allowances claimed by an employee is set forth on Form W-2. .... ___ 8.___

9. Withholding allowance certificates must be retained by employers for as long as the certificates are in effect and for four years thereafter. .... ___ 9.___

10. An employee filed a Form W-4 and claimed 22 withholding allowances. The employer should withhold 25% of the worker's gross earnings for federal income taxes until the Form W-4 is approved by the IRS.. ___ 10.___

11. Unmarried persons are distinguished from married persons under both the percentage method and the wage-bracket method of withholding. .... ___ 11.___

12. Vacation pay is to be paid at the same time as a regular wage payment. In this case, the vacation pay must be combined with the regular wage payment and federal income taxes calculated on the amount of the total payment.. ___ 12.___

13. In the IRA form of a simple retirement account, employers can contribute as much as they want into the employee's simple retirement account, even though the employee's contribution is limited to $12,000.. ___ 13.___

14. The Wage and Tax Statement must be furnished to an employee on or before February 28 following the close of the calendar year... ___ 14.___

15. If an employee who left the company requests a W-2 before the end of the year, it must be furnished within 30 days of the request or the final wage payment (whichever is later) .... ___ 15.___

16. The maximum contribution that an employee (age 40) can make into a 401(k) plan that is not taxed for federal income tax withholding purposes is $25,000.. ___ 16.___

17. Form W-3 is filed with the Social Security Administration by employers as a transmittal of the information contained on Forms W-2. .... ___ 17.___

18. Employers cannot send Forms W-2 to employees electronically................................. ___ 18.___

19. To correct errors on previously filed Forms W-2, an employer must file Form W-3. .... ___ 19.___

20. Contributions made by the employer into employees' health savings accounts are excluded from the employees' taxable income. .... ___ 20.___

2014 *edition*

PAYROLL ACCOUNTING

Bieg/Toland

SCORING RECORD

Section	Total Points	Deductions	Score
A	40		
B	30		
C	30		
Total	100		

Section A—DIRECTIONS: Each of the following statements is either true or false. Unless directed otherwise by your instructor, indicate your choice in the Answers column by writing "T" for a true answer or "F" for a false answer. (2 points for each correct answer)

For Answers Scoring

1. The federal unemployment tax is imposed on employers, and thus, is not deducted from employees' wages.. ____ **1.**____

2. Educational assistance payments to workers are considered nontaxable wages for unemployment purposes.. ____ **2.**____

3. For the purpose of the FUTA tax, members of partnerships are considered employees. .... ____ **3.**____

4. FUTA coverage does not include service of any nature performed outside the United States by a citizen of the United States for an American employer... ____ **4.**____

5. The location of the employee's residence is the primary factor to be considered in determining coverage of an employee who works in more than one state.. ____ **5.**____

6. A bonus paid as remuneration for services is not considered taxable wages for unemployment tax purposes even if the employee has not exceeded the taxable wage base................................... ____ **6.**____

7. In the case of an employee who changes jobs during the year, only the first employer must pay FUTA tax on that employee's earnings. .... ____ **7.**____

8. The maximum credit that can be applied to the FUTA tax because of SUTA contributions is 5.4%. ... ____ **8.**____

9. If an employer pays a SUTA tax of 2.0%, the total credit that can be claimed against the FUTA tax is 2.0%... ____ **9.**____

10. If the employer pays all of the state unemployment contributions after the filing date for Form 940, the maximum credit that can be claimed against the FUTA tax is 90% of 6.0%. .... ____ **10.**____

11. Employer contributions made to employees' 401(k) plans that are included in total payments on Form 940 are also then deducted as exempt payments... ____ **11.**____

12. The payments of FUTA taxes are included with the payments of FICA and FIT taxes and are paid as one lump sum. .... ____ **12.**____

13. If an employer's FUTA tax liability for the 1st quarter is $935, no payment is required for the 1st quarter... ____ **13.**____

14. If a business has ceased operations during the year, as long as the payments of the FUTA taxes have been made, a Form 940 does not need to be completed for that year.. ____ **14.**____

15. Form 940 mailed by the due date is timely filed even if received by the IRS after the due date....... ____ **15.**____

16. In certain circumstances, a FUTA tax payment can be remitted with Form 940............................. ____ **16.**____

17. All of the states allow employers to make voluntary contributions into their state unemployment fund so that a lower tax contribution rate would be assigned.. ____ **17.**____

18. Employers have to pay a FUTA tax on only the first $3,500 of each part-time employee's earnings (1/2 of the full $7,000 limit). .... ____ **18.**____

19. Voluntary contributions by employers into a state's unemployment fund in order to receive a reduced unemployment compensation rate are not permitted by all states..................................... ____ **19.**____

20. Form 940 can also be used to file an amended return... ____ **20.**____

Section B—DIRECTIONS: Determine the correct answer for each of the following problems. (5 points for each correct answer)

		Answers	For Scoring

1. Truson Company paid a 4% SUTA tax on taxable wages of $108,500. The taxable wages under FUTA were $89,400. What was the net FUTA tax of Truson Company?.................. $ _____   1. ____

2. Jason Jeffries earned $10,200 while working for Brown Company. The company's SUTA tax rate is 2.9% of the first $7,000 of each employee's earnings. Compute the total unemployment taxes (SUTA and FUTA) that Brown Company should pay on Jeffries' earnings... $ _____   2. ____

3. Caruso Company's SUTA rate for next year is 2.9% because its reserve ratio falls in its state's 8% to less than 10% category [(contributions – benefits paid) ÷ average payroll = $93,500 ÷ $971,500 = 9.62%].
   If the next category (10% to less than 12%) would give Caruso a lower tax rate of 2.3%, what would be the amount of the voluntary contribution needed to get Caruso to that next category?... $ _____   3. ____

4. Fred Stone is an employee of Henrock Company. During the first part of the year, Stone earned $4,340 while working in State Q. For the remainder of the year, the company transferred him to State S where he earned $27,000. Henrock Company's tax rate in State Q is 4.6%, and in State S, 4.0% on the first $7,000.
   If reciprocal arrangements exist between the two states, determine the SUTA tax that the company paid on Stone's earnings in State S. .... $ _____   4. ____

5. Leinart Company had taxable wages (SUTA and FUTA) totaling $175,000. During the year, the company was late in paying its state contributions of 3.6% and is subject to the FUTA credit reduction. Determine the amount of net FUTA tax. .... $ _____   5. ____

6. Englesbe Company's FUTA tax liability was $289.50 FUTA tax for the 1st quarter; $129.80 for the 2nd quarter; $123.00 for the 3rd quarter; $16.00 for the 4th quarter. The company's first required payment of FUTA taxes is .... $ _____   6. ____

Section C—DIRECTIONS: The information given below was taken from the payroll records of Clegg Company (Oregon employer) for 20--. Use the information to complete the partially illustrated Form 940 shown below. Assume that all taxes were deposited timely. (2½ points for each correct answer)

Total remuneration:
    $155,900
Included in the total remuneration is $3,000 of employer's contributions to the employees' 401(k) plans.
Remuneration in excess of $7,000: $66,670
Taxable remuneration by quarters:
1st quarter $43,700
2nd quarter $24,940
3rd quarter........ $14,360
4th quarter........ $ 3,230

Part 2: Determine your FUTA tax before adjustments for 20--. If any line does NOT apply, leave it blank.

3 Total payments to all employees ....   3 [_____] .

4 Payments exempt from FUTA tax ....   4 [_____] .

   Check all that apply: 4a ☐ Fringe benefits   4c ☐ Retirement/Pension   4e ☐ Other
                          4b ☐ Group-term life insurance   4d ☐ Dependent care

5 Total of payments made to each employee in excess of $7,000 ....   5 [_____] .

6 Subtotal (line 4 + line 5 = line 6) ....   6 [_____] .

7 Total taxable FUTA wages (line 3 – line 6 = line 7) (see instructions) ....   7 [_____] .

8 FUTA tax before adjustments (line 7 x .006 = line 8) ....   8 [_____] .

Part 5: Report your FUTA tax liability by quarter only if line 12 is more than $500. If not, go to Part 6.

16 Report the amount of your FUTA tax liability for each quarter; do NOT enter the amount you deposited. If you had no liability for a quarter, leave the line blank.

16a 1st quarter (January 1 – March 31) ....   16a [_____] .

16b 2nd quarter (April 1 – June 30) ....   16b [_____] .

16c 3rd quarter (July 1 – September 30) ....   16c [_____] .

16d 4th quarter (October 1 – December 31) ....   16d [_____] .

17 Total tax liability for the year (lines 16a + 16b + 16c + 16d = line 17) 17 [_____] .   Total must equal line 12.

Source: Internal Revenue Service.

2014 *edition*

PAYROLL ACCOUNTING

Bieg/Toland

TEST 6

Student _____

Chapter 6   Date _____

SCORING RECORD

Section	Total Points	Deductions	Score
A	40		
B	60		
Total	100		

Section A—DIRECTIONS: Each of the following statements is either true or false. Unless directed otherwise by your instructor, indicate your choice in the Answers column by writing "T" for a true answer or "F" for a false answer. (2 points for each correct answer)

Answers   For Scoring

1. In a payroll register having labor cost distribution columns, the total of each distribution column shows the amount of the gross wages or salaries for a particular department's wage expense....... ____ **1.** ____

2. The information needed in preparing a journal entry to record the wages earned, deductions from wages, and net amount paid each payday is obtained from the payroll register. .... ____ **2.** ____

3. In all computerized payroll systems, there is still the need to manually post from the printed payroll journal entry to the general ledger. .... ____ **3.** ____

4. The payroll register is used by employers in completing Forms W-2. .... ____ **4.** ____

5. The employer keeps track of each employee's accumulated wages in the employee's earnings record. .... ____ **5.** ____

6. In calculating *overtime premium* earnings at one and a half times the regular hourly rate, the overtime hours are multiplied by one-half the hourly rate of pay... ____ **6.** ____

7. When recording the employer's payroll taxes, a liability account entitled Employers Payroll Taxes Payable is credited for the total taxes owed (FICA, FUTA, and SUTA). .... ____ **7.** ____

8. The payment of the FUTA tax and the FICA taxes by the employer to the IRS is recorded in the same journal entry.. ____ **8.** ____

9. In the case of a federal tax levy, the employee will notify the employer of the amount to take out of his or her paycheck. .... ____ **9.** ____

10. FICA Taxes Payable—HI is a liability account in which is recorded the liability of the employer for the HI tax on the employer as well as for the HI tax withheld from employees' wages. .... ____ **10.** ____

11. Federal tax levies are not subject to the limits imposed on garnishments under the Consumer Credit Protection Act. .... ____ **11.** ____

12. Disposable earnings are the earnings remaining after withholding federal income taxes. .... ____ **12.** ____

13. Direct deposit of paychecks can be forced on employees in every state....................................... ____ **13.** ____

14. A garnishment cannot exceed 25 percent of an employee's gross pay. .... ____ **14.** ____

SECTION A (continued)

	For Answers Scoring

15. For the purpose of a federal tax levy, the IRS defines take-home pay as the gross pay less taxes withheld and the other payroll deductions in effect before the tax levy was received. .... ___ **15.**___

16. In the case of multiple wage attachments, a garnishment for a student loan has priority over any other garnishment. .... ___ **16.**___

17. At the time of depositing FICA taxes and employees' federal income taxes, the account FICA Tax Expense is debited for both the employees' and the employer's portions of the FICA taxes. ... ___ **17.**___

18. When union dues that have been withheld from employees' wages are turned over to the union treasurer, the account Union Dues Payable is debited. .... ___ **18.**___

19. The employers' OASDI portion of FICA taxes is included as part of the payroll tax entry, but the employers' HI portion of FICA taxes is not. .... ___ **19.**___

20. For child support garnishments, tips are considered part of an employee's disposable earnings. ..... ___ **20.**___

Section B—DIRECTIONS: Journalize each of the payroll transactions listed below. Omit the writing of the description or explanation for each journal entry, and *do not skip a line between each entry*. Then post all entries except the last one to the appropriate general ledger accounts. (8 points for each correct journal entry and ½ point for each correct account balance)

The journal page and the ledger accounts to be used in this section are supplied on the following pages. The balances listed in the general ledger accounts for Cash, FUTA Taxes Payable, SUTA Taxes Payable, Employees SIT Payable, Wages and Salaries, and Payroll Taxes are the results of all payroll transactions for the first quarter, not including the last pay of the quarter. The balances in FICA Taxes Payable—OASDI, FICA Taxes Payable—HI, and Employees FIT Payable are the amounts due from the March 15 payroll.

March 31, 20--: Paid total wages of $9,350.00. These are the wages for the last semimonthly pay of March. All of this amount is taxable under FICA (OASDI and HI). In addition, withhold $1,175 for federal income taxes and $102.03 for state income taxes. These are the only deductions made from the employees' wages.

March 31, 20--: Record the employer's payroll taxes for the last pay in March. All of the earnings are taxable under FICA (OASDI and HI), FUTA (0.6%), and SUTA (2.8%).

April 15, 20--: Made a deposit to remove the liability for the FICA taxes and the employees' federal income taxes withheld on the two March payrolls.

May 2, 20--: Made the deposit to remove the liability for FUTA taxes for the first quarter of 20--.

May 2, 20--: Filed the state unemployment contributions return for the first quarter of 20-- and paid the total amount owed for the quarter to the state unemployment compensation fund.

May 2, 20--: Filed the state income tax return for the first quarter of 20-- and paid the total amount owed for the quarter to the state income tax bureau.

December 31, 20--: In July 20--, the company changed from a semimonthly pay system to a weekly pay system. The employees were paid every Friday through the rest of 20--. Record the adjusting entry for wages accrued at the end of December ($770) but not paid until the first Friday in January. *Do not post this entry.*

December 31, 20--: The company has determined that employees have earned $19,300 in unused vacation time. Record the adjusting entry to put this expense on the books. *Do not post this entry.*

JOURNAL

PAGE 18

DATE	DESCRIPTION	POST REF.	DEBIT	CREDIT

GENERAL LEDGER

ACCOUNT **CASH** ACCOUNT 11

DATE	ITEM	POST REF.	DEBIT	CREDIT	BALANCE DEBIT	BALANCE CREDIT
20-- Mar. 31	Balance	√			4 1 9 8 4 19	

ACCOUNT **FICA TAXES PAYABLE—OASDI** ACCOUNT 20

DATE	ITEM	POST REF.	DEBIT	CREDIT	BALANCE DEBIT	BALANCE CREDIT
20-- Mar. 15	Balance	√				1 1 28 40

ACCOUNT   **FICA TAXES PAYABLE—HI**   ACCOUNT   21

DATE		ITEM	POST REF.	DEBIT	CREDIT	BALANCE DEBIT	BALANCE CREDIT
20-- Mar.	15	Balance	√				2 6 3 90

ACCOUNT   **FUTA TAXES PAYABLE**   ACCOUNT   22

DATE		ITEM	POST REF.	DEBIT	CREDIT	BALANCE DEBIT	BALANCE CREDIT
20-- Mar.	15	Balance	√				2 6 1 12

ACCOUNT   **SUTA TAXES PAYABLE**   ACCOUNT   23

DATE		ITEM	POST REF.	DEBIT	CREDIT	BALANCE DEBIT	BALANCE CREDIT
20-- Mar.	15	Balance	√				1 2 1 8 54

ACCOUNT   **EMPLOYEES FIT PAYABLE**   ACCOUNT   25

DATE		ITEM	POST REF.	DEBIT	CREDIT	BALANCE DEBIT	BALANCE CREDIT
20-- Mar.	15	Balance	√				1 1 3 0 00

ACCOUNT   **EMPLOYEES SIT PAYABLE**   ACCOUNT   26

DATE		ITEM	POST REF.	DEBIT	CREDIT	BALANCE DEBIT	BALANCE CREDIT
20-- Mar.	15	Balance	√				4 7 8 71

ACCOUNT   **WAGES AND SALARIES**   ACCOUNT   51

DATE		ITEM	POST REF.	DEBIT	CREDIT	BALANCE DEBIT	BALANCE CREDIT
20-- Mar.	15	Balance	√			4 3 5 1 9 20	

ACCOUNT   **PAYROLL TAXES**   ACCOUNT   52

DATE		ITEM	POST REF.	DEBIT	CREDIT	BALANCE DEBIT	BALANCE CREDIT
20-- Mar.	15	Balance	√			4 8 0 8 88	

The Inspector files for the *Payroll Accounting, 2014 Edition are* available on the disc packaged with the Instructor's Edition. All other instructor resources can be found on the product Web site at http://login.cengage.com.

CPSIA information can be obtained
at www.ICGtesting.com
Printed in the USA
FFOW02n1104060314
4091FF